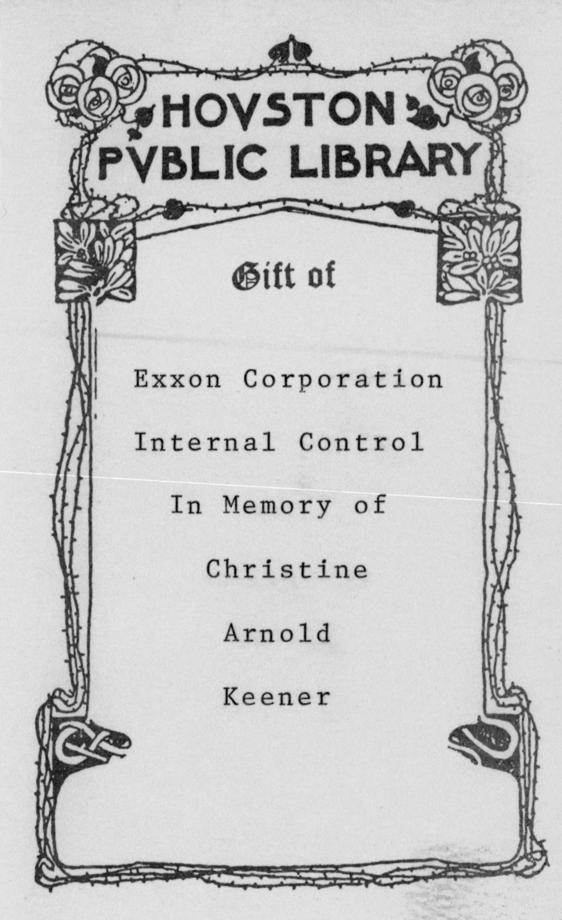

Love Lines

Love

Lines

A Romance Reader's Guide to Printed Pleasures

♥

Rosemary Guiley

♥

Designed by J.C. Suarés

Facts On File Publications
460 Park Avenue South
New York, N.Y. 10016

♥ ♥

Love Lines

BY ROSEMARY GUILEY
edited by Olga Vezeris

Cover painting by Pino Daeni
courtesy of Bantam Books

Published by Facts On File, Inc.
460 Park Avenue South, New York, N.Y. 10016

Library of Congress Cataloging in Publication Data
Main entry under title:

Lovelines.

Includes index.
1. Love stories, American—History and criticism. 2. Love stories, English—History and criticism. 3. Love in literature. 4. Courtship in literature.
I. Guiley, Rosemary.
PS374.L6L68 813'.085'09 82-7383
ISBN 0-87196-826-6 AACR2
ISBN 0-87196-724-3 (pbk.)

Printed in the United States of America

10 9 8 7 6 5 4 3 2 1

ACKNOWLEDGMENTS

The people who work in the romantic fiction business are dedicated professionals. My special thanks to those who granted interviews and contributed information and material for this book—there are more than 100 of you, and your generosity with your time and resources is greatly appreciated.

TABLE OF CONTENTS

ACKNOWLEDGMENTS V
INTRODUCTION VIII
I. THE ROMANCE WITH ROMANCE 2
1. Spice Of Life 2
2. Great Escapes 11
3. That's Entertainment 20
4. Love Boats 28
5. Test Your Romance Quotient 34
II. THE LANGUAGE OF LOVE 36
1. Once Upon A Time 36
2. Hearts On A Sleeve 46
3. Write From The Heart 50
III. LIGHTING THE TORCH 54
1. In The Beginning 54
2. The Romance Hall Of Fame 59
3. Those Avon Ladies 65
4. The Romance Reader's Library 69
IV. THE MANY FACES OF LOVE 72
1. Contemporary Romances: Not The Same Old Story 72
2. Historicals: From Virgins To Vamps 80
3. That Special Charm Of A Regency Romp 86
4. Gothics and Suspense: Twists And Terrors 89
5. Teen Romances: Young Love In Bloom 92
V. LEADING LOVERS AND OTHERS 96
1. Heroes And Heroines: They Aren't What They Used To Be .. 96
2. Rivals In Love: Sorry, Toots 103
3. New Deal Realism 106
4. It's All In A Name 110
5. Calling Cards 113
VI. PASSION PLAYS 116
1. Some Enchanted Meeting 116
2. Settings And Sensations 119
3. Sensuality: The New Byword 126
4. Silks And Sashes 141
5. And They Lived Happily Ever After 145
VII. SPREADING THE WORD 150
1. Names: Love 'Em And Leave 'Em 150
2. Harlequin: World's Largest Romance Storyseller 154
3. Silhouette: Looking To Be Number One 162
4. Love American Style 173
5. From England With Love 183

TABLE OF CONTENTS

VIII. KEEPERS OF THE FLAME 192
Jennifer Blake...Parris Afton Bonds...Rebecca Brandewyne...Sandra Brown...Candace Camp...Barbara Cartland...Jayne Castle...Elaine Raco Chase...Virginia Coffman...Catherine Coulter...Tom and Sharon Curtis...Janet Dailey...Jude Deveraux...Roberta Gellis...Brooke Hastings...Patricia Matthews...Alice Morgan...Laura Parker ...Rosemary Rogers...Maura Seger...Bertrice Small...Elizabeth Neff Walker...Linda Wisdom...Kathleen E. Woodiwiss

IX. TRUE CONFESSIONS 230
1. Also Known As 230
2. By Any Other Name 236
3. Behind Every Great Woman 246
4. So You Want To Write A Romance? 248
5. The Life—Or Death—Of A Romance Manuscript 255

X. FOR LOVE AND MONEY 258
1. Birth Of A Live Line 258
2. The Romancing Of America 268
3. Filling The Shelves 271
4. The Road To Fame And Fortune 273

XI. PACKAGING THE GOODS 276
1. The Arts Of Passion 276
2. Telling A Book By Its Cover 280
3. Portraits Of The Artists 293
4. Fitting The Most Into The Least 302

XII. LOVE NOTES 304
1. Hot Love By Cool Writers 304
2. Love By Association 307
3. Winning Words 309
4. Heart Beats 311

BIBLIOGRAPHY 315
INDEX 321

IF YOU'RE AMONG THE MILLIONS WHO LIKE TO READ ROMANCES, whether it's an occasional book or a dozen a week, you'll enjoy *LoveLines*. This is a book that, for the first time ever, puts the history and business of romances into perspective for you, today's romance reader. Romantic fiction has had a fascinating history that reaches down through thousands of years, and has of late turned into an incredible industry. While much has been written about the industry's enormous size and rapid growth (hundreds of millions of dollars in sales every year) and reasons for the books' popularity (fantasy, escape), nowhere has an attempt been made to probe behind the scenes, to explain all the hows and whys of a most remarkable phenomenon.

LoveLines does just that, from A to Z, even exploring a bit of love and romance in real life as well as in the pages of a book. Full of anecdotes, intimate details and the stories behind the stories, *LoveLines* takes you inside a fabulous world. It's a celebration of romance novels—and of romance itself.

Love Lines

I. THE ROMANCE WITH ROMANCE

Never has time been better for love—from a publishing standpoint, that is. Romances account for a hefty share of the paperback market, and without them, business would be lackluster indeed. But who's reading all those books and spending all that money on them—and why? Who's cheerleading the industry? Filmmakers, cruise lines, even the U.S. Postal Service are making the most out of the popularity of romance.

CHAPTER ONE

Spice Of Life

Romantic fiction is big business, and it's no secret that its phenomenal growth and sales is helping the publishing industry—in particular the paperback sector—with its bottom line. While inflation and rising production costs have forced most cover prices so high that consumers are noticeably resisting, romances continue to sell by the bagload. Although TV, cable and video games lure millions of people away from books as a form of entertainment, millions of romance readers remain steadfastly loyal, each buying anywhere from a handful to several dozen books a month. If there ever was a goose laying golden eggs in publishing, romance is it.

Are you ready for the numbers? They're all big, all impressive.

An estimated 20 million or more romance readers in the United States alone look over more than 150 new romance titles that hit the shelves each month. In 1981, they spent about $200 million; estimates for 1983 range as high as $450 to $500 million. It's not uncommon for a devoted romance reader to spend $60, $100, even $150 a month on an assortment of titles.

Silhouette
FOXFIRE LIG
In the wooded C
met proud-hear
His gold-flecke
his country-bor
with her city-wi
lean body chall
Her beauty was po
Men fought to touch her, ho
staked claim to her body an
Derek Hawke, once her master, now
vowed his love, promising her a plac
mistress of his English estate.
Red Nick, the cruel pirate, showere
with jewels and challenged her haut
his passion.
Jeremy Bond, renegade mercenary
charm any woman to his bed, risked
rescue her from her island prison.
AVON
AWAKENING OF LOVE
He was the surly, tough-talking star reporter. She was warm and outgoing, a creative photographer.
Josh Rettinger and Tracy Monroe couldn't have been less alike. Yet as they worked side by side on the latest news stories, their friendship blossomed. When Josh asked her to pose as his fiancée because he couldn't face Christmas with his family alone, Tracy agreed to play the part.
But their romantic playacting soon became more than make-believe. For Josh, the closeness of his "fiancée" filled him with unexpected desire. Tracy found herself falling deeply in love. She knew Josh's icy façade hid a heart that had been cruelly hurt...and she knew just as surely that she loved him with a passion that would awaken him to love.
NOW COMES THE SPRING

The books come in all types and lengths, from historical to contemporary, from short to long, from not so sexy to explicitly so. Most of them are contemporary romances, particularly brand-name lines, and in 1983, there were twenty such lines on the market or announced for launch. (A brand-name line, such as Harlequin, each month releases titles that have a fairly consistent editorial content and style, sold largely on the basis of the line's name rather than the individual

ecial Edition

Silhouette Special Edition

JANET
DAILEY
Foxfire
Light

ills Joanna
ac Wilder.
mocked her;
clashed
s. His
ner, sparking

FICTION
WARNER BOOKS

rt.

Jennifer Wilde

The long-awaited sequel to the 3-million-copy bestseller Love's Tender Fury

Love Me, Marietta

NOW
MES THE
SPRING
ANDREA EDWARDS

titles and authors.)

Brand-name romances alone account for 41 percent of total paperback sales, according to the romance newsletter *Boy Meets Girl*, and best-sellers, which include many romance titles, account for another 11 percent of the market. Consequently, romances as a whole are nearing 50 percent of the entire paperback market.

Meanwhile, other categories of paperbacks lag far behind. Male espionage, war and western books combined account for 17 percent; science fiction and occult—10 percent; general interest, including nonfiction—8 percent; mystery and detective—7.5 percent; religious and inspirational—4.5 percent; and sports—1 percent (all figures from *Boy Meets Girl*).

Silhouette Books, which publishes five brand-name lines of contemporary and young adult romances, estimates the romance market will grow at a rate of about 15 percent a year for at least several more years. (Others say the growth will slow to less than that, but the market will remain healthy and strong.)

This growth and proliferation of romantic novels is a fairly recent development. While there has always been romance in literature and the arts—and in stories passed on by word of mouth before there were books—romance as a genre and as an industry is a product of the last few decades, and mostly the last few years.

Harlequin began reprinting the British Mills & Boon Ltd. romances in the 1950s and then dedicated itself to romances in 1964, quietly monopolizing the market; big historical romances boomed in popularity in the United States in the 1970s; American publishers jumped into the market full force in the beginning of the 1980s, and the increasing competition generated a lot of press. With millions of dollars in annual sales at stake in a now very competitive market, publishers are spending big bucks on advertising and promotion—Harlequin and Silhouette alone each spend $20 million or more a year, more than the entire U.S. publishing industry spends for its advertising.

Romance readers, once discreet and almost surreptitious when buying romances, have become more open about their purchases in the face of publicity concerning the genre's popularity. "The industry came out of the closet in about 1977," says Vivien Lee Jennings, president of Rainy Day Books in Fairway, Kansas and editor of *Boy Meets Girl*. "Suddenly it became okay for a woman driving a late model car and wearing a fur coat to openly purchase a romance."

Who are these readers who have put romance on the publishing map?

Market research indicates nearly all are women and most range in age from eighteen to forty-five—although many are older. Most have a college education, are married, work and have an average annual household income ranging from $22,000 to $25,000. "These women are not television watchers, but they are avid readers, who probably belong to one or more book clubs," says Kathryn Falk, publisher of *Romantic Times*. "Romantic novels provide them with relaxation and a break from busy routine. They also provide information about history, social relations and geography, in a painless and entertaining manner."

"It's a mass audience," says Ellen Edwards, senior editor of Jove's Second Chance At Love. "Women don't find the romance they need on TV. Readers become very involved in these books." Ellen cites examples of letters that arrive daily at Second Chance offices, heart-wrenching letters written by women who say, "your books give me hope that there is love in the world."

"These love stories *are* very close to people's hearts," agrees Carolyn Nichols, senior editor of Bantam's Loveswept line. So close, in fact, that "light" readers of romances read up to twenty-five books a month, and "heavy" readers devour eighty or more, as incredible as it may seem.

Many of the readers eventually become writers,

TREVOR MELDAL-JOHNSEN

Author of ALWAYS

Barbara Ferry Johnson

om

ls

were
nted
past–
love
d been,
uld be
more...

ZEBRA 0-8217-1014-1 $3.50

FORBIDDEN ECSTASY

BY JANEL TAYLOR

AUTHOR OF SAVAGE ECSTASY

ALISHA FOUND RAPTURE IN GRAY EAGLE'S

"This is an unparalleled odyssey of survival. It is a rich tapestry of passion written across the canvas of history. A remarkable achievement told by a talented, sensitive author."
—Cynthia Freeman, author of COME POUR THE WINE

IN JOY AND IN

DELL • 14367 • 3.50

Their love was as fierce as the savage frontier!

LOVESWEPT • 7

Billie Green
A Tryst With Mr. Lincoln?

21607-4 ★ $1.95 ★ A BANTAM BOOK

, most dashi

OF HEARTS AND MARTYRS

Next to Christmas, there probably isn't a busier time of the year for the U.S. Postal Service than the period just preceding Valentine's Day. Although it didn't start out that way, the practice of sending cards and letters expressing deepest love for one another has become the true hallmark of this holiday, which is celebrated each February 14.

How a holiday started in remembrance of the martyrdom of St. Valentine, an early Christian, became linked to this sudden blossoming of love and affection is still somewhat a puzzle. The best guess of historians is that the sending of love notes began as an accident in the late Middle Ages.

One theory ties the origin of sending love greetings to a medieval European belief that birds begin to mate on February 14. Thus it seemed only right that lovers should exchange greetings and gifts on that date.

Today, the practice is ritually observed. Lovers exchange everything from simple heart-shaped cards and boxes of candy to furs, jewelry and cars. After all, there's really no limit when love's involved.

something which is more characteristic of romance than any other genre. According to Kathryn, at least 500 romance authors have published at least one book. The pay is good, ranging from $3,000 to $10,000, roughly, for a typical advance, with additional royalties estimated at another $10,000 to $20,000. Prolific stars with large followings easily earn annual six-figure incomes, and a handful of megastars earn in the millions.

Even without star status, the potential earnings are enticing, yet few professional writers have been able to make it in the genre. "It's harder to write a romance than one might think," says Carolyn. "It's a tougher nut to crack than any other genre. Some well-known writers have tried and failed—no big name has made it yet." Contrary to popular misconception, romances are not formula, fill-in-the-blanks books. "They don't have extensive plotting—all they have is a man and woman sparking off each other for 60,000 words," Carolyn says.

But readers who know and understand the fantasy can hit the mark. "They're very professional about it and many do this for a living," says Robin Grunder, editor of New American Library's Rapture Romance line. "They're interested in their craft and they're very conscientious. They're not a lot of little old ladies in Connecticut banging away on their typewriters."

Where will it all stop—or will it? How many more romances are consumers interested in and willing to buy? Women comprise 60 to 80 percent of all paperback customers (a medium that once catered to men), and ever since they discovered fiction tailored specifically to their tastes and fantasies, they haven't stopped buying. No overnight fad, this romance genre. "Romance will continue to be a major category—it has been for thirty years," notes Jacqui Bianchi, editorial director of Mills & Boon Ltd. in London, part of Harlequin Enterprises. However, it's doubtful the market is big enough for everyone who wants to be in it. Since 1980, major publishers have entered the market—especially the brand-name contemporary

FIRST CLASS LOVE

Even the U.S. Postal Service pays a tribute to love, a subject always worthy of repeat performance. In 1973, reports *Boy Meets Girl*, the Postal Service issued an 8¢ first-class stamp commemorating love that sold 3.3 million copies. In 1982, a 20¢ first-class love stamp was issued. Designed by Mary Faulconer of New York, the stamp says LOVE with flowers—daisies, red poppies, pansies, coral bells and bachelor's buttons.

Bachelor's buttons? Is there something subliminal there?

segment—and publishers already in the market have added new lines. "There are so many people jumping on the bandwagon, I'm afraid the wheels are going to fall off from all the weight," Jacqui says. "It can't go on at this pace."

What has started to happen is "churning"—the lines are exchanging customers. But eventually the stronger ones will attract and keep enough customers to push out the weaker ones. In a test of survival of the fittest, quality will win out. And that bodes well not only for customers, but for the continuation of a strong, healthy and very romantic form of fiction.

I. THE ROMANCE WITH ROMANCE

The question is always one of the first to be asked in any discussion or interview about romance novels—why are they so popular? Why are women spending up to $500 million a year on formula books about Prince Charming on a white horse?

Aha, a couple of fallacies here right off the bat. Yes, women spend millions every year—more than $1 million a day, in fact—on millions of romances. Obviously, they like them or they wouldn't keep coming back for more. "Women never spend money on anything they don't like," observes Vivian Stephens, senior editor of Harlequin American Romances.

Formula books about saviors on white horses? Maybe in years past, but the genre has changed to a large extent. "It's become revolutionized," says author Brooke Hastings. "In so many early books, there were misunderstandings that could have been cleared up with a simple question but weren't until the end. Now there's more communication between the characters and the heroines are more assertive and experienced in life."

"Formula" these days means only that the books contain a strong romance and a happy ending. Beyond that, just about anything can, and does, happen, including some fairly explicit—but always tastefully romantic—sex. "You never find unsatisfying sex in a romance," notes Ann Gisonny, senior editor of Dell Candlelight Ecstasy.

Hero and heroine are generally more equally matched, professionally, socially and economically, and endings often involve compromises.

Still, the question persists—what do these books have that strikes such a responsive chord in the female heart?

Romances offer two main attractions to readers—escape and the filling of an emotional void. They offer other things, too: entertainment, which is part of escape, and hope—hope that somewhere in the world, romantic love does indeed exist. "They're better than a lot of stuff on TV," says author Dixie Trainer. "They appeal to women because a lot of life is not very interesting or romantic." Author Tom Curtis notes, "They're the stuff of which daydreams are made."

But practically any fiction, even serious fiction, offers escape, says Pamela Strickland, senior editor of Ballantine's Love & Life line. "In romantic fiction, you get into a different world with different characters, and some wonderful things happen. Romantic fiction is entertainment, which is not to say it doesn't deal with serious themes—it does and that's what makes it strong and interesting."

I. THE ROMANCE WITH ROMANCE

Romances are often a woman's primary source of escape from boredom or the multitude of unpleasantries, large and small, in daily life. The romance fan generally isn't a soap opera fan and doesn't watch much other TV programming. "We've all got to have a change of pace and relief from stress," says Vivien Lee Jennings, president of Rainy Day Books in Fairway, Kansas and editor of *Boy Meets Girl*. "Our environment is so stressful. Romances are inexpensive, they're portable, and you can share them with friends."

The need for escape applies to all persons, men as well as women, and women certainly have other means of escape besides romantic fiction. But romances offer something much more, something uniquely and totally feminine. Through fantasy, they enable women to vicariously enjoy a courtship that may have long since faded from their real life relationship, or maybe one that never was part of it at all. "I think it's the times—there is so much uncertainty today," says Kathryn Falk, publisher of *Romantic Times*. "The future is not as hopeful as we would like it to be, and the pressures of working and raising a family are enormous."

In the last two decades, the role of women in the workplace, in society and in marriage has gone through profound upheaval. The women's liberation movement enabled women to make great strides towards realizing their full intellectual and professional capabilities, their right to equal pay, their right to independence. At the same time, it threw male-female relationships into confusion. "The women's movement has robbed womanhood of the mystery that made it so wonderful," according to author Sandra Brown, who describes herself as "a pure, dyed-in-the-wool, unrelenting romantic." "We've lost our intrigue, and that's what I like to see in a romance. Men don't have to be gentlemen anymore, [but] women are looking for that."

Furthermore, the Me First Decade of the 1970s, now spilling into the eighties, has caused entire generations, both sexes, to become immersed in self-absorption. "A lot of women don't really know what to expect in a relationship, especially younger women," says Vivian Stephens. "A woman who is twenty-four has never really been courted. Women wanted to get together with men and many don't know how. It's no longer 'Hello . . . What's your name . . . Let's go to bed,' like it was in the sixties."

The problem, says author Rebecca Brandewyne, is communication. "People do not know how to communicate on a one-to-one, everyday basis," she says. "This is why there is so much confusion, so many problems in relationships, such a high divorce rate. I believe very strongly

that the women's movement created a gigantic upheaval in the way both men and women perceive themselves, and many things were lost—all kinds of courtesies, like lighting cigarettes, opening doors and sending flowers. Men don't do those things anymore. Besides that, the economy is so bad that even if a man wanted to send a woman a dozen long-stemmed roses—how many of them have seventy-five bucks to blow on flowers that are going to be dead in a day?

"Romance," Rebecca continues, "has been taken out of our lives through social circumstances, but we still have those basic yearnings to feel loved. And when you don't get something in real life, you have to get it somewhere else."

Women seem to be caught between polarizations of what it means to be a woman—the "liberated woman" who doesn't have to depend on a man, on one hand, and the submissive "total woman" on the other. "The majority of us are somewhere in between," Rebecca observes. "We don't want to browbeat men and we don't want to be browbeaten ourselves. We'd like to be right there by our man's side."

But the popularity of romances doesn't mean women yearn en masse to give up the gains of equality; reality and fantasy are two very different things. As author Nancy Friday points out in *My Secret Garden*, the sexual fantasies women enjoy have little or nothing to do with their real lives—or real wants. Romantic fantasies are similar in a way—while many women do wish they had more courtship and romantic passion in their lives, they wouldn't necessarily throw their husbands over for a novel hero. How many men throw down their briefcases and become spies after they've read a James Bond book?

Nevertheless, the romantic fiction phenomenon provides juicy grist for all manner of sociological, psychological and academic experts who wish to speak on the state of womanhood. Men smirk at the "trash," feminists moan that the books are "pornographic" and full of sexually regressive stereotypes—the wimpy, submissive woman and the domineering, macho man. They claim the romantic fantasy encourages women to revert to weak, submissive behavior in real life—to accept male "oppression."

Yet after all the gains made by the women's movement, it's doubtful that more than 20 million women feel weak and oppressed after reading a book about the joys of romance and love.

Speaking about many of the critics, Karen Solem, vice president and editor in chief of Silhouette Books, says that "it's obvious they haven't read even the first pages of a romance. These are not 'white knight' books. Of course everybody wants to be loved in their lives, but we're not saying you should wait for the white knight to ride up. The women in these books are active, involved, happy people, but they have a lack in their life. Maybe they're not even aware of it. But suddenly a man presents himself and makes their life a little fuller.

"I don't think romances reinforce stereotypes, though they might have ten years ago," Karen says. "But there's always going to be that traditional book that the critics latch onto."

Some of the most vocal critics of romances are women. "In a day when women can do what they want to do, they're often the first critics of other women who want to read romances," Karen says. "It seems peculiar to me that women can criticize other women's taste when they don't take exception to what men read. Nobody criticizes men, like Franklin D. Roosevelt, for reading mysteries."

Karen says she hopes the misinformed preconceptions about romances will change. "I think it was Edna Ferber who said that romances will always be downgraded in their time," Karen reflects. "We call *Jane Eyre* a classic, but it was a contemporary romance in its time. I'm not saying these books are going to be classics, but they're entertainment—and more legitimate than some other forms of entertainment."

Indeed, there's little but happiness and optimism in romances. Unlike television and male adventure novels, there's no brutality, no horrible crimes, no senseless tragedies, no insoluble problems. The hero and heroine do have their difficulties and traumas, but readers always know at the outset that all will end well. "We know that these books aren't going to deal with anything terribly tragic or political," says Vivian Stephens.

Historical romances do have more adventure and violence—even rape—than contemporaries, but that element is always secondary to the romance.

What romances are not, however, is fairy tales, asserts author Sharon Curtis. "Somehow, romances have gotten equated with fairy tales, but they really don't have fairy tale endings. They have hope and happiness, but they never promise eternal bliss."

Author Maura Seger tells of a woman she met while conducting a bookstore autograph signing to promote her first romance, *Defiant Love* (Tapestry), a very sensual historical with explicit but gentle sex. "She was a 98-year-old woman who'd bought *Defiant Love* and brought it back to the bookstore for my autograph," says Maura. "There was a definite gleam in her eye."

I. THE ROMANCE WITH ROMANCE

LOVE'S LEADING LADY

There's one person who's done more single-handedly than anyone else to boost the prestige and visibility of the romance genre: Kathryn Falk, publisher of *Romantic Times;* author of *Love's Leading Ladies* (Pinnacle) and *How to Write a Romance and Get It Published* (Crown); organizer of major romance conferences; and hostess of deliciously romantic teas and wine parties. A cheerful, bubbling lady who manages to squeeze more into a single day than most people can fit in a week.

"I've been interested in romantic fiction for a long time," says Kathryn, who explains she grew up with her nose in a book, usually a romance. For years, Rhett Butler in Margaret Mitchell's *Gone with the Wind* was her image of the ideal romantic hero.

Born on December 5, 1940 in Harrisburg, Illinois—she grew up in affluent Grosse Point, Michigan—She was nearly forty before she turned her considerable energies to the romantic fiction business. Before that, she lived a full-tilt life as a romantic heroine herself, traveling the world over, meeting and being courted by rich and dashing men. She finally found Mr. Right on a steamboat trip down the Mississippi River—Kenneth Rubin, now her betrothed and the business manager for *Romantic Times.*

Kathryn graduated a history major from the University of Detroit, where she was a cheerleader and Miss Bond Bread and conducted her own on-campus radio and TV show as well as a dancing and cheerleading school.

In 1963 she moved to New York City—Greenwich Village, to be exact—and did modeling and public relations work. She took a stab at acting school, gave it up and worked as a trouble-shooter for a medical instruments firm, saving up enough money to buy two homes: one in Austria and one in the Catskills. She left the medical instruments firm to buy her own dollhouse shops in Manhattan, which she later sold. She wrote two books on dollhouses: *Miniature Needlepoint and Sewing Projects for Dollhouses* (Hawthorn) and *The Complete Dollhouse Building Book* (Bobbs-Merrill).

In 1978 Kathryn began researching romance authors for her collection of profiles, *Love's Leading Ladies*, and spent two years interviewing and compiling material. In the course of her research, she got the idea for *Romantic Times*, a full-fledged bimonthly newspaper devoted solely to romantic fiction and chock-full of articles, illustrations and photographs. "There are 20 million women who are avid fans of romantic fiction," says Kathryn, "and there was no publication catering to their interests. I love these books, too, so it has been a great thrill for me to create the first magazine in this field."

Kathryn put up $25,000 of her own money to start *Romantic Times.* Word of mouth was so strong that she had 3,000 subscribers by the time her first issue came out in July 1981. She had 6,000 subscribers by her second issue, 50,000 by her fourth and 55,000 today. The size of the paper has been expanded from twenty-four to thirty-six pages. Offices are at Kathryn and Ken's home, a Victorian carriage house in Brooklyn Heights.

But Kathryn hasn't stopped with *Romantic Times.* She created, in coordination with Long Island University, the Romantic Book Lovers Conference, the first of which, in 1982, drew an international audience of 500 people to New York City for two days of seminars, a romantic luncheon, cocktail parties, an awards ceremony and a book fair. The second, in 1983, drew more than 500 persons and featured three days of similar activities, all with spectacular special effects and romantic touches. Participants from the West Coast traveled to the New York conference aboard a special Amtrak "Love Train" that made whistle stops for author autograph signings. For 1984, Kathryn plans to begin her conference in New York and then move it to London, where it will pick up after the British Book Fair.

Kathryn and LIU also put together a Romantic Fiction Publishing Program, the first of its kind. And she is planning her own cable television show, "I'll Take Romance."

When Kathryn isn't busy with one of these projects or on the phone doing business or granting interviews on TV, she is entertaining her constant stream of visitors, many of them celebrity romance authors. "We have a wonderful English cook, Ms. Wiltshire, who serves every type of food imaginable for our parties," Kathryn says. "If Regency authors are visiting, we serve syllabub." (Syllabub is a wonderful dessert made of wine, rich cream and lemon.) Kathryn loves formal entertaining and loves to dress up for it. If she could choose to come back in another time, it would be the turn of the twentieth

Kathryn Falk

century, she says, a period of social elegance and splendor.

Where Kathryn finds the time and energy for so many activities mystifies many a casual observer. But that's been the story of her life—brimful of vigor and adventure. "You only live once," she says, "so you might as well aim high."

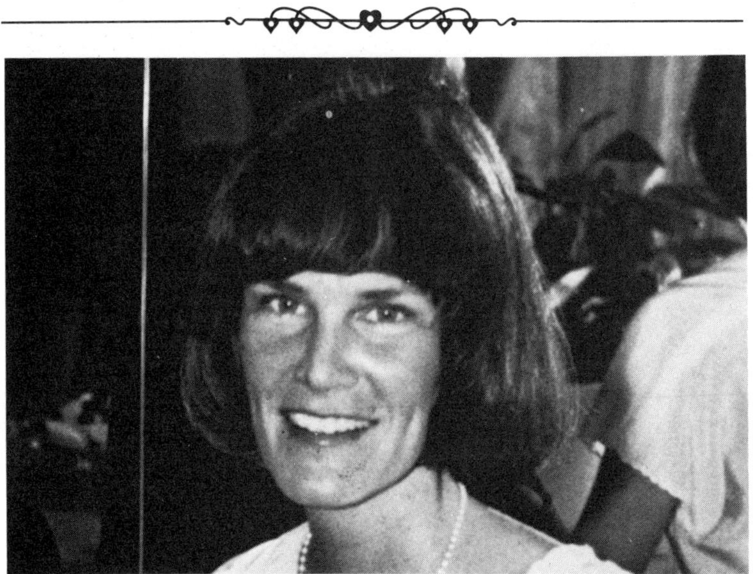

Vivien Lee Jennings

THE INDUSTRY WATCHER

From her headquarters at Rainy Day Books in Fairway, Kansas, Vivien Lee Jennings keeps close tabs on the trends and nuances of the romantic fiction industry. She reports all in her savvy newsletter, *Boy Meets Girl,* which she launched in March 1981. Each week, *Boy Meets Girl* is full of inside tidbits—the movements of editors, shifts in editorial needs, new lines in the works, the rising author stars, reports on romance conferences, the latest market data.

The newsletter is owned jointly by Vivien and her husband, Dick Jennings. Vivien is also president of Rainy Day Books, a corporation in which she is a partner along with another woman, Jane Walker Hess. Six Rainy Day bookstores are scattered throughout the Kansas City metropolitan area, and romances constitute about 50 percent of their trade.

That's by no accident, for Vivien, a native of Little Rock, Arkansas, has been reading romantic fiction since she was a teenager. "I wanted to specialize in romantic fiction because I knew it so well," she says.

The first Rainy Day store was opened in 1975 in Fairway; each subsequent store has been licensed as a separate company (the sixth was licensed in 1982).

Since 1975, Vivien has been in an ideal position to watch the romance genre expand and mature. Her customer base is diverse, she says, and many come to her and her employees for advice on what to read.

Her visibility with *Boy Meets Girl* has gotten her significant media exposure and has led to consulting jobs with publishers, for example, Jove for To Have And To Hold, its contemporary romance in marriage line, and Ballantine for Love & Life, its romance/women's fiction line. Her work takes her frequently to New York and to various romance conferences around the nation.

Boy Meets Girl previews significant upcoming books, but doesn't review them like many other romance publications. It is strictly trade news, intended to provide an overall perspective of the business. "I think if the romance business is going to succeed, people must have an overview of the business as a whole," Vivien says. "You can't just see it from the perspective of one publishing house."

A SLICE OF THE UNIVERSE

You've heard what a few people in the romance industry have to say about why romances are so popular, but what about the readers themselves? While *LoveLines* attempted no scientific polling or analysis of reader opinions, a few reader comments were provided by Myrna Armstrong, proprietor of The Bookworm's Castle in Buena Park, California. In the remarks below, they explain briefly why they like to read romances and why they prefer sexy romances to chaste ones. They're just one tiny slice of the romance universe, but their thoughts are revealing.

"It takes some of the pain and harshness out of everyday life. And it gives me an outlet to life.... Too much sweet gives me heartburn."
—G.W., *Anaheim*

"One, for the adventures; two, to read about places I've never been to or seen or might never get to see; three, escape; four, they make me feel happy after I read them, and I want to share with my friends the books I've read.... My husband is not romantic, and when I read these books it keeps me hoping and wishing and thinking maybe someday this will happen to me."
—T.L., *Buena Park*

"I like forceful men! And they help me to escape a little from my humdrum life.... It's nice to dream about it sometime."
—T.K., *Fullerton*

"They're escape from everyday trouble.... Every woman had hope at one time."
—B.B., *Anaheim*

"I hardly ever watch TV or go to movies. I can lose myself in a good book. If I've really enjoyed the book, it isn't unusual for me to re-read it several times.... I don't like them to be vulgar, but I do like them spicy."
—G.F., *Cerritos*

"Light easy reading... enjoyable, slightly erotic without being vulgar."
—B.N., *Buena Park*

"I enjoy getting away from realities!... I'm a spicy lady."
—N.W., *Cypress*

"I enjoy them, they make you forget your own problems for a while."
—P.M., *Buena Park*

"They are an escape from the world of work and worry. They are also, to my mind, better entertainment than TV and movies—they last and can be re-read whenever one desires to do so. ... They are thrilling and for a while one can live vicariously the life of the heroine."
—J.B., *Anaheim*

"It is a form of escapism and a happy ending, to become the person in the novel. I live vicariously."
—B.W., *Buena Park*

"I like them. I read 42 books a month."
—V.M., *Cypress*

"My husband was *so* romantic."
—H.O., *Anaheim (age 77)*

I. THE ROMANCE WITH ROMANCE

A book industry such as romance that has hit such heights of sales, profits and popularity does not go unnoticed or untapped by film and television folks for long. Sooner or later it had to happen: romance novels—or at least the concept of romance novels—adapted to the screen. Not just an occasional movie but daily series of mini-romances as well.

Romance fans haven't before seen many of their novels acted out on the screen. In 1976, Harlequin filmed an Anne Mather novel, *Leopard in the Snow,* and planned more films; several years later, a Barbara Cartland book, *The Flame Is Love,* was filmed and shown in the United States as well as England and elsewhere. But 1982 marked the beginning of significant film and television activity in the romance genre. Janet and Bill Dailey wrote and produced their own movie, *Foxfire Light*; Silhouette Books and Paramount Video formed *Silhouette Romance Theatre* to make movies of Silhouette novels; and Comworld Productions of Brentwood, Tennessee launched *Romance Theatre,* a daily half-hour show of romance dramas syndicated on more than 100 TV stations across the nation.

(One might also include in that list *Romance,* a series produced by PKO Television Ltd. with Telegenic of Toronto for late-night cable television. However, the nudity in that show makes it a bit sensational for true "romance" classification.)

The idea of producing love stories for TV and movie theater is certainly nothing new; love, along with crime, is one of the most common elements in all films, regardless of story or setting. Even though there are only a few variations on the theme of love—requited love, unrequited love, lost love, reunited love, betrayed love, tragic love, illicit love, sacrificed love—we never tire of them; a love story is guaranteed an audience. How many times have you or someone you know wept over the tragedy that befalls Ryan O'Neal and Ali McGraw in *Love Story*?

Many great love film classics are based on novels, such as *The Sheik, Camille* and *Anna Karenina.* The greatest and most emotion-provoking love films of all time are *Casablanca,* starring Humphrey Bogart and Ingrid Bergman, and *Gone with the Wind,* starring Clark Gable and Vivien Leigh.

On television, the series *Love Boat,* romances aboard cruise ships based loosely on the nonfiction book of the same name by Jeraldine Saunders, is one of the most successful series ever, shown in eighty-three countries. A precursor of *Love Boat* was *Love American Style,* which featured light

Elizabeth Garvie and David Rintoul in *Pride and Prejudice*

Pride and Prejudice

Rebecca, starring Jeremy Brett and Joanna David

Sorcha Cusack and Michael Jayston in *Jayne Eyre*

comedies about true love and its pitfalls and joys.

But if romance novels are so popular, why haven't more of them been adapted to the screen before now? Some of them, particularly big historicals, have sold millions of copies—why not make them into movies?

The truth is, most romance novels don't translate well to the screen, for two main reasons: action and dialogue.

With the exception of some historicals, most romances, especially contemporary romances, are not action-oriented books—they are *emotion* books. Pages and pages are devoted to the thoughts of the heroine, her feelings and her emotional reactions to the hero. Feelings and thought processes give the viewer nothing to look at. One way to handle this is to use voice-over to explain what's going on in the heroine's head, but too much voice-over only puts distance between the viewer and the story.

Many novelists can't write good dialogue, especially TV and movie dialogue, and romance writers are no exception. Comworld's *Romance Theatre* uses no romance novel dialogue because much of it is "unsayable," according to executive producer William E. Glenn.

Dialogue is more easily fixed in a screenplay than action, however. And many romances just don't contain enough turbulence to make good stories for the screen.

Romance Theatre: Alternative To Soaps

Comworld Productions is betting $7 million that women want to watch romances, in addition to or instead of soaps, on television. That's how much money the Tennessee firm has invested in its first season of *Romance Theatre*, twenty-six weeks of twenty-six shows, each story spread over five half-hour segments. It's intended for airing in late afternoons, though the syndicating stations may choose a different time slot.

Although the program's producers are veterans of soap operas—*Guiding Light* and *The Young and the Restless*—*Romance Theatre* is not another soap. It is a series of love stories, one story each week, and every story ends happily. The stories attempt to capture the "swept away" feeling women like and find in romance novels.

Louis Jourdan, the quintessential romantic hero with his tall, dark and handsome good looks and his French-accented eloquence, hosts *Romance Theatre*. At sixty-three, Louis still looks like he could knock just about any woman off her feet.

Psychologist Dr. Joyce Brothers is a guest star on the program and

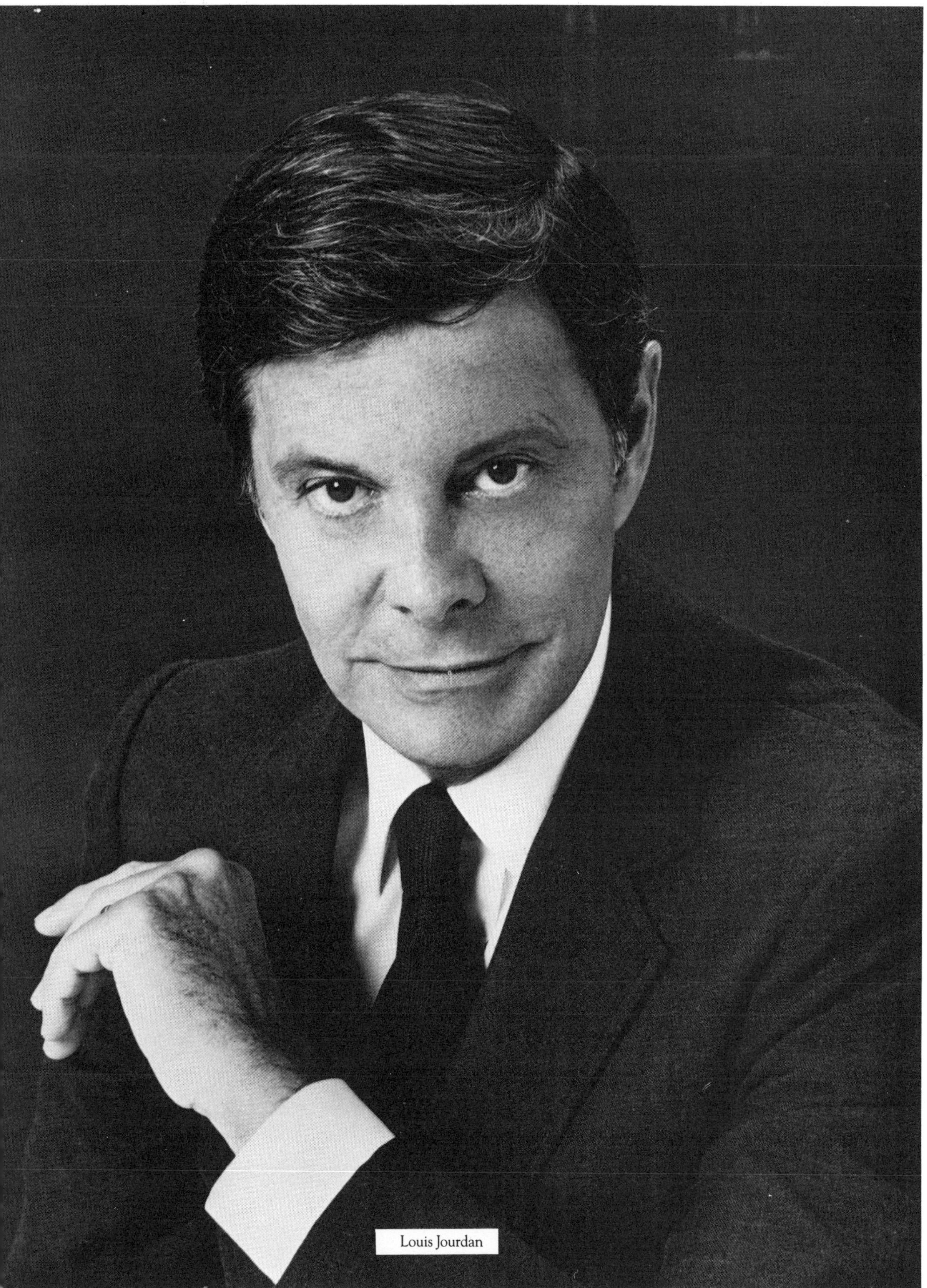

Louis Jourdan

comments on the importance of romance in relationships. She says without it "lovemaking can be no more fulfilling than a sneeze." Romance is making a comeback, she adds, for both women and men. "The young and old are going back to allowing closeness in a relationship, and they are going back to honoring the old ideals."

The idea for *Romance Theatre* came from James W. McCallum, Comworld's vice president for development and syndication. McCallum had never read a romance, but press publicity about the genre's popularity piqued his interest. He picked up a few romances, read them and thought, "Why not?"

Several attempts at adaptation of novels didn't work; now a team of writers turns out original screenplays that strive for realism while remaining true to the fantasy essence of the genre.

Among the story lines are these plots:

"Love at the Top." The heroine, an employee of a top lingerie fashion design company, is under consideration for an executive promotion to the firm's New York headquarters. Her only competition is the hero, who is married to the owner's daughter and with whom she falls in love. The choice—romance or career.

"Escape to Love" (stars Patricia Davis, President Ronald Reagan's daughter). A young American journalist, traveling in Europe, helps a famous author escape prison for speaking out against political repression in Poland. They escape under a guise of being married, and fall in love. Once they are safely in Paris, he leaves her to go back to Poland to help others in danger. Will they ever be reunited?

"Lights, Camera, Action, Love." An upcoming actress falls for a cameraman but is pursued by a famous director who could make her a star. She must make the right choice.

"The Awakening of Cassey." An artist gets deeply into a love affair with a gallery owner who admires her work, then she discovers he's married. She confronts him and his spouse and tells them their marriage is worth saving—but not at her expense. She finds love and happiness with another artist.

Silhouette Romance Theatre: Let's Go to the Movies

Hoping to tap into a whole new audience of romance fans, Silhouette Books, a division of Simon & Schuster, contracted with Paramount Video in 1982 to produce two-hour movies based on popular Silhouette novels. Paramount Video is part of Paramount Pictures Corp., which, along with Simon & Schuster, is a subsidiary of Gulf + Western Industries, Inc. The first movie is to be released in 1983 on a worldwide basis, through either pay TV, cable TV, commercial TV or movie theaters.

"By traveling into another medium with the Silhouette romance concept, we have an exceptional opportunity to capture a share of romance enthusiasts we might not otherwise have had access to," says John C. Gfeller, president of Silhouette Books.

Paramount will be the first major motion picture studio to adapt a brand-name contemporary romance to the screen. The results promise to be interesting.

Janet and Bill Make a Movie

It's always a thrill to writers to see their characters come alive in a book. It's an even greater thrill to see them come alive in film. And probably the biggest thrill of all is doing everything yourself—the book, the screenplay, the production, the distribution.

That's exactly what Janet and Bill Dailey did with one of Janet's Silhouette novels, *Foxfire Light*. Janet, America's leading romance author, wrote the screenplay, and their own production company, Ramblin' Productions, made the movie. The film, to be distributed in 1983 either on TV or in movie theaters, was shot in its entirety on location in the Ozark Mountain Country near Branson, Missouri, where the Daileys live.

"It was quite a project and an adventure, but it was worth every minute—from the agony of the casting to the ecstasy of the first rushes," Janet says. "The first time I saw the first day's rushes, I cried. There they were—my characters come to life, saying the lines exactly the way I'd heard them in my head. It worked! This great bunch of actors and crew had made the story *real!*"

Casting for the forty-two speaking parts was done in Hollywood. Stars of the film include Barry Van Dyke (son of Dick Van Dyke), Faye Grant, Leslie Nielsen, Lara Parker, Tippi Hedren and John Steadman.

Foxfire Light was screened at the 1983 Romantic Book Lovers Conference in New York, sponsored by *Romantic Times*. Kathryn Falk, publisher of *Romantic Times*, arranged for the audience to have that traditional movie fare, popcorn—appropriately colored a romantic pink.

Dr. Joyce Brothers

Barbara Mallory and Sarah Rush in "For Love of Angela"

NO SOAP TO SOAPS

People who aren't familiar with romance novels often compare them to the soap operas on daytime television, believing them to be similar in content and appeal.

They're wrong.

"Soap operas are series of continuing problems," notes Ellen Edwards, senior editor of Jove's Second Chance At Love. "Romances are happy stories with happy endings."

Soap operas do feature love. Luke and Laura, when they were together on ABC's *General Hospital,* riveted entire college populations to the tube every weekday afternoon. But Laura, played by Genie Francis, fell in love with Luke, played by Anthony Geary, after he raped her—something no self-respecting contemporary romance novel heroine would stand for today.

More often than soaps dish out love, however, they dish out reality and the seamier side of human relationships—infidelity, corruption, betrayal, drug abuse, wife abuse, casual and opportunistic sex. Gothic author Virginia Coffman loves them for their realism. "They show things that are really going on in people's lives," she says. A soap fan since 1965, Virginia prefers the daytime soaps to nighttime ones. "They're ridiculous," she says of the latter. "They dramatize extremes."

Romance readers, on the other hand, read more for fantasy than reality—a believable story about a man and woman who meet, fall in love, overcome obstacles to their love and happily commit themselves to each other in marriage. A soap opera with that as its only story line would be short-lived, indeed.

That doesn't mean romance readers don't watch soaps. Undoubtedly they do, but probably more at night because of daytime jobs. When romance publishers buy television spots to advertise their products, it's more often on prime time shows, some of which are nighttime soaps, such as ABC's *Dynasty* and CBS' *Dallas*. "We don't advertise in the afternoon anymore," says Karen Solem, vice president and editor in chief of Silhouette Books. "We don't feel there is much of an overlap in audiences."

If you want trauma, turn on a soap. If you want tenderness, read a romance.

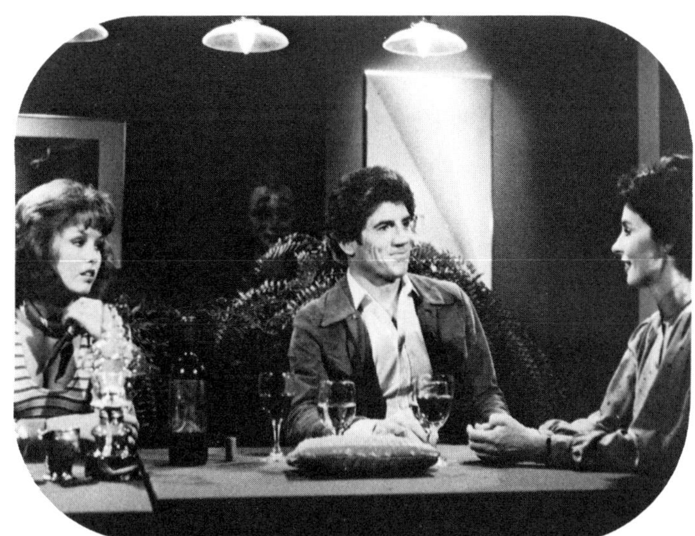

Deborah Foreman, Thomas MacGreevy and Millie Perkins in "Love in the Present Tense"

Janis Paige in "Love at the Top"

Millie Perkins

I. THE ROMANCE WITH ROMANCE

According to Princess Line Cruises, provider of television's long-running *Love Boat* series, romantic vacations on a cruise ship are big business—and no wonder. How else can you travel to exotic ports-of-call at your leisure, pampered, entertained and fed like royalty—and have the chance to meet that handsome stranger of your dreams? Whoever said "romance of the sea" wasn't kidding. Indeed, romance and sea cruises go hand in hand.

Prior to the advent of steam-powered ships, sea travel was at the mercy of wind and tides, and conditions were often less than pleasant. Even so, young boys dreamed of becoming sailors and buccaneers, and many young women waited anxiously for their dashing lovers to return from India, Africa or Cathay. In historical romances, the most oft-used vocation for heroes is that of sea captain, which enables travel to exotic locales and shifts in settings.

With steamships, transatlantic passenger travel became more common and much more luxurious, reaching its height of glory with the giant English and French ocean liners of the 1930s. The *Queen Mary* and *Queen Elizabeth*, both British registry and built by Cunard Lines Ltd., each weighed more than 80,000 tons; the only other ship that large was the French liner *Normandie*. The *Queen Elizabeth II*, by comparison, weighs 58,000 tons; the *Titanic* weighed just over 46,000 tons.

The Glorious Royal Mail Ship *Queen Mary*

The R.M.S. *Queen Mary* is the only survivor of the era of giant, supremely glamorous ocean liners. The first ship under Cunard registry that wasn't christened with a name ending in "ia"—other Cunard liners were *Britannia*, *Lusitania*, *Aquitania* and *Mauritania*—the *Mary* is 1,018 feet long, which is taller than the Eiffel Tower (984 feet) and nearly as tall as the Empire State Building (1,248 feet). She was built in Glasgow, Scotland shipyards and made her first voyage as a luxury liner in 1936. She could carry 1,957 passengers, which would fill the equivalent travel space of 65 Pullman train cars, plus 1,300 crew members, and she had over a half million pieces of glassware, china and table silver on board. The restaurants, lounges and cabins were elegantly appointed in Art Deco style; many were paneled in exotic—and expensive—woods. In fact, the ship was known as the Ship of Woods, for 1.25 million square feet of timber were used in her construction, including 56 varieties of woods from Britain's various colonies.

During World War II, the *Queen Mary* was repainted wartime gray and conscripted as a troopship; she could carry an entire division. She was able to cross the ocean in four days, an incredible pace for a troop carrier and one that enabled her to outrun enemy submarines and ships. She always took a zigzag course to further thwart enemy attack. Adolf Hitler had a standing offer of $250,000 to the crew of any U-boat that sank her.

The *Mary* also served as a hospital ship and as the "brides" ship, carrying thousands of British women to be reunited with the servicemen they had married during the war.

All in all, the *Queen Mary* transported more than a million soldiers during the war. Her first voyage carrying American troops, from Boston to Sydney, Australia, took place between February 18 and March 10, 1942; the trip was dubbed the "forty days and forty nights" voyage.

Today the *Queen Mary*, which is permanently docked at Long Beach, California, is a major tourist attraction and hotel (operated by Hyatt). She has been kept in immaculate condition—the woods shine, the brass gleams, the staterooms have their original cabinetry and appointments. It's impossible to walk on board and not be awed by the superb craftsmanship, not to imagine what it must have been like to travel first class, to spend easy days and then dine and dance the nights away. The Romance Writers of America had its 1982 annual conference on board the ship, a fittingly romantic setting.

It's estimated that it would cost about $500 million to refit the *Queen Mary* for ocean travel—if it were at all feasible to operate such a large ship. And if someone wanted to try to build a duplicate of the ship, cost notwithstanding, it couldn't be done. Many of the woods that were used are now extinct.

The End Of An Era

The *Queen Elizabeth*, the heaviest of the grand ocean liners at more than 83,000 tons, was also sold to American investors in the 1960s as a tourist attraction. Launched in 1940, the *QE* was often seen passing the *Queen Mary* in the opposite direction on the New York to Southampton crossing. Unfortunately, the stately *QE* was destroyed by fire in Hong Kong harbor in 1972.

The French ocean liner *Normandie*, fastest in the sea until the launching of the *Queen Mary* in 1936, was also destroyed by fire, in New York

harbor in 1946. The U.S.S. *United States*, pride of the American fleet but no longer in service, holds the current world record for speed at 34 knots an hour.

Faster and cheaper airplane travel seemed to sound the death knell for the grand ocean liners. But in 1969, Cunard's *Queen Elizabeth II*, or the *QE2* as she is known, made her maiden voyage. Much lighter and shorter than her namesake, the *QE2* has a cruising speed of 28.5 knots and carries about 2,000 passengers. Most of its summer traffic is transatlantic; cruises to the West Indies and South Atlantic are common in winter. The *QE2* also makes periodic around-the-world voyages, stopping in all the major ports of Europe, Asia, Africa, Australia and North and South America. The cost of passage on one of these big trips starts in the five-figure range.

Princess Marguerite

As elegant and beautifully appointed as her older sisters, the *QE2* has kept the romance of transatlantic travel alive. Like the *Queen Mary*, she's also performed military duty, carrying British troops and supplies to the Falkland Islands during Britain's war with Argentina there in 1982.

Today's Love Boats

But what are the "real" love boats? Fleets of ocean liners may no longer be practical, but lighter passenger cruisers, weighing about 20,000 tons, are taking thousands of people each year on romantic vacations and honeymoons to such areas as the Caribbean islands, South America, the Mediterranean and Alaska. One ship, the 369-foot Canadian *Princess Marguerite*, advertises its Seattle-Victoria-Vancouver cruise as the Last of the Great Romantics, playing directly to the emotional pull of romantic—and sensuous—sea adventures. There are even cruise ships that take vacationers along the coast of China to see the splendors of the Imperial Palace and the Great Wall, complete with guides and delicious Chinese cuisine.

These smaller ships have air-conditioned cabins, swimming pools, restaurants, lounges, tennis courts and even discos. They usually make seven-day trips, stopping at various ports, particularly on Caribbean tours, letting passengers disembark to see the sights. Some of the major cruise lines making these voyages are Sitmar, British Columbia Steamship Co. Ltd., Norwegian Cruise Lines, Carnival Cruise Lines and Princess Cruises.

It may be faster and more convenient to take a plane these days, but for true luxury, leisurely travel and the chance to make your dreams come true, there's nothing like a sea cruise.

Queen Mary's Queen's Salon

AN ELEGANT FEAST

The Right Honorable Winston S. Churchill, prime minister of Great Britain, crossed the Atlantic three times during World War II on the *Queen Mary*. In August 1943, he sailed to America to meet with President Franklin D. Roosevelt. Here's a dinner menu from which he ate. The original is preserved in one of the ship's museums.

Diner d'Adieu

Coupe de Melon au Kirsch
Velout Pommes d'Amour
Truite de Rivière, Grenoblaise
Grouse Rôtie à l'Anglaise
Petits Pois à la Française
Pommes Soufflées
Ruche, Queen Mary
Café
Champagne, Bollinger 1929

R.M.S. *Queen Mary*

TEST YOUR ROMANCE QUOTIENT

To find out just how much you know about romances and the romance publishing business, take this quiz. It starts off easy and moves on to some tougher questions. By reading *LoveLines,* you should be able to answer every question. When you're done, see next page for the correct answers and scoring. All but two questions are one point each; numbers 10 and 17 are two points each. Good luck!

1. The largest publisher of romances in the world is ______________________________.
2. The biggest American publisher of brand-name contemporary romances is __________.
3. Her nickname is "Sunny," and she writes sexy historicals such as *Skye O'Malley* and *Unconquered* (Ballantine). The author is ______________________.
4. The largest romance newspaper, published by Kathryn Falk, is ______________.
5. Harlequin's headquarters are in ______________________.
6. The biggest romance publisher in England is ______________________.
7. Tapestry Romances are (choose one) *contemporary* or *historical?* ______________
8. The late British author who created the Regency romance was Georgette __________.
9. In 1980, Dell started a line of sexy romances called ______________________________.
10. The initials of both these authors are J. D., and you know them by their "Velvet" and "Calder" books. They are ______________________ and ______________________ (two points).
11. Best known for medieval romances such as *The Roselynde Chronicles* is author Roberta ______________________.
12. RWA are the initials for what organization? ______________________________
13. The former Avon Books editor who discovered Kathleen E. Woodiwiss, Rosemary Rogers and other authors is Nancy ______________________________.
14. She is Harlequin's biggest author, with more than 90 million copies in print, and one of her latest books is *Stormspell.* Her name is Anne ______________________.
15. The name of Barbara Cartland's home in England is ______________________________.
16. Rapture Romances are published by ______________________.
17. The real-life identity of Robin James, pseudonymous author of *The Golden Touch* (Second Chance At Love) is ______________________________. (two points)
18. How many books has Harlequin sold since its beginning in 1949? ______________.
19. Bantam Books started this line of contemporary romances as Circle Of Love, then revamped it and renamed it ______________________.
20. This author of contemporary romances likes to work with her pet cockatiel perched on her shoulder. Her name is Linda ______________________.
21. Name the author who's also a mercenary soldier and a body guard. ______________
22. The name of Janet Dailey's first movie is ______________________.

I. THE ROMANCE WITH ROMANCE

ANSWERS

1. *Harlequin*
2. *Silhouette*
3. *Bertrice Small*
4. *Romantic Times*
5. *Toronto, Ontario*
6. *Mills & Boon Ltd.*
7. *Historical*
8. *Georgette Heyer*
9. *Candlelight Ecstasy*
10. *Jude Deveraux and Janet Dailey*
11. *Roberta Gellis*
12. *Romance Writers of America*
13. *Nancy Coffey*
14. *Anne Mather*
15. *Camfield Place*
16. *New American Library*
17. *Tom and Sharon Curtis*
18. *197 million*
19. *Loveswept*
20. *Linda Wisdom*
21. *Tom Townsend (aka Tammie Lee)*
22. *Foxfire Light*

SCORING

20–24 Exceptional—pat yourself on the back
14–19 Superior—you know the genre
9–13 Excellent—a good romance fan
0–8 Admirable—study up—read *LoveLines!*

II. THE LANGUAGE OF LOVE

Ah, love! It has remained essentially the same throughout the years, the centuries and the ages. Despite the changes brought by science and technology, despite wars and the rise and fall of cultures and empires, lovers today love much the same way they did thousands of years ago. Their hearts soar in rapture with love fulfilled; their hearts bleed in pain and in vain over love lost or unrequited. For the sake of a love, great works of art have been wrought and great deeds done; battles have been fought, crimes committed and political treacheries spawned. "Who loves, raves," observed Lord Byron.

Here are ten famous romances taken from history, from the ancient days of Rome and Egypt to the present world of princes and princesses. Some of these tales are happy, others are tragic.

CLEOPATRA (69 B.C.–30 B.C.) & MARK ANTONY (83 B.C.?–30 B.C.)

Cleopatra and Mark Antony had all the makings of a modern celebrity couple: a young, beautiful, intelligent queen of Egypt and a respected leader of the Roman Republic, a man of fine, virile physique with an eye for women. Their blind ambition for power, however, sealed their unhappy fate and contributed to the end of the Roman Empire.

Cleopatra possessed a sensuous mouth, dark, liquid eyes, a firm chin and a voice, wrote the Greek biographer Plutarch, "like an instrument of many strings." She also possessed a keen desire to rule the world, which made her suspect in the eyes of Rome. Cleopatra set out to conquer Rome by charming its leaders—most notably Julius Caesar, who fell under her spell and fathered a son by her. After Caesar was murdered, she turned her charms on his close associate and heir apparent, Mark Antony, who was engaged in a power struggle with Octavian, Caesar's nephew and adopted son.

For her famous meeting with Antony in Tarsus, Cilicia, Cleopatra spared no expense. Dressed as the love goddess Venus, she sailed up the Cydnus River in a lavishly decorated barge laden with gifts. Antony, bewitched, postponed a military campaign, abandoned thought of his third wife back in Rome and returned to Alexandria with Cleopatra, where the two engaged in a life of revelry, debauchery and dissipation. Cleopatra gave him three children and he gave her Eastern kingdoms.

Antony brazenly married Cleopatra in 36 B.C. while still married to a Roman woman. In another brazen move, in 34 B.C., Antony and Cleopatra crowned themselves "King of Kings" and "Queen of Queens." An outraged Roman Senate declared war on Antony.

The lovers were unlucky in battle, however, and their combined forces lost a naval encounter with Octavian. The couple fled to Alexandria with the

victorious Octavian in pursuit. There, with their dreams of world power crumbling, they ended their lives. Antony fell on his sword and died in Cleopatra's arms. She, now Octavian's prisoner, barricaded herself in her mausoleum and committed suicide, probably with an asp smuggled to her inside a basket of figs.

HELOISE (1097?–1164) & PETER ABELARD (1079–?1144)

Alas, poor Heloise and Abelard—their tragic, all-consuming love was doomed from its very beginning.

Abelard, son of a Britanny knight, was one of the most famous and controversial theologians and teachers of his age, holding the chair of philosophy and theology at Notre Dame in Paris. With his gift for poetry and his handsome looks, he was enormously popular with women.

Around 1113, at the peak of his teaching career, he met Heloise, a pretty, bright teenager who lived with her uncle, Canon Fulbert, a Paris clergyman. Instantly infatuated with her, Abelard got himself hired as her private teacher and arranged to live in Fulbert's house. There he seduced Heloise and a passionate affair began, creating a love in Heloise that was so intense she described it as madness. She was willing to do his every bidding, even if it meant plunging into the flames of Hell.

Their affair became public and scandalous, infuriating Fulbert and causing him much grief. Abelard, lost in love, put aside his scholarly work and devoted himself to writing and singing romantic ballads about Heloise. To appease her family, he pressed her for marriage, but she resisted, arguing that it would ruin his career. After she bore his illegitimate son, Heloise finally agreed to a secret marriage. The wedding vows, however, came too late to placate her uncle, who had Abelard attacked and savagely castrated.

Their lives shattered, Abelard forced Heloise to enter a convent and take the veil, while he retired to a monastery. For the rest of their days, they sanctified themselves in the Church, maintaining contact through letters. Abelard submerged himself in religion, but Heloise never could forget the passion that had taken them to the heights of ecstasy and the depths of despair.

"Of all wretched women I am the most wretched," she wrote to Abelard, "and amongst the unhappy I am unhappiest. The higher I was exalted when you preferred me to all women, the greater my suffering over my own fall and yours, when I was flung down; for the higher the ascent, the heavier the fall."

ANN BOLEYN (1507–1536) & HENRY VIII (1491–1547)

For more than six years, Henry VIII was obsessed with love and desire for the wily Anne Boleyn. It was an obsession that gave impetus to a massive political and religious upheaval, the English Reformation.

Young Anne, a 19-year-old court attendant and sister of one of Henry's mistresses, first caught the king's roving eye in 1526. Tall, muscular and athletic, Henry, 35, had tired of his wife, Catherine of Aragon. At 41, Catherine, his brother's widow, had produced no male heir.

Henry began sending Anne love letters in 1527, proclaiming his true love and swearing he would be faithful to her alone if she would be his mistress. No fool was Anne; if the king was to have her, it would have to be as his wife. But the Pope refused to grant an annulment to Henry, a staunch Roman Catholic. Anne, well versed in court intrigue, held out for marriage.

In the ensuing political turmoil to free himself from his marital fetters, the king executed those seen as threats to his position and replaced them with sympathizers. Finally, in 1531, Henry had Catherine imprisoned and took Anne as his mistress. The following year, the Church of England, with Henry as its head, split from Rome. Henry and Anne were wed secretly in 1533, shortly before the king's annulment became official. Soon thereafter, Anne gave birth to a daughter, Elizabeth.

Anne delighted in her triumph, alienating court members with her arrogance. But her triumph was short-lived. She could not produce a male heir, and Henry soon grew bored with her. To amuse himself, he took a mistress, Jane Seymour, who was to become his third wife, and then erased Anne from his life. She was accused, probably falsely, of incest with her brother and adultery with various members of the royal court. On May 19, 1536, she was beheaded at Tower Green in London, protesting her innocence right up to the fall of the ax.

EMMA HAMILTON (1761–1815) & HORATIO NELSON (1758–1805)

Vice Admiral Horatio Nelson was one of England's greatest naval commanders, a brilliant, magnetic man revered by his crews and adored by his loving spouse, Fanny, whom he married in 1787 as the "perfect wife" for an aspiring naval officer. He was away at sea for all but five years of their married life, during which Fanny remained steadfast in her devotion to him. Nelson created an international scandal when he lost his heart and head to Lady Emma Hamilton, a young, vivacious former courtesan who was married to Sir William Hamilton, England's elderly ambassador to the court of Naples.

In 1798, fresh from a stunning victory over Napoleon's forces in the Battle of the Nile, Nelson put in at Naples for repairs. There Emma, whom he had briefly met five years before, gave him an emotional welcome, fussed over his minor wounds and then turned him into a local celebrity. Placed on a pedestal before society and the royal court, Nelson was flattered by all the attention. He was dazzled with Emma, as she was with him, despite the fact that he'd lost his right arm and the sight of his right eye in previous battles.

In the thrall of infatuation and then love, Nelson stayed on at Naples for two years, openly conducting an affair with Emma while Sir William looked the other way. He neglected his naval duties, which angered his superiors in England, and hence was recalled to London in 1800. Arriving with Emma and Sir William, Nelson was hailed as a hero by the public. But high society snickered at his affair, and royalty snubbed him.

Nelson didn't care. He, Sir William and Emma carried on a menage a trois for three years while Fanny pleaded in vain for a reconciliation. After Sir William died in 1803, Emma and Nelson bought a luxurious house, where they lived with their daughter, Horatia, until Nelson was summoned back to duty two years later.

Again joining battle with Napoleon's naval forces, he demolished the French fleet in the Battle of Trafalgar, thereby establishing England as ruler of the seas. But the victory cost him his life. Nelson's last request as a dying man was that Emma be granted a pension from his estate, but the British government refused, awarding everything to Fanny and his brother. Emma died penniless, nine years later in Calais.

• II. THE LANGUAGE OF LOVE •

GEORGES SAND (1804–1876)
ALFRED de MUSSET (1810–1857)

The love affair between writer George Sand and poet Alfred de Musset was passionate, tortured, brief and violent. Called "the wildest love affair of the century," it stimulated some of the most creative works of each artist. For slightly more than a year, their hearts were inexorably locked, but they could live neither with each other nor without.

George Sand, born Amandine Aurore Lucie Dupin, married a baron at age 18. During nearly a decade together, they scarcely got along. In 1831, she left her husband and, sustained by an allowance from him, went to Paris to live the life of a bohemian artist. She was an alluring woman, with black hair, olive-hued skin and intriguing, enormous dark eyes. She chose, however, to dress like a man, smoke cigars and adopt a man's name, under which she published her novels of romantic feminism. Despite her masculine airs, she attracted numerous male lovers, many of them famous.

Alfred, one of France's great love poets and dramatists, achieved fame by age 17. A golden-haired Apollo and a moody dandy, he was determined to experience everything he possibly could.

They met at a dinner party in June 1833; he was 22 and she was 28. Within weeks they were lovers. Both brilliant talents, George and Alfred loved intensely, each one mirroring the other's image. They read to and wrote about each other. In December, the couple embarked on what was to be a glorious lovers' journey to Italy. However, they both fell ill, Alfred denounced his love for George and she took another lover. They returned to Paris separately—Alfred alone and George with her new lover. Although apart from one another, the memory of their passion remained strong, and they sent each other anguished letters of love.

The next year was marked by a series of joyous reconciliations, violent fights and recriminations and tortured partings. Finally, George put an end to it. To console themselves, each turned to writing. "Love and write," George had once told Alfred, but while she continued to prosper as a writer for the rest of her long life, he did not. He never was able to put his tempestuous affair with George behind him. After a creative spurt that resulted in some of his best work, Alfred's last two decades were marked by bitterness, ill health, debauchery and the deterioration of his artistic career.

ELIZABETH BARRETT (1806–1861) &
ROBERT BROWNING (1812–1889)

"How do I love thee? Let me count the ways," begins one of the most famous love sonnets of all time. It was written by poet Elizabeth Barrett Browning as part of *Sonnets from the Portuguese,* a love tribute to her husband, Robert Browning, also a poet. The Brownings enjoyed what was probably the sweetest romance of the nineteenth century until Elizabeth's fragile health ended it.

The lovers first met—by mail—in January 1845, when Robert sent Elizabeth a note praising her newly published and highly acclaimed *Poems.* "I do, as I say, love these books with all my heart," enthused Robert, "and I love you too." He begged to see her, but she declined. Weakened by a chronic respiratory ailment and under the tyrannical domination of her father, Elizabeth had confined herself to her room for the past five years. During that time, she had seen no one.

The two corresponded heavily through the following months, with Elizabeth's ardent admirer persisting in his desire for a meeting, which she finally consented to in May. Their love blossomed, and bolstered by Robert's encouragement, Elizabeth ventured out into the world again.

Her father would not allow marriage for any of his children, so the lovers wedded secretly in September 1846. They left England for the warmer climate of Florence, Italy, which Elizabeth needed for her health. Her father never forgave her and refused to read or answer her letters for the rest of his life.

In Italy, Elizabeth and Robert enjoyed years of marital happiness, professional success and a stimulating social and literary life. Elizabeth thrived under the warm Italian sun, but her health declined rapidly after the death of her sister in 1861. She died in Robert's embrace on June 29 of that year. But her *Sonnets from the Portuguese,* the story of their touching and tender courtship, has lived on for lovers the world over.

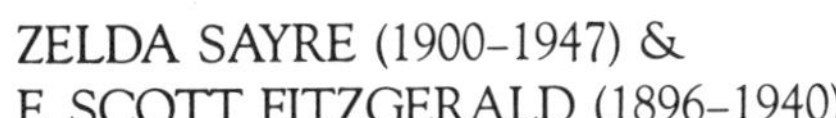

ZELDA SAYRE (1900–1947) & F. SCOTT FITZGERALD (1896–1940)

F. Scott and Zelda Fitzgerald were the prince and princess of America's Jazz Age, and they played their roles to the hilt in a fever pitch of extravagant living. Their meteoric rise to fame was followed by a long, slow deterioration into alcoholism for Scott and insanity for Zelda, but their love remained steadfast to the end.

Scott met Zelda in 1918, when the aspiring novelist was in the Army and stationed near Montgomery, Alabama. Zelda was ravishing, charming and a trifle spoiled—the quintessential Southern belle. Together, they made a handsome pair. They fell head over heels in love, and upon his discharge in 1919, Scott went to New York to become an "instant success," which would enable them to marry. Success didn't come instantly—in fact, Zelda grew impatient and broke their engagement. But with the publication of *This Side of Paradise* in 1920, Scott realized his dream of fame and wealth. Their honeymoon was one big, gaudy spree.

The next decade was their wildest, happiest and, for Scott, the most creative. A daughter, Scottie, was born in 1921. They filled their days and nights with drunken parties and outrageous behavior—dancing on cafe tabletops, riding atop a taxi down New York's Fifth Avenue, plunging into the fountain outside The Plaza hotel. The couple lived abroad in Europe for several years. During this period, their intense love was matched by equally intense quarrels.

In 1930, life for the Fitzgeralds began to unravel. Scott, who had become dependent on alcohol, hit a long sterile stretch, and debts mounted. Zelda suffered a mental breakdown; the diagnosis was incurable schizophrenia. Two years later, she had another breakdown, one from which she never fully recovered and which condemned her to spend most of the rest of her life in sanitariums. Scott tried desperately to hold their lives together, but he slid further into alcoholism.

In deep financial trouble by 1937, Scott moved to Hollywood and got a job as a scriptwriter, but he experienced continual frustration and failure. Mourning Zelda's illness and his inability to make a comeback, the distraught writer began an affair with gossip columnist Sheila Graham. He suffered a fatal heart attack in her home in 1940. Zelda lived until 1947, when a fire at a sanitarium in Asheville, North Carolina took her life.

• II. THE LANGUAGE OF LOVE •

WALLIS SIMPSON (1896?–) & EDWARD VIII (1894–1972)

For royalty, marriage has often been a matter of expediency, designed to cement political alliances, gain wealth or ensure bloodline succession. But for Edward VIII, marriage was a matter of the heart, and he paid his lover, Wallis Simpson, the ultimate compliment by giving up the throne of England in order to marry her.

Wallis, an American raised in Baltimore, married her second husband, Ernest Simpson, an English businessman, in 1928. Their home in London was frequently the scene of lively parties where diplomats, businessmen, aristocrats and celebrities mixed in stimulating conversation. The Simpsons met Prince Edward in 1930 while staying in the country with friends. Soon the prince was attending dinners and parties at the Simpsons' home.

Although not a beauty, Wallis possessed a natural grace and dignity, and was startlingly well informed about politics, current events and the theater. She never hesitated to argue her views, and her spirited independence enchanted the prince. They shared a keen zest for living and spent an increasing amount of time together, dancing, partying and traveling. Around 1934, their friendship developed into love.

Their balloon burst in 1936. Edward ascended the throne on January 20, and eleven months later, he announced his intention to marry Wallis as soon as she was divorced from Ernest. His ministers balked—this was a serious matter of state. Not only did Wallis lack royal blood, but her divorce would not be recognized by the Church of England, of which Edward, as king, was head. It quickly became apparent that the only way for Edward to have Wallis without causing a major political crisis was to give up the throne.

Wallis, prepared to endure "rivers of woe, seas of despair and oceans of agony" for Edward, urged him to give her up. But Edward, unyielding in his love, abdicated on December 11, 1936, and the lovers immediately left England. As the Duke and Duchess of Windsor, they spent most of their remaining years together living in splendor in France. Years later, the duchess stated, "Any woman who has been loved as I have been loved, and who, too, has loved, has experienced life in its fullness."

GRACE KELLY (1929–1982) & PRINCE RAINIER III (1923–)

Their union seemed destined. Prince Rainier III of Monaco had once casually remarked that when he found his dream girl, she would be blond and feminine and have "clever blue eyes"; a prominent Monaco fortune teller later predicted the prince would marry a movie star. In 1955, Rainier met his dream-girl-movie-star: Philadelphia-born Grace Kelly, a beautiful, elegant international film celebrity.

They were brought together by the Paris magazine *Match*. For a photo feature story, Rainier had agreed to give Grace a guided tour through his thirteenth-century 180-room castle in Monte Carlo. While the photographers clicked away, the prince became star-struck (though he later denied it was love at first sight). Grace and Rainier found each other refreshingly different from their gossip-column images—she was not a spoiled movie star and he was not a good-time playboy. They were both Catholics and basically shy.

After her visit, the prince could scarcely talk of anyone else. One of his close associates, Father Francis J. Tucker, an Irish-American priest who was also a friend of Grace's parents, discretely played Cupid. He arranged for Rainier, incognito, to visit Grace and her family in the United States. Rainier followed Grace from Philadelphia to New York and proposed to her on New Year's Eve, 1955. He was 32 and she was 26.

They were married April 18, 1956—in the "wedding of the century"—in the cathedral at Monte Carlo. More than 1,800 journalists and photographers flocked to the tiny principality to cover the event. Upon her marriage to the prince, Grace retired from the screen (much to Hollywood's regret) and devoted herself to her family and royal affairs. Over the next decade, the couple had three children: Caroline (born 1957), Albert (born 1958) and Stephanie (born 1965).

In the ensuing years, Grace acted as a goodwill ambassador for Monaco, established a foundation to help local artists and worked on behalf of numerous charities. Her life ended tragically on Sept. 14, 1982. Her brain dead following a stroke and car crash, she was taken off life support machines by her agonized family.

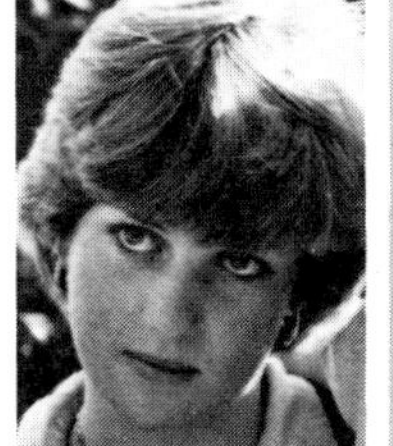

DIANA SPENCER (1961–) & PRINCE CHARLES (1948–)

Grace Kelly and Prince Rainier's "wedding of the century" was eclipsed on July 29, 1981, when England's "bonny" Prince Charles married lovely Lady Diana Spencer before a live television audience of 750 million people. The marriage, which was the culmination of a storybook romance, was accompanied by lavish and colorful celebration, pomp and pageantry.

Charles and Diana first met as children. As the daughter of Earl Spencer, Diana belonged to a family that had served as courtiers for generations. But there were about 13 years separating her and Charles, and it wasn't until she was sixteen that "Shy Di" caught the interest of the prince.

As one of the world's most eligible bachelors, Charles had been linked romantically to a number of willing young women, all of whom eventually fell by the wayside. Diana, however, stayed in the picture, and in the summer of 1980, the two discovered they were in love. Diana was ideally suited to the future king: tall, slim and athletic like him, of good parentage and possessing a spotless reputation. She held up with grace under the relentless scrutiny of the press, and she had a knack for charming crowds—important assets for the wife of a man who must spend a good part of his life participating in goodwill ceremonies and public events.

And so the prince proposed to her one August evening over dinner at Buckingham Palace, not at all certain, he said later, that she would accept. She did, immediately. (Is there a lass alive who wouldn't want to be queen?)

They took their vows in St. Paul's Cathedral (Westminster Abbey has for centuries been the traditional wedding place for England's royalty, but St. Paul's held more people). The bride's stepgrandmother, Barbara Cartland, the pink-attired "Queen of Romances," declined to attend, fearful that she would draw attention away from Diana. The couple started a royal family without delay, with a son arriving in the summer of 1982. "With Charles beside me," proclaimed Diana, "I cannot go wrong."

Aphrodisiacs: Fact or Fiction?

Since ancient times, people have tried to enhance their amorous adventures with aphrodisiacs (from Aphrodite, the Greek goddess of love and beauty), usually a food, spice or potion believed to stimulate sexual excitation. There is little scientific evidence that aphrodisiacs really work, though some belief in them persists to this day. Here are ten, some that you ingest, and some that you, well. . . .

1. MANDRAKE ROOT

This forked root, which resembles a man's shape, was once thought to have dark, magical power. According to legend, it screamed when pulled from the ground, and touching it could make a woman pregnant. Mandrake contains a poisonous narcotic.

2. OYSTERS

Oysters and certain fellow products of the sea supposedly provide sexual potency, which they derive from Venus, the Roman goddess of love (also known as Aphrodite) who sprang from sea foam. Oysters were much championed by the famous lover Casanova, and still enjoy popularity as aphrodisiacs.

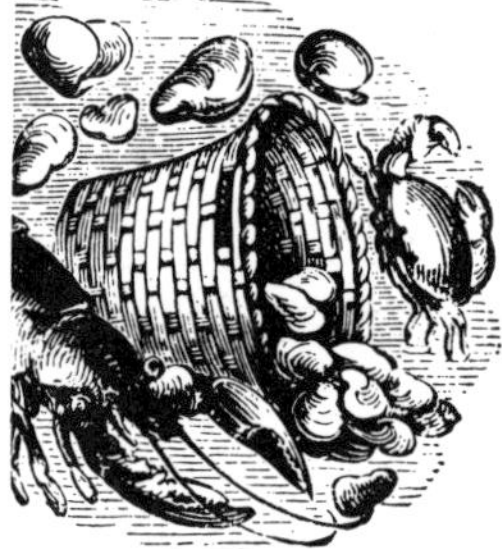

3. GARLIC

Three for the price of one with this member of the lily family: lure a lover, ward off vampires and other evil spirits and cure a few ills. Although the bulb contains an antiseptic, it doesn't do much for a lover's breath.

4. GINSENG

For centuries the Chinese have considered ginseng a sexual stimulator as well as a cure-all for most ills. The aromatic herb is often used to brew tea. The root, like the mandrake root, sometimes resembles a man's shape.

5.

CANTHARIDES

Also called Spanish fly, this aphrodisiac does create a physical reaction, but it's hardly one of sexual arousal. When ingested, the dried *Cantharis vesicatoria* beetle painfully irritates the genito-urinary tract. It can be fatal.

6.

CORIANDER

A member of the parsley family, this plant produces aromatic, seedlike fruits used to season such dishes as curry. Its sexual powers were cited in *1001 Arabian Nights.*

7.

ABSINTHE

Popular during the 1800s, absinthe was a highly intoxicating alcoholic drink with twice the punch of whiskey. It was flavored with wormwood oil, anise, fennel, coriander seeds and hyssop. Because of the severe health hazards associated with its consumption, the United States banned it in 1912. Modified versions are pastis, Pernod and ouzo.

8.

YOHIMBINE

The bark of the yohimbe tree in Central Africa yields a crystalline substance that for centuries was used by the natives as a male aphrodisiac. Veterinarians have employed it in bull breeding. In sufficient doses, it can be toxic.

9.

MONEY

One of the best, most enduring aphrodisiacs of all time, money works not on the body but on the mind. It's by far more effective than anything ingestible on this list.

10.

POWER

Power often, but not always, goes hand in hand with money, and also works psychologically rather than physically. Be it corporate, political or social, power is more potent than dozens of oysters or gallons of ginseng tea.

II. THE LANGUAGE OF LOVE

CHAPTER TWO

Hearts On a Sleeve

"In a man's letters . . . his soul lies naked," Samuel Johnson, the famous eighteenth century lexicographer and author, once wrote to his lover, Mrs. Thrale. "His letters are only the mirror of his heart."

Ever since men and women first began to commit thought and sentiment to paper, the love letter has bared soul after soul. Lovers have celebrated their joy and lamented their anguish in letters to one another, expressing their deepest feelings, which perhaps they never would have found the courage to speak aloud.

The written word is a wonderful medium for love sentiments. It is intimate and personal; it has the power to conjure up vivid images and feelings. It can be read slowly and savored, and reread as often as desired. Unlike the disembodied voice on the telephone or soft whispers in the ear, the written word lasts, never fading in intensity. Love letters written hundreds of years ago are still fresh and poignant when read today.

More's the pity that lovers don't write as often as they did in days gone by.

Letters, of course, were once the only means of communication when face-to-face meetings weren't possible, and so they were written more frequently. It was not uncommon for lovers to write daily or, if a message had only to be delivered across town, even several times a day. Napoleon, in the thick of battles as he conquered his way across the Continent, retired to his tent nearly every night to write his beloved wife Josephine a passionate letter. But she didn't feel the same about him, and her lack of reciprocation kept him in a frenzy of worry and jealousy each time they were separated.

Elizabeth Barrett and Robert Browning, whose relationship began with a letter from Robert, wrote to each other often during their crosstown courtship—long letters, sometimes a thousand words or so, filled with sentiments. Robert got right to the point in his first missive with a sincere declaration of love—before they had ever set eyes on each other.

Communicating love is much different today, much less formal. It's easier to pick up the telephone or buy a card that expresses feelings than it is to sit down and compose a message that lays bare the soul. Nevertheless, the love letter endures, because lovers will always need to make some kind of permanent record of their feelings.

What's in a love letter? Endearments, confessions, one's innermost secret thoughts, descriptions of one's passion. Horatio Nelson, England's greatest naval hero, declared that his lover, Emma Hamilton, was his "Alpha and Omega." Lord Byron, smitten by young countess Teresa Guiccioli, told her he wished she'd stayed in her convent. "Think of me, sometimes, when the Alps and ocean divide us—but they never will, unless you *wish* it," he wrote her.

The all-time prize for the most profuse and unusual endearments probably goes to Heinrich von Kleist, a German romantic poet who lived around the time of Goethe, in the late eighteenth and early nineteenth centuries. The object of von Kleist's affection was Henrietta Vogel, and one letter to her consisted of nothing but a string of endearments, 59 of them altogether. Besides such typical ones as "my heart-blood," "star of my eyes" and "my all and everything," he came up with "my entrails," "my goods and chattels," "my tragic play" and "my posthumous reputation."* In despair over Henrietta's incurable illness, von Kleist committed suicide at age 34, a year after writing that letter. He probably had no idea how much his passion for her influenced his "posthumous reputation."

Love letters also make promises and beg promises. Henry VIII promised Anne Boleyn, "I shall take you as my sole mistress, casting off all others than yourself out of mind and affection, and to serve you only." Perhaps if Anne had had any idea she would be but number two out of eight wives and would lose her head in the bargain, she might have paid no heed to

* Can you imagine receiving a letter addressed to "my dearest, my entrails"?

SONNETS FROM THE PORTUGUESE: 43

By Elizabeth Barrett Browning
(1806–1861)
English poet

How do I love thee? Let me count the ways.
I love thee to the depth and breadth and height
My soul can reach, when feeling out of sight
For the ends of Being and ideal Grace.
I love thee to the level of every day's
Most quiet need, by sun and candle-light.
I love thee freely, as men strive for right;
I love thee purely, as they turn from praise.
I love thee with the passion put to use
In my old griefs, and with my childhood's faith.
I love thee with a love I seemed to lose
With my lost saints—I love thee with the breath,
Smiles, tears, of all my life!—and, if God choose,
I shall but love thee better after death.

• II. THE LANGUAGE OF LOVE •

VENUS: GODDESS OF LOVE

The Greeks called her Aphrodite, the Romans called her Venus. As goddess of love, beauty and fertility, she was one of the most important deities of ancient times. She commanded the largest temple in Rome, and the most brilliant planet in the sky was named in her honor.

According to ancient myth, Venus arose from foam that was generated when Uranus, the personification of the heavens, was castrated by his son and his genitals were thrown into the sea. Although she represented the epitome of perfect female beauty, she married the ugliest of gods, the lame blacksmith Vulcan. Her lovers included the gods Mercury, Mars and Jupiter and the physically flawless mortal Adonis. From these unions came Venus' offspring: Cupid, god of love; Aeneas, a Trojan leader; Hymen, god of marriage; and Priapus, god of fertility.

Besides overseeing love, beauty and fertility, Venus was the patroness of prostitutes and the protector of seafarers. She was worshipped as the mother of the Roman people, and Julius Caesar boldly claimed to be a direct descendant of her.

During the Middle Ages, Venus was associated with sensual love. Today, we use the term *Venus* to describe dazzling female beauty, and the term *aphrodisiac*, a derivative of her Greek name, to describe anything that enhances sexual ardor.

CUPID: GOD OF LOVE

In today's language of courtship and romance, Cupid is a whimsical winged cherub whose invisible arrows strike love into human hearts. He goes about this task with a cheerful, smiling face—but he wasn't always such a pleasant little fellow.

The Greeks and Romans, well aware that love is invariably accompanied by pain and that a fine line exists between love and hate, added a dark side to Cupid's nature. According to one myth, he was the son of Venus, goddess of love and beauty, and Mars, god of war.

The Greeks, who called him Eros (from the Greek word for sexual desire), depicted him as a handsome young man who wielded whips and axes to strike lust into both gods and mortals. Later, he switched to gentler tools—bows and invisible arrows—and sprouted wings. Sometimes he carried a torch to symbolize the fiery hazards of love.

The Romans named him Cupid, and over the centuries, his image changed and softened. He was never a virtuous deity and was often portrayed as vulnerable to bribes. He wasn't particularly concerned about accuracy either, shooting his arrows blindfolded.

Cupid grew younger in mythology, until by the fourth century B.C. he was a child archer. Today, we think of him as a mischievous and capricious cherub and associate him with happy love, romance and Valentine's Day.

the ardent king. French novelist Stendhal begged his married lover, Clementine Curial, for letters and meetings, and Sir Richard Steele, an Irish-born English playwright and essayist, beseeched Mary Scurlock to present him with one of her fans, gloves or masks "or I cannot live." In wooing Mary, he wrote her, "Methinks I could write a volume to you; but all the language on earth would fail in saying how much and with what disinterested passion I am ever yours."

Some love letters, unhappily, are filled with anguish, as were Esther (Vanessa) Vanhomrigh's to her cruel lover, English novelist Jonathan Swift. An irascible man, Swift abruptly dropped Vanessa for another woman. She wrote him: "'Tis impossible to describe what I have suffered since I saw you last. I am sure I could have bore the rack much better than those killing, killing words of yours." She died shortly after their split, perhaps of a broken heart.

Anguish knew no bounds in the pitiful letters that crossed between Heloise and Abelard after he was castrated on orders from her angry uncle and they both committed themselves to the church. "Letters were first invented for consoling such solitary wretches as myself," wrote Heloise from her convent, ". . . I will still love you with all the tenderness of my soul till the last moment of my life." Said Abelard: "I have not triumphed over that unhappy passion. In the midst of my retirement I sigh, I weep, I pine, I speak the dear name of Heloise, and delight to hear the sound."

Some of the most impassioned love letters never reached the hands of the one to whom they were written. After Beethoven died in 1827, three letters were found in his effects. All were addressed to an anonymous "Immortal Beloved" but apparently never posted. The brilliant composer spent his life as a solitary, moody man, but he poured his heart out in these letters. "Even in bed my ideas yearn toward you," he said, ". . . I can only live, either altogether with you or not at all. . . ." Unfortunately, for melancholy Beethoven, it was "not at all."

Lovers of today, pick up your pens and keep the love letter alive. Express your deepest desires, your most secret confessions—do not be embarrassed! Save them, preserve them, tie them up in a bundle with red satin ribbon and, some day decades away, relive through them that sweet passion that once filled your heart and soul.

THE AGONY AND ECSTASY OF NAPOLEON

Napoleon Bonaparte, the "little general" who made himself emperor of France, was able to conquer entire nations, but he failed miserably to conquer the heart of his wife Josephine.

Napoleon, six years younger than Josephine, was blind with passion for her, though she was more interested in being a celebrity than in loving him. From his many battlefields, he inundated her with letters, frantic in their pleas for a reply and sizzling from the heat of his ardor. She filled him with "intoxicating frenzy," he said; "[your kisses] set my blood on fire" and "[your tears] burn my blood."

Typical of his passionate declarations was, "I hope before long to crush you in my arms and cover you with a million kisses burning as though beneath the Equator." When she didn't write back, he accused her of having other lovers. "My heart, obsessed by you, is full of fears which prostrate me with misery," he confessed.

But as long as she could be empress, Josephine had no intentions of casting Napoleon aside. Ironically, it was he who divorced her—though with a heavy heart—because she was unable to provide him with a male heir. Although Napoleon remarried, his subsequent *billets d'amour* were never as passionate as the ones he'd written to his first wife, Josephine.

II. THE LANGUAGE OF LOVE

Writing a love letter is serious business. It isn't like sitting down to dash off a note to a relative or an acquaintance, nor should it be approached the same way as a chatty, "here's the latest news" report. A love letter takes a little thought and planning, the right setting and the right mood. Here are a few tips on how to go about writing something straight from your heart:

1. **Decide what type of love letter you want to send.** Not all love letters need be eloquent and passionate—they can be light and humorous or even downright sexy. Which tone will best help get your message across, and more importantly, which will get the best reception from the object of your love?

2. **Select the proper stationery and writing utensil.** The kind of love letter you want to write will determine your tools. For eloquence, perhaps a rich, high-quality parchment paper, a fountain pen and brown ink would produce the right effect. Stationery lightly scented with your cologne or perfume may conjure up special memories and emotions. It's important not to overdo the fragrance, however, because a strongly odoriferous letter sitting in a mailbox may embarrass rather than titillate your lover. For humor, stationery printed with a cute drawing or cartoon might be best. Greeting cards, with or without printed messages, can also set the stage. Whatever you choose, it should convey a feeling of intimacy. *Never, never type a love letter!*

3. **Set the right mood.** Pick an unhurried time of day or night to write. Shut the door and take the phone off the hook. Your sentimental reverie should be uninterrupted. Gaze at a picture of your lover and, perhaps, play the favorite music you share. For sexy letters that will make him blush to read, don a sexy nightgown and compose something like "*Dearest darling, whenever I wear that little black lace nothing you like so well—and I've got it on now as I write this letter in bed—I think of the*

HEART THROBS

In romances—real and fictional—love letters have always figured prominently. Now from Ruby Street, a New York paper goods company, comes a novel greeting card to spice up a romantic message to your loved one.

Called Heart Throbs, these greeting cards are designed to look like exotic, steamy historical romance book covers, done in purples and reds with gold-foil embossing. Tongue-in-cheek messages are printed inside, but there's plenty of room left to add your own humorous love note.

The cards sport titles such as "*Passion's Flame*" and "*Taste the Savage Wind*," and scenes such as sailing ships tossing on stormy seas and knights in armor astride galloping horses.

A tastefully racy way to say "I love you."

wonderful sensation of your touch as you. . . ." You get the idea.

4. **Be spontaneous.** It may take you a few false starts, but once you get going, let your words and feelings flow honestly and spontaneously. If you rework and rework a draft, it may come out sounding stilted. Let your letter be you!

5. **Send it.** Sometimes words of heartfelt emotion and passion seem embarrassing once they cool. It's only natural—you've got your heart on the line. But don't wait for second thoughts to sway you into placing your letter in your diary instead of the mailbox. Don't be like Beethoven, who composed beautiful love letters to an anonymous lover, the "Immortal Beloved," and then deprived her of the pleasure of reading them by never sending them to her.

6. **Research for inspiration.** Go to the library and look up collections of love letters written by well-known men and women, either from centuries past or the present. Styles of expression vary from person to person as well as from era to era, and you may find some particularly to your liking. Let them inspire you to write better love letters of your own.

III. LIGHTING THE TORCH

The role of romance in literature has a long and fascinating history. It wasn't until the twelfth century that a fictional knight named Sir Lancelot became a model for the chivalrous hero. Throughout the centuries, romantic fiction has been continually maligned—even today, with its millions of fans and millions of dollars in sales.

The big business of romantic fiction may be a fairly recent development, but romantic stories are certainly nothing new. They've been told and retold since human emotions were first recorded. Tales of passion have been kept alive in fable, myth, song and book; indeed, the love story has been at the center of all arts. Some stories are universal. For example, variations of *Cinderella*, the story of a downtrodden girl who, thanks to magic, catches the eye of a prince, are found throughout Eastern and Western cultures; the same is true of *Beauty and the Beast*.

Today, romances are generally defined as love stories about women, written from a woman's point of view. (Although the field is almost exclusively controlled by women, there are some male authors who write romances.) Romances focus on emotions, desire, sensuality, sex and commitment, and the heroine invariably wins her man in the end, no matter what obstacles are placed in front of her.

In Western culture, today's romance novels have their roots in twelfth century literature, when tales of both courtly and illicit love began to gain fashion. Interestingly, many romance writers of that time were influenced by Ovid, a Roman poet who lived around 43 B.C. to 17 or 18 A.D. Among Ovid's enduring works are *Amores*, *Heroides* and *Ars amatoria*, which contain love stories, advice on how to find and keep a mistress, and love letters from women to their husbands and lovers. Ovid's influence can be seen in the courtly love poems that medieval men wrote to the women of their fancy as well as in some of the works of such writers as Chaucer, Shakespeare, Milton and Tennyson.

The father of the medieval romance, however, was Chretien de Troyes, a French writer known chiefly for his embellishments of the legends of King Arthur and his creation of the gallant knight Sir Lancelot, the fictional lover of Guinevere. De Troyes, too, was inspired by Ovid, but his primary influence was Queen Eleanor of Aquitaine, wife of King Louis VII of France, and her daughter, Marie de Champagne. The royal ladies wanted stories about dashing knights who loved their women above all else, who would defend their honor to the death and who would be forever subservient to them. While de Troyes was opposed to the idea of illicit love, he was more or less coerced into writing about it by Eleanor and Marie. Thus, Lancelot serves King Arthur in battle and services his wife in bed.

De Troyes wrote other types of romances and was widely copied, and his stories won incredible popularity, even spreading throughout England. As is true today, critics then were not kind to romantic tales, which were denounced as mind-warping trash that would encourage extramarital affairs. The powerful clergy, alarmed at the defection from the reverence for spiritual love to the celebration of physical love, decried love poetry and novels as obscene and tried to suppress them. Some clergymen even attempted to substitute other, "chaste" stories for the more popular romances. One of the more laughable efforts was that produced by the abbey of St. Denis in France, which pushed tales like *Song of Roland*, in which the hero chooses his sword over the ladies—sort of like a cowboy who prefers his horse. Roland lavishes much praise and affection on his sword, named Durendal, and dies with it in his arms. Not exactly the kind of story that would make a lady swoon with emotion, is it? Despite the efforts of the abbey's members and others of the clergy, popular interest in stories about human passions could not be subdued. The romance was here to stay.

It wasn't until the eighteenth and nineteenth centuries, however, that romantic literature began to take on many of the characteristics associated with today's romances. The central characters were women, and the books dealt with their emotions and sexuality. Some were even written by women.

Perhaps one of the earliest prototypal books of this period was *Pamela*, subtitled *Virtue Rewarded*, written by Samuel Richardson, an English printer who died in 1761. Richardson actually had a mission, which was to write a book that would warn working-class girls about seductive employers and convince them that keeping their virtue would have its rewards. He based his book on a true story he had heard about a landowner who was notorious for seducing his servant girls. One resisted, however, and the landlord was so impressed that he married her. So the heroine, Pamela, resists the advances of her employer, Mr. B, and wins his hand in marriage.

Pamela was enormously successful, so much so that it inspired Henry Fielding (*Tom Jones*) to write a satire, *Joseph Andrews*, in which a footman fends off the advances of his lecherous employer, Lady Booby. Richardson went on to capitalize on his success with another novel, *Clarissa*. The heroine of that novel is raped after she faints, and she becomes so distraught about her ruin that she kills herself. Richardson was adept at analyzing female emotions, and his women readers adored him.

The talented Brontë sisters made significant contributions to romantic literature during the nineteenth century. Emily Brontë's Heathcliff in *Wuthering Heights* became a model for brooding, self-destructive heroes nursing dark secrets. Charlotte Brontë's noble *Jane Eyre* was panned as immoral trash by critics upon its publication in 1847. The book was called "anti-Christian" and the character of Jane was termed "unregenerate and undisciplined." Jane, a governess, stands up for herself and is uncharacteristically outspoken for a woman in nineteenth century England, but she demonstrates the ultimate in compassion, love and unselfishness by returning to her employer, Mr. Rochester, and marrying him even though he has been blinded.

Jane Austen's novels, most notably *Pride and Prejudice* and *Emma*, go far beyond romance to astute social satire. Nevertheless, the story lines deal chiefly with getting husbands.

Shortly after the turn of the twentieth century, Mills and Boon was founded in London and began publishing a wide variety of titles, including romances. Georgette Heyer, whose name has remained synonymous with Regency romances, began her prolific career in 1920 with *The Black Moth*, which was published by Mills and Boon.

For several decades, most of the popular romances were historicals, written by such authors as Kathleen Winsor, Thomas B. Costain, Frank Yerby and Anya Seton, among others. Two of the biggest best-sellers were Margaret Mitchell's *Gone with the Wind*, in which a spunky Southern belle meets her match in a man during the Civil War era, and Winsor's *Forever Amber*, which chronicles the rags-to-riches rise of a seventeenth century English peasant girl who seduces a succession of aristocrats. In many of these novels, romance was not necessarily the only element; they also contained a lot of action and adventure. But at the same time, the "pure" romance, in which the central character was a woman and the entire plot revolved around how she met and captured the Big Love of her life, was gaining readership.

In 1949, Harlequin was founded in Toronto, and among its early and varied titles were Mills and Boon reprints. As romance titles continued to grow in popularity, Harlequin began increasing publication of them until, by 1964, romances were its exclusive product under that imprint. Most notable were its contemporary romances: sweet stories in which sexually inexperienced secretaries and teachers met the men of their dreams—usually in some exotic locale—and got married, with the promise of living happily ever after. Also popular were doctor-nurse themes.

For American publishers, romances, both historical and contemporary, enjoyed a steady market for many years. However, in the 1960s, the notion of "romance" fell out of fashion as Americans grappled with a number of social issues, such as civil rights, war protests, feminism and liberated sex. By the end of the decade many people—and women in particular—had had enough and turned their attention to less strident concerns. Perhaps that's what made conditions during the 1970s so ripe for a renaissance of happy-ending romantic novels. Avon Books struck a mother lode with Kathleen E. Woodiwiss' *The Flame and the Flower* in 1972. In 1971 Harlequin merged with Mills and Boon and began a period of rapid growth and aggressive market expansion. American publishers started jumping on the romance bandwagon in the mid- to late 1970s.

The romance category has expanded and subdivided to the point that there is now a type of romance for just about every possible taste. But whether they're historicals or contemporaries, with lots of sex or moderate sex, romances all have one thing in common: the lady always gets her man.

LOVE AT FIRST SIGHT

"Who ever loved, that loved not at first sight?"

—Christopher Marlowe (1564–1593)
English poet and dramatist

It happens all the time in the world of fiction—countless Romeos are smitten by love at the first sight of their Juliets. But does love at first sight actually happen in real life? There is evidence aplenty that it does—but not often.

The symptoms of love at first sight are nearly the same as those of infatuation or a strong physical attraction. The heart beats faster, breathing quickens, the face becomes flush, hands tremble, knees weaken. If it's only infatuation, such responses fade over time, and a couple may discover they really aren't compatible with one another after all.

But couples who fall instantly in love experience a much stronger, deeper reaction—the bond goes beyond physical chemistry. Such lovers may feel they've known one another all their lives and as though they are not "whole" unless they are with each other.

The chemistry can last for years, even lifetimes. The glow of romantic love seldom dims for such couples, and decades into marriage, they are still unhappy whenever they are separated. For these lucky lovers, love remains a sweet and pleasing madness.

THE FACE THAT LAUNCHED A THOUSAND SHIPS

How many women have ever possessed the type of beauty that could start a war? Fair Helen of Troy, who had beauty secrets known only to the gods, caused the Trojan War and the downfall of Troy.

No one knows just how much of the legendary Trojan War is fact and how much is fiction. It supposedly took place sometime between 1334 B.C. and 1150 B.C.

Paris was the son of Priam, king of Troy, a city in Asia Minor. One day, Venus, the goddess of love and beauty, promised him that he would have the fairest woman on earth as his wife—Helen, wife of King Menelaus of Sparta. Paris deserted his own wife and set out to capture Helen, whom he seduced and carried back to Troy.

The enraged Menelaus called upon his Greek allies to help him rescue his wife, and an armada of a thousand ships or more set sail for Troy. The war dragged on for ten years.

A lover and not a fighter, Paris was a coward in battle. He suffered an unheroic death when he was felled with a poisoned arrow.

The Greeks finally triumphed by hiding soldiers inside a huge wooden horse, which the Trojans foolishly accepted as a gift and took inside their city walls. The Greeks then slipped out of the horse and sacked and burned the city. Those Trojans who weren't slain were made slaves.

Helen, meanwhile, reconciled herself with Menelaus. The couple sailed back to Sparta, where they resumed their regal life of comfort and splendor, scarcely giving a thought to the destroyed kingdom across the sea.

III. LIGHTING THE TORCH

Nothing is more enjoyable, more enchanting or more engrossing than a rich tale of love—nothing except the real thing! Throughout the ages, people have never tired of a good love story, especially those in which lovers face all kinds of obstacles and tragedies. Thousands upon thousands of love tales have been spun through the centuries of recorded history, and the best of them have endured the test of time, being passed on from generation to generation, thrilling each new heart that discovers them for the first time. Stories of forbidden love are always a favorite, as are tales of lovers torn apart by events beyond their control, such as wars or untimely deaths.

Speaking of death, how many fictional lovers have died in the arms of their beloved or together in each other's arms? Untold numbers! True love endures to the very last breath, and many lovers hope to find in death what life denies them.

Here are 10 of the most famous stories of love, ecstasy and woe, from the ancient mythology of Greece and Rome to the modern-day novel. They have come to us from a variety of sources: some verse-memorized and recited; some set to music; some written for the stage; and some published in book form. Whatever their form, whatever their age, these stories continue to enchant and entertain.

ORPHEUS & EURYDICE
A Greek myth, recorded by Roman poets Virgil and Ovid
Setting: Thrace, a region north of Greece, during ancient times

Could there ever be a greater love than that of the anguished Orpheus, who travels to the black depths of Hell to try to reclaim his treasured Eurydice?

Orpheus' joy knows no bounds. A talented musician, the son of a Muse and a Thracian prince, he charms men, beasts and the very rocks beneath his feet with the beautiful music he makes on his lyre. His captivation of the fair Eurydice elates him beyond description. But hours after their happy wedding, she is fatally bitten by a snake and descends into the realm of the dead.

The distraught Orpheus goes after her, for without Eurydice, life is meaningless. With his lyre, he beseeches Pluto, god of the dead, to give him back his love. So moved is Pluto that iron tears fall from his cheeks. He grants the request—on one condition: Eurydice will follow Orpheus back to the land of the living, but he is not to turn around until they are both out of darkness or she will return to Hell forever.

Orpheus is ecstatic, but along the way back, he grows anxious and impatient to see his beloved. As he steps into sunlight and the world of the living, he turns to Eurydice. A thousand woes! She is still in darkness. "Farewell!" she cries before vanishing, reclaimed forever by the Lord of the Dead.

The inconsolable Orpheus wanders aimlessly until a band of angry women tears him apart limb from limb. Sorrowful gods place his lyre in the heavens as the constellation Lyra.

CLAIR DE LUNE

A Troubadour romance

Setting: Somewhere in Europe during the Middle Ages

Beware should you hear a strange, soft melody on a night lit by a full moon . . . for it is on such a night that Lady Clair de Lune lures her jealous lover to a mysterious fate.

The handsome Duke of Picardy decides it is time to take a wife. He desires a woman whose beauty won't pale in the moonlight, but though he searches far and wide, he finds no damsel who suits his fancy.

Then one night when the duke returns home from a feast, he comes upon a great forest glistening in the light of a full moon. Among the trees dance women fairies, their faces luminous and bewitching. The spellbound duke impulsively proposes to one, Lady Clair de Lune. She agrees to wed when the moon has waned—provided the duke agrees never to question her whenever she leaves him nor ever to follow her. He consents.

So they wed, and every time the moon is full, the duke is lulled to sleep by strange, sweet music. When he awakes, his lady is always gone, not to return until the moon has waned again.

The jealous duke suspects her of having a secret lover. The next night of the full moon, he feigns sleep and follows her to the edge of the glistening forest. She spies him and tells him he has broken his pledge. She swears she never again will come to him and that he will be doomed forever to follow her "'round the world and back again."

She disappears and the saddened duke goes home. But at the next full moon, he hears strange music that falls on no one else's ears—it is the Lady Clair de Lune calling to him! The music lures him into the forest and he is never seen again.

TRISTAN & ISOLT

A Chivalric romance

Setting: Britain and Ireland during the Middle Ages

Alas, poor Tistan and Isolt. After falling in love, they mistakenly drink a potion that binds their hearts together for eternity—but cruel fate separates them.

Tristan, a distinguished knight in the service of King Mark of Cornwall (a region in southwestern Britain), lands in Ireland by mistake after his ship is blown off course by strong winds. However, when he sees Isolt, the stunning daughter of the King of Ireland, he swears it is no mistake. He is haunted by her beauty and, upon his return to Cornwall, raves about her to King Mark. The king decides he wants Isolt for his bride and sends Tristan back to Ireland to fetch her.

Tristan complies reluctantly—he'd love to have the beauty for himself. On the return voyage to Cornwall, he and Isolt fall in love. Then their fate is sealed when they accidentally drink a love potion that was intended for Isolt and the king.

Isolt marries King Mark, but her continuing love for Tristan enrages the monarch and he banishes the knight. After many adventures, Tristan eventually marries another damsel, but he still yearns for his true love.

One day Tristan is seriously wounded in battle. The wound worsens, and he sends a ship for Queen Isolt, knowing she alone can heal him. If the ship returns with her, it is to hoist a white flag in the harbor; if not, a black sail will fly.

Tristan's jealous wife intervenes. When the ship arrives flying a white flag, she tells him it is black. Her scheme tragically backfires when Tristan dies in despair. Queen Isolt rushes to his chamber, but it is too late. She cradles her dead lover in her arms and expires from grief.

ROMEO & JULIET
A drama by William Shakespeare
Setting: Verona, Italy during the fifteenth century
First performed: 1595

Love knows no boundaries, as Romeo and Juliet, two star-crossed young lovers discover.

When Romeo Montague first sets eyes on the exquisite Juliet Capulet, it is love at first sight. But he cannot court her openly, for the Montagues and Capulets are bitter enemies. He manages to steal a kiss but is seen by Tybalt, a Capulet, who becomes angry.

Undaunted by family feuds, the lovers conspire to marry secretly with the help of sympathetic Friar Lawrence. After the ceremony, Romeo unfortunately slays Tybalt in a fight, and is forced to flee the city. Juliet's father, meanwhile, betrothes her to another man.

Juliet and the friar devise a desperate plan: she will drink a potion that will put her in a deathlike trance. While she lays in her family's open tomb, Romeo, who will be notified of the plan in a letter from the friar, will rescue her and the two will escape.

Juliet takes the potion but the friar's letter doesn't reach Romeo. Shattered by news of her "death," Romeo goes to her tomb and kills himself with poison. As he dies, Juliet rouses from her trance. Horrified by the sight of Romeo's still-warm corpse, she tries to kiss the poison from his lips, then takes his dagger and plunges it into her breast.

JANE EYRE
A novel by Charlotte Bronte
Setting: Northern England around 1800
First published: 1847

This gothic of gothic tales reveals the dark side of romance, as the heroine,

Jane Eyre, unravels the mystery of Edward Rochester.

Jane, a poor girl, becomes governess in the employ of mysterious Edward, who resides at Thornfield, a huge manor. Edward is handsome but often somber and moody, and strange events happen at the house. Most disturbing is a demented woman who lives locked up on the third floor.

Although Edward seems to be courting a lady, Jane can't help falling in love with him. Her wildest dream comes true when he suddenly and very tenderly confesses his love for her and proposes.

But the wedding is stopped at the altar by the revelation of Edward's dark secret: the insane woman is his wife! Despite his anguished pleas, Jane leaves him and wanders about the countryside.

Time passes, and Jane declines another marriage proposal. Then she dreams that Edward is calling her name, and she feels compelled to go to him—only to find tragedy. Thornfield has been gutted in a fire set by Edward's demented wife, who perished in the flames. Edward was blinded trying to rescue her.

His sightlessness doesn't stand in the way of their true and tender love, however, and they marry at last. Happily, two years later, he regains sight in one eye, in time to see their firstborn son.

CAMILLE
A novel by Alexandre Dumas (son)
Setting: Paris and its environs during the nineteenth century
First published: 1852

A loser at cards but a winner at love . . . or was she? Pity poor, fragile, dying Camille Gautier.

A Parisian working-class girl with a bad reputation, Camille is luckily befriended by a wealthy duke who introduces her to society. She leads a gay life but loses heavily at card games and cannot repay her debts. An admirer, a count, offers to pay her debts if she will become his mistress.

Before Camille decides, she meets Armand Duval, who falls wildly in love with her. She scorns him at first because he has no money, but she soon realizes that love is more important than money. Because of her failing health, they go the the countryside, where they live an idyllic life.

One day while Armand is away, his father appears and begs Camille to leave him. Armand's sister is engaged, but her fiance has threatened to back out unless Camille is purged from the family. Camille is crushed, but she agrees. She writes a letter telling Armand she has gone back to Paris and the admiring count, and leaves.

The letter devastates Armand, then angers him. Camille, meanwhile, grows increasingly weaker as she pines away for her love. At last, Armand's father takes pity on the lovers and tells Armand the truth. Armand rushes to Paris, where he finds Camille on her deathbed in a shabby flat. He throws himself on her, vowing eternal love, and she dies peacefully in his arms.

ANNA KARENINA
A novel by Tolstoy
Setting: Russia during the nineteenth century
First published: around 1875–77

Sometimes love hits with the force of a runaway locomotive, as beautiful Anna Karenina tragically finds out.

Anna, a mother and the respectable wife of a politician, visits her sister in Moscow, where she meets the dashing Count Vronsky. The count is supposedly a suitor of her niece, but upon meeting Anna, he is smitten. He relentlessly pursues Anna, following her home to St. Petersburg. She finds him irresistible, and they are seen together often.

The gossip is nasty. Alexei, Anna's cold husband, warns her to be careful, but she has already lost her head as well as her heart. She becomes pregnant; Alexei refuses to grant a divorce, because it would ruin his career.

After Anna gives birth to a daughter, she takes her baby and goes to live with Vronsky. But the lovers' relationship is strained—Anna has been disowned by Alexei and ostracized by society. Sinking into bitterness and despair, she clings desperately to Vronsky. He callously withdraws from her, and she becomes convinced he has taken another lover.

Poor Anna! Her once-ordered life is in shambles. Everything dear to her has been lost. She goes to a railway station and watches a train approach. Suddenly, she throws herself under its wheels.

CYRANO DE BERGERAC
A drama by Edmond Rostand
Setting: France during the seventeenth century
First presented: 1897

In his own words, it is not a nose but an island. Despite this accident of nature, Cyrano de Bergerac tries to win the heart of Roxane, his lovely cousin.

Cyrano, a French soldier, is often mocked because of his large nose, and so he keeps his love for Roxane secret. One day she tells him she is in love, and for a fleeting moment, he thinks he is the lucky man. But no, she loves Christian de Neuvillette, another soldier. Cyrano's heart sinks.

When Christian discovers that Cyrano is Roxane's cousin, he asks for his aid in wooing her. Cyrano, who is a gifted poet, ghostwrites love letters to Roxane for Christian and helps bring about their marriage.

Then Cyrano and Christian are called to fight against the Spanish. Cyrano risks his life to send love letters to Roxane, letters that express his own tender feelings but are signed by Christian. Eventually, Christian realizes Roxane is in love with the emotion expressed in the letters and not with him, and he begs Cyrano to tell her the truth. But Christian is killed and Cyrano swears himself to secrecy.

Fifteen years go by. Roxane, who has retired to a convent, is visited weekly by Cyrano. One night he arrives mortally wounded from a brick dropped on his head by enemies. As a final love tribute, he takes Christian's last letter to Roxane and reads it to her. Suddenly, she realizes it is too dark for him to see the words—Cyrano knows them by heart because he wrote them! As he dies, she tells him she must have loved him, not Christian, all along.

GONE WITH THE WIND
A novel by Margaret Mitchell
Setting: The South during the Civil War and Reconstruction
First published: 1936

If the South had had a general named Scarlett O'Hara, Sherman never would have completed his march to the sea . . . but would Rhett Butler have given a damn?

Spoiled Scarlett, belle of a Southern plantation, uses men the way some women use clothes, tossing them aside when she tires of them. In the genteel, mannerly days before the Civil War, dozens of beaus court her, but her heart belongs to Ashley Wilkes, although his heart belongs to his wife, Melanie. Their marriage doesn't faze Scarlett and she continues to carry a torch for Ashley. Meanwhile, Rhett, an insolent Yankee blockade-runner, is amused and intrigued by impetuous Scarlett; yet his ardor fails to light a fire within her. After Scarlett goes through two husbands, Rhett succeeds in becoming number three.

Lo and behold, she falls in love with him, but their love never seems to be in sync. Eventually, Rhett tires of always playing second fiddle to Ashley in Scarlett's heart. Just as she renounces her passion for Ashley—to herself—Rhett tells her he doesn't "give a damn" and walks out. But plucky Scarlett is unconcerned, for tomorrow is always another day.

DOCTOR ZHIVAGO
A novel by Boris Pasternak
Setting: Russia during the Russian Revolution
First published: 1958

Just as the Russian Revolution splits a nation in two, Yurii Zhivago's heart is rent by his love for two women: his gracious, attractive wife, Tonia, and his dazzling mistress, Lara.

Yurii, a doctor and a poet, marries Tonia and settles down to a respectable life in the splendor of Moscow society. Then the Russian Revolution destroys his comfortable world. At a war-zone hospital, where he serves as a doctor, Yurii is assisted by nurse Lara, and the seeds of their destructive passion are sown.

As the revolution ravages Moscow, Yurii and his family retreat to the Ural Mountains. In a village there, he is overjoyed to find Lara, and abandons his family to live with her for months. The guilt of his infidelity is crushing, however, and at last, he decides to leave Lara for good and confess all to Tonia. But before he reaches home, Red Army troops capture him and press him into service in their guerrilla war. For three years, Yurii's whereabouts are unknown.

When he finally escapes, Yurii goes straight to Lara, but he is grieved to learn his wife and two children have been deported to Paris. Lara herself is in danger of arrest, and after a painfully short reunion, he sadly sends her away to safety. He never sees any of his loved ones again and never learns that Lara has borne him a daughter.

Broken in heart and spirit, Yurii returns to Moscow and allows his life to deteriorate. He "marries" a young woman but nurses hope that someday he will be reunited with Tonia. Just when it seems possible, a heart attack claims his life.

On the day of Yurii's funeral, Lara comes to Moscow and discovers his death. She sobs over his coffin and then quietly vanishes forever.

III. LIGHTING THE TORCH

CHAPTER THREE

Those Avon Ladies

In New York City, on a summer day in 1970, history was made in romantic fiction. The executive editor of Avon Books, Nancy Coffey, picked a thick manuscript off her mountainous pile of unsolicited manuscripts and took it home to read over a steamy weekend. She could never tell if "the slush pile" would yield a treasure or a disaster, but this time, Nancy struck gold. The manuscript proved to be as steamy as the weather. She began to read:

> Somewhere in the world, time no doubt whistled by on taut and widespread wings, but here in the English countryside it plodded slowly, painfully, as if it trod the rutted road that stretched across the moors on blistered feet.

What a romantic, lyrical beginning! The manuscript, titled *The Flame and the Flower*, was submitted by an unknown writer named Kathleen E. Woodiwiss, from Princeton, Minnesota. And from its very first page, Nancy Coffey was hooked.

Kathleen's historical romance centers around the love, lust and misunderstanding between the petite, voluptuous Heather Simmons and the strong, handsome and rich Brandon Birmingham. In England in 1799, Heather is an innocent lass when Captain Birmingham gets his hands on her, literally, forcefully takes her virginity and makes her pregnant. Her influential relatives demand a shotgun wedding. Thus married, Heather and Brandon spend almost the entire book certain of each other's hatred and resentment—when actually they have fallen deeply in love. Happily, they discover their true feelings and find heaven on earth in one another's arms.

Published in 1972, *The Flame and the Flower* became a quick and phenomenal best-seller, surprising Avon and touching off a boom in romantic fiction publishing that has continued to this day.

Nancy, now editor-in-chief of The Berkeley Group, remains singularly modest about her role in shaping and propelling today's romantic fiction industry. "At the time," she explains, "we were looking for good original novels rather than 'romances' in particular. I'd never read *Gone with the Wind* or *Forever Amber*. But I figured that if I would keep reading this story, other women would too. I really didn't think of it as starting a new genre."

Not that romances hadn't been around before that. Regencies, Gothics, Harlequins and other contemporary romances, for example, had enjoyed a certain market success, but nothing of the magnitude of what was to come. No one in publishing had any inkling that romances had the potential of becoming the largest selling category in the industry, generating hundreds of millions of dollars in sales each year and accounting for 40 percent of all paperbacks sold. A market was waiting; legions of women were ready to devour novel after novel after novel about passion and romance—from a woman's point of view.

The Flame and the Flower went on to sell more than three million copies, and with its success, other romance manuscripts began arriving at Avon. One, addressed to "the editor of *The Flame and the Flower*," catapulted secretary Rosemary Rogers to fame as a best-selling author. Rogers' *Sweet Savage Love* chronicles the torrid lust and love between Ginny Brandon, a refined, desirable lady, and Steve Morgan, a rugged, macho adventurer who is also rich. Steve seduces the virgin Ginny and they despise each other for most of the book—or think they do, at any rate. But their mutual lust always wins out over hate, and by the end of the tale, set in Mexico during revolutionary days in the late 1860s, they confess their undying love. As Ginny might say, "*mon Dieu*, it is a sexy tale!"

Following *Sweet Savage Love*, it appeared that a new market trend was taking shape. "We must have hit a spark," says Nancy. "Women were ready for this kind of book. We were as

KATHLEEN E. WOODIWISS
By the author of A ROSE IN WINTER
THE FLAME AND THE FLOWER

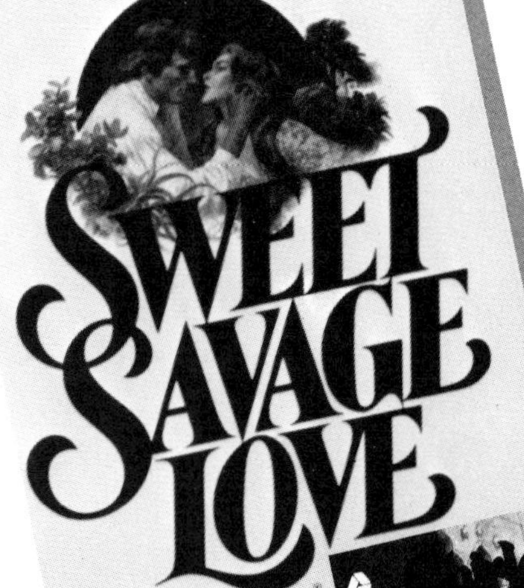
ROSEMARY ROGERS
Author of DARK FIRES and LOST LOVE, LAST LOVE
OVER 3 MILLION COPIES IN PRINT!
SWEET SAVAGE LOVE

Author of LADY VIXEN and GYPSY LADY
SHE HAD NEVER KNOWN DESIRE... UNTIL HIS LOVE AWAKENED HER TO ECSTASY.
While Passion Sleeps

surprised as anyone that the books sold as well as they did. Our only reaction was, how can we top this?"

The letters from readers indicated that Avon had indeed struck a responsive chord. And they arrived by the sackload. "All of them were incredibly positive," recalls Nancy. "They said things like, 'You took me out of my humdrum existence, away from the screaming kids and my beer-drinking husband sitting in front of the TV all night.' They poured their hearts out."

Along with the letters came an increasing number of romance manuscripts, many of them addressed to Nancy's attention. As Avon published more romances, its romance writers became known in the industry as "the Avon Ladies." Among them, besides Kathleen E. Woodiwiss and Rosemary Rogers, were Laurie McBain, Shirlee Busbee, Patricia Gallagher, Johanna Lindsey, Joyce Verrette and Bertrice Small. Some of these authors are still with Avon, while others have moved to different publishing houses.

Male authors also tried their hand at writing these female romances, but Nancy says she could usually spot them even when they used female pseudonyms. "They always had their heroines looking into mirrors and admiring their 'luscious breasts.' Women don't do that—they look in a mirror and say, 'Oh, my legs are too fat,' or something like that."

Avon began to publish more romances, mostly taken from the slush pile. Other publishers began to cash in on the flourishing market, until nearly every major tradebook publisher in America was producing romances. While historicals held sway in the early stages of the boom, the market began to spread and divide into subcategories. Eventually, there was a type of romance tailored to almost every possible interest and taste. Today, there are sweet, or fairly chaste romances; sexy, spicy romances; historicals; suspense romances; Regencies; sagas and contemporaries; romances for the second time around; romances for mature women; and romances with both foreign and American settings.

Regardless of differences in format and setting, they all have one thing in common: they all concern heroines who are highly desirable to men and who are pursued, wooed and loved—but never left—by handsome, masculine heroes. In the end, the lady always gets her man.

It's a fantasy that invariably makes a good story, and according to Nancy, it was only a good story—not a revolution in women's fiction—which she sought that summer day in 1970.

Still, perhaps Nancy needn't be so modest. Someone has to light the fuse to set off the explosion. Best-selling author Bertrice Small voices the feelings of many when she says the credit for today's romance market should go to Nancy. "If it hadn't been for Nancy Coffey," says Bertrice, "there wouldn't have been a romance revival."

ROMANCE AVON STYLE

Recognize any of the following authors and titles? They've all been published by Avon Books. The list shows a sampling of the romance pacesetters turned out by Avon since *The Flame and the Flower* was published in 1972. Some of the authors have moved from Avon to other publishing houses. This list does not include titles by these authors that have been published by other houses.

Shirlee Busbee
Gypsy Lady
Lady Vixen
While Passion Sleeps

Jude Deveraux
The Enchanted Land
The Black Lyon
Casa Grande

III. LIGHTING THE TORCH

Patricia Gallagher	*Shadows of Passion* *Castles in the Air* *Mystic Rose* *The Thicket* *No Greater Love* *All for Love*
Johanna Lindsey	*Captive Bride* *A Pirate's Love* *Fires of Winter* *Paradise Wild* *Glorious Angel* *So Speaks the Heart*
Laurie McBain	*Devil's Desire* *Moonstruck Madness* *Tears of Gold* *Chance the Winds of Fortune* *Dark Before the Rising Sun*
Rosemary Rogers	*Sweet Savage Love* *The Wildest Heart* *Dark Fires* *Lost Love, Last Love* *Wicked Loving Lies* *Love Play* *The Crowd Pleasers* *The Insiders* *Surrender to Love*
Bertrice Small	*The Kadin* *Love Fair & Wild*
LaVyrle Spencer	*The Fulfillment*
Joyce Verrette	*Dawn of Desire* *Desert Fires*
Kathleen E. Woodiwiss	*The Flame and the Flower* *The Wolf and the Dove* *Shanna* *Ashes in the Wind* *A Rose in Winter*

III. LIGHTING THE TORCH

Every avid reader of romantic fiction should have a well-rounded library. Your bookshelves, of course, reflect your own preferences—the kinds of books you enjoy reading most. But if you're like many romance fans, you enjoy poking around bookstores for both new and used books, looking for certain titles that will help complete your collection. Perhaps you want to collect all of Janet Dailey's titles or the out-of-print works of Elsie Lee, for example. Whatever your interests, here are a few titles that belong in every romance library. Some are classics from another century and some are contemporary products.

Moura by Virginia Coffman
Gothic tale with a twist—a man accepts the guilt for his sister's death, then protects his niece, the real culprit. Heroine tracks down the culprit and discovers what a monster she is.

No Quarter Asked by Janet Dailey
City girl yields to arrogant Texas rancher in this first novel (Harlequin) by America's First Lady of Romance.

Love's Tender Fury by Jennifer Wilde
Beautiful English lass wrongly sold into slavery manages to master her masters.

Dust Devil by Parris Afton Bonds
Illicit love, tragedy and triumph for white women and Indian men in frontier New Mexico.

Black Sheep by Georgette Heyer
A lovable rogue turns proper Bath society upside down with his eccentric manners and wins the hand of a high-spirited lady by playfully abducting her.

Poinciana by Phyllis Whitney
Mystery, tension and danger surround a wealthy but corrupt man who marries a girl because he loved her dead mother.

Angelique by Sergeanne Golon
The first of nine novels about the adventures of a saucy, green-eyed beauty who entrances King Louis XIV but refuses to yield to him.

Gentle Pirate by Jayne Castle
In this contemporary Dell Candlelight Ecstasy Romance, a hook instead of a hand doesn't stop the hero from being oh-so-sexy.

Temporary Bride by Phyllis Halldorson
A-baby-for-hire scheme unites the hero and the heroine in love and matrimony in this contemporary Silhoutte Romance.

• III. LIGHTING THE TORCH •

Forever Amber by Kathleen Winsor
A rags-to-riches tale about a sexually liberated English peasant girl who seduces a king and becomes a duchess, but still carries her heart on her sleeve for another.

Sweet Savage Love by Rosemary Rogers
Well-bred girl falls for macho rake, set against revolutionary war adventures in Mexico.

The Flame and the Flower by Kathleen E. Woodiwiss
Rich Yankee sea captain is forced to marry English lass after he rapes and impregnates her; they manage to fall in love anyway.

Penmarric by Susan Howatch
Unsuspecting bride gets sucked into a dark whirlpool of family hate, infidelity and rivalry.

Jane Eyre by Charlotte Bronte
Governess falls for irascible employer and stands by him in the face of ruin and blindness.

Wuthering Heights by Emily Bronte
Brooding hero suffers family contempt, then rejection from his love. Death proves to be the only solace.

Pride and Prejudice by Jane Austen
Independent lass defies social-class lines and wins handsome, wealthy man.

Gone with the Wind by Margaret Mitchell
Headstrong Southern belle survives Civil War devastation by wrapping men around her pinky—except one.

Pamela by Samuel Richardson
Servant girl fends off amorous employer and is rewarded with marriage.

Skye O'Malley by Bertrice Small
Frisky Irish heroine goes through several husbands, becomes a pirate, and does a stint in a harem and angers a queen.

Rebecca by Daphne duMaurier
Bride encounters mystery surrounding suspicious death of her husband's first wife.

The Golden Touch by Robin James
A Second Chance At Love in which a sexy, glamorous rock star pursues a widowed minister's daughter with style, wit and sensuality.

Captive of Desire by Alexandra Sellers
In this superromance a British journalist and a Soviet dissident pump a lot of steam into a stormy love affair.

The Rebel Bride by Catherine Coulter
The first Regency to contain explicit sex, featuring a hero and heroine who are married.

CHAPTER ONE

Contemporary Romances: Not The Same Old Story

It's the final page, page 192, of *Devil in a Silver Room*. Throughout the book, Margo, a governess, has shared a few hot and heavy kisses with Paul, the dark and ruthless master of a French chateau. But Paul knows Margo is the woman for him, and on the last page, he proposes. "How I love you, Margo," he proclaims. "My passionate puritan!"

Devil in a Silver Room, written by Violet Winspear, was published by Harlequin as a Harlequin Presents in 1973. Juxtaposed against today's fare of racy and sexually explicit romances, it sounds quite tame. But it was with novels about virtuous but passionate "puritans," such as Margo, that Harlequin built its publishing empire and established a loyal following of readers around the world. And it was those formula, Cinderella-ish, happy ending novels that for years defined contemporary romances.

Contemporary romances still have happy endings—it's a fantasy genre, after all—but the generalization ends there. "American readers have greatly influenced changes in contemporaries," says Alicia M. Condon, Silhouette senior editor. "They like more independent women, more humor. Almost anything can be done as long as it's handled right."

Contemporaries comprise the largest and fastest growing segment of the romantic fiction market. They generally take place in the everlasting present, that is, not dated by history or events. Most contemporaries are "category" or brand-name novels, in which characters and plots follow certain guidelines established by the publisher. Category romances, such as those published under the Harlequin, Silhouette and Second Chance At Love names, for example, are sold more by the brand name of the line than by title or author. Noncategory romances, such as those written by Danielle Steel and some by Janet Dailey, lean more toward mainstream women's fiction, with greater length, more characters and more complex plots and subplots. More and more, brand-name romances are moving toward mainstream, offering readers more than romance.

Harlequin, still the world's largest publisher of romances, commanded nearly all of the contemporary market until 1980, when more American publishers began competing for readers. Founded in 1949 in Winnipeg, Ontario, Harlequin had an early line that was a mix of mysteries, westerns, adventures, cookbooks and reprints of romances published by Mills & Boon in London. The romances, short, light and happy, were so successful that Harlequin published more and more, until by 1964 the Harlequin name appeared only on romances (other types of books

FINDING
MR. RIGHT
AVON
83311
$2.75
COULD
SHE FOLLOW
HER HEART AND
STILL KEEP
LOVE FOR
THE TAKING
BETH CHRISTOPHER

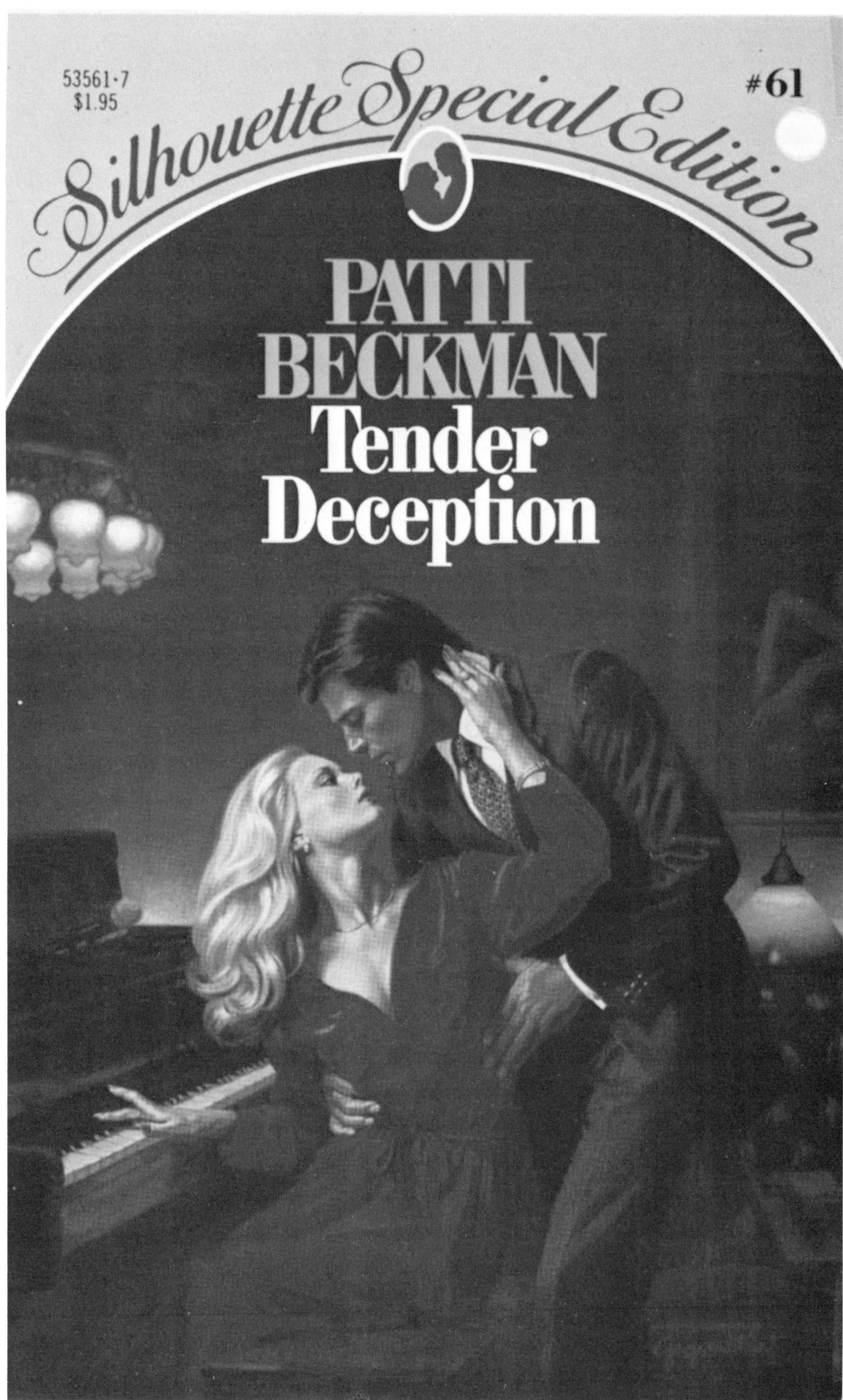
53561-7
$1.95
Silhouette Special Edition
#61
PATTI
BECKMAN
Tender
Deception

published by the company appeared under other imprints). Harlequin merged with Mills & Boon in 1971 (the Mills & Boon imprint is still retained in England).

During the 1950s, 1960s and even the 1970s, contemporary romances were fairly easy to stereotype. The heroines were usually young teachers, nurses, secretaries, governesses and the like who were swept off their feet by older, wiser, more sophisticated and affluent businessmen, doctors and nobility. The heroes were dark, moody and smoldering and did a lot of mocking, especially of the heroine. Sexual encounters were chaste—mostly a lot of kissing and heavy breathing. If the heroine didn't start crying or fight off the hero, or if he didn't exercise some supreme self-control and back off, the two were usually interrupted by an external occurrence. The obstacles that kept the would-be lovers apart were often misunderstandings, particularly over other women and other men. Strangely, the lovers never asked the questions that could have cleared up the misunderstandings until the novel's end.

Those days, for the most part, are gone. The contemporary romance has matured to reflect modern mores, values and problems—and the sexual revolution. With the 1980s, the heroine has become bolder, smarter, more independent, sexually experienced and, even though she yearns for passion and true love, less willing to sacrifice all for Mr. Right. When she's certain she loves the hero, she indulges in sex before marriage—and enjoys it without guilt. The hero is no longer physically flawless, doesn't have all the answers and is allowed to be emotional and vulnerable. And the areas of conflict are seldom contrived misunderstandings. Love triangles still exist, but the central characters can also be at odds because of differences in life styles, goals, ethics or values.

American publishers are responsible for the "liberation" and "sexualization" of contemporary romances. When Harlequin fired Pocket Books (Simon & Schuster) as its U.S. distributor in 1979, Simon & Schuster set up a new division, Silhouette Books, which came out with its own line of contemporary formula romances in 1980. It wasn't the first such American line, but it was the first to be heavily advertised and promoted. Early Silhouette Romances closely resembled Harlequins in style and then began offering more independent heroines, to reflect American life styles. Favorable reader response was enormous. "We realized quickly that readers were tired of submissive, weak heroines and dominating heroes," says Silhouette editor Leslie Wainger.

Sex became bolder, more frequent and more graphic, though the heroines still resisted seduction before marriage or, at least, the promise of marriage. Then, under the guidance of editor Vivian Stephens (now at Harlequin), Dell went even further with Candlelight Ecstasy Romances, which came out in December 1980. Dell later claimed to be the first to consummate sex without an interruption. Vivian suspected that readers, like she, wanted to go beyond the threshold of the bedroom door, not necessarily in terms of explicit sexual description but in terms of passion and emotional satisfaction.

Initially she put out just two Ecstasy books: *The Tawny Gold Man* by Amii Lorin and *Gentle Pirate* by Jayne Castle, without publicity. Through word of mouth, they sold out within a week, and the sensuality trend was on.

Sex and sensuality, or the trappings and emotions of seduction, riveted readers to the pages, and Ecstasies began selling by the millions—30 million copies a year by the end of 1982, according to Dell, which ranks third in the romance market share behind Harlequin and Silhouette.

Along with more liberated sex, contemporary heroines now enjoy more liberated lives. They actively pursue professions, from bush pilots to corporate presidents to college professors; they're more self-confident and are able to think for themselves. They can be almost any age.

Settings need no longer be exotic to serve as a backdrop for romance; an author no longer needs to fly her heroine to the jungles of South America or sunny Greek isles. Readers are perfectly happy with novels set anywhere in the United States, from New York City to Los Angeles to Boise to San Antonio. "Almost any setting can be sensual and romantic," states Ellen Edwards, senior editor of Jove's Second Chance at Love.

Today, there's something for everyone in contemporary romances. Twenty lines (either launched or planned as of 1983) offer different themes and/or varying degrees of sexual activity and description, from the traditional chaste, or "sweet," end to the racy, or "spicy," end. There are books for women on the second time around, due to death, divorce or a jilting lover; there are plots in which the heroine chooses between potential mates, neither of whom is perfect but both of whom offer something desirable; there are romances involving older women coping with life changes; there are even romances concerning married couples. In some lines, the romance is mixed with adventure and suspense, although the romance always dominates, of course.

LOVESWEPT • 5
Carla Neggers
Matching Wits
21605-8 ★ $1.95 ★ A BANTAM BOOK
LOVESWEPT • 6
Dorothy Garlock
A Love for All Time

IV. THE MANY FACES OF LOVE

As the contemporay romance subcategory has matured, the old formulas are falling by the wayside. Guidelines have loosened and become short and general, thus giving writers more freedom to portray characters and situations that appeal to contemporary women. The results, happily, are romances that are increasingly realistic yet retain the fantasy element that appeals to romance fans.

ETHNIC ROMANCES

Traditionally, the lovers in romances have been Caucasian. Hero and heroine are almost always Anglo-Saxon, particularly the heroine, although she may sometimes fall for an American or Eastern Indian or a Latin, for example. But ethnic romances, in which *both* hero and heroine are non-Caucasian, have scarcely been done—until recently, and then with mixed results in the marketplace. The jury is still out as to what and how much of a role ethnics will play in the romance genre, but editors believe there is room for at least a few such titles on their lists.

Their success may be limited just by the sheer demographics of romance readers. Harlequin senior editor Vivian Stephens notes that the world's population may be mostly non-Caucasian, but in the United States most paperback buyers are white women—overwhelmingly so—more than 90 percent, according to a leading market research firm. And they buy white romances.

However, says Vivian, every American, regardless of race or ethnic origin, wants to be middle class and live the American Dream of prosperity, love and happiness; romance knows no racial boundaries. In 1980, while she was at Dell, in charge of the Candlelight and Candlelight Ecstasy Romances, Vivian brought out several wholly ethnic American romances—black, Hispanic, Indian, Chinese—with the intent of publishing them regularly. But the market response was not enthusiastic enough, and the idea was quietly dropped.

Interest in ethnic romances did not, however, disappear. There may not be enough of a market to sustain a dedicated line of ethnics, but editors of contemporary and young adult lines are actively looking for such manuscripts to intersperse among the Caucasian romances. Watch for them in the near future.

OVER ONE MILLION
JANELLE TAYLOR
BOOKS IN PRINT!

SEARING PASSION
BOUND THEM
TOGETHER—
JEALOUS FATE
TORE THEM APART!

BRAZEN ECSTASY

BY JANELLE TAYLOR

Historical romances have a special appeal. Not only do they transport you to another locale, often several around the world, they sweep you away to another time, when all things were different: dress, manners, morals and everyday life. It's so easy and so enticing to suspend disbelief, to forget about bills, the economy, politics and liberated sex—and plunge into the fantastic world of another era.

Lost in another place and time, a reader can identify with a heroine who undoubtedly wears exotic and often elegant clothing; who is courted by an aristocrat or an appealing rogue (the latter either has blue blood or wealthy roots or comes into money during the course of the novel); and who may have all sorts of adventures, such as being kidnapped by pirates, sold into slavery or sold into an Eastern harem. Wars are always good for a little intrigue—spying, perhaps, or falling in love with a soldier who wears the wrong colors. And because historicals are not bound by reality in the same way as contemporaries, they tend to have characters who are much larger than life.

Historicals have been around as long as storytellers; historical romances are largely a recent phenomenon. What distinguishes a historical novel from a historical romance novel?

It's often hard to say. Any good story has a love line to it, but in historical romances, the love line *is* the story, written from a woman's point of view, exploring a woman's emotions, intended for women readers. Their slant is different: they're more romance with adventure than adventure with romance, though the dividing line is often a subtle one.

Let's take a hypothetical example. A medieval earl plots to overthrow the king and secretly mobilizes an army. He also happens to be the lover of the king's cousin, who can either help him or betray him. Jeopardy! A historical novel would focus on his plot and its successful execution; oh, yes, he wins the woman, too. A historical *romance*, on the other hand, would focus on the love affair between him and the heroine, the king's cousin, basically from her point of view. Her blood ties and his ambition would be the obstacles to their love—will they or won't they come together in the end? Oh, yes, he becomes king, too.

Among the contemporary historical writers whose works have influenced authors in the romance genre are Anya Seton, Frank Yerby, Taylor Caldwell and Thomas Costain. The amount of historical detail in a romance varies with the author. Some do painstaking, extensive research to weave accurate facts with fiction, while others use history more as a backdrop for a love story.

The treatment of sex also varies. Some authors, such as Barbara Cartland, write their historical romances sweet, with a kiss and an embrace or two, and other authors, such as Bertrice Small, make them very sexy. In general, historical romances tend to have more sex than contemporaries, and the sex is frequently more risque and may involve a variety of partners. The heroines aren't "wanton," mind you. Readers like to view their heroines as basically virtuous women—"promiscuous by accident," as Barbara Dicks, executive editor of Ballantine's/Crest Books, puts it. But a lass may be raped by an unscrupulous villain or may have to surrender to a man for self-protection, meanwhile remaining faithful *in her heart* to the hero, from whom, alas, she has been separated.

There *are* one-man one-woman historical romances, but considering the length and complexity of most historical plots, episodic sex seems to serve them well.

Many historical romances have been labeled "bodice rippers" or "sweet/savage" romances, the latter term taken from Rosemary Rogers' popular first novel, *Sweet Savage Love* (Avon Books). The labels have been unfairly applied in many cases, for not all historical romances feature lust-driven brutes ripping women's clothes off. Bodice rippers are usually long on sex and short on historical detail.

Since the early 1970s, when historical romances took off in popularity, the treatment of sex in them has been changing, from forced and violent to more sensual. "They're friendly persuasion novels instead of Captain Blood," says Kate Duffy, Pocket Books senior editor in charge of Tapestry Romances.

Then there are the nearly sexless romances, the Regencies. They take place between 1811 and 1820, the years when England's Prince George (later to be King George IV) reigned as prince regent while his father, King George III, spent his last years in seclusion, blind and ill. The setting is usually England but can involve France or even America. Regencies are characterized by witty repartee, high-society elegance and social conventions, the violation of which causes acute embarrassment. The trappings of the wealthy—clothes, balls, manors and the like—are described in great detail. The Regency style was set by the late Georgette Heyer, who wrote more than 50 books before her death in 1974. Her own favorite period was the Middle Ages; she also wrote suspense. But it was

FOR LOVE AND VALCOUR

The compelling saga of three sisters who rose from the ravages of war—to seize a passionate dream!

DOROTHY DANIE
Author of The Sisters of Valcour

WARNER BOOKS 30-256 $3.50

AMBER
TREASUR

BY ELAINE A. BARBIERI
AUTHOR OF AMBER FIRE

SHE WOULD
FOREVER BE
HIS CAPTIVE
PRINCESS!
ZEBRA/0-8217-1202-0/$3.50
LOVE
STONE
BY

her Regencies that made her famous and set the standards for all such novels to come.

It's interesting to note that while Regency novels portray very proper and upright social manners, the prince regent himself lived a most dissolute life. Disliked by his subjects, George drank to excess, squandered money and ruined two marriages (one secret, one "official") because of his habitual and flagrant infidelity. What a contrast to the prim and refined conduct of the Regency heroine and hero!

Regencies have had their cyclical ups and downs in popularity, but they have maintained a steady core of fans who enjoy their style and tone. Authors such as Joan Smith, Catherine Coulter, Elizabeth Chater, Marion Chesney, Elizabeth Mansfield and Elizabeth Neff Walker have followed in Georgette Heyer's footsteps.

Somewhat less popular than Regencies are novels set in the Georgian, Victorian or Edwardian eras of England (sometimes the term "Regency" is applied to novels set in the latter two periods as well). King George III was born in 1714 and held the throne from 1760 to 1811. The Georgian period is portrayed with more raucous behavior than the Regency period, a time when dueling was a popular means of settling disputes and avenging affronts, and spies were common. The reign of Queen Victoria, from 1837 to 1901, was one of repressed morals, and consequently, few romances are set in this era. Indeed, romance fiction itself waned in popularity during Victoria's rule. The Edwardian period was brief—King Edward VII held the throne from 1901 to 1910, though the period generally extends to the start of World War I in 1914.

Other periods in history that attract readers are America's Revolutionary War and Civil War and its pioneer age of the late nineteenth century. The medieval times of England and Europe have served well for such popular authors as Roberta Gellis, whose novels include *The Royal Dynasty Series* and *The Roselynde Chronicles* (Playboy), and Jude Deveraux, whose novels include *The Velvet Promise* (Richard Gallen/Pocket Books) and *Highland Velvet* (Pocket Books).

Saga historicals are family epics of passion, turmoil, treachery, glorious success and bitter failure, told with multiple points of view. Susan Howatch, who started out as a prominent writer of Gothics, became a master of sagas, with such novels as *Cashelmara* and *Penmarric* (both Simon & Schuster). Janet Dailey, who cut her writer's teeth on short contemporary category novels for Harlequin before moving into mass

market paperback romances, enjoyed best-selling success in 1982 with her first multivolume saga, the Calder series (Pocket Books), which sweeps from historical to contemporary times in Montana. Sagas are often the stuff of which best-selling blockbusters, rather than romances, are made.

CHAPTER THREE

That Special Charm of a Regency Romp

If you've never read a Regency romance, you've missed a tremendous treat. There's a special quality about these novels that makes them particularly fun to read—a pleasant break from whatever your usual book fare may be. The stories usually take place in England, with English characters, between 1811 and 1820, when Prince George ruled as regent in place of his ill and incapacitated father, King George III. Although there was much political turmoil at the time—Napoleon was conquering his way through Europe—the novels usually reflect an unruffled, gracious and sumptuous life enjoyed by the wealthy and privileged. Some Regency plots may include a little political intrigue, but by and large the characters are preoccupied with social concerns and the pursuit of pleasure. It was a grand period of shaking loose the rigid behavior and clothing that prevailed in the eighteenth century and of trying new things. Women got rid of their stiff, layered petticoats for the freer Empire style of dress, and men dressed more colorfully.

The vast majority of Regencies don't contain much sex—a major element in most other romances—but it's scarcely missed. Instead, heroine and hero match their wits in a series of misunderstandings and clashes, all framed within the most delightful, witty period dialogue. (Usually, the heroine manages to take the typically arrogant and chauvinistic hero down a notch or two.) The clothes are elegant; the trappings luxurious; the social engagements, balls and country visits glamorous; and the manners impeccable.

While the heroine and hero often do little more than kiss—in accordance with the strict courtship rules of the day—there's still a sexual tension in Regency novels that's very appealing to many readers, notes Barbara Dicks, executive editor of Ballantine's Crest Books and an experienced Regency editor. "It's all in the talk—the sex and the charm are really in the conversation."

But sex isn't absent in all Regencies. In 1979, NAL/Signet published *The Rebel Bride*, Catherine Coulter's second novel, which contained explicit, sensual sex scenes between a husband and wife, and the husband and his mistress—just about the only two acceptable ways to include sex in a Regency plot. The enormous success of that book encouraged other writers to produce more sensual Regencies.

The late Georgette Heyer, in the fifty-plus novels she wrote between 1920 and 1974, established the standards for Regency characters. The heroes, "Corinthians" in the lingo of the times, are tall (over six feet), muscular and physically fit. Their broad shoulders *never* need padding. They box, fence and race horses to stay in shape. They're wealthy, of course, prime catches, and they're much sought after by young lasses with matrimony on their minds. The heroes "become very cynical, very sardonic about it," says Barbara. "They're skeptical of all these mothers pushing their daughters at them."

The heroines are beautiful, though in some cases they get by with being a bit on the mousy side. Most importantly, they are very intelligent—more than a match for the heroes, much to their masculine surprise. Barbara notes, "Even though being an intellectual was frowned on for women in this period, the Regency heroine is often what they called a 'bluestocking,' someone interested in intellectual matters."

Both sexes are, naturally, quite gracious, charming, well mannered and *virtuous*. In fact, the manners and stiff propriety often aggravate the misunderstandings that develop: conversations are polite, never pointed; to be direct is unspeakably, unthinkably rude. That's part of the fun of Regencies, the improbable situations which could never happen today because of the confrontational nature of our society.

For example, in Elizabeth Mansfield's *A Regency Match* (Berkley), the heroine is crushed

SIGNET REGENCY
Diana Campbell
Lord Margrave's Deception
A LOVELY YOUNG LADY IN NEED MAKES A SCANDALOUS ALLIANCE WITH AN OUTRAGEOUSLY RAKISH LORD
SIGNET REGENCY ROMANCE
THE THREE GRACES
JANE ASHFORD
IT'S TRIPLE TIME FOR ROMANCE WHEN EACH OF THREE ENCHANTING SISTERS SEEKS HER OWN KIND OF LOVE
Your Warner Library of Regency Romance
Pretty Kitty
Zabrina Faire
The London ton was the field of honor, but she was an American determined to fight for her English lord's love.
12
Your Warner Library of Regency Romance
The Wicked Cousin
Her fiancé was tall, dark and handsome. A pity! When she wanted someone witty, kind and gentle.
Zabrina Faire

7
Your Warner Library of Regency Romance
The Romany Rebel

when she accidentally overhears the hero describe her as a "shatterbrained hysteric." It's a wrong impression created by unfortunate circumstances, but she certainly can't confront him about it. Instead, out of indignation, she decides to do her best to live up to his impression and cause him trouble and embarrassment. She accomplishes her objective, in a series of "accidental" mishaps and madcap adventures, but gets more in the bargain—he falls wildly in love with her and proposes.

In Georgette Heyer's *Faro's Daughter,* the heroine runs the faro table at her debt-ridden aunt's gaming house. The hero suspects she's a fortune hunter after his gullible cousin, and attempts to buy her off. She has no interest in marrying the doting cousin but is so outraged at the hero's bribe offer that she plays along with it and defies him to stop the "marriage." When the muddle is finally straightened out, the cousin elopes with another lass, and the hero kisses the heroine and proposes.

Tone and language are crucial to Regencies, and writers must have an ear for the speech cadence of the time as well as a good knowledge of the everyday vocabulary and colorful slang. There's no central reference source that lists Regency slang expressions; writers pick up the language and tone from reading dozens and dozens of Regencies, learning by inference and osmosis.

To help Regency readers along, Elizabeth Neff Walker, an experienced Regency author, prepared this list especially for *LoveLines.*

broke: pockets to let, not a feather to fly with, bellows to mend, rolled-up, in Dun territory

depressed: blue devilled, in the dismals, green and yellow melancholy, Friday-faced

drivers: competent whip, mere whipster, top sawyer; also, actions such as sticking to your leaders, featheredging a corner, handling the ribbons

drunk: foxed, bosky, disguised, in his cups

dying: slipping his wind, having his notice to quit, put to bed with a shovel

fighting: plump his daylights, draw his cork, milling, handy bunch of fives, drawing claret

fool: cork-brained, gudgeon, paperskull, ninnyhammer, slow-top, sapskull

good horses: prime goers, beautiful steppers, high bred 'uns

a lie: bouncer, banger, loud one, bubble, bag o' moonshine

loose woman: demi-rep, Paphian, light-skirt

man about town: Corinthian, sprig of fashion, nonesuch, nonpareil, bang up to the nines, top-of-the-trees, tulip of fashion, buck of the first head, of the first consequence, slap up to the mark, of the first stare, a swell

marrying: getting buckled, leg-shackled, caught in parson's mousetrap

miser: a nip-cheese, clutch-fisted, close as wax

praise: great gun, complete hand, pluck to the backbone, all the crack

reckless riders: bruising, neck-or-nothing

rich: hosed and shod, born with a silver spoon in one's mouth, beforehand with the world, well-blunted, well-breeched, plump in the pocket

romance: throwing out lures, dangling after, dalliance, having a *tendre* for, trifling with

to scold: clapperclaw, comb one's hair, ring a peal over, come the ugly

seduction: slip on the shoulder

teasing: gammoning, quizzing, bamming, roasting, hoaxing, humbugging

upset: in the boughs, on her high ropes, daggers drawn, overset, in a pucker, in a rare taking, vexed, in a fret, in the fidgets, at sixes and sevens

youngster: scarcely breeched, green one, whelp, halfling, downey one, bantling

CHAPTER FOUR

Gothics and Suspense: Twists and Terrors

The Gothic period in Western Europe ranged from about the twelfth to the sixteenth centuries and was characterized architecturally by massive structures with pointed arches, flying buttresses and ribbed vaulting. In literature, the classic Gothic story evokes this period to create a feeling of mystery and horror.

Gothic tales have been around for a long time; their popularity goes back to the eighteenth century. In classic Gothic tales, a dark, forbidding mansion, castle or other dwelling dominates the story, which usually takes place in the 1700s or early 1800s. Mysterious events occur, and supernatural elements are sometimes part of the plot, which doesn't necessarily include romance. The heroine is a young, beautiful and innocent girl, the hero a mysterious, moody and strong-willed man harboring a secret. The mystery puts the heroine in jeopardy. The ending has a twist: for example, the suspected evil isn't the real evil—the "hero" turns out to be the villain and the villain the real hero who saves the girl. If there's a romantic element, it doesn't clutter the story with much sex—the sinister hero just sort of smolders away at arm's length. Horace Walpole's *The House of Otranto* is a classic Gothic; Charlotte Bronte's *Jane Eyre* has Gothic elements, as does Daphne du Maurier's *Rebecca*. Gothics written more recently usually play up the romantic angle.

Among present-day authors, Virginia Coffman ranks among the leading writers of Gothic-type novels. Coffman's novel *Moura*, published by Crown in 1959, was influential in renewing interest in the subcategory. While *Moura* follows a classic Gothic theme, the ending has a double twist: the "sweet and innocent" young heroine turns out to be the monstrous villain of the tale.

During the 1960s and part of the 1970s, Gothics experienced a raging boom that suddenly went bust. The market was flooded with them, many badly written and published in haste, unfortunately, and soon customers grew wary of being burned. So, books that sported covers with terror-stricken lasses fleeing from sinister looking houses (dark except for a light in a single upstairs window) were left unsold on bookstore shelves. "Gothic" became a tainted term.

Enter romantic suspense, which combines romance with mystery or Gothic mystery. Often there's a fine line between "Gothic" and "romantic suspense"; not all mysteries have the dark, evil Gothic elements. Shortly after *Moura* proved to be a hit, Doubleday published *The Mistress of Mellyn* by Victoria Holt, a historical romantic suspense with Gothic

The spirit of a long-dead actress possessed her—setting her body afire with its lust and consuming her soul with its evil.
Moths
"Could be a young Daphne DuMaurier... Fans of Rebecca will be moths to the flame."
—Publishers Weekly
A LITERARY GUILD ALTERNATE SELECTION
PRINTED IN U.S.A.
FICTION
WARNER BOOKS
$1.95
Moths
Rosalind Ashe
0-446-89447-8
195
Rosalind Ashe
Moths
WARNER BOOKS
Daughters of the Misty Isles
Aola Vandergriff
Silhouette Special Edition
#38
NANCY JOHN
Web of Passion
From the author of the bestselling NO GENTLE LOVE
BECCA BRANDEWYNE
Forever my Love
A tale of two headstrong lovers whose forbidden passion set the Highlands aflame.

overtones that also quickly became a success. For years Doubleday closely guarded the real identity of "Victoria Holt," a pseudonym, thus adding a little mystery to the mystery. (Victoria is Eleanor Hibbert, who also writes under Jean Plaidy and Philippa Carr.)

Romantic suspense enjoyed a boom along with Gothics, bringing fame to Mary Stewart and Phyllis A. Whitney, who prefers to set her suspense novels in contemporary times. Although Phyllis' work is labeled "romantic suspense," some of it has modern Gothic elements. *Poinciana* (Doubleday), for example, takes place in a huge, forbidding Florida mansion filled with secret passageways, dark stairwells and mysterious occupants. The hero, strong-willed and moody, reveals himself to be a villain; he dies suddenly under mysterious circumstances. The heroine is threatened by unknown sinister people until she is rescued and romanced by a man who at first seems to be a villain but turns out to be a hero instead.

When Gothics went down, romantic suspense began sinking, too—much to the dismay of dedicated fans. Nevertheless, big-name authors, such as Phyllis, Mary, Victoria and Virginia, who were firmly established, continued to publish.

But trends in publishing are cyclical, and now that there's been a dearth of Gothics and suspense on the market, publishers are once again beginning to experiment with the themes. Silhouette, Dell Candlelight Ecstasy and Scholastic Books' Windswept young adult line are publishing some "modern Gothics"; a strong entry into romantic suspense is planned by Avon Books with a dedicated line, tentatively called The Velvet Glove. The line will be packaged by The Denise Marcil Literary Agency in New York. All of this renewed interest bodes well for the writers and readers who enjoy mystery along with their romance.

CHAPTER FIVE

Teen Romances: Young Love In Bloom

Remember when you were in high school, how confused you were about so many things—yourself, your parents, your future, growing up and, most of all, *boys?* Those mysterious creatures who could evoke a whole panoply of emotions from you, from rapture to despair to disgust? It really doesn't matter what your generation is, or what decade comprised your tumultuous teen years, for some things never change. Mores, social habits, attitudes, sophistication—yes, those things change with the times. But the murky uncertainties of boy-girl relationships never change. Teenage girls invariably spend part of their time fascinated by and preoccupied with boys. It's inevitable, and it explains in part the enduring appeal of young adult romances.

Since 1980, at least six publishers have either launched teen romance lines or planned to do so, and as more of the books have appeared on the market, sales have jumped tremendously. For the B. Dalton Bookseller chain, young adult romance sales doubled in volume between 1981 and 1982, accounting for 25 percent of all nonadult paperbacks sold.

Scholastic Books led the field and set the trend. Young adult romances had been popular titles during the 1950s and into the 1960s, but they fell out of grace when "realism" struck in the 1970s. Heavy-hitting books by authors like Judy Blume dealt with such issues as drug and alcohol abuse, premarital sex, birth control, unwanted pregnancy and parental divorce. They were popular, but somewhere along the line, publishers forgot that teens were still interested in simple infatuation, romance and courtship. A primary concern of teenage girls, says Scholastic senior editor Ann Reit, is boy-girl relationships.

Noticing that romances continued to be strong sellers in its Teenage Book Club, Scholastic launched a special line of paperback romances, dubbed Wildfire, in 1980. It was so successful that the publisher followed with Wishing Star in 1981; this line featured romance but with more problem-oriented plots. The same year, Bantam joined the field with Sweet Dreams; Silhouette came out with First Love; and Dell brought out some of the backlisted titles in its twenty-year-old Laurel Leaf line, adding to the covers a gold heart-shaped locket inscribed "Young Love." In 1982, Ace Tempo launched Caprice, which allowed room for problems along with romance; Scholastic started Windswept, which it termed "modern Gothic"; and E.P. Dutton announced plans for a teen line, Heavenly Romance.

Clean romance is the appeal of these novels. If the plots include problems, such as with parents or rival siblings, they never steal center stage from the romance. There's no sex in these books—physical encounters are limited to a few kisses and embraces. There is no profanity and little slang (slang dates a book, and these young adult romances have a strong backlist longevity because of their appeal to each new crop of readers). Heroines can range in age from thirteen to seventeen (but are usually fifteen to seventeen) and heroes are just a little older.

Who reads these books? Girls eleven to nineteen, weighted toward the younger years. "They love them," says Nancy Jackson, senior editor of Silhouette's First Love. Teens, she adds, are looking for values, and the romances portray self-respect and respect for other individuals.

And young adult romances encourage some nonreaders to start reading.

The fantasy romance element doesn't reduce these novels to "will-I-get-a-date-for-the-prom" books. There are "prom" books, but for the most part, the heroines usually either have a sense of their goals or experience

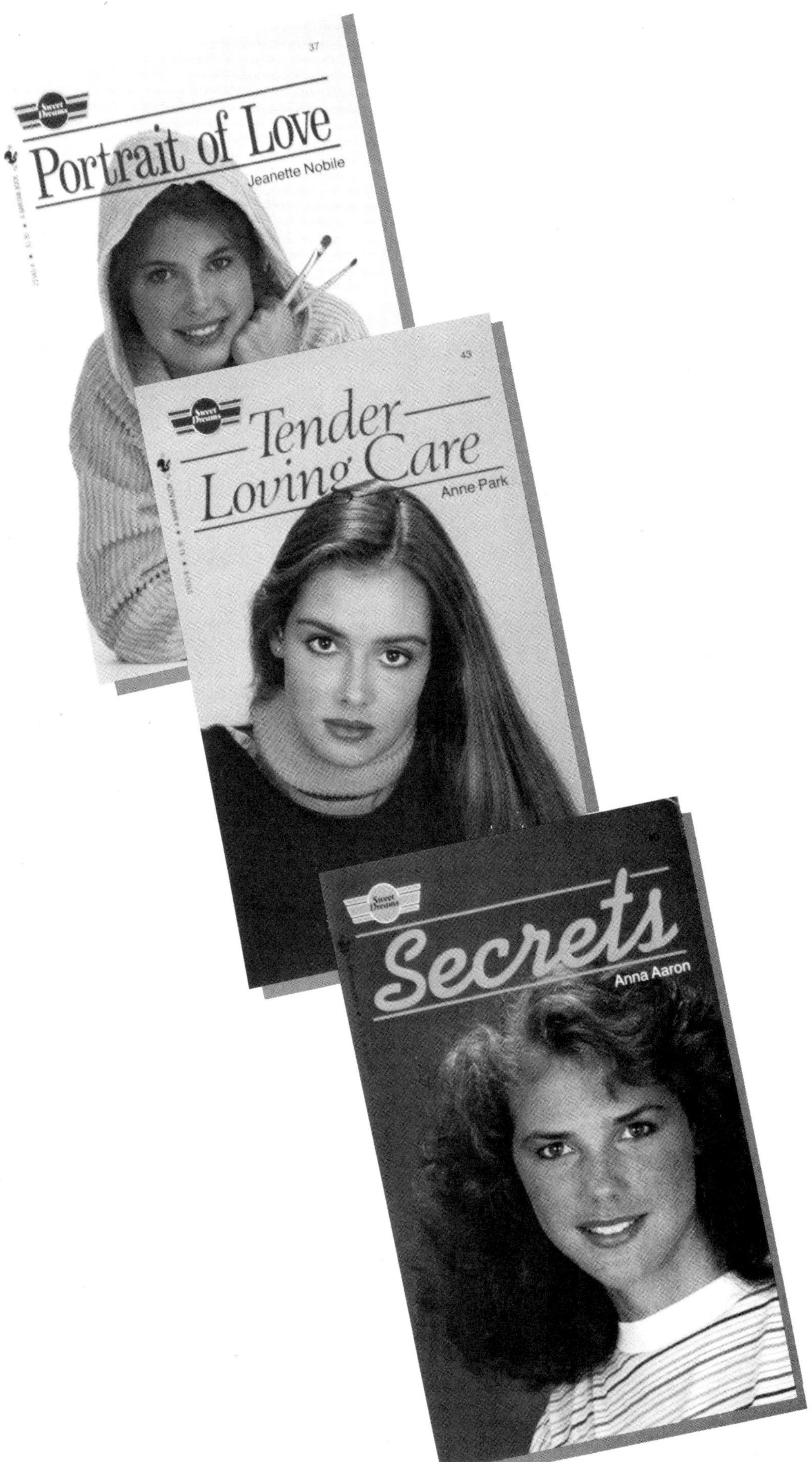

37
Sweet Dreams
Portrait of Love
Jeanette Nobile
43
Sweet Dreams
Tender Loving Care
Anne Park
Sweet Dreams
Secrets
Anna Aaron

some kind of self-discovery. For example, in Elaine Harper's *We Belong Together* (First Love), the heroine realizes and develops her artistic talent for painting, which plays a role in the romance. And not all boy-girl relationships in the books must be romantic ones. Male-female friendships are portrayed, as are group social activities and "dates," as in Maud Johnson's *Saturday Night Date* (Wildfire). The heroine of that novel is dropped by her longtime steady and has to learn to keep on going and form new relationships. One of the biggest selling romances, with more than half a million copies in print, Barbara Conklin's *P.S. I Love You* (Sweet Dreams) features a heroine, an aspiring writer, who tragically loses her boyfriend to cancer.

What's more, the teen characters don't run to adults for help but grapple with their own dilemmas and generally demonstrate some kind of personal growth or maturation by the end of the novels. "Parents, teachers and other adults should not solve the young person's problems," notes author Emily Hamlin.

Nevertheless, the books are still meant to be fun to read and are still fantasies, just as adult romances are fantasies. Humor is always appreciated by the editors, and sometimes gimmicks are used as interesting plot devices. In *Ask Annie* (Sweet Dreams), for example, the heroine's common-sense outlook unwittingly leads her to become a popular Ann Landers, which causes her problems when the boys flock to her for advice about girls.

As long as teenage girls are interested in the opposite sex, young adult romances are sure to have a place on the bookshelf.

V. LEADING LOVERS AND OTHERS

Times have changed for the cast of characters in romance novels. The heroes and heroines, other women and other men, have different personalities and jobs than they did in years past, and behave differently—women are stronger, men more vulnerable. The changes open up some intriguing avenues for writers and editors to explore.

CHAPTER ONE
Heroes and Heroines: They Aren't What They Used To Be

Once upon a time, the characters who populated romances were a different breed than the ones who live on the pages today. In bodice-ripper historicals, the arrogant hero raped the spirited—but resistant—heroine until she realized she loved him; after that it wasn't rape anymore. In contemporaries, sullen, sophisticated macho men dominated naive, virginal girls, forcing themselves physically on their prey and treating them cruelly until a sudden burst of tenderness at the end led them to propose marriage. That old, traditional breed of leading lovers hasn't vanished, but it has been joined in increasing numbers by Modern Man and Woman, thanks largely to American readers and writers.

Since the 1950s, most traditional contemporary romances have been written by English and Canadian authors and published by Toronto-based Harlequin, virtually the only name and game in romance publishing until 1980. That year marked the beginning of heavy competition from American publishers, particularly in contemporary romances. Since the Harlequin characters and plots had been so successful for so long, the early American romances closely followed their structure. But American writers felt too limited by traditional characters and plots, and readers weren't timid with their opinions.

"The hero used to be enigmatic—totally unfathomable," says author Brooke Hastings. "That was okay when the heroine was a girl of sixteen or seventeen and had very little sense of self and experience with men. But you take a heroine who's twenty-eight, or thirty-two, who's had a career and is self-confident, who deals with men in business and who might have had other lovers, and it just doesn't work."

Thus began the evolution of the hero and heroine, a trend to better mirror the reality of modern times yet still retain the traditional fantasy of ideal love. "It's time to leave the old stereotypes behind," says Ellen Edwards, senior editor of Jove's Second Chance At Love. "We're tired of macho heroes with no hint of sensitivity until the very end, and of heroines who run away from the heroes instead of confronting them."

So nix, then, to the macho man who is always fabulously wealthy and worldly. Nix to the arrogant fellow who has all the answers, the Greeks and sheiks who are physically flawless and always TDH (tall, dark and handsome) or BBB (bronzed, blond and beautiful). Nix to the moody, mean-tempered, nasty man—who in their right mind would want to fall in love with a beast?

That doesn't mean the New Hero is a wimp. He is still successful, but not necessarily wealthy; is still older than the heroine, but not as much; is still good looking, even tall, dark and handsome, but not necessarily in a drop-dead way; is still confident, often arrogant, but has weaknesses and even admits he's wrong. He can show great sensitivity to the heroine's feelings and even be emotional himself. If he's ill tempered, it's due to a passing reason, not his basic disposition. Above all, he respects the New Woman. "He isn't going to grab the heroine the first time he sees her," says Robin Grunder, editor of New American Library's Rapture Romances. "She wouldn't put up with it."

The New Heroine is no longer the sweet young thing emerging from the protection of her parents' nest, someone who never smokes, drinks only white wine (and that rarely), cringes when she hears a profanity and can't comprehend the fluttering in her stomach whenever she's near the hero. She has no longer been "sealed in cellophane for seventeen years," observes

THE UNIQUE ANGELIQUE

The most famous historical romance heroine of all time certainly must be Angelique, a seventeenth century French beauty whose nine books sold more than 80 million copies in thirty countries between 1956 and 1980. Blonde, green-eyed, gorgeous and willful, Angelique has become a role model for historical heroines.

She was created by Serge and Anne Golon, French husband and wife writers who used the pseudonym Sergeanne Golon (Serge is now deceased). The first of the nine novels, *Angelique,* was published in Germany in 1956 and was an immediate success. (In the United States, Angelique books have been published by E.P.

author Dixie Browning. She's no longer a fragile, petite thing with porcelain skin who fails to recognize her attractiveness or understand her sexuality. "Romances are more realistic in depicting the way women are now," says Ann Gisonny, senior editor of Dell Candlelight Ecstasy Romances. "It's not Betty Friedan, but rather a filtered-down feminism."

The New Heroine is older—mid-twenties to early thirties and even older in some cases—and established in a job or career. She's more mature in her experience and outlook on life as well as her expectations. She has a mind of her own and is capable and resourceful.

"This is the girl who gets up to the dock and sees the boat leaving for the island, knowing the ferry goes only once a week," Robin Grunder describes as an example. "Does she stand there and cry? Of course not. There's a wonderful-looking guy nearby in a speedboat, and she jumps in and says, 'Ten dollars if you can get me to the ferry!' She doesn't shrink from getting things done."

Furthermore, she doesn't allow misunderstandings to fester unresolved. The traditional heroine may say nothing about the hero's apparent interest in the other woman, instead biting her pretty little nails down to the quick in worry and despair. Not the New Woman. "She has a mind of her own and she's going to use it," says Robin. "She's going to ask the hero, 'Say, are you still seeing that floozie in the other department?'"

The change from simper to sass is refreshing, comments author Ellen Langtry. "The heroine may still be verbally abused by the hero, but now she stands up, pulls her shoulders back and tells him where to get off."

Both hero and heroine may have physical flaws, from small imperfections to major handicaps. Or a heroine may not be able to bear children. In *Gentle Pirate* (Dell Candlelight Ecstasy) by Jayne Castle, the hero is a wounded Vietnam veteran who has a hook instead of a hand.

Another new element in romances is humor—readers enjoy characters who can laugh at themselves, make

Dutton in hardcover and Bantam Books in paperback.)

Angelique lives during the reign of King Louis IV, known as the Sun King for his patronage of the arts. It is a glittery, opulent, romantic period, yet also one fraught with political upheaval. Angelique has no trouble entrancing men, including the Sun King himself. But she will be dominated by no one, not even the monarch, and eventually aids the Huguenot Protestant uprising against him.

Her adventures have been so often mimicked that they now seem like stock fare. She sails to Africa, is kidnapped by ruthless pirates and sold as a slave. Escaping, she is captured again and sold to a sultan for his harem. She escapes that, too, and returns to France, only to leave again for the New World with yet a new lover, of course, and the feeling that anything is possible. With Angelique, anything is.

THE ANGELIQUE BOOKS

1. *Angelique*
2. *Angelique and the King*
3. *Angelique and the Sultan,* or *Angelique in Barbary*
4. *Angelique in Love*
5. *Angelique in Revolt*
6. *The Countess Angelique*
7. *The Temptation of Angelique*
8. *Angelique and the Demon*
9. *Angelique and the Ghosts*

silly mistakes and engage in clever repartee.

They don't turn their romance into a comedy of one-liners, however; humor has to be subtle and natural, part of a writer's style.

Making History With Historicals

Historical romances have more adventure and fantasy than contemporaries, and the characters are usually larger than life. The stereotypes are the heroes who swagger, brood and issue commands, and the heroines who are either meek and submissive or proud and defiant (usually the latter). Hero and heroine tame each other, in their own ways.

Author Roberta Gellis, well known for her many medieval romances, creates her characters based on research of historical biographies, scholarly analyses of historical events and prominent people and original historical chronicles. "I look for what people wanted in their heroes back then—the medieval hero was considered to be brave and gentle—and then add human faults," Roberta says. "No man is a saint."

While Roberta is one author who does not condone violent sex, many historical heroes force themselves on the heroines, at least initially and in some way, before becoming gentler. In bodice rippers, such as *Sweet Savage Love* (Avon) by Rosemary Rogers or *Love Me, Marietta* (Warner) by Jennifer Wilde, the hero, in addition to other men, may force himself on the heroine repeatedly.

Bodice rippers, however, no longer command the market they once did; even historical romances in general have dwindled under the onslaught of contemporary romances. But at least one romantic fiction editor believes that interest in historicals will regenerate—but only if the characters are more sympathetically portrayed, and sex is a mutually desirable act. Pocket Books senior editor Kate Duffy, who launched a new line of historicals, Tapestry Romances, in late

1982, prefers gentler tales of love. In *Defiant Love* by Maura Seger, a Tapestry introductory title, the medieval hero never once brutalizes his heroine, instead using tenderness to overcome her resistance and fear.

"It's a very sensual romance, but no physical violence is done to the heroine," says Kate. "She isn't slapped around and the hero isn't Conan the Barbarian, a mysterious person you'd fear because of the rage lurking in his eyes. We've tried to keep these as relationship books—people who get to know each other, have problems and solve them together. Not a heroine who pouts and a hero who's enigmatic."

THE NEW LOOK

Stiff macho men and brooding Heathcliffs have yielded to strong and sexy yet sensitive men—men who aren't afraid to acknowledge their emotions, even show them. The New Hero even weeps on occasion, and no one, least of all the heroine, calls him a sissy. Heroines, meanwhile, have matured from innocent flowers who languish unfulfilled without a man into savvy, accomplished, attractive women who know how to appreciate a good man when they see one. The New Heroine isn't marking time until Mr. Right sets the world on fire; she intends to set it on fire herself. It's so much the nicer, however, when they fall in love and do it together. Below are some characteristics that typify the traditional leading lovers and their newer versions.

HEROES		**HEROINES**	
TRADITIONAL	**NEW**	**TRADITIONAL**	**NEW**
Antagonistic	Appealing	Fragile	Accomplished
Arrogant	Assertive	High-spirited	Assertive
Brutal	Athletic	Idealistic	Attractive
Domineering	Attractive	Inexperienced	Capable
Enigmatic	Aware	Intelligent	Experienced
Masterful	Caring	Likable	Independent
Moody	Dynamic	Passive	Intelligent
Quick-tempered	Masculine	Petite	Mature
Rich	Sensitive	Pretty	Resourceful
Rugged	Sexy	Proud	Sensitive
Tall, dark & handsome	Strong	Self-assured	Successful
Virile	Successful	Virginal	Vivacious
Worldly	Witty	Vulnerable	Witty

THE OLDER WOMAN

Readers may want older and more mature heroines in their romances, but how old is "older"? Is there an age limit beyond which reader interest evaporates? One romantic fiction expert says yes.

"Do women really want to relate to someone their own age, or would they rather fantasize back to what they probably considered their prime years?" asks Vivien Lee Jennings, president of Rainy Day Books in Fairway, Kansas, editor of *Boy Meets Girl* and romance industry consultant.

While romance readers span all ages, most of them are in their mid-thirties or older. "When romance readers read to fantasize, they want to imagine themselves in that prime time of life, twenty-five to thirty, maybe even late thirties," Vivien says. She cites a New York ad agency survey that indicates most middle-aged people think of themselves as being five to fifteen years younger than they really are. Consequently, they think of themselves as being thirty to thirty-five.

Vivien points out that Americans worship youth culture. "People don't like to be reminded of aging. Romances recall a time when all things were possible. Your heroine can't be preoccupied with loose fitting dentures."

Romance heroines have matured from late teens and early twenties to late twenties and early thirties. Even at that age span, all things are still possible.

But are they for a heroine who's forty or more? Some romances feature such older heroines as well as younger ones in their early thirties. The plots are less fantasy and more real life, with heroines facing various life crises: divorce, relocation and "second careers" in midlife; hysterectomies; the desire for a baby but not a husband; the decision to sacrifice marriage for a career and, years later, doubts about whether the decision was right; distintegrating marriages and unfaithful husbands. A new or reborn romance is the main element in the resolution of the problems, but the books are designed to appeal to women who want something *more* than romance.

But Vivien thinks that introducing too many middle-aged heroines will result in the loss of readers. "You can't have too much gray hair, too many wrinkles or bodies too much out of shape."

CHAPTER TWO
Rivals In Love: Sorry, Toots

Business is no longer brisk in contemporary romances for the "other woman" and "other man"—you know, those rivals for the affections of the hero and heroine who conveniently disrupt their relationship. More and more, they're sitting on the shelf instead of making nuisances of themselves. If they're allowed an appearance at all, it's as different characters than the traditional ones we've all come to know and hate.

Other men and other women appear in historical romances as well as contemporaries, but they've made their fame in the latter. In historicals, it's always possible to let war, political intrigue, piracy and travel sustain tension between hero and heroine. But in less adventurous contemporaries, rivals have been a reliable, tension-creating device, especially in traditional plots. The rivals are a persistent lot but never the winners. They're appearing less often because the conflicts that keep the main characters apart are changing, from contrived misunderstandings to problems closer to real life.

In traditional romances, conflict is sustained largely through misunderstanding and lack of communication between hero and heroine. Thus, it's easy for the heroine to assume the hero is as enamored with the other woman as the rival claims he is (haughtily, of course). Conversely, it's easy for the hero to write off the heroine as infatuated with that wimp of a guy, the other man. They never ask each other, they just assume, and then they somehow manage to dispel the misunderstandings at the very end.

The traditional other woman is always older, which means thirtyish, for traditional heroines usually are barely into their twenties. She's ultra-sophisticated and thus fits perfectly into the worldly life style of the hero. She's glamorous, dresses in provocative clothes, polishes her talons to a sheen and is thoroughly mean, nasty and catty: "Keep your hands off Lance," she snarls, "he's mine!" She terrorizes the heroine and delights in embarrassing her, humiliating her or catching her in compromising circumstances. The heroine feels like a meek frump around her—no wonder the hero is mesmerized! The other woman constantly clings to his arm, flicking her eyes possessively over him, and he remains oblivious to her bitchiness. Why he's even mildly interested in such a vile woman is a mystery, especially when he falls for the heroine, a virtuous, truly wonderful thing the complete opposite of her rival.

The other man comes in two main versions. Occasionally he's a villain in disguise, making a false play for the heroine to further his own grasping ends or take revenge on the hero. If he's of this breed, it's preferable for him to redeem himself by nobly dropping his evil ambitions when he sees how right the hero and heroine are for each other.

More often, the other man is just a nice guy who bumbles his way through the plot, often offstage, trying valiantly to impress the heroine but never succeeding. He's younger than the hero and not as sophisticated or successful—and usually not as rich. But he is attractive and often is very ambitious and on his way up in a promising career—the heroine certainly couldn't go wrong by marrying him. The trouble is, he's boring, and his kisses fail to send a fire roaring through her blood.

Sometimes jealousy motivates the nice-guy other man to try to spoil things. He fails and then makes up for his folly, proving that he's really a decent chap after all.

For instance, in *Captive of Desire* (Superromance) by Alexandra Sellers, the jealous other man puts the heroine, a journalist, in jeopardy with both her job and her love affair with the hero, her news source. He makes it appear that she has betrayed the hero's confidences, which naturally causes a considerable rift between the two. Later, smitten by a guilty conscience and the realization that he'll never win the heroine, the other man confesses to the hero.

The other woman and other man used to have their own place in editorial guidelines, but no more; if they're mentioned at all, they're lumped in with "other characters." Increasingly, they're taking a back seat to other kinds of conflicts confronting the leading characters, such as careers, children, life styles or personal philosophies.

The new other man can be as old, successful and sophisticated as the hero; the new other woman can be the same age as or younger than the heroine. They may even have a few good points.

The other woman still has the power to rattle the heroine, however. The sudden appearance of the hero's old flame in *Keys to Daniel's House* (Silhouette Special Edition) by Carole Halston makes the heroine feel inadequate and dowdy compared with the other woman's "exquisite" and perfect dress, makeup and coiffure. The heroine runs off to shampoo her hair, change clothes and put on makeup, only to discover the other woman has gone by the time she returns. She thinks the hero is still in love with his old flame; he realizes this and lets her believe it—but just for a short time.

Rivals now can be more fully developed and presented more sympathet-

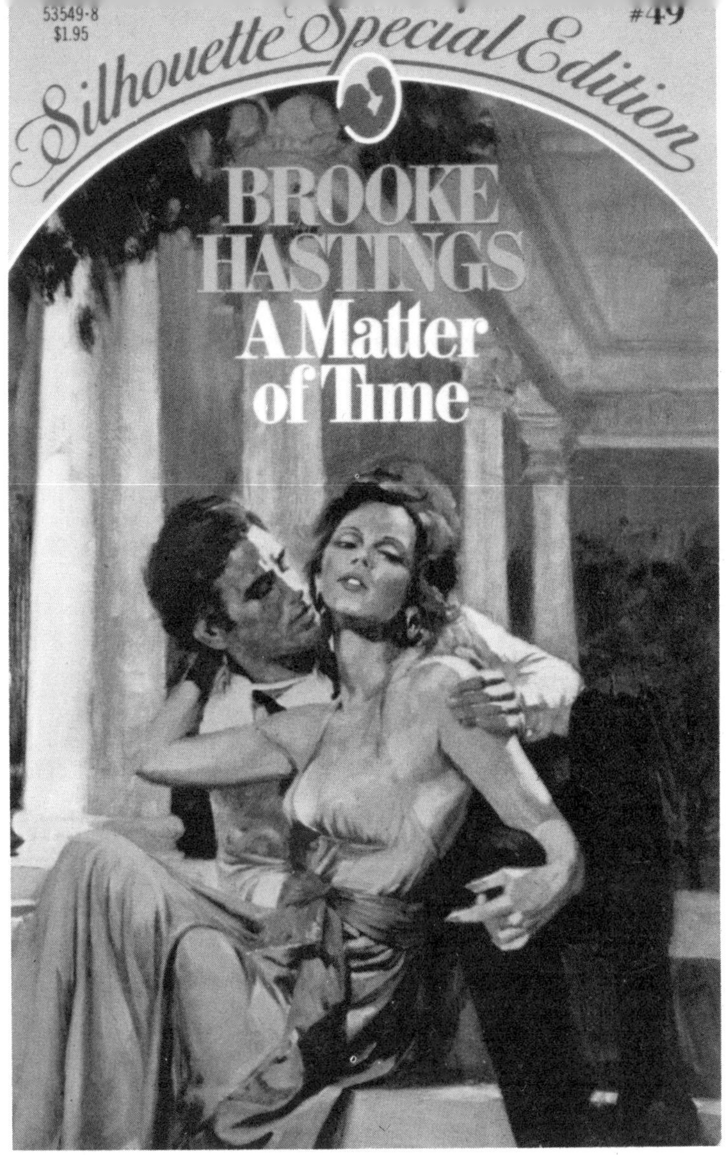

ically, without stealing the show, of course. A rival may be a previous lover whose relationship with the hero or heroine has mellowed to close friendship and mutual respect. She or he can't be all bad, otherwise why did the hero or heroine become involved with that person?

In *A Matter of Time* (Silhouette Special Edition) by Brooke Hastings, the heroine deals with two other women: one who steals her husband at the beginning of the book and one who has been the hero's latest lover. While Sylvie, the heroine, will never be chummy with the husband-stealer (even if she *did* relieve her of a bad marriage), she does raise her opinion of the woman when she discovers some of her good qualities. And she soon discovers that the relationship between the hero and his latest lover has long since cooled to friendship; the other woman, in fact, becomes very supportive of Sylvie.

While that may still be an idealized version of what goes on in real life, it is more believable than the old stereotypes.

The other man and other woman may have fallen a bit out of favor, but they'll never become obsolete. As long as there is love and passion, there will be love triangles, unrequited love and jealous lovers.

V. LEADING LOVERS AND OTHERS

CHAPTER THREE
New Deal
Realism

There's a great deal of talk buzzing around romance circles these days about "realism" in contemporary romances. And there's a great deal of disagreement over what "realism" is.

Is it fewer contrivances, such as the arranged marriage and the overheard conversation? Is it sex before marriage—all the way and without guilt? Is it characters who aren't classically good looking and physically perfect? Is it the writing—more graphically described sexual encounters, fewer fade-outs as the lovers near the bedroom door? Just what *is* realism? And doesn't the intrusion of reality mar the fantasy readers are seeking in the first place?

While "realism" seems to be defined largely according to the subjective, personal preferences of individual writers and editors, nearly everyone agrees that it means fresh plot ideas and more fully developed characters who reflect today's society. "The basic situation must be believable in the contemporary world," says Ellen Edwards, senior editor of Jove's Second Chance At Love. "Once you've established that world in your book, you can get away with a little more, stretch people's credulity a bit."

Whatever else "realism" may be, everyone seems to want it and be looking for it.

Ballantine's Love & Life romances, for example, seek to appeal to the "realistic contemporary woman" of the 1980s, whose primary concerns are work, love and family. Jove's To Have And To Hold line (to be introduced in the fall of 1983) will offer romance in marriage, a realistic, if not sobering, setting.

By all accounts, the lady who deserves the credit for putting more realism into the sweet, traditional romances is Vivian Stephens, now senior editor of Harlequin American Romances. Vivian, who wanted romances to describe what happened *after* the heroine and hero headed for the bedroom instead of fading out just as they got there, introduced the Dell Candlelight Ecstasy Romances in 1980. Ecstasies offered a dash more realism and a lot more sensuality than any other contemporary-brand romance on the market, and their phenomenal success started a whole new trend.

Vivian's slogan for the Ecstasies was "romance within the realm of possibility." Now, at Harlequin, her slogan is "romance within the realm of reality," and she intends to take Harlequin American Romances even closer to real life. According to Vivian, they glorify the average middle-class American man and woman. "Why not?" she says of her ground-breaking line. "If you're going to fantasize, it might as well be about

Pamela Strickland

something that's within reach. I want the woman reading the book to be reassured she made the right choice if she's married or involved with someone. After all, there's only one Tom Selleck and one Prince Charles."

It's okay, Vivian tells her writers, to give your hero a slight paunch or a receding hairline; an attractive man doesn't have to be a glamorous one. There are no rules for her line, she insists. "Rules have been relaxed in real life, so I see no reason why they can't be relaxed in fiction," Vivian says.

Of Love & Life, which Ballantine introduced in 1982, senior editor Pamela Strickland describes the books as closer to high-quality magazine women's fiction than the romance genre but says they still retain a fantasy element. "A terrific hero who is human and could be real is a lot sexier than the cardboard tall-dark-and-handsome guys," she points out.

To Have And To Hold also promises to be closer to midlist women's fiction. The hero and heroine begin the plot married to each other and then face and resolve a conflict, which may involve separation or even divorce, and reconciliation. "It is more realistic," says Ellen Edwards. "When you're dealing with a marriage, you have to be more realistic, although our aim will be to idealize marriage to a large extent. Part of the appeal of these books will be that they'll show that love and romance, and fun and excitement, all can exist within a marriage."

Another new line offering more realistic romances is Avon's Finding Mr. Right, introduced in early 1983. The concept of the line is that no one person is the perfect choice. The heroine must make a believable and sympathetic choice between two heroes who are both attractive yet have shortcomings and flaws. She may make love with both of them, she may not. The introductory title, *Paper Tiger,* by Elizabeth Neff Walker, concerns a heroine who is a woman's rights activist, and much of the plot and dialogue has to do with women's rights and choices. That kind of realism appeals to some romance readers but not to others.

"Believable" is a term often interchanged with "realistic" in romance realism discussions, but for senior editor Carolyn Nichols, who has resurrected Bantam Books' short-lived Circle Of Love line as the more sensual Loveswept line, there's a vast difference between the two words. "I've been horrified to hear the word 'realistic' applied to any of these books," Carolyn says. "Realism is a killer. These books don't have anything to do with the hard facts of real problems that are insoluble—they have nothing to do with realism." It's the job of the writer, Carolyn says, to make an idealized romance *believable.*

"Who knows what 'realism' really means?" says literary agent Denise Marcil, who packages Finding Mr. Right for Avon Books. "I think it means more creativity, something fresh—getting away from tired, overused plot devices and characters. But romances aren't reality. Reality is, it's hard to find a man, and these ladies don't have any problem finding a man. On page one, there he is."

Does realism ruin the fantasy? It can. Readers seem to want more "realistic" and "believable" romances, but at the same time they still want to identify with heroines who are swept off their feet by idealized men. That's what fantasy is all about—becoming, for a while, someone else, and believing that something wild and wonderful is possible. Fantasy takes us away from the real world—realism brings us back. A murky gray area lies in between.

Will realism sell in the romance market? Says one editor, "We'll find out."

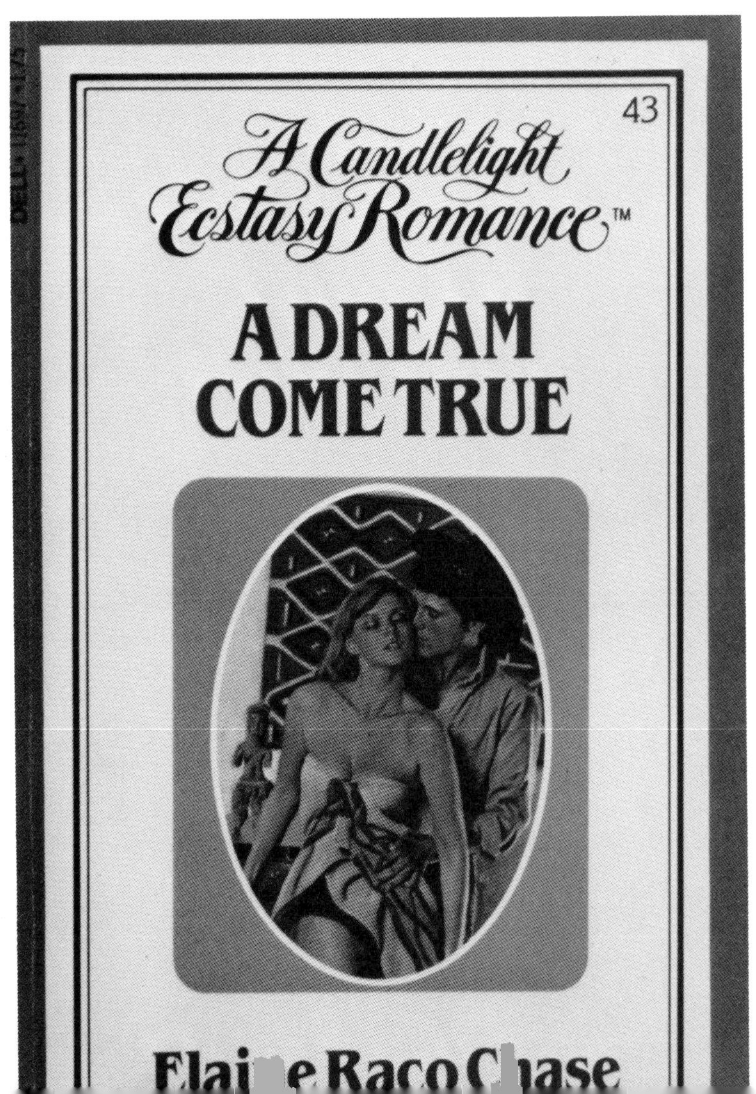

•V. LEADING LOVERS AND OTHERS•

You're at a party, and a dazzlingly handsome, well-built man catches your eye and strikes up a conversation. He appears dominant, masterful, supremely confident, yet sensitive and tender—in short, *the* Mr. Right. Your mind cooks up instant fantasies of crushing embraces, bruising kisses, moonlit nights.... You ask his name. And in his resonant, commanding baritone he replies, "Elmer Milksop." Your fantasies fizzle like air rushing from a balloon, and you stammer an excuse for making a speedy escape.

Would your reaction be different if the fellow had had a different name, perhaps one that better fit his appearance and demeanor? It's unlikely that love and power rise and fall on the sheer strength of a name, but admit it—names *do* influence our impressions of and reactions to others. Which is precisely why Marion Morrison changed his name to John Wayne.

Marshall McLuhan once said that a man's name "is a numbing blow from which he never recovers," and scores of books and articles have been written about the make-you-or-break-you power of a name. It's nothing new. For thousands of years, people have attached great significance to names, and fortunetellers have used them to predict the future. Ancient Egyptians believed names literally had a life of their own, separate from the human entity. Ancient Greeks sometimes judged others according to the odd or even number of vowels in their names; Romans gave infants descriptive names and believed they would live up (or down) to them. Augustus, for example, means "exalted," while Claudius means "lame" and Cassius "vain." Puritans preferred virtuous but awkward names, such as Patience and Chastity, in the belief that they would fortify religious values. Today, it's not uncommon for celebrities and business moguls—or anyone—to discard bland or awkward names for memorable, impressive ones that roll nicely off the tongue.

It's therefore not surprising that names are given a

THE NAME GAME

Here's a little exercise for all of you well-read romance fans. Match the names of the lovers on the left with the books they belong to on the right. Answers below—don't peek!

1. Nicole Ashford
   Captain Saber
2. Erienne Fleming
   Lord Saxton
3. Kalinda Brady
   Rand Alastair
4. Lanna Marshall
   Jim Blue Hawk
5. Bronwyn MacCarran
   Stephen Montgomery
6. Ruth Jason
   Dominic Howard
7. Alys of Marlowe
   Sir Raymond d'Aix
8. Felicite Lafargue
   Morgan McCormack
9. Casey Reynolds
   Travis Craig
10. Annmarie Duvall
    Sloan MacAllister

great deal of attention in romantic fiction. No Elmer Milksops sweeping ladies off their feet in this genre. Appealing lovers must have appealing names. "Naming your characters deserves the same attention as naming your own baby," says author Jayne Castle, who always tests out the "sound" of a name. "Names carry a lot of power and meaning."

Common names, no matter how appealing, don't quite fit the bill, however, Romance writers usually strive for unusual as well as pleasant sounding names; one of the most heavily thumbed books on their shelves is a dictionary of names and their etymological, or linguistic, origins. Unusual names, especially for the heroine, help make a novel more memorable. "A reader may have a common name and wish she'd been named something else," surmises author Diana Haviland. "Something else" could be Tanis, Lissa, Kalinda, Chelsie, Leoni or Brandy, all of which have appeared in romance novels.

Interestingly, "other women" tend to have "M" names, such as Monica, Mona, Marsha, Margot, Martina, Marina, Marla and Melissa. Perhaps "M" names connote an aggressiveness more appropriate to the rival female than the heroine.

Names may be chosen strictly for their etymological meaning, which may be important to the story. Perhaps a heroine named Clarissa, which means destined for fame, is on the rise in her career, and fame becomes the obstacle between her and the hero. Or a name may enhance a character's personality. You'd expect a Rebecca ("ensnarer") to act and dress differently than a Vanessa ("butterfly"). "The name must fit the character," says author Linda Wisdom. "You wouldn't use the same kind of name for the other man or other woman as you would for the hero or heroine." William Shakespeare knew that as well. Would *Tybalt and Juliet* have been as memorable as *Romeo and Juliet?*

While a hero's name invariably suggests masculinity and strength, a heroine's name can suggest anything

A. **Night Way** (Pocket Books) by Janet Dailey

B. **Embrace and Conquer** (Fawcett/Columbine) by Jennifer Blake

C. **Stormspell** (Worldwide Library) by Anne Mather

D. **A Rose in Winter** (Avon Books) by Kathleen E. Woodiwiss

E. **Lady Vixen** (Avon Books) by Shirlee Busbee

F. **Corporate Affair** (Silhouette Desire) by Stephanie James

G. **Highland Velvet** (Pocket Books) by Jude Deveraux

H. **Wild Honey** (Pocket Books) by Fern Michaels

I. **Double Occupancy** (Dell Candlelight Ecstasy) by Elaine Raco Chase

J. **Winter Song** by Roberta Gellis

Answers: 1-E; 2-D; 3-F; 4-A; 5-G; 6-C; 7-J; 8-B; 9-I; 10-H

from a dainty flower to an assertive businesswoman. However, says Jayne Castle, "women should not have unisex names, because their sexuality comes through in their names. They shouldn't be so soft that they sound girlish."

Girlish names appear more often in historicals, in which names must fit the times and locales. Throughout history, names have fallen in and out of popularity; medieval characters, for example, should have medieval names. Still, authors try to choose names that sound right to modern-day ears. Thus, a thirteenth-century Norman hero is better off with Gerard than Bevis or Ivo. Lush, exotic names, especially those ending in "a," such as Selena or Alexandra, are preferable for heroines, notes Diana Haviland, while heroes tend to get sturdy names, such as Brandon, Adam or Stephen.

In American contemporary romances, names are overwhelmingly Waspish; Harlequins have more foreign heroes, whose names reflect their heritage. Since American publishers of contemporary romance lines are beginning to experiment more with ethnic romances, ethnic names may be seen more often.

While some names seem more appropriate for fictional lovers than others, the final appeal of a name is a personal, subjective matter. Most of us go through life wishing we were named something else; a few of us are motivated to change our names. In a romance novel we can, for a while, become someone else—with a different name, a different life and a different fate.

Heroines of contemporary romances once worked only as nurses, secretaries, teachers and governesses, and they met the man of their dreams at a new job, a vacation abroad or at an elegant soiree. Maybe they didn't work at all—they were just some couple's young daughter, still at home with their family. Regardless of the heroine's station in life, the hero was always above it, wealthier, more famous, an aristocrat or a leader in his profession. Latching onto him meant a better life for the heroine, and not just in love.

When Mr. Wonderful proposed, the heroine's job, if there was one, went out the window in favor of setting up a homey little nest. "No wife of mine is going to work!" growled many a traditional hero.

Now the heroines are growling back. More and more, they're on an equal footing with the heroes, not only in age, sophistication and experience but in the work arena as well. They're holding more unusual jobs and are more dedicated to careers and professions—and they're very unwilling to toss it all aside for a man. Sometimes it's the hero who makes the professional sacrifice, such as Drew Bradford does in *Of Passion Born* (Silhouette Desire) by Suzanne Simms. Drew moves part of his electronics company to a college town so that he can be with Dr. Chelsie McBride, an English literature professor. A few years ago that would have been unthinkable.

The emphasis on occupations, especially for the heroine, is confined to contemporary romances. In history, it's a simpler matter—women didn't work unless they had to. Historical romance heroines may be temporarily reduced to servitude or slavery through cruel twists of fate or vicious relatives, but they are rescued by the heroes, who are aristocrats, royalty, sea captains, military officers, plantation owners or wealthy businessmen. Occasionally a hero may be rogue, such as a pirate or a highwayman, but he's usually a blue blood and invariably reverts to type by the end of the novel. He patches things up with his estranged wealthy father, reclaims his wrongfully seized riches/land/title or comes into a new fortune, and he and his lady are set up for a life of splendor.

In contemporary romances, it's another matter. When it comes to breadwinning, almost anything goes—provided it's legal and moral, that is. Things haven't changed much for the heroes, who have always been able to be and do anything, as long as they are extremely successful, but things have changed for the heroines. There are two major reasons why.

One is simply variety. "It's a way to add a fresh element," says Ellen

Edwards, senior editor of Jove's Second Chance At Love. Dozens of contemporary romances are published each month, and readers would find it quite tiresome to see heroines stuck in a few occupational ruts. Competition among publishers is fierce, and a heroine with a novel job just may hook an undecided book buyer. Hence, occupations are often plugged on the back-cover copy: "Beautiful, tempestuous and newly-divorced, Storm Reynolds is determined to succeed as a bush pilot in Alaska," reads the copy for *Untamed Desire* (Second Chance At Love) by Beth Brookes.

The second, and more important, reason for this trend is that work-oriented heroines are symbolic of the Equal Woman, someone who can make it on her own, and romance readers have made it clear they want to see more of that in their books. They write letters, make phone calls, answer surveys, fill out questionnaires in the backs of books. What they like is women who are more independent, says Alicia M. Condon, senior editor of Silhouette Books.

Decisions involving whether or not to have children and how to juggle career and family concern American women daily, says Karen Solem, vice president and editor in chief of Silhouette Books. "More than 50 percent of the women in this country work," Karen points out. "It's unrealistic to present a character who's going to meet a man, get married, and then live happily ever after and never have to work a day in her life. The reality is that she has to work to help maintain a family—and she *wants* to work."

The push into new career territories has come in stages. The first departures from traditional occupations fell into several main areas: the arts, fashion, travel and real estate. Different but "acceptable" roles for women, they included models, writers, reporters, actresses, singers, photographers, real estate agents, travel agents, resort owners. However, cautioned one set of now-defunct editorial guidelines, if a heroine had one of these "glamorous" occupations, she had to be a beginner—*not* a top executive, ace reporter or owner of a stable of racing horses. She had to be a *struggling* artist, a *minor* actress, a *junior assistant* resort hotel manager. The main exception to not being the boss was if Daddy bequeathed her the company, but even then, she struggled against formidable odds just to stay afloat. Along came the hero to restore stability and order.

When these types of careers reached the saturation point, vitually anything became acceptable. The sky was, and is, the limit, literally. "We were the first to put a heroine into outer space, and not only in bed," says

Ann Gisonny, senior editor of Dell Candlelight Ecstasy Romances, referring to a female astronaut in *Dance the Skies* by Jo Calloway. Today's heroine can still be a real estate agent or an actress, but she may also be a policewoman, lawyer, Pulitzer Prize-winning reporter, architect, corporate president (a competent one, that is), jet fighter designer, engineer, tennis pro or ad executive. "It's nice if she's a ground breaker and her job is not so much glamorous as interesting," says Robin Grunder, editor of New American Library's Rapture Romances. Rapture's introductory title, *Love So Fearful* by Nina Coombs, features a veterinarian heroine who is hired and then wooed by a Montana rancher and champion rodeo cowboy.

Even a few novel occupations have cropped up for heroes. Author Jayne Castle, for instance, has created men who are bodyguards, magicians and corporate raiders. The corporate world, says Jayne, is a largely unmined source of jobs and plots. For ideas, she reads the *Wall Street Journal.*

For Harlequin American Romances, senior editor Vivian Stephens prefers heroes who "typify the average American male," and the average man is *not* president of the company. He is ambitious and successful, the kind of man the average American woman—and reader—is likely to meet.

While the emphasis on careers gives heroines a more realistic and better balanced life, it does not detract from—or supersede—the romance. "The heroine is not looking for marriage to be her career," says Vivian, "but regardless of how successful she is in her $100,000-a-year job, she still wants a husband—just as the man who makes $100,000 a year still wants a wife."

VI. PASSION PLAYS

From meetings to marriage and what takes place in between—read all about it in the following section. Find out how and where heroes and heroines meet; how they love; the rise of "sensuality" and the debate over how much sex readers really want in a romance; and finally, the happy ending that awaits all lovers.

CHAPTER ONE

Some Enchanted Meeting

In just about any romance, hero and heroine meet in Chapter One, as close to Page One as possible if the book is short. Their encounter sets the bells ringing—alarm bells, that is. They are, of course, instantly and strongly attracted to each other, but there's also some obstacle standing between them. After all, there wouldn't be much of a romance if a conflict didn't sustain sexual tension for a few hundred pages. Even though the reader knows the hero and heroine will get together in the end, the fun is in seeing how they do it.

In contemporary romances, the means of meetings have undergone many changes as these books have matured. At one time the initial encounter always set an antagonistic tone between the hero and heroine, and the antagonism and misunderstandings that resulted from it kept them apart. The heroine was usually at a disadvantage and flustered her way through the encounter; the hero mocked or scorned her, often in a sexually threatening way. Now first meetings can be sensual and even humorous as well.

In the traditional romance, which once dominated the contemporary field, the Collision is a favorite type of first encounter. The heroine, distracted or in a hurry, plows headlong into a massive chest. She can't miss noticing how ultramasculine the man is. He laughs or snarls at her, and she spits a caustic remark back and flounces off. She doesn't realize that fate will throw them together again—only then she will be at his mercy. She vows to hate him forever, even if he *is* irresistibly tall, dark and handsome. Collisions still show up in more modern, sensual romances, though they may be handled differently—the characters may not automatically growl at each other, for example.

The Rescue is another old standby. The heroine, once again distracted or in a hurry, steps in front of a speeding car and.... When she recovers consciousness, she finds the driver somehow managed to stop in time, leaped from his car and carried her to safety. The trouble is, he turns out to be Victor Vile, the last man on earth she wants to be beholden to.

Then there's the Inheritance Dispute. The heroine, learning she has been bequeathed a Scottish manor, Caribbean resort or giant conglomerate, travels to an exotic foreign place to claim her inheritance only to find that the hero is staking a counterclaim. She may even have to marry him to get her inheritance or protect the family name.

The Overheard Conversation also brings characters together while keeping them at bay. The heroine discovers, to her horror, that the hero is conspiring to take over or ruin her father's business—or at least that's what she *thinks.*

The Arranged Marriage is guaranteed to cause fireworks—nasty at first because the bride is unwilling and resentful, then passionate as the characters fall in love. Sometimes the bride may not even see her betrothed before the wedding ceremony. Arranged marriages are seldom used in contemporary romances anymore, but they're justifiably common in historicals, for nearly all marriages were arranged in centuries past.

Finally, there's the Assignment On Location meeting. The heroine, a journalist, photographer or scientist, meets the hero because of a professional assignment. Perhaps she's supposed to do an expose on him, or they're stuck together for a two-week expedition through Amazon jungles, and he doesn't like the idea of looking out for a woman.

While these are some of the older, tried-and-true devices for meetings, heroes and heroines don't have to get acquainted in such ways anymore. They don't have to suffer hostile encounters, although the meeting does have to generate conflict and tension as well as attraction and guarantee that the two will be forced together throughout the book. In *Love with a Perfect Stranger* (Silhouette Special Edition) by Pamela Wallace, the hero and heroine meet and indulge in a capricious affair, then try to develop a relationship that keeps threatening to end before it really begins.

In *Heaven's Price* (Loveswept) by Sandra Brown, the first meeting compromises the heroine in a comical way. A dancer, she calls a local "Y" for a masseur, and when a handsome man shows up, she undresses and he obligingly gives her a sensual, if not satisfactory, massage. Then the real masseur shows up. Oops.

The heroine in *No Easy Way Out* (Dell Candlelight Ecstasy) by Elaine Raco Chase is a stuffy doctor of physics and mechanical design engineer who transforms herself into a sexy bunny for a Halloween costume party. She meets an attractive "bandit" and, under a gorgeous and romantic harvest moon, the two get quite carried away. The bandit, however, turns out to be her new colleague at work. And now that he's enjoyed some intimacy with her—well, how embarrassing.

Modern heroes and heroines meet in bars, as in *Masquerade of Love* (Dell Candlelight Ecstasy) by Alice Morgan. In that book the attraction is instant and unfettered by any immediate conflict, and the characters hit the sheets within the first few pages. The seduction, however, is part of a secret plan—the heroine has chosen the hero to father a child she desperately wants. She tries to disappear with her secret safe, but he tracks her down.

Hero and heroine still meet as a result of relocations, new jobs and new job assignments. The journalist heroine in *Floodtide* (Harlequin Presents) by Kay Thorpe sets out to interview a famous but moody sculptor. A flood traps them together in a house, long enough for passion to explode between them.

Leading lovers also meet on retreat or vacation. Determined to test her own inner strength on the raging white-water rapids of the Rogue River in Oregon, the city-girl heroine in *River of Love* (Rapture Romance) by Lisa McConnell is swept away by the hero, a handsome, arrogant river guide.

More often than hostile misunderstandings, first encounters involve conflicts of interest. Immediately, hero and heroine are on opposite sides of the fence on an important issue, and intend to stay that way. The lawyer heroine in *Matching Wits* (Loveswept) by Carla Neggers puts her job in jeopardy when she opposes a developer who intends to tear down a historic hotel in Boston. Other conflicts can be life style oriented: career versus family; desire or lack of desire to have children; city versus country living.

Whatever the conflict, whatever the meeting that brings the hero and heroine together, we know from the instant they see each other that a wonderful romance is inevitable.

Formerly, romances always had to be set in some exotic, lush locale. In historicals, that was no problem, because virtually anything set in the past takes on an exotic air, no matter where. Not so in contemporaries—it was verboten to set a romance in Gary, Indiana. Instead, the setting had to provide an imaginary vacation of sorts for the reader—a Swiss chalet, tropical isle, African jungle, Middle Eastern casbah, French winery, Greek isle, Australian sheep station. The novels were packed with facts and trivia about the locale and some of its history, which enriched a reader's knowledge—sort of a painless geography and social studies lesson tucked in with the romance. Whenever the tension between the hero and heroine began to sag, the heroine took a little side trip and learned fascinating facts about her surroundings. The setting was almost as important as the story itself.

Since 1980, two significant changes have occurred in the role of the setting in romances. First, settings more often complement the story rather than intrude on it. Certainly the setting must be described in enough detail to become vivid and real to the reader, but there are fewer timeouts for history lessons and tourist trips. Readers, impatient when the conflict between the hero and heroine is not on center stage, tend now to skip over such sections. "The setting is becoming less important than the story," says Ellen Edwards, senior editor of Jove's Second Chance At Love. "A travelogue is not the way to use a setting."

The second change is the acceptance of American settings, thanks to American romance publishers and the burgeoning ranks of American romance writers. Before 1976, a contemporary romance rarely, if ever, had an American setting. Harlequin claimed nearly the entire romance market, and it generally refused American writers until 1976, when it published Janet Dailey's first novel, *No Quarter Asked*, set in Texas. When American publishers began competing with Harlequin, American settings became common.

The obvious glamour settings were the first to be used frequently, some to excess, such as New York City, San Francisco and Hollywood. Other popular settings include New Orleans for its Old World flavor; the Southwest, especially Texas, for its frontier ruggedness; Alaska for its primitiveness; and Hawaii for its tropical beauty.

Now any place in the nation, or in the world, is acceptable as long as it adds to the romantic tone of a story. "It all depends on how it's handled," says Ellen. "Small towns and out-of-the-way places may not have glitter

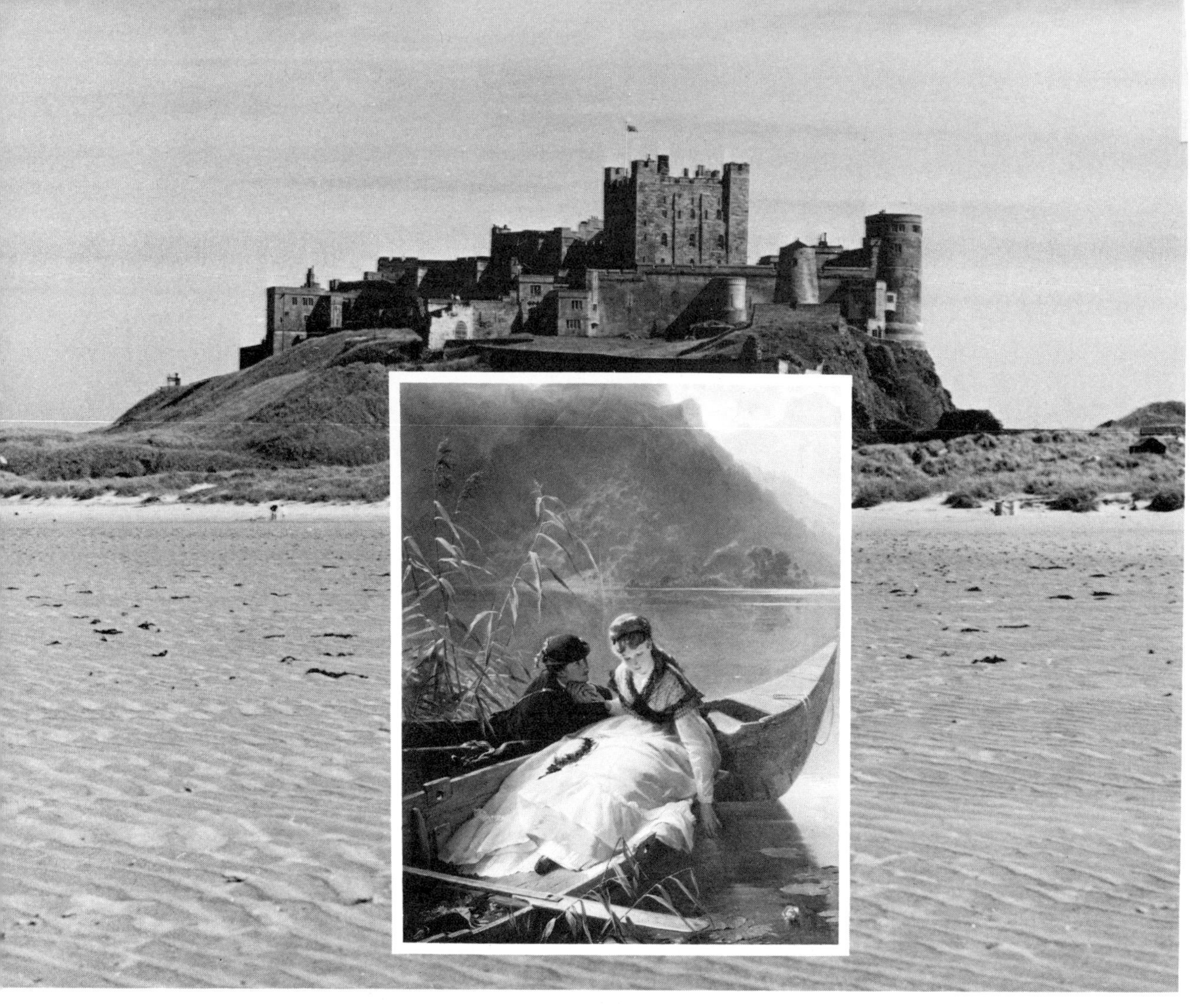

and glamour, but they have a certain exoticism all their own—and the customers seem to enjoy reading about them just as much as they do about Paris in the springtime." One of Ellen's titles, *The Golden Touch* by Robin James, proves her point. Set in Apple Grove, Wisconsin, it concerns a small-town woman living a comfortable, predictable small-town life until she meets a famous rock idol. Most of the action takes place either in Apple Grove or the backwoods of Tennessee.

For oft-used locales, a new twist makes all the difference between a stale setting and an intriguing one. In Pamela Wallace's *Love with a Perfect Stranger* (Silhouette Special Edition), the heroine, who owns a gift shop in San Francisco, goes on a buying trip to Europe. A last-minute whim leads her to travel on the Orient Express on her way from Italy to London. It is on this famous train, so rich in history, mystery and romance, that she meets the hero, an art buyer for a museum in Los Angeles. The train is an irresistible setting for romance. Plus, the brevity of the trip—they have only one night together before the hero disembarks in Paris—heightens the sexual tension. The Orient Express establishes a romantic aura that carries over to the action that takes place in the commonly used settings of Paris and London.

Whatever the settings, vivid descriptions of them are important in romances, not only to help bring the story alive but also because romance readers like details. They like to know exactly what the heroine is wearing, what she orders for dinner, the fact that the tables have pink linen cloths, not white. They like to know the specifics about furnishings in a room, the color and texture of cloth. They want descriptions of smells—the hero's musky aftershave, for example.

Sensory descriptions "are very important to a woman's enjoyment of these books—they experience the sensual enjoyment of things vicariously," according to Ellen. "It helps create the atmosphere of romance."

Many people unfamiliar with romances think the use of detailed descriptions is part of a formula. However, Vivian Stephens, senior editor of Harlequin American Romances, says, "It's not so much a formula as a style that's developed according to what women respond to. Women respond to descriptions, such as how he looked and what he wore. The books really glorify the five senses, and I think that's something everybody likes. You can't really get the five senses from watching television or movies. But when you read, you can conjure up in your mind exactly what his hair felt like, or the smell of the veal piccata. That's a bonus. That's a celebration."

THE WORLD'S MOST ROMANTIC CITIES

There are some cities in the world whose very names mean romance. Just thinking about San Francisco, Paris or Venice brings to mind moonlit water, long candlelit dinners or gondola rides for two. And just reading about the balmy evenings on the beach at Rio de Janeiro can make you feel as if you're there, even if you're thousands of miles away. Although any place can be romantic if you're with the right person, here are eleven of the most romantic cities in the world, in no particular order. The list was originally meant to contain ten, but an extra one was included for those romantics who think ten just isn't enough.

1. **PARIS.** Parisians have always felt that romance is their specialty—remember Leslie Caron, in the movie *Gigi*, singing that Parisians live for love? Fabulous art and architecture abound: there are rococo cherubs smiling down from ornate palaces and Notre Dame, where Victor Hugo's Hunchback supposedly died for love—what a beautiful city for love to blossom in. Atop the Eiffel Tower, you can look out over the entire city, from the cafes on the Left Bank of the River Seine to the wide boulevard of the Champs d'Elysee. Even French cuisine is romantic, shared in an intimate restaurant with a fine bottle of French wine or champagne.

2. **VENICE.** Venice has always been a place for romance. Britons and Russians flock to its sunny plazas to escape the chill of northern winters and to glide peacefully in gondolas along one of the city's famous canals, serenaded by Italian musicians and accompanied by discreet gondola oarsmen. The pace of living is slow in this Mediterranean environment—people take time to meet each other, to sit

for hours in a cafe and have a glass of wine or a cup of espresso. And who knows? The person sitting next to you may be a descendant of a Venetian count!

3. **ROME.** This warm Italian city draws on its immense role in history for its atmosphere of romance and power. The ruins of the Coliseum bring to mind festivals of the Roman Empire era, while the palaces and piazzas of the medieval period call up images of knights and their ladies, velvets and furs and lavish banquets. Romans claim that one who tosses a coin into the Fountain of Trevi is granted a wish; perhaps all wishes for romance are granted in Rome.

4. **NEW YORK.** The most populous city in the United States is also the most exciting. Walking in New York's bustling neighborhoods is like touring the world on a zigzag route: you can go from China to Italy to the Middle East to India to old Dutch New Amsterdam in a matter of blocks. The lights of Broadway beckon to the "I-know-I-could-be-a-star-if-I-could-just-get-the-chance" in everyone. And what could be more romantic than a carriage ride at dawn through Central Park, followed by a champagne breakfast at the Waldorf-Astoria?

5. **LONDON.** London, on the banks of the River Thames, is steeped in swashbuckling romantic history. Windsor Castle, built in the Middle Ages, has housed a succession of monarchs who helped build England's vast empire and made its navy the greatest in the world. Landmarks abound—Westminster Abbey, Buckingham Palace, the Tower of London, Big Ben, Parliament—and medieval pageantry and pomp and circumstance live on.

6. **BANGKOK.** There's something inherently romantic about the Far East. Perhaps it's because of the silken robes, the enigmatic smiles or the musky fragrances. Or perhaps it is because Westerners have always known so little about this exotic area and so mysterious a culture. Bangkok was once called the Venice of the East because of its many canals, which have since been filled to form boulevards. As the capital city of Thailand (formerly Siam), Bangkok brings to mind Buddhist temples, beautiful silks and jade and the lovely face and graceful arms of the dancing Siva, deity of destruction and reproduction.

7. **SAN FRANCISCO.** The City by the Bay has been sung about, painted and photographed from every angle to show how enchanting it is and how much it means to the people who've left their hearts there. The Golden Gate Bridge is breathtaking, whether shrouded in fog or illumined by a full moon over the water. One of the city's most romantic attractions, the cable cars, are temporarily out of service for repairs. But residents and visitors alike believe the cars are a nostalgic link to the past, and they'll soon be back.

8. **RIO DE JANEIRO.** Brazilians share the Latin love for music, fun and romance. The people of Rio, or *cariocas,* would rather lie on the beach all day and party all night than do anything else. Rio is a sexy city, full of bronze women in tiny string bikinis and suntanned men. The city's most striking geographical feature, Sugarloaf Mountain, guards the entrance to a beautiful harbor, a city that never sleeps.

9. **VIENNA.** In nineteenth century Europe, Vienna was the center of education, medicine and high society. It was the home of Sigmund Freud, Johann Strauss and others who've left their mark on the world. In its golden era, there were many elegant balls, where dashing Austrian soldiers and their ladies, princes and princesses and dukes and duchesses waltzed 'til dawn. Like the Italians, the Viennese take time every day to enjoy each other's company and watch the world go by while savoring a cup of strong coffee and a sweet, rich pastry.

10. **MONTE CARLO.** Monte Carlo is the capital and only city of Monaco, a tiny principality on the French Riviera. The countryside is ruggedly beautiful, with twisting roads and breathtaking views.

The city is dedicated to the good life, with first-class hotels and casinos that attract European, Arab and American jet-setters alike. But most of all, Monte Carlo is a romantic place because of her late Serene Highness Princess Grace.

11. LISBON. Lisbon was once the "end of the world" for Europeans; it was the last major city on the continent. There is a sad sweetness there today. The Portuguese dream about the wealth and fame that was theirs in the sixteenth century, and they experience a *saudade,* or melancholy memory, of lost loves, romantic voyages to the Far East and past greatnesses. Strains of fado music fill the air from the old Arab quarter, the Alfama, as you walk to the harbor past the Castle of St. George, which dates from the fifth century. Watching the lights twinkling over the River Tejo, you can almost see a ship laden with gold and spices returning from Africa and points beyond.

STATES OF THE UNION

Since American settings have become popular in romances, one author, superstar Janet Dailey, has set a novel in every state in the nation, earning her a place in the *Guinness Book of World Records.* What's even more amazing about this record is the fact that Janet just started writing romances in 1975. Not only has she turned out a book for each of the fifty states, she's written more than twenty-five other romances, for a total of over seventy-five books; she has 90 million copies in print in seventeen languages. Most of Janet's books have been published by Harlequin, which she left in 1979 to write for Simon & Schuster's Silhouette and Pocket Books divisions.

Janet has been able to write authoritatively and accurately about her settings because she actually lived in every state while researching her novels. She and her husband, Bill, traveled around the country in a trailer, parking in communities where they could do research at local libraries and museums and talk to residents. For her Calder saga (Pocket Books), which includes *This Calder Sky, This Calder Range, Stands a Calder Man* and *Calder Born, Calder Bred,* Janet and Bill spent a month in Montana familiarizing themselves with the people and landscape.

Bill did much of the legwork while Janet wrote in the trailer. Details of local places and color, history and folklore have been scrupulously accurate.

Traveling around the nation has had another benefit for Janet, America's most popular romance writer. It has enabled her to be visible and stay in touch with her audience—and that's partly what success is all about.

Here are all of Janet Dailey's books, as of 1983; her publishers; the dates of publication; and, where available, the states in which the stories take place.

POCKET BOOKS

Touch the Wind, May 1979, Mexico
The Rogue, February 1980, Nevada
Ride the Thunder, July 1980, Idaho
Night Way, January 1981, Arizona
This Calder Sky, August 1981, Montana
This Calder Range, April 1982, Texas/Montana
Stands a Calder Man, January 1983, Montana
Calder Born, Calder Bred, not scheduled, Montana

SILHOUETTE ROMANCES

The Hostage Bride, May 1981, Missouri
The Lancaster Men, October 1981, North Carolina
For the Love of God, December 1981, Arkansas
Wildcatter's Woman, May 1982, Louisiana
The Second Time, September 1982, Florida
Mistletoe and Holly, December 1982, Vermont
Separate Cabins, March 1983, Mexican Riviera
Western Man, June 1983, Colorado

SILHOUETTE SPECIAL EDITIONS

Terms of Surrender, February 1982, Texas
Foxfire Light, July 1982, Missouri
The Best Way to Lose, not scheduled, Mississippi
Leftover Love, not scheduled, Nebraska

HARLEQUIN PRESENTS

No Quarter Asked, January 1976, Texas
Boss Man From Ogallala, March 1976, Nebraska
Savage Land, May 1976, Texas
Fire and Ice, July 1976, California
Land of Enchantment, August 1976, New Mexico
The Homeplace, October 1976, Iowa
After the Storm, December 1976, Colorado
Dangerous Masquerade, January 1977, Alabama
Night of the Cotillion, March 1977, Georgia
Valley of the Vapors, March 1977, Arkansas
Fiesta San Antonio, June 1977, Texas
Show Me, August 1977, Missouri
Bluegrass King, September 1977, Kentucky
A Lyon's Share, October 1977, Illinois
The Widow and the Wastral, November 1977, Ohio
The Ivory Cane, January 1978, California
The Indy Man, February 1978, Indiana
Darling Jenny, March 1978, Wyoming
Reilly's Woman, April 1978, Nevada
To Tell The Truth, May 1978, Oregon
Sonora Sundown, June 1978, Arizona
Big Sky Country, July 1978, Montana
Something Extra, August 1978, Louisiana
Master Fiddler, September 1978, Arizona
Beware of the Stranger, October 1978, New York
Giant of Mesabi, November 1978, Minnesota
The Matchmakers, December 1978, Delaware
For Bitter or Worse, January 1979, Texas
Green Mountain Man, February 1979, Vermont
Six White Horses, March 1979, Oklahoma
Summer Mahogany, April 1979, Maine
The Bride of the Delta Queen, May 1979, Mississippi River
Tidewater Lover, June 1979, Virginia
Strange Bedfellow, July 1979, Rhode Island
Low Country Liar, August 1979, South Carolina
Sweet Promise, September 1979, Texas
For Mike's Sake, October 1979, Washington
Sentimental Journey, November 1979, Tennessee
Land Called Deseret, December 1979, Utah
Kona Winds, January 1980, Hawaii
That Boston Man, February 1980, Massachusetts
The Thawing of Mara, February 1980, Pennsylvania
Bed of Grass, March 1980, Maryland
The Mating Season, May 1980, Kansas
Lord of the High Lonesome, June 1980, North Dakota
Southern Nights, July 1980, Florida
Enemy in Camp, August 1980, Michigan
Difficult Decision, October 1980, Connecticut
Heart of Stone, November 1980, New Hampshire
One of the Boys, December 1980, New Jersey
Wild and Wonderful, March 1981, West Virginia
A Tradition of Pride, April 1981, Mississippi
The Traveling Kind, May 1981, Idaho
Dakota Dreamin', August 1981, South Dakota
Northern Magic, January 1982, Alaska
With a Little Luck, February 1982, Wisconsin
That Carolina Summer, March 1982, North Carolina

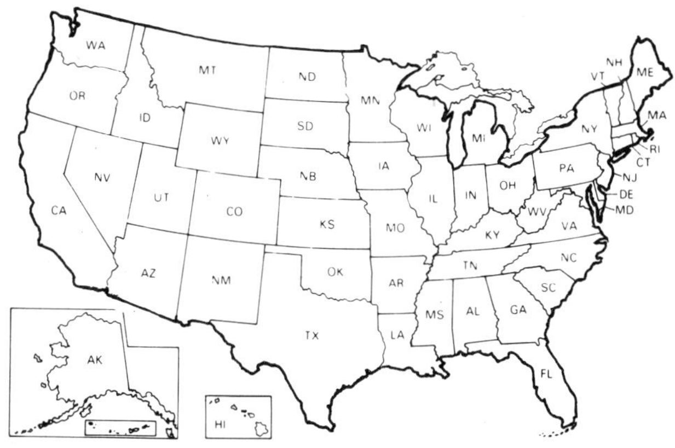

A romance is a love story, and love naturally involves sex, sooner or later. That's no problem in historicals, which have always been on the sexy side. But in contemporaries, it's another story—sex used to mean *never before marriage*, and since the proposal came on the last page, the consummation was left to the reader's imagination.

There isn't much left to the imagination anymore. A 1980s trend towards "sensual romances," as a sexy romance is known in the business, has had a powerful impact on contemporaries. Many contain love scenes so hot and explicit they blister the page. Most, however, fall somewhere between the old blushing chastity and the new blunt eroticism—stories in which the lovers indulge in and enjoy sex, with or without marriage, in a rich celebration of emotion and pleasure of all senses.

Before we go any further in this discussion of sex and sensuality in romances, let's define a few terms. The emphasis today is on "sensual" sex and not mechanical sex or graphic descriptions. A sensual experience involves all the senses and, in romances, is wrapped heavily in emotion. Sensuality goes beyond the physical act of sex to include such elements as courtship, the sexual spark in eye contact or a soft touch as a gesture of affection and intimacy. A romance can be sensual without being explicit.

Profanity and crude anatomical descriptions are generally avoided; euphemisms are still used for genitalia. "Women want moonlight and roses and how the air smells, not how he took her dress off," observes Karen Solem, vice president and editor in chief of Silhouette Books.

"The feeling, the woman's emotions, is the crucial difference," according to Ellen Edwards, senior editor of Jove's Second Chance At Love. "Women read these books to get emotionally involved, to live these feelings vicariously. They want to strongly identify with the heroine and feel all of her feelings, not just the sexual stimulation, but the feelings of love and tenderness."

Ann Gisonny, senior editor of Dell Candlelight Ecstasy Romances, comments: "Sensual romances are a woman's fantasies about great lovemaking. There's no sex for the sake of sex, no promiscuity. Descriptions are more anatomical, but there's also a communication that's going on between the hero and heroine on other levels, spiritually and emotionally."

Contemporaries owe some of their liberation to historical romances. "That's what brought the romance genre back—sex," says historical author Bertrice Small. Back in the 1940s, Kathleen Winsor scandalized people with the sexual escapades of her heroine in *Forever Amber.* But it wasn't until the 1970s that sexy historicals hit the market in force, with many of them becoming best-sellers.

The trend was started by two books: Kathleen E. Woodiwiss' *The Flame and the Flower* and Rosemary Rogers' *Sweet Savage Love,* published by Avon Books in 1972 and 1974 respectively. *The Flame and the Flower* begins with an attempted rape followed by an actual rape, and then hero and heroine hardly touch each other for several hundred pages, until they work out their misunderstandings. In spite of its initial violent sex and subsequent avoidance of sex, it's considered to be a sexy, sensual book because of the erotic tension Kathleen sustains throughout the entire story. It's also a one-man-one-woman book, in that the hero and heroine never bed anyone else after they discover each other.

Not so in *Sweet Savage Love,* which contains much violent sex. The heroine is raped repeatedly, not only by the hero, but by villains as well. Its bodice ripping was widely imitated, giving rise to the label "sweet/savage" for similar books. "I think that was the first book that had a lot of sex in it totally from a woman's point of view," says Hilary Ross, senior editor of New American Library, who, as a free-lancer, edited *Sweet Savage Love* for Avon.

Not all historicals published in the 1970s were bodice rippers, although many people confuse the two. Bodice rippers were characterized by "no-no heroines and macho, violent heroes," as Bertrice puts it, and were not too different from Harold Robbins-style books. Author Catherine Coulter calls them "sweet/sour" books. "The heroine gets raped on eight continents, or else she's raped by a dozen Indians and then gets up, dusts off her skirts and says, 'Oh, that was terrible.'" For the most part, bodice rippers were out of style and out of favor by the end of the 1970s.

"I'm partially responsible for soothing things down," says Bertrice. "I don't like violent sex, although I know there are going to be times when you can't avoid it. But I think we've seen the end of the macho men." One device to allow the historical heroine to have many sexual experiences without sinking to the level of a whore is to give her an assortment of husbands. "I have always felt that explicit sex with your own husband is not pornographic," Bertrice says. In her novel *Adora* (Avon Books), for example, the heroine, a fourteenth-century Byzantine princess, has three husbands, two of whom she passionately loves and one of whom she is

117

A Candlelight Ecstasy Romance®

WHEN NEXT WE LOVE

DELL • 19588 • 1.95

Heather Graham

forced to endure. Her first husband, an old goat of a sultan and a cruel brute to boot, has her tied down and deflowered by a club-wielding slave. Fortunately for Adora, husbands two and three are gentler and more passionate. She loses number two to poisoning by enemies; number three buys her as a slave. He keeps her in his harem for quite a while before she convinces him to marry her, and a tender, caring relationship develops between them.

While historical romances of the 1970s didn't shirk from describing sex, contemporary romances were squeaky clean. The hero and heroine sometimes came close to losing control, but something always happened to cool down their ardor—the phone rang, someone knocked on the door, the hero magnanimously decided he was being ungentlemanly, or the heroine had a sudden seizure of conscience and began either to cry or to struggle and beat the hero's chest. Sometimes, they did little more than breathe heavily. In any case, readers were never allowed to view what went on behind closed bedroom doors.

But real life male-female relationships in the 1960s and 1970s were *not* squeaky clean like their fictional counterparts. The Pill, the women's movement, the soaring divorce rate, the acceptability of remaining single, all led to a loosening of restrictions concerning sex. Sex before marriage and with more than one partner did not ruin a woman for life. "Real men and women go to bed without the benefit of the clergy," points out Vivian Stephens, senior editor of Harlequin American Romances.

Vivian Stephens

For sex, readers who liked contemporary romances had to turn to historicals or bodice rippers. Author Sharon Curtis says, "People put up with the brutality [in bodice rippers], but they obviously wanted something else they weren't getting in contemporaries."

Senior editor Carolyn Nichols, of Bantam's Loveswept series, agrees, adding that editors should have taken the cue from the sexy historicals that readers would welcome sexy contemporary romances.

The Ecstasy Breakthrough

The movement towards more sex in contemporary romances was glacial, however, until American publishers began to compete in earnest with Harlequin. In 1980, Dell published two romances that changed the industry. The books were released quietly, without fanfare, and no one expected them to have such incredible reverberations throughout the romantic fiction business. They were an enormous catalyst for the growth of sensuality in romances, a trend ripe and ready to happen.

The books were *The Tawny Gold Man* by Amii Lorin and *Gentle Pirate* by Jayne Castle, the first two Dell Candlelight Ecstasy Romances. They were discovered by Vivian Stephens, then senior editor of Dell Candlelight Romances.

"I was as surprised as everyone else," says Vivian about the books' impact. "I received these two manuscripts in which the sexual tension was so consistent from beginning to end that there was no relief for the reader. I decided to ask the writers to take it one step further—what happened next, beyond the passionate kiss at the end. I wanted that something extra, if not in bed, then what happened after we knew the characters had sexual intercourse.

"I wasn't interested in the intercourse itself, because I knew the reader wasn't, but in the *emotional satisfaction*—were these two people now satisfied with each other? I put these two books out without any publicity and they sold out within a week. I was shocked."

Ecstasies took off like rockets, and soon the new line was, and still is, the leading seller in the field of contemporary romances. The line's success encouraged other publishers to follow suit, and authors quickly began writing more and longer sexual encounters in increasingly explicit detail. Several sex scenes per book became de rigeuer. It wasn't long before the successors to *Gentle Pirate* and *The Tawny Gold Man* made those two books look mighty tame.

As explicit as they have become, the spicy romances, as they are called, still rely on euphemisms for sexual anatomy below the belt. The intrusion of clinical terms, it seems, ruins the fantasy element.

Too Much Of A Good Thing?

As is often the case when businesses try to cash in fast on a hot trend, there has been a certain amount of overkill. Even lots of sex becomes stale after a while, and readers grow bored and jaded. Some become offended. "The trend toward more sensual romances has come to an end," says Ann Gisonny. "Readers don't want one love scene after another."

"I think there's a flaw in a lot of the books we've been seeing," comments Carolyn Nichols. "They're rip-off books that are emulating the original sensual books, and they've gone too far. What you have is a string of sexual episodes between the hero and heroine with very little romance. I firmly believe women want to read good emotional sex, but it must not be devoid of romance."

Says Robin Grunder, editor of New American Library's Rapture Romances, "Premarital sex was needed in these books to reflect real life, but the books have gotten about as sexy as they can, and there's already a backlash reaction. Readers are interested in falling in love, not necessarily in what goes on in the bedroom."

Some authors have pulled back a bit, emphasizing sensual encounters rather than sex. "I like books to have sensuous detail, but so many contemporaries seem to have women who are sexually addicted to a man, and I don't want to portray that kind of sexual involvement," says author Elizabeth Neff Walker. "I like heroines who are mature, but not willing to give up their independence."

There's no evidence, however, that sensuality will fade completely from the scene—it's too much a part of contemporary life. "I think sensuality will be here to stay," states Ellen Edwards, "unless society changes drastically."

"The pendulum won't swing back to sweet romances unless something replaces sensuality," says Carolyn. "There will always be a market for sweet romances, but it will be small."

While the sensuality boom has added sex to contemporaries, it has in a way toned down many historicals. "There's less violence, but the sex isn't less hot," says Page Cuddy, Avon Books editorial director. "But the brutal, unfeeling hero is not popular."

"I write more sensuous books now, with less violence," reports historical author Jennifer Blake.

The romance reader now has a wide spectrum of sexual contents and tone to choose from in today's romance market. There are still traditional contemporary romances; there are others with a dash of sizzle and others with a lot of sizzle. The same can be found in historicals.

"If I've given anything to the industry," says editor Vivian Stephens, "it's that I've made sensuality all right. It is in our lives every day, but a lot of people don't acknowledge it, I think because of the Puritanical background of most Americans. Yet they take part in sensual exercises every day—we do see, smell and touch people. These books just put it in words."

VI. PASSION PLAYS

FIRST KISS

Lips do many things in romances. They quiver, burn, brush, bruise, hesitate, plunder, nibble, lick, tease, cover, claim, meet, seek, demand, beg, conquer and trace the curves and hollows of a body. Lips can be greedy but are seldom stingy. They're almost always full; they only thin out in anger and irritation. Lips kiss, but it's never sufficient simply to say that they kiss—it isn't exciting enough, nor does it evoke enough emotion. It's much better to have someone's lips plundered by another's or to have a hot, moist pair of lips greedily cover another pair of willing, parted lips.

The first kiss in a romance is quite significant, for it acknowledges the sexual tension between and mutual desire of the hero and heroine, even though the heroine may be trying to deny it. It can be rough and forced, such as in a bodice ripper or a traditional romance, with the heroine fighting not only the hated hero but the rise of passion awakened in her by the kiss. It can be light and teasing. Or it can be stupendous, an oh-God-why-did-we-wait-so-long kind of kiss. With the first kiss, a virginal heroine realizes she never dreamed that passion could be *so good.* If she's more mature and experienced, she's still likely to be knocked off her feet, although not because she'd never really been kissed until the hero came along.

A first kiss can also be tentative and may not even evoke much of a passionate response, especially if the heroine is reluctant or suspicious about the hero (they make up for lost time later). Even if the first kiss is a real bell ringer, it's seldom as good as the ones that come later, as the emotion and passion deepen and the lovemaking progresses. Brutal kisses become tender, cool kisses become hot, hot kisses become hotter.

LOVE'S PHILOSOPHY

By Percy Bysshe Shelley
(1792–1822)
English poet

The fountains mingle with the river,
  And the rivers with the ocean,
The winds of heaven mix forever
  With a sweet emotion;
Nothing in the world is single;
  All the things by a law divine
In one another's being mingle;—
  Why not I with thine?

See the mountains kiss high heaven,
  And the waves clasp one another;
No sister flower would be forgiven
  If it disdained its brother;
And the sunlight clasps the earth,
  And the moonbeams kiss the sea;
What are all these kissings worth,
  If thou not kiss me?

IN DEFENSE OF OLD-FASHIONED VALUES

Sensual sex, and lots of it, is definitely "in" in romances. But best-selling author Barbara Cartland, the doyenne of today's romantic fiction, is sticking to her virginity-before-marriage guns—and has the sales figures to prove that plenty of women around the world agree with her.

Barbara, whose 350-plus books (most of them romances) have sold some 350 million copies, firmly believes that a sterner morality is what's needed these days. You won't find *her* heroines slipping between the sheets with the men they love before the wedding rings are slipped on their fingers. Even then you won't find any sexual scenes in Barbara's books; she gracefully leaves that up to the imagination of her readers. What women want, she says, is the idealistic, romantic love described by poets, painters and composers throughout history.

"Love is the most beautiful, sacred and divine emotion we can experience in life," says Barbara. "Love between a man and a woman, which is both physical and spiritual—the perfect love—is something we all yearn for and is the nearest thing we get to the love of God.

"Of course, love has been debased, sneered at, made obscene, and become, through pornography, ugly and vulgar. But I am convinced that every young woman and man start by believing they will find in their lives the perfect love, which is both beautiful and good."

Barbara asserts that double sex standards for men and women are a medical fact of life and will never change. For men sex can be a purely physical act that can be enjoyed and forgotten. But for women "making love" is always an emotional experience. "That is why for a young girl to sleep about affects her character and her personality," she says.

"We have to get back to fundamentals, and the most fundamental thing of all is the belief in the stability of marriage and the responsibilities of parenthood. These are quite simply based on the love between a man and a woman."

SONNET 116

By William Shakespeare
(1564–1616)
English dramatist and poet

Let me not to the marriage of true minds
Admit impediments. Love is not love
Which alters when it alteration finds,
Or bends with the remover to remove.
O, no! it is an ever-fixed mark,
That looks on tempests and is never shaken;
It is the star to every wand'ring bark,
Whose worth's unknown, although his height be taken.
Love's not Time's fool, though rosy lips and cheeks
Within his bending sickle's compass come;
Love alters not with his brief hours and weeks,
But bears it out even to the edge of doom.
  If this be error, and upon me prov'd,
  I never writ, nor no man ever lov'd.

NEW 174
BARBARA CARTLAND
Help From The Heart
NEW 173
BARBARA CARTLAND
Gypsy Magic

SEX AND THE REGENCY

Sex may be commonplace in most romances today, but there's still one genre of book in which a no-sex barrier has been tough to break down—the Regency. Nevertheless, sex has come to Regencies, albeit in a limited fashion.

In accordance with the mores of the period—early nineteenth century English society—and the parameters of the Regency novel established by the late author Georgette Heyer, hero and heroine usually do little more than kiss when they become engaged at the end of the book. Instead the books focus on witty repartee, silly misunderstandings and social concerns. But in the late 1970s, sex began to sneak into Regency plots.

The author who deserves most of the credit for liberating these drawing room comedies of manners is Catherine Coulter, whose first Regency, *The Autumn Countess,* was published by NAL/Signet in 1979. That novel was slightly racier than those written by Georgette Heyer, and there was more to come in her second book for Signet, *The Rebel Bride.*

Catherine recalls that she brought the subject up over lunch with Hilary Ross, senior editor for Signet, in a restaurant in New York City's staid Wall Street district—the epitome of male-dominated conservatism. Her request—"Can I put explicit sex in this book?"—came during a lull in the conversational noise in the restaurant. Heads turned. "Hilary," the author remembers, "looked rather taken aback and said something about the little old ladies in sneakers in Iowa." Then she decided, why not? One man, on his way out, stopped by their table. "Would you let me know when your book comes out?" he asked. "I'd like to read it!"

If he ever did read it, he was likely disappointed—*Valley of the Dolls* it wasn't. But for a Regency, it was hot. It included a forced seduction scene between the hero and heroine, who are married. He forces himself on her because she won't let him near her, due, unbeknownst to him, to a rape she suffered as a young child. It was one of Catherine's best sellers, and it influenced other Regency writers to remove the shackles from the genre.

But the opportunities to portray consummated sex in the Regency period are few and far between and usually require a marriage. "The period was less hidebound than the Victorian period, but there were strict social mores for young girls and definite rules of courtship," says Catherine. Promiscuity prevailed among the aristocracy, but it was largely confined to men having mistresses, an acceptable custom in those days. Women, however, would ruin themselves by having affairs or by having sex before marriage.

Readers apparently like having a sexual element in the books, where appropriate, of course. "I have taken very few liberties," Catherine says. "It is just that I have opened the bedroom door for the readers. But you have to be careful, or it ceases to be a Regency."

"I have sometimes wondered," Catherine concludes, "how Georgette Heyer would have handled sex—probably beautifully. I understand that editors are now encouraging authors to write more sensual sex scenes in Regencies, so a new trend has been born and accepted. I believe that this type of Regency is now being referred to as the 'realistic' Regency novel. In any case, so long as the sex flows naturally from the plot, I think most readers will continue to believe that the change in the genre has been a change for the better."

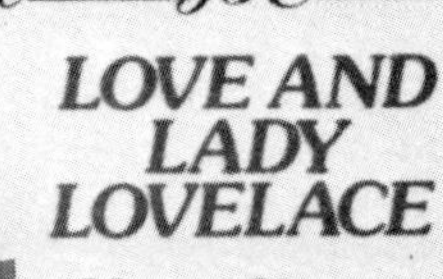

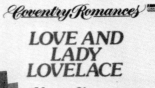

LOVE AND LADY LOVELACE

Marion Chesney

SIGNET•451-AE1623•$2.25

SIGNET REGENCY ROMANCE

THE MARCHINGTON SCANDAL

JANE ASHFORD

A REBELLIOUS YOUNG LADY FINDS THE PRICE OF AVOIDING SCANDAL SHOCKINGLY HIGH

VI. PASSION PLAYS

DEFINING SENSUALITY

"Sensual" is the term generally used to describe romances which contain consummated sex, but the term is not necessarily interchangeable with "sexy," which means "erotic." "Sensual" means "devoted to pleasing the senses," which goes far beyond mere sexual gratification. Here's how a few editors, authors and agents describe the essence of sensuality:

Vivian Stephens, *senior editor, Harlequin American Romances:* "A lot of people confuse the two words 'sexy' and 'sensual.' 'Sexy' means you have a lot of physical activity going on, a lot of intercourse. 'Sensual' is the interaction between the two characters with a lot of sexual overtones, physical and verbal."

Jayne Castle, *author:* "Sensuality goes beyond mere physical beauty. . . . There's no bed-hopping. Sex is explicit but with the glow of romance."

Ann Gisonny, *senior editor, Dell Candlelight Ecstasy Romances:* "'Sensual' means heightened emotions and a sense of commitment and love, not graphic, mechanical sex."

Ruth Cohen, *agent:* "A sensuous relationship involves subtle yearnings and startling passions. Whether they are lovers or not, there is an ardent magnetism in every encounter—a hunger to touch, to taste, to memorize each expression, to delight again and again in the marvelously exhilarating and totally engrossing joy of mutual discovery."

Ellen Edwards, *senior editor, Jove's Second Chance At Love:* "A sensual romance reflects the love lives women have and the love lives they dream of having."

Karen Solem, *vice president and editor in chief, Silhouette Books:* "Sometimes sensuality is just a matter of two people looking at each other—it doesn't have to be the mechanics. It's more the emotions that are involved in a situation. It's the feeling of being swept away."

Elaine Raco Chase, *author:* "Sex doesn't always have to be hot in a romance. It really comes last, after love, compassion and intimacy."

Robin Grunder, *editor, New American Library's Rapture Romances:* "Sensuality is the aura of being in love—everything glows."

SHE WALKS IN BEAUTY

By Lord Byron
(1788–1824)
English poet

She walks in beauty, like the night
Of cloudless climes and starry skies,
And all that's best of dark and bright
Meet in her aspect and her eyes;
Thus mellowed to that tender light
Which heaven to gaudy day denies.

One shade the more, one ray the less,
Had half impaired the nameless grace
Which waves in every raven tress
Or softly lights o'er her face,
Where thoughts serenely sweet express
How pure, how dear their dwelling-place.

And on that cheek and o'er that brow
So soft, so calm, yet eloquent,
The smiles that win, the tints that glow
But tell of days in goodness spent,
A mind at peace with all below,
A heart whose love is innocent.

RAPE IS A FOUR-LETTER WORD

"I do not write about rape—it really turns me off. The only woman in my books who was raped killed the man who raped her and enjoyed doing it. She would have gelded him first, but she was in a hurry. No woman I ever wrote about fell in love with the man who forced her. Rape is not funny—it's an abomination, it's disgusting."

The speaker is Roberta Gellis, author of medieval romances. She acknowledges she's written some rough love scenes, but mention rape in romances, and she is swift to attack it: "I become rabid on that subject," she says, and from the fire in her eyes, you know she means business. Roberta speaks for many in the romance field, readers, writers and editors alike, who feel romances have no room for rape (or "forced seduction," as it's sometimes called if it occurs between hero and heroine). "Rape is not a woman's fantasy," says Karen Solem, vice president and editor in chief of Silhouette Books.

Rape was once gratuitous in bodice rippers and still appears in some historical romances. "There are rape scenes and there are rape scenes," says historical author Bertrice Small, pointing out that one must look at the way women were treated in times past—and they often were forced to have sex with men and husbands not of their choosing. "I do not like rape, yet I have some rape sequences in my books," she says. "For the most part, they're not violent rapes, they are emotional rapes." For example, her heroine in *Love Wild & Fair* (Avon) is forced to receive the king, even though she objects. However, notes Bertrice, "violence is definitely out."

In traditional contemporaries, the hero sometimes attempts rape but rarely consummates it. He is always interrupted, fought off by the heroine or suddenly becomes too much of a gentleman. Even in lesser physical encounters, the hero usually has the role of forcing himself on the heroine—grabbing her, pushing her against a wall or down on a bed, kissing her even though she struggles. As contemporaries have matured, the element of force has decreased but not vanished. Readers don't like swaggering macho behavior, and they've said so, vociferously, in letters and calls to editors: cut out the violent sex.

"Sexual violence is enormously offensive," says author Maura Seger. "I think a good argument can be made that the bodice rippers of the past sold *despite* their reliance on violent sex, rather than because of it. With recent improvements in the quality of romances, readers have become far more discriminating. In both contemporaries and historicals, they are looking for strong, tender heroes and heroines who take active responsibility for their own lives rather than simply waiting for Prince Charming to show up."

Violent sex has always been more a part of historicals than of contemporary romances, and more accepted in historicals (not all historicals are bodice rippers, which generally contain more violence than either romance or history). Yet readers have begun to object when violence occurs in historical romances. For example, *Devil's Embrace,* the first major historical for Regency author Catherine Coulter, published by NAL/Signet in 1982, contains a violent rape scene after the heroine, Cassie, is kidnapped by four men. The rape scene disturbed some readers and reviewers, although the book was touted. "I was taken aback," says Catherine, who describes herself as a feminist. "I have never cared for long historicals that have the heroine lose her virginity to the hero by page thirty and then separate them until the end of the book. There is no relationship between them, simply an accounting of the 'perils of Pauline.' With *Devil's Embrace,* Anthony and Cassie are together for the majority of the novel. This, of course, requires that there be a sustained tension between them—it would be quite boring to have sweetness and light for 150,000 words. Their relationship had developed to a point where it was a necessity to have something totally unexpected, something highly dramatic, occur. Given the feedback I've gotten from readers, though, I think now that I would try to handle it differently."

Page Cuddy, editorial director of Avon Books, the leader in historical romances, says rape is acceptable in historicals "because it's not without a strong romance component. In the good books the hero realizes the heroine is more than he thought her to be, and then he's not so brutal. There's a certain amount of rape that's acceptable—readers will accept it from some writers and not from others." What they don't like, however, is brutal heroes without any glimmer of feeling, according to Page.

Not everyone agrees that rape is acceptable in historicals. Kate Duffy, senior editor at Pocket Books, intends to steer clear of violent sex in her line of historical romances, Tapestry, believing that historical fans are ready for gentle-sex historical romances.

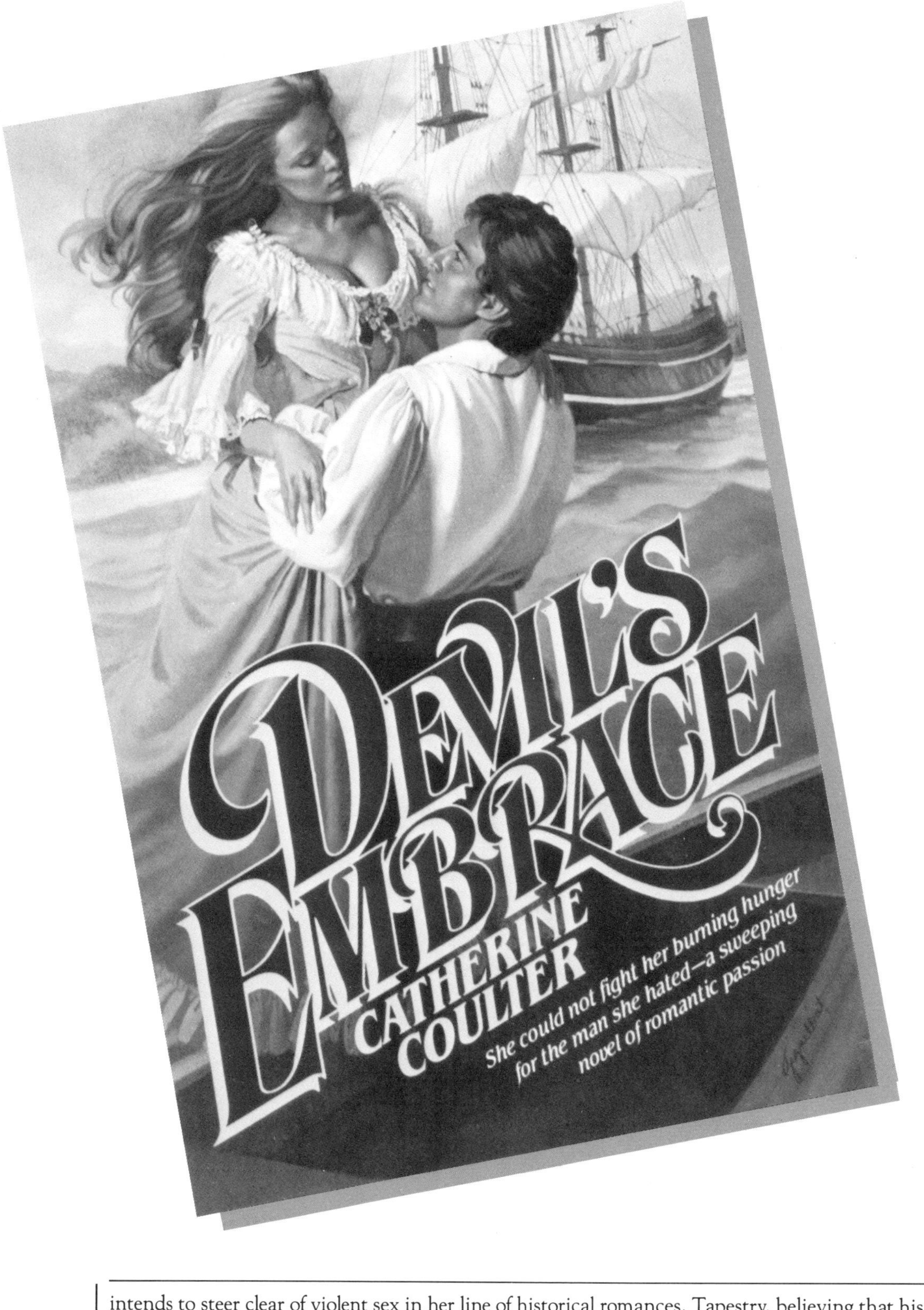

"So many things happened to the poor heroine in the bodice rippers that nobody in their right mind would want to have happen to them," Kate says. "She was pinched, prodded, picked on, slapped, humiliated and abused, and then all of a sudden fell into the hero's arms at the end. I don't believe it." Kate adds that in Tapestry novels, there are no Captain Blood or Conan the Barbarian heroes.

Clothes make the heroine. Even if she doesn't have the money to dress richly, she dresses tastefully. Readers love descriptions of the heroine's outfits, from lavish period ball gowns to modern-day slacks and blouses. Usually the heroine gets at least one chance to dress up and really shine during her story, much to the appreciation of the hero.

Historical heroines wear the period clothing of the day, of course, and their gowns reflect their social and economic station. For contemporary heroines, who live in a time when anything goes, the emphasis is on good taste and classic styles. The typical modern heroine doesn't go for trendy, offbeat clothes or designer labels. If she's a career woman, she buys the best she can afford, such as silk blouses instead of polyester. Even when she dresses casually, her jeans are neat, never ratty. When she dresses up specifically for a man—a fancy, low-cut or clingy dress for a party or intimate dinner—her outfit may be sexy but never risque.

Details, including colors, fabrics, textures and names of styles and garments are important, and that means some research on the part of the authors. Historical romance authors are automatically at a disadvantage—they can't merely watch people on the street or flip through a fashion magazine to describe the garments their characters wear. Their research is often long and painstaking, involving the reading of historical and costume texts and visiting museum exhibits. Author Jude Deveraux, however, takes it all one step further—she actually designs and sews doll-sized period costumes before she starts a novel. It's research from the skin out, she explains, from underwear to hats, bags and scarves, and it helps her understand the role and influence of clothing in daily life.

Jude spends literally thousands of hours on her doll clothing, in what started as pure work-related research and grew into an absorbing hobby. She has accumulated a library of some 200 costume books plus slides and sketches, which she uses to make patterns for her seventeen-inch and five-and-a-half-inch dolls. She shops for just the right fabric with small enough print, even if it's expensive, such as wool challis at $35 a yard or high-grade silk. She sews the garments, weaves sashes and scarves and even beads bags. For an American frontier pouch that measured 1 x 1.5 inches, Jude sewed on 946 beads that were one-third the size of seed beads, using beading needles from England that were scarcely thicker than a human hair. "I think I cursed at every one of those beads," she laughs.

Her interest in making period clothing began in the late 1970s when she started her second novel, *The Black Lyon* (Avon Books), which she intended to set in medieval times. "The Middle Ages spanned hundreds of years and I decided to set the story at a time when castles were at their peak, before they became white elephants," Jude says. "Unfortunately, I soon discovered that when castles were at their very best, women wore horned headdresses. For the life of me, I couldn't visualize my heroine tearing from one adventure to the next wearing a three-foot, veiled horn on her head. So, I set the book in 1283, a time of luxurious fabrics and simple clothes."

By the time Jude started her next medieval novel, *The Velvet Promise* (Gallen/Pocket Books), she was thoroughly intrigued by costume research and had acquired a small library of books on the subject. She chose to set the book in the sixteenth century, then learned that the clothes of that period were "atrocious—heavy, cumbersome and worn over steel corsets," she says. "After a lot of work, I at last found some illustrations of clothes of the first ten years of the century, and they were beautiful."

Jude soon found that her small library was inadequate. "I began to order tons of material. I discovered the Costume Society of America, which I later joined, and they, in turn, introduced me to new sources. By then my interest in clothing had become a full-fledged addiction. I would spend hours with curators and at museums and was tempted to make the costume library at the Metropolitan Museum of Art in New York my second home."

Then Jude discovered mail-order dolls that came with kits containing hairstyles of different time periods, and she got the idea of outfitting dolls as inspiration for her books. "I loved doing it and soon I began to acquire more and more of these mini-mannequins," says Jude. "I've always done a lot of sewing, so creating the costumes themselves isn't a stumbling block. In addition, the extra research required to dress the dolls properly leads me to all kinds of new information.

"For instance, with each one I've had to study underwear, fabrics and hats along with the basic dress styles. This leads to understanding the limitations or freedoms imposed on women during different eras based on their style of dress, and reinforces the importance of climate in determining dress and life style.

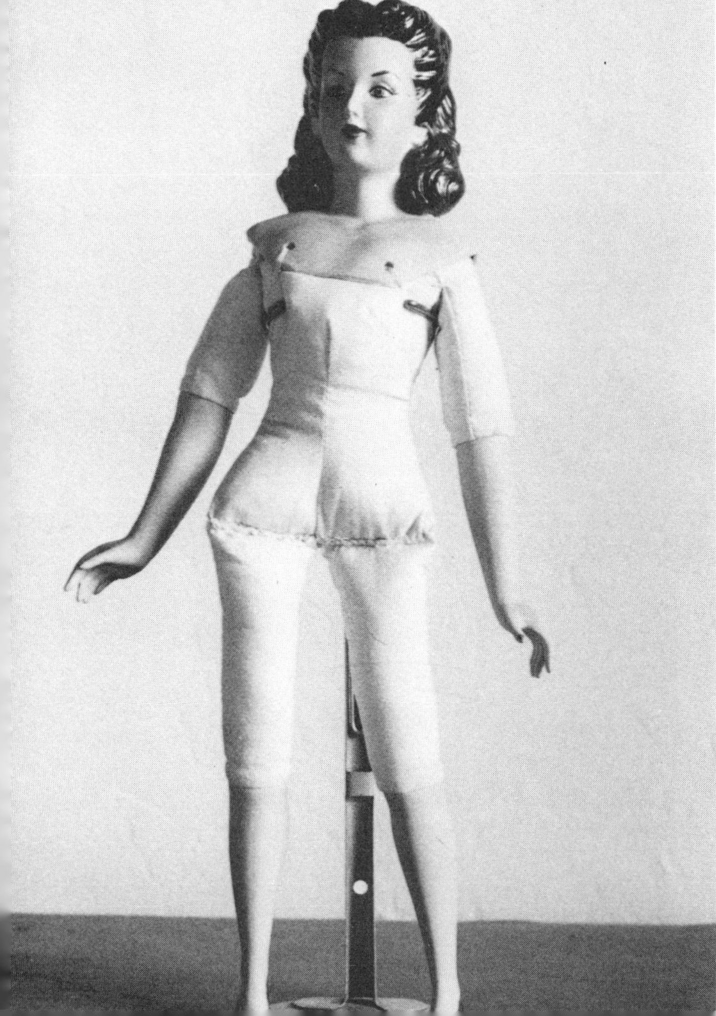

"Today," she continues, "we don't appreciate how simple, easy and sturdy our clothes are. Silk looks good and feels good, but it snags just by touching it at times. A woman would have had to walk slowly and carefully if she wore satin or she'd ruin her gown in hours."

The sewing alone averages sixty hours per doll, and research and shopping add many more hours. Her costumes originally were made for heroines only, but for a forthcoming series set in eighteenth century Virginia, Jude began designing clothes for her heroes as well. She's done about a dozen dolls altogether.

In addition, she constructs model dwellings of various time periods from kits. She has two entire villages, one medieval and one eighteenth century Virginia plantation, plus about a dozen houses. The villages measure about four square feet each.

"It's absolutely absurd how much time it takes," Jude says jokingly of her research/hobby. But she knows it's well worth it.

VI. PASSION PLAYS

Theresa Vaughn, an English polygamist, had sixty-one husbands. Martha "Calamity Jane" Burke, a nineteenth-century American frontierswoman who dressed like a man and drank and swore with the roughest of them, went through twelve husbands. Most of us, however, will happily settle for one good one—if we can find him.

The venerable institution of marriage is alive and well despite the battering it took in the 1960s and 1970s and the advent of free sex, "swingles," communal living and "shacking up." Although the divorce rate is soaring, women still want the security and comfort of marriage. Their desire for this kind of commitment is reflected in romance novels, which, almost without exception, end happily with the promise of marriage. "Romances uphold traditional values," says Karen Solem, vice president and editor in chief of Silhouette Books. "They're about middle-class American people—about all of us in a way—and people like to see commitment."

These days men and women marry chiefly for love, and marriage is supposed to be a happy, if not equal, union. Throughout history, however, marriage was often at best a duty for women and at worst a living hell. Women were sometimes bound and kidnapped and forced into marriages that were little more than slavery. Parents arranged marriages for their offspring while the children were still in their infancy, and sometimes the betrothed never saw each other until their wedding day. Women were chattels to their husbands, who could do with them as they pleased, even kill them. To make matters worse, women who fled abusive husbands were scorned by society and forced to return to their tormentors.

Not all marriages were unpleasant, however. Marriage was generally regarded as a socially accepted institution that allowed for procreation and sex. Love was a surprise bonus. Author Roberta Gellis says that in medieval times "many marriages were very happy, particularly when you consider that the girl came to the marriage expecting to have her teeth knocked in. If she didn't, then her husband was an angel and she loved him dearly. A man might expect a girl to be ugly or a shrew, and if she was a decent young woman who wished to please him, then he was delighted.

"I think there were probably as many happy marriages as there are now. In a sense, there might have even been more, because it was inevitable that if your husband wasn't a monster, you were happy with him. You couldn't divorce him, you couldn't leave him. There was no place for a woman to go, except into the Church."

Thankfully, marriage has improved considerably for women, at least in Western civilization. Marriage is something most women look forward to, from the time they are small girls.

Finding Mr. Terrific is not all that easy, however, as any single woman knows. The romance heroine has it much easier than her real life counterpart. She has little difficulty meeting and attracting a wonderful, sexy prospective husband, usually just when she is ready to give up on love and men. (Although she professes a desire to marry for love, she conveniently falls for someone her equal or better, although he can be younger.)

Unlike real-life men, most romantic heroes can't wait to get to the altar once they're in the throes of love. There are no second thoughts, no doubts, no foot dragging, no suggestions to live together for a while first; and no preliminary negotiating about who's going to do the vacuuming, take out the trash or empty the cat box. Romances, mercifully, are not concerned with these mundane facets of real life. The hero and heroine can thrash out their daily routines offstage—after the final curtain, after the reader has been entertained, as promised, by a romantic fantasy.

The marriage happy ending is an unwritten guarantee that comes with virtually every romance. "Readers know in advance what's going to happen in the end," according to Leslie Wainger, editor of Silhouette Books. "Their expectation is that the book will deliver a good fantasy and that it will be enjoyable getting to the end."

"You want to identify with the heroine, fall in love with the hero and have a darn good story," says Pamela Strickland, senior editor of Ballantine's Love & Life line, which straddles the romance genre and mainstream women's fiction. In keeping with its more "real-life" focus on relationships, Love & Life is perhaps the one exception to marriage endings. Pamela requires a happy ending, not necessarily a wedding, "in terms of the eighties."

The marriage ending applies to both historicals and contemporaries. (Young adult romances generally do not end in engagement or even going steady; rather, the heroine is left with the happy feeling that she's found a "special" relationship, and who knows where it will lead or what's in store for her.)

The reinforcement of marital commitment is reassuring. "I'm very old-

A YOUNG LADY'S DOWER HER WEIGHT IN PINE TREE SHILLINGS.

THE PINE TREE SHILLING.

THE LORD BALTIMORE SHILLING.

fashioned and I truly believe in marriage," says author Sandra Brown, who has been married about fifteen years. "I think most of the women who read these books feel better knowing that the hero and heroine are going to get married in the end. It gives them a sense of well-being to know they'll live happily ever after."

"In romances, a happy ending always means marriage," comments Vivian Stephens, senior editor of Harlequin American Romances. "We've been programmed for it since Adam and Eve."

In *The Devil's Dictionary* Ambrose Bierce defined a bride as "a woman with a fine prospect of happiness behind her." Millions of romance fans would like to disagree.

RITES OF PASSAGE

There's probably no greater testament to the universality of love between men and women than in the way people the world over celebrate their marriage. From country to country, from culture to culture, despite the differences in language and custom, the wedding ceremony—no matter where it is performed—has a remarkably similar look.

The fact is that many customs of modern weddings, such as cakes, veils, prayers and presents, owe their origins to pagan rituals, which today have entirely different meanings.

The most common wedding customs fall roughly into three groups:

1. Customs stressing marriage as a transition from one form of life style to another
2. Practices symbolizing the fertility aspect of marriage
3. Rituals to ensure good luck for the new couple

Of those three groups, the first—designed to signify the transition from the single to the married life—is perhaps one of the most widespread of marriage customs. It takes many forms. For example, the practice we know best—carrying the bride over the threshold—underscores the fact that both partners have left their parental homes and are starting anew in their own dwelling. Similarly, the mere act of the father "giving away" the bride during the wedding ceremony is a gesture that marks an important transition in the lives of both parents and children.

The fertility aspect of marriage and the ways it is symbolized in the wedding ceremony is as old as marriage itself. After all, marriage was initially designed as a way to propagate society, to ensure its continuation. The practice of throwing confetti or rice, which we do today because it would hardly be a wedding celebration without it, started because early societies and cultures believed such acts ensured that new families would multiply and be fruitful. In fact, in some countries, such as Spain, Ireland and Greece, it is still common to throw fruit at the departing couple.

Finally, there is the warding off of evil. This simple act can take the form of a prayer for the health and welfare of the new couple, as is generally the case in this country. Or it can be symbolized by the wrapping of horseshoes in silver paper, an ancient practice that still survives in many Christian countries. In other countries, China, for example, women with mirrors and lights search the bride's carriage for evil spirits; in India archers fire arrows to scare off any lurking demons.

A GIRL'S BEST FRIEND

The bestowing of the engagement ring is one of civilized man's oldest social customs. But the diamond, mined for thousands of years, didn't really become synonymous with engagement and wedding rings until the twentieth century.

In centuries past, engagement rings were plain or decorated bands made out of whatever material was handy or popular. They were not symbols of love, for marriage once was a matter of service to the family and state, but were signals to men that a female was off the market. At the time of marriage, the engagement ring, a single band, became the wedding ring.

The ancient Egyptians, for whom the ring is the symbol of eternity, fashioned their betrothal and wedding rings from ivory, amber, silver, copper, bronze and, if poor, rushes. The Greeks used iron, as did the Romans until about the second century B.C., when they began using gold as well. Roughly cut diamonds from India, nothing like the brilliant-faceted stones we know today, appeared on a few Roman rings as early as the fourth century B.C.

The first known discovery of diamonds, the hardest natural substance in the world, was made in ancient India. Alexander the Great was familiar with the gem; in fact, diamonds derive their name from the Greek term *adamas*, which means invincible. It was commonly believed that those who wore diamonds would be invincible in battle and would be protected from poisons and pestilence.

Due to their scarcity and unimpressive appearance, rough Indian diamonds seldom were used on jewelry. In fact, in medieval times, diamonds were ranked lower in worth than pearls, rubies and emeralds. Meanwhile, betrothal bands, still largely made of silver, gold or other metals, became

"HE WAS A MAN WHO KNEW HIS OWN MIND."

increasingly ornate, with engraved designs, such as clasped hands and twin hearts pierced with an arrow.

It wasn't until the seventeenth century that an Italian lapidary produced the first "brilliant cut" round diamond, with 58 facets that showed off the gem's splendor to its fullest. The brilliant cut is the most common style today for engagement and wedding rings, followed by pear, marquis and emerald cuts.

Even with that development, diamonds seldom appeared on jewelry because they were still rare. In 1725, large diamond reserves were found in Brazil. Another major diamond discovery occurred in South Africa in 1867. Diamonds began appearing more on rings and other jewelry, but the gem didn't achieve its status as the "marriage stone" until after the turn of the twentieth century.

The hand of marriage. Throughout history engagement rings have usually been placed on the third finger from the thumb of the left hand, which is supposed to be the weaker, "feminine" hand and which, in tradition, indicated the woman's subservience to the man. A legend believed up to and through the Middle Ages held that a "love vein" flowed from this ring finger directly to the heart. The Egyptians believed the vein was in the right hand, and so they wore their betrothal and marriage rings on that hand, as did some Europeans in medieval times. In 1549, the Church of England officially established the left hand as the "hand of matrimony."

Double rings—that is, half the ring worn during engagement and the other half added at marriage—weren't introduced until the sixteenth and seventeenth centuries, becoming particularly popular in Germany and Scandinavia. In the United States, double rings have been traditional since World War II.

VII. SPREADING THE WORD

Harlequin Enterprises once claimed nearly the entire romance market, but since 1980, American publishers have made a strong showing, most notably Silhouette Books, a division of Simon & Schuster. Their stories are here, as well as those of several other publishers in the United States and England.

CHAPTER ONE
Names: Love 'Em and Leave 'Em

What should the name of a romance line convey—sentiment, passion, commitment? Should it sound nostalgic, in an old lace and lavender way; romantic, in a chocolates and red roses way; or sexy, in a heart throbbing way? Most importantly, what's going to lure the customer? The classiest name in the world is worthless if it has no cash register appeal.

These are some of the questions publishers face when naming a romance line. They may spend thousands of dollars on market research testing dozens of candidates—or someone in house may casually suggest a name that everyone thinks hits the mark. Among the goodies, some odd ones have cropped up over the years.

Let's take a look at a few romance line names, some predictable and some not so predictable, and at how several publishers chose their names. A special thanks goes to Vivien Lee Jennings and her newsletter, *Boy Meets Girl*, for providing some of the historical information that follows.

Besides cash register appeal, the name should fit the personality of the line. "The name of a line is important for the visual images that carry through a theme," says Carolyn Nichols, senior editor of Bantam's Loveswept line. In Loveswept's case, the name was chosen to convey the "swept away" exhilaration and passion of love and is used in conjunction with a rainbow wave of colors on every cover.

It shouldn't therefore surprise customers that Loveswept is a sexy line, as are Dell Candlelight Ecstasy Romance, New American Library's Rapture Romance and Silhouette Desire; or that Jove's Second Chance At Love features stories about heroines who manage to find love again. To Have And To Hold, another Jove line scheduled for launch in the fall of 1983, implies marriage vows, and the line indeed concerns married couples who solve problems to strengthen their commitment to each other. Ballantine's Love & Life, as close to mainstream women's fiction as to the romance genre, suggests more realism. Avon's Finding Mr. Right (originally Looking For Mr. Right, not quite as optimistic as its successor) predictably features heroines who choose between two suitable heroes. Dell's Temptation, announced in 1982, hopes to tempt customers with its sexy innuendo. And Superromance, a Harlequin imprint published by Worldwide Library, promises, well, a super romance. Scarlet Ribbons (NAL/Signet) suggests sensual historicals, and Jove's Camfield Romances is strictly for Barbara Cartland, named after her home, Camfield Place.

On the teen side, there are First Love (Silhouette), Sweet Dreams (Bantam), Wishing Star, Wildfire and Windswept (Scholastic) and Heavenly Romances (E. P. Dutton), among others, which appeal to teen dreams and fantasies.

All of the names mentioned thus far are for lines which are new since about 1979. What about some names from the past?

Ballantine undoubtedly gets the prize for the most unusually named romance line: Beagle. If anyone thought it strange that romances were published under an imprint that brings to mind hounds and foxes, they weren't put off from buying the books. Beagle lasted from about the 1940s or 1950s to the 1970s before it finally was laid to rest (Ballantine did use other more romantic names, such as Valentine and Red Rose). Second prize goes to Pinnacle, which launched Dear Miss Lonelyhearts in 1974. By 1980, Miss Lonelyhearts had pined away and Pinnacle was using Ashton Hall. Finally, third prize goes to Ace, which, in the 1970s, tried out An Adult Romance for the Modern Woman, which sounds more like medicine than romance.

Other names that have come and, in some cases, gone include Cameo Romances, Airmont Books, Hamilton House Romances, Dove Hill, Satinwood, Coventry Romances, Encore, Rainbow, Silverbell, Tiara and MacFadden Romances. Zebra Books once had 'Round the World Romances; now it has Leather And Lace, a line that is as sexy as it sounds.

Harlequin's name, established in Canada in 1949, has become synonymous with romance, although its namesake has more to do with light entertainment than romance. In sixteenth century Italian comedy, Harlequin was a clown who wore multicolored tights, a black mask and a cape and entertained the audience with slapstick and acrobatics. The name was appropriate in Harlequin's beginning, for its lists were a mix of genre fiction and nonfiction. Since 1964, the Harlequin imprint has been used solely for romances. A line of romantic suspense novels named Mystique Books was launched by the Canadian publisher in 1979 only to be discontinued about two years later because of poor sales.

When romance lines are launched, they often don't have the names

originally given them in planning stages; tinkering is constant. Bantam considered several names, including Stardust, for its ill-fated line of sweet romances introduced in 1982. The line came out as Circle Of Love, which symbolized a wedding ring and evoked a feeling of security and commitment. But by 1982 the romance market had shifted to sensual books, and Circle Of Love bit the dust later the same year. In 1983, it rose from its ashes as the sexier Loveswept.

That name was chosen through an in-house contest at Bantam. "I think almost every person in the company entered," says Carolyn. "The prize was a gift certificate, but naming the line was the real motivation for entering." Several employees came up with the winner.

Bantam is also planning a minor line of contemporary romances tentatively named Dawn Star Romances. The line will be published under a new imprint, Golden Apple.

Silhouette's Desire line had two predecessor names that were seriously considered: Rapture and Rendezvous. Both were tested in market research; Rapture didn't do well, and Rendezvous was unfocused. "You could rendezvous at the tenth parallel or you could rendezvous in space," says Karen Solem, vice president and editor in chief of Silhouette Books. "What does that word really mean to people?"

Even though Silhouette pays an ad agency to test and suggest names, "We usually come up with one that I suggested or someone else in the company suggested," Karen says. Special Edition and First Love were in-house suggestions.

As for the name Silhouette Books, Simon & Schuster hired an ad agency to suggest names for its new division, formed in 1979. The agency came up with dozens of them. "Some weird and some not so weird," says Kate Duffy, senior editor of Pocket Books' Tapestry Romances, who headed Silhouette at the time of its launch. "The name Silhouette suggested a logo, and I liked the way it sounded." The final decision was made by Richard Snyder, chairman and chief executive officer of Simon & Schuster, and Ron Busch, president of Pocket Books.

The fact that Rapture didn't test well for Silhouette didn't stop New American Library from choosing it for its line of sensual contemporary romances, launched in January 1983. Rapture, says editor Robin Grunder, "evokes sensuality, the aura of being in love. When you're in love, you're on a different plane—you're enraptured." Meanwhile, a predecessor to Rapture, Adventures in Love, may or may not continue, depending on the market.

NAL may launch another contemporary line with more mature heroines, referred to in house as September Romances. If the line does indeed come out, it's likely to be under another name, perhaps something that doesn't suggest to a woman that she's nearing the twilight of her life.

For Tapestry Romances, a line of historicals that Pocket Books started in the fall of 1982, Kate Duffy tried in vain to think of a suitable name. "I come up with the worst titles in the world," she confesses. "I wish I could take credit for the name, but I can't. Joan Schulhafer, our publicity manager then, came up with it. She was sitting in my office with two or three others and me, and as soon as she said 'Tapestry,' we all looked at her and said, 'That's it!' It was just the right name." After a bit of corporate lobbying, the name stuck.

Before that, says Kate, "I'd been coming up with Unicorn, Pendant, Swan, Heirloom, Heiress, Champagne, Phoenix, Dove, Orchid, Pockett—I was in a real cute mood that day—Velvet, Brocade... I was really floundering."

Tapestry, she adds, "is a nice word, says a lot, and doesn't limit me as an editor."

Furthermore, Tapestry has real historical significance. In the days before women learned to read and write, they embroidered tapestries to record events and tell stories, of hunts and feasts and of chivalrous knights and their fair ladies. The tapestries were hung on walls, and many have survived to the present day. "Romance books are like tapestries," says Kate. "They are created by women and contain a blend of myth and reality. They're a weaving together of ideas, mores and history, telling the basic love story that has endured in literature for centuries."

VII. SPREADING THE WORD

Richard Henry Gardyne Bonnycastle probably had little inkling that he was founding an international publishing empire when he established Harlequin Books in Winnipeg, Ontario in 1949. The first mayor of Winnipeg and a flamboyant printing entrepreneur, Richard owned a company that produced American paperbacks for distribution in Canada. He astutely realized that even though the market was modest, there was a greater demand than supply. Some thirty years later, Harlequin Enterprises Ltd. had sold a total of more than one *billion* copies of 3,000 titles around the world—in more than ninety countries in twenty-three languages—with an astonishingly low return rate (the percentage of unsold copies that bookstores send back to a publisher) of 20 to 25 percent (the average return rate for paperback publishers is 35 to 40 percent). It was publishing under more than thirty imprints and had cornered the romantic fiction market, so much so that the term "Harlequin" had virtually become generic for romance novels.

In addition, Harlequin had achieved a number of "firsts" in the publishing business: it became the first major line to sell through supermarkets; the first to advertise on national and prime time television; the first to treat books as a brand-name consumer product; and the first to give away books with other consumer products, such as laundry soap.

But back in 1949, romances were probably the furthest thing from Richard's mind as he set up his new company, which he intended to have publish a grab bag of fiction and nonfiction. He named it after Harlequin, the proper name of a stock character from Renaissance Italian comedy theater who provided light entertainment to his audience. For an emblem, Richard chose a Harlequin figure enclosed in a diamond.

He brought out twenty-five titles his first year, mostly reprints of westerns, mysteries and thrillers. Book number one was *The Manatee* by Nancy Bruff, subtitled *Strange Loves of a Seaman*. (One could wonder about that—a manatee is a tropical sea mammal that resembles a tuskless walrus.)

Other titles included *Here's Blood in Your Eye*, by Manning Long; *Crazy to Kill*, by Ann Cardwell; *Wolf of the Mesas*, by Charles H. Snow; *Virgin with Butterflies* by Tom Powers; and *No Nice Girl*, by Perry Lindsay.

Success was modest, but enough for Richard to keep going. Romances, however, had yet to make much of an appearance. Harlequin's first decade was dominated by male-oriented fiction, such as *Rats with Baby Faces* (W. Stanley Moss), *Yucca City Outlaw* (William Hopson) and *No Wings on a Cop* (F. Cleve Adams). Mixed in were some original fiction titles, cookbooks, how-to books, history and health (the latter included *The Normal Child*, by Dr. Elizabeth Chant Robertson and Dr. Alan Brown, and *Health, Sex and Birth Control*, by Dr. Percy Chase).

A few famous names appeared on the lists, among them mystery writers Sir Arthur Conan Doyle, Agatha Christie, James Hadley Chase, Edgar Wallace and Harry Whittington; Canadian journalists Kate Aitken and Ralph Allen; and novelists W. Somerset Maugham, Brian Moore and Jean Plaidy (better known as Victoria Holt).

Romance titles were sprinkled throughout the early years' lists, including books by an American novelist, Lucy Agnes Hancock, whose first of twenty novels was published in 1953. But it wasn't until 1957 that Harlequin published its first Mills & Boon romance reprint, *Hospital in Buwambo*, by Ann Vinton. Mills & Boon Ltd., established in London in 1908, was well known for its hardcover romances, all written by women, most of them British. These romances, what Richard's wife, Mary, called "nice books with happy endings," sold well. Mary favored them, and it was largely due to her influence that romances began to dominate Harlequin's lists by 1960.

Three short years later, the last nonromance book appeared under the Harlequin imprint: *Never A Day So Bright*, the autobiography of Kate Aitken. The following year, 1964, the Harlequin imprint was devoted solely to romances by Mills & Boon authors. Ninety-six titles were issued.

After that, the Harlequin name became synonymous with romances. The books featured young, usually virginal heroines pursued by older, more sophisticated, usually arrogant men. The heroines always won a marriage proposal, usually after their pristine virtue subdued the challenge from a nasty "other woman." The books were exceedingly chaste by today's standards—mostly the heroines just got kissed, grabbed, pushed around and sexually threatened by the heroes.

But female readers loved them. They were romances with a little armchair travel thrown in, for most took place in an exotic setting foreign to a North American audience, such as Spain, Greece, Australia or Britain.

Richard Bonnycastle died in 1968, and Harlequin Books became a publicly held company (today Richard's son, Richard A.N. Bonnycastle, is chairman of the board, though he is no longer active in management). Company headquarters were moved to Toronto.

The Boom Years

The 1970s marked the beginning of a phenomenal growth period for Harlequin: international expansion, mass marketing, new lines and acquisitions. Throughout the 1960s, the company had had a small presence in the United States. In 1970, it began moving into the United States in a big way by establishing a distributorship with Pocket Books, the mass market paperback division of Simon & Schuster. And in 1971, Richard A.N. Bonnycastle hired a new president: W. Lawrence Heisey, a Harvard Business School grad and marketing whiz who sometimes referred to himself as "an old soap salesman from Procter & Gamble." Lawrence, who had spent thirteen years at Procter & Gamble, brought with him the brand-name, mass marketing strategies which have made that company so successful and began applying them to the book business.

In his first years as president, Harlequin and Mills & Boon merged, forming Harlequin Enterprises Ltd. The merger assured Harlequin of a steady supply of hardcover romances for its Harlequin Romance line.

New programs and product lines were rapidly initiated—a Harlequin Reader Service to handle direct-mail sales of backlisted titles; a Scholar's Choice division to distribute educational materials throughout Canada; new imprints for collections of popular backlisted titles; and a major new line, Harlequin Presents, started in 1973 as a vehicle to showcase popular authors and provide more sophisticated stories. Initially, only three authors were featured—Anne Mather, Anne Hampson and Violet Winspear—but the ranks eventually swelled to more than fifty by the end of the decade. Harlequin Romances, meanwhile, continued to offer traditional or "sweet" romances.

By 1973, Harlequin was the world's largest publisher of romances, and its market share continued to grow until it claimed about 80 percent.

While the company was tapping more and more Americans as readers, it was shutting them out as writers. Since 1964, Harlequin had exclusively published reprints of Mills & Boon romances. But in 1976, it broke with tradition and published a romance by an unknown American author, Janet Dailey, who had been reading Harlequins since 1968. Janet had finally decided to write a romance herself and sent her first manuscript to Harlequin in innocence, unaware of the Mills & Boon exclusivity. In addition, *No Quarter Asked* was set in Texas, a far cry from the Greek isles and other requisite exotic settings so familiar to Harlequin readers. But published it was, and the book marked the beginning of Janet's meteoric rise as a romance novelist, paving the way for more American authors to get published in the genre. During the next four years, Janet wrote more than fifty novels for Harlequin, all set in the United States, before she was lured away to write for a new competitor on the scene: Simon & Schuster's Silhouette Books, formed in 1979.

Marketing Books As Consumer Goods

Early in the go-go decade of the 1970s, Harlequin began employing the same mass marketing principles used to sell toothpaste, soap, deodorant and a host of packaged goods. National television advertising, which began in Canada and the United States in 1975 and was supplemented by print ads, emphasized the brand-name reliability and quality of the Harlequin line rather than the appeal of a particular title or author. Harlequin books were positioned as "romantic fiction in good taste," and the consumer knew exactly what she was getting every time she bought one, regardless of title or author: a romance with a happy ending (marriage), without explicit sex or offensive language.

Specially designed racks to encourage multiple sales were installed in stores wherever possible, and Harlequins were offered as free premiums with various consumer products, such as laundry detergent. Advertising was extensive, especially on TV, and by 1982, Harlequin was allocating $15 million a year to buy television time (including network prime time) and consumer and trade print space.

Expansion and Acquisitions

Until the 1970s, Harlequin had licensed foreign rights for some of its books. Then the idea of establishing its own publishing presence in other countries, besides the United States, became attractive. Expansion was bolstered by an influx of cash in 1975, when Harlequin sold controlling interest—53 percent—to Torstar Corp., a diversified communications and entertainment company that owns the *Toronto Star* and other newspapers; Comac Communications, Canada's second largest publisher of consumer magazines; and part of Infomart, which is involved in electronic publishing.

Also in 1975, foreign expansions began in earnest; they included the Netherlands, Germany (a joint venture with a German publisher), France, Japan, Greece, Scandinavia, Mexico and Brazil. By the end of the decade, the foreign operations were bringing Harlequins to readers in ninety-eight countries in eighteen languages. The United States, Canada and the United Kingdom remained Harlequin's largest market, with the United States accounting for more than half its net revenues by the end of the 1970s. France, Germany and the Netherlands became the largest non-English-speaking markets.

Besides romances (contemporary and historical), Harlequin Enterprises was publishing educational materials, mysteries, thrillers and science fiction books under non-Harlequin imprints.

Acquisitions made in the late 1970s included the Ideals Publishing Corp. of Milwaukee, Wisconsin, publisher of inspirational magazines and books, cookbooks and greeting cards; Marshall Editions of London, an international book packager; the Miles Kimball Co. of Oshkosh, Wisconsin, a mail-order business of gifts, household goods, books and assorted products; and a controlling interest in the Lauffer Co., a North American publishing group that puts out entertainment and teen magazines.

In addition, Harlequin Magazines, Inc. was established in New York City and acquired "substantial holdings" in *ARTnews*, *Antiques World*, *Weight Watchers Magazine*, *Photo Life* and *Snow Goer.*

Harlequin also entered the film industry, first in 1976 with *Leopard in the Snow,* a feature film based on an Anne Mather Harlequin by the same title. Plans were made to produce several more films, all based on the publisher's own romances, of course.

Harlequin's growth was impressive and steady but also quiet. In the United States, what little press attention there was on romances focused on the booming market in historicals and bodice rippers. Harlequin had no significant competition for the market in short (50,000 to 60,000 words) contemporary romances—particularly its style of brand-name romances. It had an estimated 80 percent of the international market; its annual sales had increased from less than 25 million copies at the start of the seventies to nearly 200 million by the beginning of the eighties, nearly a tenfold growth in readership; and it had achieved a 75 percent brand awareness among women eighteen years and older. Its advertising theme, "No one touches the heart of a woman quite like a Harlequin," was getting to be a household slogan. "They let everyone believe that only a small number of women were reading these books," says one U.S. publishing executive, and another adds, "They were doing it very quietly and laughing all the way to the bank."

A Monopoly Comes To An End

But the secrets of success couldn't be kept forever, and Harlequin's golden era came to an end at the close of the 1970s. In 1979, Harlequin executives decided the company would handle its own U.S. distribution, and Pocket Books was fired. "It was just a marketing decision," says Josh Gaspero, formerly president of Harlequin's North American Division and now an industry consultant. "Simon & Schuster did a good job over the years, but as we got into market expansion and other categories, we wanted to control our own distribution. The Pocket Books sales force also distributed titles that were in conflict with titles we wanted to publish."

But Richard Snyder, chairman and chief executive of Simon & Schuster, and Ron Busch, president of Pocket Books, were not about to let go of a good and lucrative market. They created a new division, Silhouette Books, to compete with Harlequin on its own turf, the brand-name contemporary romance, and in a big way, backed with a heavy advertising budget.

At this same time, the U.S. market was ripe for harvesting by U.S. publishers. The success of historical romances had set the stage for a move into the contemporary field. Dell Candlelight Romances, operating at low speed for a number of years, came out with a sexy new line, Dell Candlelight Ecstasy, that zoomed to success. Jove launched Second Chance At Love, a contemporary line with yet another twist—the heroine who's already been around the track once. Suddenly, nearly every major publisher in the United States wanted one of the goose's golden eggs, and the fierce competition quickly cut Harlequin's market share down to about 58 percent (Harlequin's estimate based on 1982 sales).

For Harlequin, the decade of the 1980s began with consolidation, because of competition, worldwide recession and an increase in book returns (although 1981 net sales of books reached an all-time high of 197 million copies, the rate of return of unsold books was higher than it was in 1980). The company made a strategic decision, according to the Torstar Corp.'s annual report in 1981, "to get back to basics and concentrate on what it knows best"—romances. Accordingly, some unprofitable properties were divested, including the Laufer magazines and Scholar's Choice. Imprints that hadn't met expectations were discontinued, including Mystique Books (romantic suspense) and Raven House (mystery).

Consolidation didn't preclude expansion in certain areas, however, particularly the popular "sensual romance." The Harlequin Presents line hadn't kept pace with the spicy books rolling off American presses, and so a new line of longer, more sophisticated books with more sensual detail, Superromance, was launched in 1981 under the Worldwide Library imprint, with a $4 million advertising budget. By mid-1982, production of the successful line had been boosted to four releases a month. In 1983, another more sensual line, Harlequin American Romance, was launched with a $5 million ad campaign. The longer, sexier books were designed to compete directly against American romances on their home ground.

Since 1980, Harlequin has also increased its promotional activity, including a series of "thank you" luncheons for readers in cities around the United States; sweepstakes and contests; and greater visibility of its authors. For example, Anne Mather, one of Harlequin's most popular authors with more than eighty titles published and some ninety million copies in print, wrote a lead title for Worldwide Library, *Stormspell,* published in 1982.

Although American competition has significantly cut into the romance pie, Harlequin is still a leading seller with a staunchly loyal audience. B. Dalton Bookseller, the second largest chain of bookstores in the United States, ranked Harlequin Presents and Harlequin Romance as the second and sixth top selling lines of 1982, respectively. (Dell Candlelight Ecstasy was first; Silhouette's Special Edition, Romance and Desire lines were third, fourth and seventh, respectively; and Jove's Second Chance At Love ranked fifth.)

Publishers expect the mid-1980's to be shake-out years in the romance genre; not all the lines on the market now are expected to survive the long haul. There's no doubt the grandmother of them all will continue to be a leader. But will it be as Number One—or as Number Two?

A LITTLE FUN WITH SOME HARLEQUIN FACTS

1. In 1981, Harlequin sold 197 million books—almost six books a second.

2. Harlequin has sold one billion books in the last ten years, and if you set out to read all of them at a rate of two books per hour, you'd be reading for the next 250,000 years.

3. If all the Harlequin books sold in a single day in 1981 were stacked on top of each other, the pile would be sixteen times higher than the 102-story World Trade Center in New York City.

4. If all the pages of the one billion books sold in the last ten years were placed end to end, they could cover the entire states of Colorado and Pennsylvania.

5. If all the words in the 197 million books sold in 1981 were laid end to end, they would stretch 1,000 times around the earth, 93 times to the moon and halfway to the sun.

Fred Kerner tosses bridal bouquet

SYMBOL OF AN ENTERTAINER

No one at Harlequin purports to know exactly why founder Richard Bonnycastle chose Harlequin to be the name and emblem of his fledgling publishing enterprise. Whatever his reasons, the choice was appropriate, for in Renaissance times, Harlequin was a stage character who amused and entertained people. Richard probably chose it because it symbolized what he hoped to do with his books—entertain.

The origins of Harlequin (the character's proper name) actually date back to the theater of ancient Rome. It was customary for all characters to wear masks; actors who portrayed foreign slaves and did slapstick covered their faces with soot.

In sixteenth century Italy, traveling bands of actors put on shows called *commedia dell'arte.* The troupes played standard characters, including a hunchback and two clowns, one of whom was Harlequin. A wild, zany character, Harlequin provided the comic relief and performed acrobatics. In skits he was often a man's valet and the suitor of a maid.

By the early to mid-eighteenth century, the *commedia dell'arte* had picked up popularity in England. The harlequinade, as it was known there, usually consisted of a pantomime in which Harlequin and his maid lover, Colombine, were chased by her father, Pantaloon, and his servant.

Harlequin wore a black mask, and his original costume was simply long pants and a peasant's shirt covered with colored patches. Eventually the clothes became more tight fitting, and the patches evolved into patterns of triangles and diamonds. His cap, originally a simple, soft one, became double-pointed.

The Harlequin emblem for Harlequin books wears no cap, but he does have a black mask and tights with diamond-shaped patches. He sits cross-legged inside a diamond.

The Harlequin name was a better fit for Richard's first decade or so, for his lists then were an eclectic bag of adventures, mysteries, mainstream fiction, history, cookbooks, westerns and science fiction as well as romances. Since 1964, the Harlequin imprint has been used solely on romances, which have indeed entertained millions of readers around the world.

ROAD SHOW IN PINK

The hotel tables are set with pink linen tablecloths, shiny crystal and china and pretty arrangements of pink and white flowers. The guests, between 200 to 350 of them, nearly all women, are here to discuss one of their favorite topics, romance—in particular, Harlequin romances, since Harlequin is the host of this gathering, footing the bill of some $12,000.

What's this all about? With competition from American romance lines pressing on all sides, Harlequin has found a novel way to reach out directly to readers—invite them to "thank you" luncheons.

The luncheons, begun in 1980, are staged in a dozen or so cities around the United States each year. Harlequin runs an advance ad in the local newspaper inviting people interested in attending to fill out an entry blank and opinion poll (who do you think is the most romantic man in America, for example). At least 1,000 people usually respond, and from those entries the guests are selected in a random drawing. There is no cost to attend. It's all frothy fun for guests but serious promotion for Harlequin.

The program consists of spiels on the merits of Harlequin novels—"No one touches the heart of a woman quite like Harlequin," as its ad slogan goes—and includes an author or two who speak on their work and on the genre. Results of the opinion poll are announced. In 1982, actor Tom Selleck *(Magnum P.I.)* was a big winner as most romantic man, and actress Jane Fonda was often named most interesting woman.

After lunch, a huge pink and white frosted cake is brought out, and women who've recently celebrated wedding anniversaries help cut it. There's romantic mood music, and as a finale, Fred Kerner, vice president of publishing, tosses a bridal bouquet of roses and baby's breath into the crowd. All guests are sent home with little hot-pink bags containing sample Harlequin books.

The publicity value of these "thank you, loyal fans" gatherings is enormous. Harlequin has a captive audience for its pitch and always gets press coverage, which reaches thousands more than actually attend. To help the publisher's now-competitive search for new talent, prospective authors are invited to send manuscripts. And the free book samples go to receptive consumers, who, if they like what they read, might be encouraged to pick up an extra Harlequin or two on their next trip to the store—or choose Harlequin instead of the competition.

Pantaloon
Columbine
Harlequin
Clown
Clown

VII. SPREADING THE WORD

CHAPTER THREE

Silhouette: Looking to Be Number One

Short and sweet—that's the history of Simon & Schuster's Silhouette Books: conceived in 1979; born in 1980; snared the lead in the American romance publishing business by 1981; multiplied to four lines by 1982 and five lines by 1983. By the end of 1982, just two and a half short years after its launch, Silhouette was publishing more than twenty titles a month, was licensed in seventeen foreign countries and claimed to have 39 percent of the U.S. romance market. It had boosted annual domestic advertising expenditures to some $22 million for 1982—not only more than Harlequin spent but more than the entire U.S. publishing industry spent. And it expected to overtake Harlequin for the Number One spot in contemporary romances. "We set the tone for what this category is all about," says Al Lieberman, senior vice president of marketing.

Yes, the rise was short and sweet, but not necessarily easy. Cracking a monopoly market—and Harlequin had a monopoly—seldom is. "It's been a tough struggle," acknowledges Karen Solem, vice president and editor in chief. "We came out with one line and six books a month, while Harlequin had twelve books a month and they'd been in the business for years. We were the new kid on the block and had to overcome enormous obstacles, from booksellers who would only carry Harlequins to readers who considered 'Harlequin' as a generic name for romances. We've made some incredible accomplishments."

Consider these figures: from a zero starting point, 21 million books—$35 million retail—were sold in the United States in Silhouette's first year, on the strength of a single line, Silhouette Romance. The second year, sales nearly tripled—60 million copies worth $100 million retail, plus another 1.8 million copies sold in foreign markets. For its third year, the division was projecting 80 million copies worth more than $144 million retail, representing approximately 42 percent of the domestic romance market.

Silhouette had a bit of a bumpy start, however. The division was created to compete with Harlequin after the Toronto publisher fired Simon & Schuster's Pocket Books as its U.S. distributor in 1979. Simon & Schuster had spent a decade developing the U.S. market for Harlequin. "We created the Harlequin success here in the U.S.," says Al. "We have a powerful sales force, and we got them into supermarkets and drugstore chains." When Harlequin pulled the plug, Simon & Schuster was not about to let a lucrative chunk of business slide out the door. The profitability of romances was receiving increased press attention, Harlequin seemed to be minting money on the heart throb theme, Simon & Schuster had developed mass marketing techniques... why not go for a piece of the action?

Which it did, immediately. The Silhouette Books division was created, market research was initiated and the first Silhouette Romance titles appeared in May 1980 with the advertising theme "It's your own special time."

The concept and name for Silhouette Books were developed and approved by Richard E. Snyder, chairman and chief executive officer of Simon & Schuster, and Ron Busch, publisher and president of Pocket Books. The romance genre had been treated like a stepchild at most other American publishing houses, but Richard and Ron were willing to invest heavily in research, advertising and promotion. "Silhouette is a case history of how two people changed the whole publishing business around," says Al.

In September 1980, John C. Gfeller was named executive vice president and general manager, and in 1981 president, of the new division. John had previously been the senior sales and marketing executive for Gulf + Western's Consumer Products Division and vice president-marketing for G + W's Madison Square Garden Corporation (G + W is Simon & Schuster's parent company).

Several months after launch, Harlequin filed a suit in the U.S. District Court claiming that

Silhouette's cover design infringed on Harlequin's, constituting unfair competition. Simon & Schuster countersued, claiming Harlequin was attempting to block distribution and sale of Silhouette novels (Simon & Schuster earlier had filed another suit against Harlequin involving commissions claims as Harlequin's U.S. distributor). As a result of the suit, the Silhouette cover design was changed, from all white to white with a purple spine and border.

Not surprisingly, the early Silhouette Romances resembled the format of Harlequin romances, which had set the standards and ruled the industry for so long. The first writer's guidelines asked for young, inexperienced heroines and older, more sophisticated heroes, who often were hot-tempered or moody in a Gothic sort of way. Sexual foreplay almost always had to be interrupted.

"Of course the books were like Harlequins," says Kate Duffy, the first editor in chief of Silhouette and now senior editor of Pocket Books' Tapestry Romances. "That's what the writers had been reading for years, and that was our competition. These were writers who'd submitted to Harlequin and were turned down on the basis of their manuscripts or the fact that they were American. We had a whole raft of writers who had manuscripts sitting on their shelves and no outlet for publishing them. If we'd come out with something different, we wouldn't have been able to woo the readers away from Harlequin and Dell Candlelight, the two major lines at that time."

Kate credits her successor, Karen, with realizing the expansion possibilities for Silhouette, such as longer books and sexier books. A major market study finished by November 1980 helped pinpoint reader ages and preferences, which helped strategy development. Each new line was directed at its own audience, with some overlap. "We coined the phrase, 'brand-name category romance,' " says Al.

Reader response to Silhouette's launch was tremendous and positive, and it also clued in the editors that there was a waiting and ready market for more sophisticated romances. Given the changes in society wrought by women's lib and sexual lib, the heroine who was pure as driven snow didn't seem plausible to many readers. "People were just begging for more romances that really met their needs," says Karen. "It was important to them to read stories about people they could identify with, so we made some immediate changes. Silhouette heroines were not going to be the eighteen- and nineteen-year-old heroines you found in Harlequins but would be more career-oriented, older and better educated.

"Traditional romances have been around in the same format since the 1950s. But a lot of changes have taken place in society and in day-to-day living, and we tried to incorporate some of those changes and issues into our next line, Special Edition (launched in February 1982). Special Editions had less of a category feel and also touched upon topics previously taboo in contemporary romances, such as women getting out of abusive marriages and making a new life for themselves.

"Another major change we made in Special Edition was in the characters. The heroine was twenty-eight or thirty, maybe even in her early forties, and there wasn't a big age disparity between her and the hero," Karen says. "He wasn't going to be the father figure to her that he is in so many traditional romances."

Gradually, writer's guidelines became less and less specific. Now, says senior editor Alicia M. Condon, "almost anything can be done as long as it's done well."

Silhouette added a young adult line, First Love, in 1981; a sensual "short read" line, Desire, in 1982; and a longer sensual line with elements of suspense and adventure, Intimate Moments, in 1983.

While the spotlight has shifted to the more realistic, sexier lines Silhouette offers—Special

#213
JANET
AILEY
eparate
abins
Romance
Silhouette Special Edition
#31
53531-5
$1.95
Tears of
Yesterday
Silhouette Romance
57207-5
$1.75
#207
SUZANNAH
WINDHAM
More Precious
Than Pearls
Silhouette Romance
Silhouette Special Edition
#12
53512-9
$1.95
TRACY
SINCLAIR
Never Give
Your Heart

Karen Solem

John C. Gfeller

Edition, Desire and Intimate Moments—"there's still a big readership for the traditional Silhouette Romance, though they've become sexier, too," notes editor Leslie Wainger. "We have something for everyone."

Indeed, that's exactly the way Silhouette has positioned itself in the marketplace: whatever your preferences are in contemporary brand-name romantic fiction, Silhouette claims to have it: short and sweet (Silhouette Romance); short and sexy (Desire); long and sexy (Special Edition); long, sexy and adventurous (Intimate Moments); or young adult (First Love). The editors strive for diversity in plot and setting so that not all books coming out in a particular month are about divorcees living in Texas, for example.

Silhouette editors tread carefully the trend towards realism and sensuality in romances, feeling that both can be overdone. "There's a fine line between realism and fantasy, and some romances on the market have gone over that line," says Alicia. "In a romance, you must keep the fantasy, yet it must be real enough for the reader to sympathize and identify with the character. People don't read romances to find what's going on in the world—they have newspapers for that. They want to indulge their fantasies."

Realism means keeping contrived circumstances out of the plots, says Leslie, in favor of characters who face believable problems and act convincingly. "They have to ring true, but they don't necessarily have to be probable or even possible situations. Mimicking real life situations can be boring."

A fine line also exists for sensuality, Karen says. "It's a matter of good taste. We try to do nothing that would offend anyone, although there's always that small percent of readers who's going to think something is an outrageously racy story. But I believe very strongly in not publishing anything that's graphically explicit—that's not my job. My job is to publish romances. We have tried to meet the demand for heightened sensuality, and we've come out with some pretty sexy stories."

Readers will tire of too much sex in romances, observes Alicia, stressing that a sensual book can evoke a good emotional response without detailed descriptions of sexual encounters. She cites as an example the positive reader response to *The Cowboy and the Lady* (Desire) by Diana Palmer, in which the hero and heroine never make love, though they try twice, yet the sexual tension is sustained throughout the novel.

The Cover Story

One of the most important elements in a successful line is the cover design. The design for Silhouette's five lines was done by Milt Charles, vice president and art director of Pocket Books, who is responsible for creating more than 300 covers a year for Silhouette alone, plus covers for Pocket Books. Milt has introduced some innovative techniques in paperback cover design, such as distinctive die cuts, which helped Janet Dailey get established in mass market. For those unfamiliar with the term, a die cut cover has a cutout space showing an illustration underneath.

The basic design format for each Silhouette line went through as many as fifty variations before a final choice was made, says Milt. "We've made a lot of authors and a lot of books strictly on the covers, but covers don't do all of it. Covers will get a lot of people to pick a book up, but finally, the book itself has to deliver."

Milt uses between fifteen and twenty prominent illustrators to render the covers. "The more artistic the cover, the more the audience loves it," he says. "Each book is read carefully, a reader's report is submitted to me, and the illustrator and myself are careful to uphold the author's integrity—we're not going to put a sexy cover on a book that isn't." In spite of the

Silhouette Desire
#5
JUDITH BAKER
When Last We Loved
Silhouette Desire
#2
NICOLE MONET
Love's Silver Web
Silhouette Desire
#4
SUZANNE CAREY
Kiss and Tell
Silhouette Desire
#3
RITA CLAY
Wise Folly
Silhouette Desire
#6
KATHRYN MALLORY
A Frenchman's Kiss
Silhouette Desire
STEPHANIE JAMES
Corporate Affair

Silhouette Desire
JUDITH BAKER
When Last We Loved

high monthly volume, Milt says that "you can't ever be dogmatic. You have to be sensitive and have a high regard for the people reading the genre."

A Writer's Choice

Silhouette now has about 185 writers, and manuscripts, solicited and unsolicited, arrive at a rate of 450 to 600 a month, more than any other American romance line. All manuscripts go through a first reading by trusted free-lancers, who write a report and make a recommendation. Then someone in house goes over the reports to make sure they're on target, particularly if the recommendation is negative. Those manuscripts which pass the initial screening receive more readings in house. "If we're interested in buying something, it may go through six or eight readings," says Karen.

Most of Silhouette's authors were discovered from the unsolicited manuscripts, known unromantically in the business as the slush pile. "The best authors are the readers of romances, not the professional writers who can handle just about anything but can't capture the romance," Karen says. "The best writers don't have to be told what the format is—they know it from reading the books."

"Professional writers often don't understand the essence of romances," agrees Leslie. "There are no men's sex fantasies and no women sleeping their way to the top. These books are full of emotion. The reader should want to be the heroine and have her romantic fantasy."

A few of Silhouette's published writers are men, but the editors say that most male-authored submissions miss the mark. They either have too much graphic sex, they contain rape scenes—an anathema to the readers—or they are inadequate in descriptions of emotions and sensual detail.

While romances have been almost entirely from the heroine's point of view, more and more books are bringing in the hero's viewpoint, to a limited extent. "The readers like that," says Leslie. "Getting inside his head makes him more human and helps the reader understand his actions—but it's still a woman's fantasy."

Advertising, Promotion And Expansion

Like its chief competitor, Harlequin, Silhouette is investing substantial sums in advertising and promotion. In the United States alone, $22 million were allocated for 1982, including $15 million for the adult lines and $7 million for First Love. Most of the money is spent on television spots, including network and prime time. Network TV ads are run twenty-one days a month, says Al, and are supplemented by print ads and direct mail. Advertising is rotated to feature each line. For the launch of Intimate Moments, $1 million was allocated for advertising, mostly network television ads.

John brought in A.C. Nielsen to monitor Silhouette's penetration in the mass market, supermarkets and drugstores, and relies on bookstores to report its penetration in them. He began hiring food brokers in 1981 to help keep racks full in supermarkets.

Beyond books, there are movie opportunities. In 1982, Silhouette contracted with Paramount Video, a unit of Paramount Pictures Corp., to produce full-length movies of Silhouette novels, to be shown in theaters or on television. Filming is scheduled to begin in 1983.

Other ventures may include tie-ins with such products as swimwear or apparel.

Within its first two and a half years, Silhouette either licensed foreign rights in or began exporting to seventeen major countries, including Canada (including French Canada),

Britain, Australia, New Zealand, Germany, France, Brazil (Portuguese), Greece, Turkey, Israel, Italy, Japan, Denmark, Sweden and Taiwan (Chinese). Distributors in those nations in turn send Silhouettes elsewhere, so that the books appear in just about every country in the world. The Netherlands, where Harlequin is a strong presence, was the first country to buy foreign rights. Silhouettes appear there under the name Story Roman.

In 1982, Silhouette sold an estimated 1.8 million copies outside the United States. Approximate sales in the major markets in foreign editions were Germany—87,000; France—70,000; Italy—35,000; Britain—30,000; Japan—30,000; and the Netherlands—25,000.

The Silhouette Romance line is the most widely distributed, but there is an increasing interest in Desire, says Marcella Berger, vice president and director of foreign rights for Simon & Schuster. The American taste for sexy romances seems to pose no problem. "I think the Europeans are ahead of us on acceptance of that," comments Marcella. Interestingly, Japan, seemingly a staid and conservative nation, was the first non-English-speaking nation to take Desire.

When a foreign publisher buys the rights to Silhouette, it produces its own books in whatever format is appropriate for its market—but changes in titles, jacket copy and content are limited to cultural and translation reasons. "They don't censor them," Marcella says. "They can't make changes without our permission."

For the most part, little is changed. In Japan, market research indicated the Desire covers might be too sexy, and so they were altered. "They thought that women would be embarrassed to have them around the house where children could see them," Marcella explains.

In Germany, Silhouettes are published in magazine format, about the size of *Reader's Digest*, with photographs on the covers instead of illustrations. The books are called Natalie instead of Silhouette—women respond more to female names on publications—and the advertising theme is "Say yes to love, say yes to Natalie."

Advertising and promotion vary by country, too. Most nations in Europe have restrictions on television advertising, so print and radio are used heavily. In Germany enormous posters are used to a large extent. In Japan one of the nation's most popular female singers asked Silhouette for permission to cut a record about the romance line. The song, "Silhouette Romance," was recorded on a 45 rpm and hit number seven on the pop charts.

The foreign publishers undertake their own advertising and promotion, though Silhouette provides them with advice and help. Al Lieberman travels around the world consulting with various publishers on what techniques will get the best results.

Meanwhile, letters from readers continue to roll in. Some announce they're going to name their babies after characters in the books. "One woman said she was going to name her baby Silhouette," says Karen. "If it was a boy, she was going to name him after her favorite hero. I thought that was priceless."

GROWING UP WITH FIRST LOVE

Young adult romances, popular in the 1950s, are enjoying a resurgence, and at least six publishers offer lines targeted to this audience. But Silhouette's First Love Line, launched in late 1981, goes far beyond the basic boy-meets-girl plot.

"They're not simplistic books, they're really existential books," says Nancy D. Jackson, senior editor of First Love. "They help kids find out about themselves by taking them on a voyage of self-discovery. Kids are looking for values, and these books teach self-respect for the individual and respect for others."

"Though we call them 'First Love,' they're not really romances for kids," adds Karen Solem,

Ogilvy & Mather Partners, Inc.
380 Madison Avenue, New York, New York 10017 • Telephone: (212) 687-2510

CLIENT: SIMON & SCHUSTER
PRODUCT: SILHOUETTE
TITLE: "IMAGINATION"
COMM'L NO.: XXOM 2733

1. (MUSIC UNDER) WOMAN: (VO) Romance (SFX: CLICK) can take you many places but only so far.

2. Beautiful (SFX: CLICK) as it is,

3. it has limits

4. but Desire starts (SFX: CLICK) where romance leaves off

5. and bursts into something beyond.

6. Something Silhouette Books

7. (SFX: CLICK) now captures

8. in a startling new series about love.

9. Silhouette Desire.

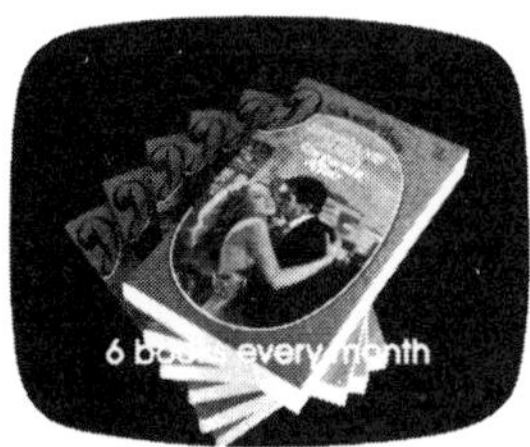

10. Beyond romance, where the possibilities are limited

11. only by your imagination.

12. Silhouette Desire. (MUSIC OUT)

Silhouette vice president and editor in chief. "They're about growing up, making friends and planning for the future. They're not really problem books, either—they're where the problems end, that you can make a better life for yourself and be responsible for yourself. You see solutions and hope in these books."

The girl doesn't necessarily get the boy in the end, either. Perhaps she decides she's not that interested in him, after all, or she doesn't want to change for him.

"We felt the 'get a date for the prom' books were outdated," comments Nancy. "Kids today don't wait around the telephone—they're more independent and they work at jobs more. They don't go steady much; they go out in groups. They're interested in relationships, but romance is not the whole focus of their lives—they're too much grounded in reality." Consequently, says Nancy, "you can't get away with fantasy as much as you can in the adult books."

Silhouette expected an audience of primary fifteen- and sixteen-year-old girls but found a much broader range, from eleven to nineteen, with more of the readers weighting the younger end.

"It's a fabulous market," says Karen. "The kids are wild about the books. They like characters they can relate to who speak their language and who are going through the same things they are. When you're that age, you feel so alone, and problems and situations are so awesome you feel you can't deal with them.

"About 50 percent of our mail is from kids, and they write heartwarming, heartwrenching letters," Karen says. "Things like, 'You'll never know how much this book helped me.' "

As in most books in the young adult romance category, sex is a minor element in First Love, usually limited to a little kissing or hugging. "We try to put forth the idea that you can be friends before you get more involved with someone," says Karen. "These books aren't particularly sexy."

From her three dozen or so writers, Nancy insists on good English in the books, permitting only a little slang.

The plots do not always portray white middle-class, college-bound teenagers growing up in comfortable suburban areas with both Mom and Dad under the same roof. On the other hand, they don't focus on juvenile delinquents, crime, drug abuse, premarital sex and unwanted pregnancy, as did many "problem" young adult books of the 1960s.

"These are books about the good, normal kids," says Karen. "They're sensitive, warm books."

THE FIVE FACES OF SILHOUETTE

Silhouette Romance
Launched May 1980
Features the traditional romance format of a young, inexperienced heroine and older, more sophisticated hero. Popular authors: Nora Roberts, Janet Dailey, Dixie Browning, Anne Hampson.

Silhouette Special Edition
Launched February 1982
Longer, more sophisticated and more realistic plots centering on the developing relationship between hero and heroine. Heroines tend to be older and more independent than in Silhouette Romances. Popular authors: Brooke Hastings, Sondra Stanford, Janet Dailey, Linda Shaw.

Silhouette Desire
Launched May 1982
Sensual books with the sophistication level of Silhouette Special Editions but shorter in length. Popular authors: Stephanie James, Suzanne Simms, Nicole Monet.

Silhouette Intimate Moments
Launched May 1983
A combination of the heightened sensuality of Desire plus the length and depth of Special Edition, with added elements of adventure, suspense, glamour and melodrama.
Popular authors: Kristin James, Parris Afton Bonds, Nora Roberts, Barbara Faith, Stephanie James, Pat Wallace.

Silhouette First Love
Launched October 1981
For girls in their teen and pre-teen years, upbeat stories about growing up and first romantic encounters, set in America. Popular authors: Elaine Harper, Caroline Cooney, Dorothy Francis.

VII. SPREADING THE WORD

Besides Silhouette, two other contemporary, brand-name American lines greatly influenced the shape of the romantic fiction industry at the beginning of the 1980s: Dell Candlelight Ecstasy and Jove's Second Chance At Love. Both lines introduced new elements to the traditional romance story line. Ecstasy introduced more sex and sensuality, and Second Chance the heroine who's more of a modern woman, is more experienced in life and has already had a major love that ended for one reason or another. Second Chance At Love also offered more sensuality.

Bantam, which entered the brand-name romance market much later than Dell and Jove, began with a sweet, wholesome product whose potential customers had switched to the sexier books. Circle Of Love went down in flames, but Bantam quickly bounced back with Loveswept, a sensual line.

A Lot Of Ecstasy

Considering the thousands and thousands of dollars that romance publishers spend on market research to find out just what readers want to buy, the success of the Ecstasy line is remarkable. The spicy romances were the idea of an editor, Vivian Stephens, and the first books were published with no fanfare. An immediate sellout, the concept was expanded and continued, and in 1982, B. Dalton Bookseller ranked Dell Candlelight Ecstasy as the top selling line, ahead of Harlequin, Silhouette and a host of others. The line accounts for 25 percent of Dell's overall sales. By November 1982 Ecstasies were being released at an annual rate of 30 million copies.

Ann Gisonny

Before Ecstasy, Dell had been publishing a Dell Candlelight Romance line, which was launched in July 1967 with *Ellen Mathews: Mission Nurse,* by Ralph E. Hayes. The line was a mix of doctor-nurse books, intrigues, Gothics, Regencies and sweet contemporary romances. "They were the basic governess-gets-her-man plots in which the heroines all go to Greece for the summer," comments Ann Gisonny, senior editor of the Ecstasy line. "Then two books hit the stands and forever changed the face of romance."

The two books were the first Ecstasies: *The Tawny Gold Man* by Amii Lorin and *Gentle Pirate* by Jayne Castle, which were published in December 1980. Vivian was editing the Candlelight Romance line at the time, and she felt instinctively that American readers wanted more realistic treatment of sex in romances, though not necessarily blow-by-blow descriptions. She was right—the first titles sold out within a week.

Two years and millions of copies later Dell increased its Ecstasy titles to eight a month and printings from 250,000 copies per title to 300,000 copies—"a lot of ecstasy," Ann notes. By 1982, sales had increased 450 percent since the line's beginning. That year Dell committed more than $1 million to consumer and trade advertising and promotion.

In addition to Jayne Castle and Amii Lorin, popular Dell authors include Jo Calloway, Rachel Ryan, Elaine Raco Chase and Bonnie Drake.

Influenced by the success of Ecstasy, other publishers spiced up their romances or launched new lines of sexier books, creating the fastest growing segment of the romance market. Many of today's spicy romances make the early Ecstasy titles look tame by comparison. However, says Ann, the trend towards hotter and hotter books has ended, though romances continue to be sensual. Readers, after all, want a good story and romance, not just a series of love scenes.

Ann receives between 100 to 200 submissions a month. "All are read very closely by either free-lancers or someone in house," she says. She agrees with other romance editors that the

116

A Candlelight Ecstasy Romance®

CAUGHT IN THE RAIN

DELL•10999•1.95

Shirley Hart

best writers are true fans of the genre. Typically they're between twenty-five and thirty-five years old. "They see something in the genre that they think they can do better," says Ann. "Professionals can see the mechanics and structure, but often not the blood and guts of a romance.

"We're not prescriptive about the love scenes," she adds. "We just want them to be an intense experience for the reader."

The cover design of the Candlelight Ecstasy line—an illustration inside an oval inside a square—is an updated version of the covers of the old, more sedate Candlelight Romance line, according to associate art director Patty Pecoraro. Nothing modest about the illustrations of embracing couples, however; some of them are pretty hot and zingy.

Dell plans to expand its sensual horizons with two new lines: Dell Candlelight Ecstasy Supreme and Temptation. The Supremes, under Ann's stewardship, are longer books than Ecstasies and feature subplots, multiple perspectives, shifts in location, adventure and other elements that move them out of the pure category romance area. Each Supreme is intended to stand on its own rather than be part of a series, Ann says. Temptation will be short, sensual contemporaries—"frankly erotic"—with subplots and more emphasis on secondary characters.

To Love Again

The Second Chance At Love theme was the idea of Carolyn Nichols, the line's first senior editor, and the first titles were published in June 1981. The books feature heroines who are more realistic than the inexperienced girls who populate so many traditional romances, and they also feature more sensuality. "A woman experiences a lot of trials and errors before she finds the right man," says senior editor Ellen Edwards, Carolyn's successor. "Our heroines resemble real women because they have histories. They've loved before, and have lost that love for one reason or another. Every Second Chance At Love heroine has suffered through a bittersweet relationship of some kind, and it's this experience that shapes her attitudes toward a later relationship that develops in our novels."

Ellen Edwards

Heroes, she says, are not macho men, but strong and sensitive men who may even cry at intimate moments.

"We like the characters to make love about halfway through the book and then several times after that," Ellen says. "But that's flexible, depending on the story. As for sensuality, they're as sensual as anything on the market."

Second Chance At Love had a modest debut in terms of advertising and promotion support. "It took a while to get on its feet, but it's been steadily catching on ever since," says Ellen, noting a continual rise in sales figures. By the end of 1982, Jove was publishing six Second Chance titles a month and advertising the line on national cable television and in trade print ads. The line is also carried by RCA Direct Marketing, which advertises it on commercial television. "We've grown steadily from the very beginning and are now a serious presence in what has become a very crowded market," Ellen says.

The design for the Second Chance At Love covers came together in about seven or eight tries, according to art director Lee Fishback. "We needed an overall series look that wouldn't be imitative of something else on the market," she says. It features a double panel, an identifying butterfly logo and the words "Second Chance At Love" in a romantic, scripted type. The illustration is enclosed in the second, inside panel, while the outer panel flows out from the butterfly's head into a border. "We also wanted a key or 'kicker' color to pull out of the painting to accent the art," Lee says. The kicker color is used for the outer panel, and

changes from book to book, depending on the colors in the artwork.

Lee uses about ten artists for the six books that come out each month. All the covers are done in oil. "I like a lot of color, but that doesn't mean using many bright colors on a single painting," she says. "I'm after the effect of one bright or rich color, not something that looks cartoony."

Lee has to make certain there's variety in the covers of each month's releases, as well as variety from month to month. She strives for a balance of poses, settings and colors. She's often used her own clothes, even sheets, as well as the belongings of friends for various covers.

The sensuality of the covers hasn't changed much since the line was launched in 1980. "They were never chaste," she says. "There's a little more flesh showing now, but it's still romantic. I try to get as much cleavage as possible in the [photographic] shots—I think it helps."

For 1983, expansion is planned with a new line, To Have And To Hold, sensual and realistic books about love and romance within marriage. The launch title is *The Testimony* by Robin James, whose *The Golden Touch*, Second Chance At Love, was a big seller in 1982. (Robin James is a pseudonym for husband and wife Tom and Sharon Curtis.) To Have And To Hold covers will also bear the butterfly logo.

Love Loses Sweetness At Bantam

When a market starts to get crowded, new entrants look for a niche that's empty or weakly guarded. Such a niche enables a base to be built, strengthened and expanded, for in a crowded market, only the strong survive over the long haul. Bantam, with its chaste Circle of Love Line, mistakenly went for a niche that disappeared before the publisher got there.

A rapid and tremendous market shift occurred in 1981, once the American romance consumer realized there were sexier contemporary books available. By 1982, the spicy contemporary romance was the hottest thing going in the genre—even in paperbacks in general. The sweet traditionals were still around, but the sexier books had opened up a whole new segment of the market—a competitive free-for-all.

In the face of this trend, Bantam launched a brand-name line early in 1982 that was strictly traditional and sweet. Circle Of Love, with its cover that suggested homey embroidery, met with strong consumer rejection. In some instances, customers returned the books, and some booksellers dropped the line. Circle Of Love staggered along under bad press and poor sales for seven or eight months before being gently laid to rest.

The reasons why Bantam, a publisher with a fine reputation, misjudged the market are a combination of misinterpretation of market research and unfortunate timing. "There were no romance specialists at Bantam," explains senior editor Carolyn Nichols, who left Second Chance At Love to revamp Circle Of Love. "When Bantam decided to get into series romance publishing, they went to a reputable firm and had market research done on which they based the line. It was completed just as the first two Dell Candlelight Ecstasy books were about to come out. With more explicit sex, more interesting stories and more mature heroines, they were instantly gobbled up. A few months later, the Second Chance At Love line was launched. Therefore, the market research was obsolete the moment it rolled off the typewriter."

Carolyn Nichols

Furthermore, says Carolyn, "some of the questions in the study were ambiguous and could be interpreted in many ways. A chief example is, a random sample of women indicated they would like better-written romances. To consumers, well-written means creative, but to people in publishing, it would mean the prose, vocabulary and the expertise with which the books were edited. My impression was that there was a gap of understanding between the respondents and those who were interpreting the information.

"What really happened," Carolyn continues, "is that the market shifted before the research was finished. Once the American consumer was offered a choice in the marketplace, she quickly showed what her preferences were—Ecstasy and Second Chance. There wasn't a ghost of a chance that a line coming into the market with sweet romances—the trembling, 18-year-old virgins—would have a crack at success.

"Bantam handled the whole Circle Of Love situation in a most admirable way," Carolyn notes. "They told the truth. They said the line was not living up to expectations and they were fixing it."

"The heartaches that went into that line," recalls Bantam art director Len Leone. "Everything, including the packaging, was wrong. It was too wholesome—there was no passion, just a controlled cool." At first there was talk of salvation, of dividing the line into three "seasons": spring, summer and fall, featuring different heroines for different audiences—the young, chaste girls; older, more experienced young women; and more mature women—each with different cover variations and sexual content. But that complicated idea was scrapped.

Instead, Circle Of Love was discontinued, and Carolyn went to work resurrecting Bantam's presence in contemporary romances with a new, sensual line, Loveswept, which was launched in May 1983 with six titles. Production was scheduled for three titles a month during the rest of 1983. Carolyn chose manuscripts that were sensual and believable—"emotional books that make the reader either laugh or cry."

The cover design features passionate illustrations set against waves that sweep up from the base of the cover. The background color is different for each title in each month's release—red, orange, blue, green—an entire rainbow. "We came right off disaster with Circle Of Love," says Len. "I read the first six Loveswept titles myself." He was impressed, he says, with the "sensitive sensuality" of the books. The wave on the covers was an inspiration from the name Loveswept. "When I heard what the name was going to be," Len says, "the first thing I thought of was the movie *From Here to Eternity*—the famous love scene on the beach."

"With Loveswept," says Carolyn, "we have anticipated the wave of the future, particularly in a market that's so glutted. I believe strongly that romance consumers will be buying more and more in that tried-and-true manner of book lovers everywhere, by author. So, I've tried to get the best writers, plus new and fresh talent." Author Sandra Brown provided the first title, *Heaven's Price*; other talent lined up by Carolyn includes Dorothy Garlock, Helen Mittermyer, Carla Neggers, Noelle Berry McCue, Tom and Sharon Curtis and Billie Green.

There are no writer's guidelines, and authors are published under their own names rather than pseudonyms. "I'm not really interested in those writers who want to write under a pseudonym because they consider themselves to be a certain kind of writer and not a real romance writer," comments Carolyn. "Often you find their books aren't the best, anyway." Also, the inside front and back covers are used to showcase the authors with their photos and biographies.

There are plenty of real and willing romance writers wanting to be published by Loveswept. Even before launch, Carolyn was receiving approximately 150 manuscripts a month, and she expects that figure to jump considerably during 1983. She also expects to hit the mark with consumers. "The formula business has been overdone," she says. "Women are getting tired of all that stale stuff out there."

ZEBRA'S RECIPE FOR SUCCESS

When others in the romantic fiction industry said the market for historicals was gone except for the big-name authors, Zebra Books quietly went about proving them wrong. Their long, sexy historicals, written largely by unknown writers, are given terrific covers and lots of promotion where they are sold. The result: some of the authors are no longer unknown, regularly selling up to 500,000 copies of each book they write. What's more, many of Zebra's romance titles are backlisted—that is, they stay in print, long after other publishers' romances have come and gone.

"We've found our niche with the historical market, and we hope our books and following will get better and better," enthuses publisher Roberta Grossman. "We'd like to stay on this track—we don't have the means or the desire to compete in contemporary romances with Harlequin, Gulf + Western [owner of Silhouette] or Hearst [owner of Avon Books]."

Zebra's success with sexy historicals has come after a few trials and errors. The publisher began issuing both contemporary and historical romances in the mid-1970s. "They weren't blazing hot," Roberta says. "Some of them were reprints of English books and were too genteel. It took us awhile to get to know what the market wanted."

In the late 1970s Zebra tried contemporary romances with photographic covers. They all had one-word titles, such as *Whispers* and *Embraces,* and they were ahead of the market in terms of realism and independent, older heroines," Roberta notes. "They were about 100,000 words, not short enough for a [brand-name] contemporary and not long enough for a major book. They were wonderful, but the sales numbers just weren't good enough." The books were discontinued.

Zebra discovered—almost accidentally—that there was untapped treasure in the historical market around 1980–81, when it published *Passion's Paradise* by Sonya Pelton and *Tides of Ecstasy* by LuAnne Walden. Both were more than 500 pages long and carried a then-hefty cover price of $3.50, at a time when similar-length paperbacks were going for $2.25 and $2.50. They sold astonishingly well, considering the price and the fact that the authors were unknown.

"We decided then to go into longer historicals, and saw we didn't have to be as prudish as we once had been," Roberta says. "The market for historicals was still there."

Zebra now publishes three to four historical romances a month. The books are racy but go to no extremes in treatment of sex, according to Roberta. Fan mail seems to prove the company's on the right track.

"Other publishers have strict guidelines, but we're more open," says Roberta. "We believe books are books, not formula material that's churned out. If it's a good story, it'll sell even if it's different from others on the market. We have no guidelines for sex scenes—we just want an attraction between the hero and heroine that carries the reader through the book."

Other romance-related books in Zebra's line include American frontier sagas, such as American Dream, "adult westerns" from the woman's perspective, and Leather And Lace, a line of combination western-romances with female protagonists that was launched in the summer of 1982.

Art director Vincent Priore makes certain that great care is lavished on the covers, which has paid off at the check-out counter. Leading illustrators, such as Pino Daeni and Walter Popp, do many of the covers, which have eye-catching embossed and foil type. "The foil adds to the mood and goes with the hot colors," Roberta says, "though books without it have been just as successful."

Zebra prefers to work with new authors because they're "more flexible and willing to take direction," she observes. "All our writers are people you wouldn't expect to find writing this kind of book; they're down-to-earth, family-oriented women. Most are housewives, and some are young grandmothers. They all started out as fans, and they're voracious readers."

Zebra's four biggest writers are Sylvie Sommerfield, Janelle Taylor, Elaine Barbieri and Sonya Pelton. Janelle Taylor's first book, *Savage Ecstasy,* was published by Zebra in 1981. Her manuscript about a white woman and a Sioux Indian was so long it was broken into two books, and the second was published as *Defiant Ecstasy.* "The books did so well and we got so much mail that we asked Janelle to continue the characters—it's truly a romantic saga," Roberta points out. With her fifth book, *Tender*

ZEBRA / 0-8217-1013-3 / $2.95
TEXAS FLAME
HER PASSION BLOSSOMED LIKE A ROSE IN THE DESERT!
BY CATHERINE CREEL
SAVAGE ECSTASY
THEIR LOVE WAS FANNED BY FORBIDDEN FLAMES
BY JANELLE TAYLOR
TENDER ECSTASY
BY JANELLE TAYLOR
AUTHOR OF SAVAGE ECSTASY

Ecstasy, Janelle has begun the second generation: the son of Gray Eagle and Alisha Williams, Bright Arrow.

Sylvie Sommerfield, first published in 1980 with *Aaron's Ecstasy*, says she has built an "enormous following" with her seven or eight books. B. Dalton Bookseller once did a special promotion for her that included all of her backlisted titles. "It's been rewarding to see someone like Sylvie grow from a print order of less than 100,000 copies to more than 500,000 copies," notes Roberta. "And that's in a market everyone said wasn't there anymore."

MORE GENTLE SEX

Historical romances have taken a turn for the gentle, with heroes who aren't brutal and heroines who aren't forced to do things they'd rather not do. More or less. Pocket Books brought out a line of gentle sex historicals in 1982 called Tapestry Romances; New American Library joined the market in 1983 with Scarlet Ribbons.

The general guidelines for the line are "no rape or violence and no semi-promiscuous behavior," says NAL senior editor Hilary Ross. "It's not a format, it's a question of emphasis—that seems to be what the readers want." Also frowned upon are long separations between hero and heroine, which are characteristic of long historical romances. The length of Scarlet Ribbons books is about 125,000 to 150,000 words, compared with about 85,000 for Tapestry.

The introductory title is *Kimberley Flame* by Julia Grice, whose three big historicals for Avon Books—*Emerald Fire*, *Lovefire* and *Wild Roses*—have sold more than 1.7 million copies. Other authors under contract for Scarlet Ribbons include Kathleen Maxwell, Kay Cameron, Maggie Osborne, Catherine Coulter, Helene Thornton and Alyssa Wells.

Although Scarlet Ribbons books have a brand name—largely for marketing purposes, to enhance customer identification—they "are not like category romances," stresses Hilary. "They're not like jelly beans—they're more 'booksy.' "

LOVED AND LEFT

Richard Gallen Books has bid adieu to its first serious love, romantic fiction. The packager blazed a path of longer (100,000 to 125,000 words), sexier romances at a time when most romances were short (50,000 to 60,000 words) and sweet. But now everybody's in the long and sexy game, and Gallen executives decided in 1982 that it was time to get out. Gallen's new love is computer software books packaged for Dell plus other projects. The last Gallen romances will be distributed by Dell in 1983.

Star Helmer, Gallen's former editor in chief, is now editorial director for Harlequin's Superromance line, which is published under the Worldwide Library imprint.

Gallen, formed in 1977, launched its own imprint of romances in late 1979 with two books a month, packaged for Pocket Books. The first books were historicals; contemporaries were introduced in April 1980, and then four new titles, two historicals and two contemporaries, were published each month.

The contemporary heroines were spirited, independent women with glamorous, often unusual jobs. They ranged in age from eighteen to thirty, didn't have to be virgins and could be interested in more than one man (limit: two, total). The format doesn't sound so unusual now, but remember, this was early 1980. It wasn't until 1981–82 that the more mature, sexually experienced, independent heroine replaced the demure, sweet young thing in most contemporary American romances. Even when other romances caught up, Gallen still went a step or two further. In *By Invitation Only* by Monica Barrie, for example, two minor characters become involved in a homosexual affair.

"It took us a long time to figure out what worked," acknowledges Judith T. Sullivan, vice president and editor in chief, noting that the packager experienced some bombs as well as successes. A reader poll showed that readers not only disdained rape and bed hopping, but also excessive wholesomeness. While the books were sensual, they named "no bodily parts below the waist," notes Judith.

The covers, designed by Milt Charles, vice president and art director of Pocket Books, bore distinctive lettering and borders in-lined with gold. Sometimes the contemporary women were placed in the dominant position, contrary to most other male-dominant romance covers.

The Gallen imprint featured some fine and well-known authors, among them Jude Deveraux; Amanda York and Katherine Kent (pseudonyms of Joan Dial); Kristin James (pseudonym of Candace Camp); Barbara Faith; Dorothy Garlock; Devon Lindsay (pseudonym of Cynthia Wright); LaVyrle Spencer; and Laura Jordan (pseudonym of Sandra Brown).

Well, *c'est la vie*. Sometimes love means knowing when it's time to say good-bye.

VII. SPREADING THE WORD

The roots of today's romance novels date back to nearly the turn of the century in England, long before any American publisher ever thought romances would constitute a major market—or even knew what a "romance" was—and long before Harlequin was conceived and established. The roots go back to Mills & Boon Ltd., established in 1908, a company which early on recognized a market for romances and which began systematically studying and analyzing the romance readership as early as 1968.

By far the largest British publisher of romances today, hardcover and paperback, Mills & Boon sells more than 30 million copies of its red rose-decorated romances per year to one in three women in Britain, and 250 million of its books are distributed around the world in twenty-three languages. Many of its followers pick up every title issued every month without hesitation. "They trust the quality," says Jacqui Bianchi, Mills & Boon editorial director.

Other major British publishers of romances include Robert Hale, which issues hardcovers only of light contemporary and historical titles, commonly called "cardigan romances" because of their lack of explicit sex; Hodder and Stoughton, which publishes Mary Stewart; and Corgi Books and Hamlyn, which both issue paperbacks. (Hamlyn titles are packaged as Sapphire Romances in the United States and are distributed by RCA Direct Marketing. American-published romances such as Silhouette, Dell Candlelight Ecstasy and Jove's Second Chance At Love are also distributed throughout the United Kingdom.)

As in the United States, romances are proving to be a financial boon to a troubled publishing industry. In spite of overall depressed book sales, Mills & Boon has regularly increased its sales.

"Romances are on the verge of booming in England the way they have in the United States," says author Jean Saunders.

While much of the boom may be stimulated by the tremendous activity in the American romance market, the entire beginnings of it still took place here, in London. Mills & Boon was established by Charles Boon and Gerald Mills with a mere £1,000 in capital. Originally, Charles, a theater buff, was interested in modeling his books on the Haymarket Theatre style of play that was popular then.

Mills & Boon was the first to publish the late Georgette Heyer, in 1920, with her first Regency romance, *The Black Moth*. Georgette went on to write more than fifty novels, not all published by Mills & Boon, and elevated the Regency to a state of art in itself. Other notable authors whom Mills & Boon published in its early days were P.G. Wodehouse, Horace Walpole and Jack London.

It wasn't until the 1930s that the company began concentrating on romances. Reading became a favored form of escapism during the grim days of the Depression and on into World War II. Mills & Boon sold everything it could produce, though paper was scarce and rationed during the war.

Trouble hit in the 1950s, when libraries, a major source of sales, began to close, and Mills & Boon was left "like playwrights without theatres," as company spokesmen are fond of recalling. At the time, there were no romance paperbacks—everything Mills & Boon published was in hardcover. A new market was found, however, with a fledgling paperback firm called Harlequin, based in Winnipeg, Manitoba. Mills & Boon provided the hardcover books and imported Harlequin's paperback reprints for distribution. Doctor-nurse titles, a popular theme in the 1950s, were the first to be contracted. Later, Mills & Boon began producing paperbacks on its own, as well as hardcover books.

The Mills & Boon romances were a tremendous success for Harlequin, so much so that by

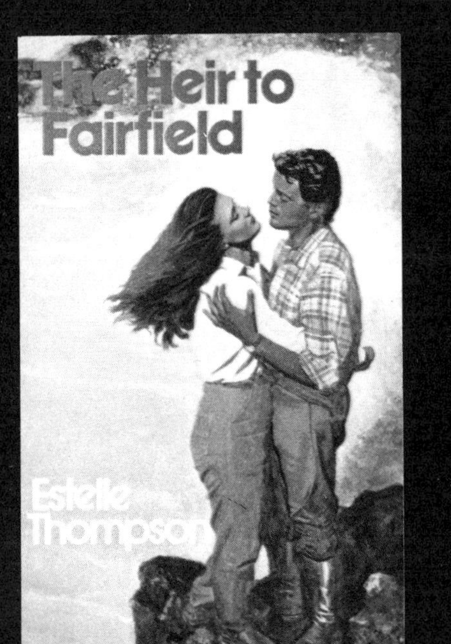

MARRIAGE
BY
BEQUEST

Elisabeth Carey

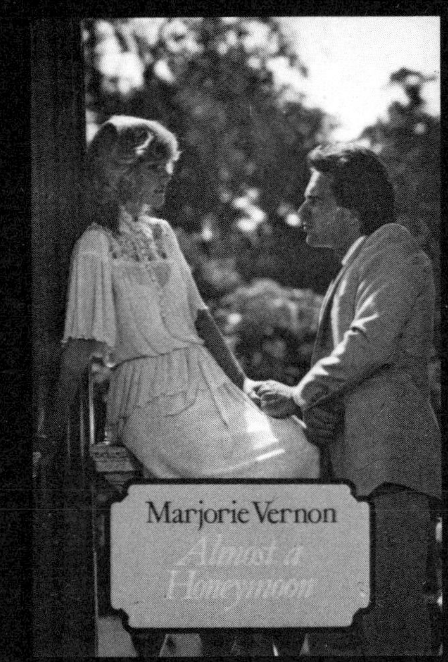

Frances Fitzgibbon

RUSTIC VINEYARD

Kathleen A. Shoesmith

1964, the Harlequin imprint was given over solely to Mills & Boon reprints. Mills & Boon merged with Harlequin in 1971.

Today, Mills & Boon still publishes doctor-nurse romances as well as other contemporary romances and historicals. The firm's comfortable offices are located in Brook's Mews in London; champagne is sometimes served to visitors.

The books are sold largely in variety stores—Woolworth is Mills & Boon's largest outlet—card shops and newspaper shops. "A lot of bookstores still feel romances are beneath them," explains author Nancy John. Many romance readers still rely on lending libraries for their books—they don't buy as much of what they read as many Americans do.

Mills & Boon receives about 3,000 unsolicited manuscripts a year, but from that stack only a handful are purchased. The company is very solicitous of its contracted writers, maintaining close relationships. Once a year, they take authors out to lunch in the countryside, chauffeured in limousines.

Even though Mills & Boon pays only a 4 percent royalty, press runs are "well over" 100,000 in the United Kingdom alone, and authors stand to earn an average £20,000 per book.

In 1982, the publisher stepped up efforts to add more American authors to its almost exclusively English stable, and Jacqui, making regular trips to the States to meet with established and aspiring writers, expected to have at least sixteen American authors being regularly published by mid-1983. American authors, she notes as an aside, are much more detail-oriented than English authors, who usually drive the plot forward with "an economy of language."

Putting In The Steam

In its decades of romance publishing, Mills & Boon has seen many trends come and go; indeed, one could get a picture of the entire history of romance just by looking over a progression of the publisher's titles. As society's sexual mores have changed and romances have become sexier, so have Mills & Boon novels. "Anyone who thinks differently hasn't read our latest books," says Jacqui. Although Alan Boon, group editorial manager, initially was dubious of the notion that a heroine could feel guiltless and moral sexual attraction, he changed his mind when he saw the success of sexier books. Now Mills & Boon heroines can go to bed with their heroes—but only if marriage results in the end, of course.

"Love can be conveyed through sex," says Jacqui, "but sex without love is pornographic."

The sexier books are called "throb" titles, and when Mills & Boon editors decide they'd like more throb in a story, they call it "putting in a bit more steam." "Sometimes there's so much steam around that it isn't clear if the couple did do 'it' or whether they just heavy-petted," says author and journalist Celia Haddon.

Sexual description still tends to be more implied than it is in many American romances, however. "Several of our books are in fact *more* sensual than either Dell Candlelight Ecstasy or Silhouette Desire, but the terms in which they are written aren't so explicit," Jacqui says. "What some of our more powerful writers achieve by implication fairly sizzles, but we aren't in the business of describing exactly what goes precisely where. It's sometimes more fun to imagine it. However, several of our books by Charlotte Lamb, Anne Mather and Helen Bianchin are definitely sensual and appreciated accordingly." The English economy of language, apparently, doesn't prevent the creation of some fairly steamy passages.

Mills & Boon strives to maintain a broad range of books that will appeal to all tastes. When Jacqui reviews manuscripts, she gives them her acid test: "Would I be prepared to pay money

The editorial team at Mills & Boon

for this? I try to think of the housewife with $3 left of her household money. Would she spend it on this book or would she save it for something else?"

One holdout on putting sex in romances—not a Mills & Boon author—is Barbara Cartland, whose unrelentingly sweet and chaste romances have sold 350 million copies around the world. Her publishers have asked her to "go modern," she says, but she flatly refuses to write what she calls "filth." Love, Barbara asserts, is a Holy Grail for both men and women, not to be sullied. When young women fantasize, she says, they dream of moonlight, roses and romantic balconies—not bedroom acrobatics.

Knowing The Market

English women are far more reticent than their American counterparts about buying romances. They tend to feel they shouldn't be spending money on escapism in a depressed economy. They still buy the books, however, quietly stuffing them down in the grocery sack. "American women are more liberated in the sense of commanding their own lives and spending money without feeling that they're taking something away from the household money," says Nancy. "English women tend to apologize for reading romances."

Another reason for the apologetic attitude is the sneering way the media view the genre. Most critics, however, actually haven't read any—or more than a few—romances. Most of them read only a narrow field of books, according to Dr. Peter H. Mann, a sociologist from the University of Sheffield. Peter has done extensive readership surveys and analyses for Mills & Boon since 1968, research that has destroyed many of the myths about romance readers and provided the publisher with valuable data on their target audience—for example, the fact that readers need to identify with the heroine within the first five pages of the book, and the fact that readers demand consistent punctuality in the distribution of each month's new titles.

Before 1969, says Peter, there was almost a "conspiracy of silence" about romances. They were purchased in enormous quantities by a silent army of loyal readers who seemed to feel that their reading tastes shouldn't be mentioned in "polite circles." Readers aren't quite that furtive today, and the genre has gained some respectability. The arrogance of self-appointed critics used to annoy him greatly, Peter says, but in recent years journalists and interviewers have loosened up a little. The popularity of romances, he concludes, has just gotten too big to ignore or dismiss.

Peter produced a major study on romance readers in 1969 and has updated his findings over the years. Most importantly, his work has shattered some misconceptions, such as:

Romances appeal mainly to spinsters
Romances appeal to women with too much time on their hands
Romances appeal only to factory girls
Romance readers never read anything else
Romance readers buy indiscriminately and don't know one book from another.

Wrong on all counts, says Peter. The typical reader is between nineteen and forty-four, representative of a cross-section of the female population, married and working, most likely in an office or clerical job. She may prefer romances but still reads other types of fiction and nonfiction. While many buy all Mills & Boon romances issued in a single month, most choose by author and jacket blurb. (Interestingly, while American publishers seek to woo customers with elaborate and expensive cover illustrations, English romance covers are much simpler and plainer—customers seem to pay more attention to the back-cover blurb.)

The Rose of Romance

Although Mills & Boon claims that nineteen out of twenty romance readers name it first before any other romance publisher—what would seem to be a comfortable brand awareness—marketing efforts never stop. In 1982, £1.5 million was budgeted for television and radio advertising and special promotions throughout the United Kingdom and Ireland. Covers, last revamped in 1971, were redesigned in 1981, replacing what was considered to be an "old-fashioned" red panel at the top with a modern white panel and pink and white stripes; the stylistic, identifying pink rose is at the top of every book.

The American competition promises to get stronger, and like its symbolic rose of romance, Mills & Boon promises to stay on top.

AN ENGLISH ROMANCE GALLERY

England boasts many fine romance writers, some of whom are also famous in the United States. Here are a few of them. (Barbara Cartland, England's best-known romance writer, is profiled in Section VIII of this book.)

MARY BURCHELL

Romantic adventures do happen in real life, insists Mary, who's written well over 100 books for Mills & Boon/Harlequin. As a young woman, she took an adventurous trip to New York to hear a great opera star sing, which later led to her first romantic serial, *Wife to Christopher.* Her interest in opera and her travels to Austria and Germany during World War II provided her with a gold mine of material for subsequent novels.

CATHERINE COOKSON

She grew up in poverty in England's north country near the Scottish border, and once she left, she swore she'd never go back. Yet she does, time and time again in her historical novels about ordinary, working-class people. Her books are full of intense emotion—she's England's Danielle Steel—and have sold more than 27 million copies in paperback. Catherine didn't publish her first novel until she was forty, and she has since become a well-known author in the United States.

JILLY COOPER

Romance with humor is Jilly's specialty, and her six books have sold more than 1.25 million copies in paperback alone. All have women's names for the titles: *Harriet*, *Octavia*, *Emily*, *Imogen*, *Bella* and *Prudence.* She models all her heroes on her husband, Leo. Beyond romance, she wants to write a serious novel, perhaps one without a happy ending.

ANNE HAMPSON

Her 120-plus Mills & Boon/Harlequin novels have done her well—a Mercedes, a house in Surrey and an exotic mansion in the Bahamas. But at one time, after she got divorced, she struggled to make ends meet. Anne began writing at age forty and burned a stack of rejected manuscripts before finally selling a book to Alan Boon. Alas, he wanted everything else she'd written.

VICTORIA HOLT

In real life, she's Eleanor Hibbert, a private woman who doesn't like to be interviewed. As Victoria Holt, her best-known pseudonym, she writes Gothic suspense; as Jean Plaidy, historicals; and as Philippa Carr, sagas. More than thirty books by her have been published under several other pseudonyms; all in all, she's done close to 100 books. For respite, she loves to take cruises—but always takes a manuscript with her. Almost all her titles make the most prestigious American best-seller lists.

CHARLOTTE LAMB

She once came close to death, and she promised herself that if she survived, she would become a novelist, as she had always wanted to do. Charlotte (her real name is Sheila Holland) did both, writing more than fifty-five novels for Mills & Boon and Silhouette Books. The rewards have been great—a twenty-room mansion on the Isle of Man, for one. And now she dreams of owning her own recording studio.

JEAN SAUNDERS

A former writer of short stories and confessions—she penned some 600 of them—Jean turned to romance novels in the mid-1970s, writing thirty-three in seven years. An agent told her that her first novel, *Ashton's Folly*, was unmarketable, but she sold it herself on the fourth try to Robert Hale (published in the United States as a Bantam Circle Of Love). She uses three pen names: Jean Innes, Rowena Summers and Sally Blake.

MARY STEWART

The Queen of Romantic Thrillers, Mary has more than a dozen books to her credit, all of them best-sellers and most of them on both sides of the Atlantic. She was born a vicar's daughter and married a distinguished geologist, Sir Frederick Stewart, making her Lady Stewart. Mary now lives in Edinburgh, Scotland. She's written historicals and children's books, but it's her suspense, such as *Touch Not the Cat*, that has made her famous.

GEORGETTE HEYER, QUEEN OF THE REGENCY

To the end of her long and prolific life, Georgette Heyer insisted she was not a romantic, yet her endearing novels of light romance set in England's Regency period attracted an enormous international following and set standards for every writer who followed in her path. By the time she died in 1974 at seventy-one, Georgette had long reigned as the Queen of the Regency romance. She had written more than fifty novels, including historicals set in medieval England and detective stories. But most of her books were set in her favorite period, the Regency years of 1811 to 1820, a time of political turmoil, aristocratic glitter and high style and manners. "She is really tops and a great talent," says Regency and historical author Catherine Coulter. "I can pick up one of her books for the fifth time and still derive great enjoyment from it."

An intensely private person, Georgette shunned publicity throughout her life, rarely granting interviews and often refusing to be photographed. She felt that personal publicity was "nauseating," in her words, and that anything anyone needed or wanted to know about her could be found in her work. She was meticulous in her research, and her attention to historical detail, even military strategy, made her novels great favorites of male readers as well as females. Of her women fans, however, Georgette had little tolerance for those who gushed over the romanticism in her books.

VII. SPREADING THE WORD

Georgette was born on August 16, 1902 in Wimbledon, England, to George Heyer, M.A. (Master of Arts) and MBE (Member of the Order of the British Empire), and Sylvia Watkins Heyer. The oldest of three children, she had two brothers, George Boris and Frank Dmitri, whose names reflect the family's Russian ancestry (George Heyer's father was from Kharkov). Georgette was very fond of her father, and he encouraged her to publish. His first glimpse of her talent came when she was seventeen, and he heard her tell a story to one of her brothers during his convalescence from a long illness. The story later became her first novel, *The Black Moth*, published in 1920.

By the time Georgette married Ronald Rougier, a mining engineer, in 1925, she'd published a second novel, *Powder and Patch*. Ronald's work took him to Tanganyika and Macedonia; Georgette accompanied him and kept up with her writing, publishing *These Old Shades* and *The Masqueraders*, besides two novels she didn't like and later suppressed, *Simon the Coldhearted* and *The Great Roxhithe*.

In the early 1930s, Ronald and Georgette returned to England, where their only child, Richard, was born in 1932. Ronald had begun reading for the bar, and he became a lawyer in 1939, eventually rising to Queen's Counsel. Their son, a Cambridge scholar and excellent bridge player, followed in his footsteps, also rising to Q.C.

During her later years, Georgette preferred to write about the medieval period rather than the Regency period, but high British income taxes forced her to continue turning out commercially successful Regencies. She was compiling a medieval trilogy about John, Duke of Bedford, last of the great lords of the House of Lancaster, when poor health and tax problems caused her to drop her research. She died before she could finish her grand project; the first book in the trilogy, *My Lord John*, was published posthumously in 1975. Ronald finished the last chapters of the book based on Georgette's notes.

Of all her work, her legacy is her Regency romances. Her extensive research and knowledge of the period gave the books that most elusive of qualities—a real world for her characters to come alive in, a world filled with everyday detail and vivid language. Her manuscripts were immaculate and always delivered to her publisher on time. No editor made the mistake of correcting her use of Regency language or vocabulary—no one knew the period as well as she. Over the years she'd collected voluminous notes on small details, such as styles and colors of dress, boots and hats, what shops were like and prices of the day. She even knew how much it cost to keep a carriage: £213 in the country; more than £500 in the city.

In some ways, Georgette's romances were an escape for her as well as her readers. She disliked the modern world and seemed to create a writing and life style that were barriers to the realities outside. She was often characterized as forceful and sometimes frightening to younger women. Even the Queen Mother, who bought Miss Heyer's books for Christmas presents, described her as "formidable" to the Harrod's salesclerk. But Georgette never saw herself that way and was incredulous at the remarks. In her own mind, Georgette was merely intensely private and not too serious about herself or her work.

The most lasting tribute to her work came in a letter written by Rachel Law, Lady Ellenborough, to Ronald after Georgette's death. In the letter, Lady Ellenborough said that Georgette's books remained readable even under the worst circumstances—"even when one is in hospital beds awaiting drastic surgery."

Georgette's Regency comedies have an understanding of human nature and a common sense that sustain the reader, when higher literature, such as Shakespeare, has lost its meaning, and light, sexy books seem pointless. Georgette knew the value of her escapist stories, adhering, according to one critic, to the three English virtues: good taste, quiet courage and the saving joke.

The ranks of romance writers have swelled considerably with the expansion of the genre. Most of them have come directly from the legions of readers, bringing with them a strong understanding of romances and some definite ideas about the kinds of things they themselves want to see in the novels. The majority of them have written little, if any, fiction before trying their hands at romance. They entered the field because they enjoyed it and wanted to improve upon what they were reading. Now many a former reader makes a full-time living—in some cases, quite a lucrative one—from writing.

With the proliferation of lines and titles (some 150 titles issued every month), a fair number of writers have come and are coming into prominence, both in the historical and contemporary fields, particularly the fast growing latter. Although it's impossible to catalog them all in this book, this section features sketches of twenty-four writers, some long established and famous and others new and rising. With the exception of one or two hard-to-reach or publicity-shy authors, all were interviewed especially for *LoveLines*.

JENNIFER BLAKE

Growing up in a tradition-steeped Louisiana family has given Jennifer Blake (nee Patricia Ann Ponder) an understanding and knowledge of the South that has served her well as a romance novelist. Patricia—she doesn't go by her well-known pseudonym—has often drawn on the history of the South and her home state environs in the twenty-plus novels she's written since 1970. She counts some best-sellers on her list, among them *Love's Wild Desire* (Popular Library), *Golden Fancy* (Fawcett) and *Embrace and Conquer* (Fawcett).

Her family roots go back to the 1830s in Louisiana's inner swamp country. Growing up in an extended family with such a long heritage gave her "a constant feeling of your place in the scheme of things in the South," she says. "Being Southern is different, and I didn't realize how different until just the last few years when I began to get out of the South and travel."

Patricia was born on March 9, 1942 in Goldonna, Louisiana, at the aged cottage of her grandparents, who, because of their remote location, had no electricity or plumbing service until the 1950s. "Visiting them (later) was like going back into the nineteenth century," she recalls.

She married young, at age fifteen. Her husband, Jerry Maxwell, romantically wooed her by sending her intriguing but anonymous poems. Then the babies came, three of them by the time she was twenty (a fourth followed several years later). Patricia was plenty busy but still had time to read a wide variety of books, including Gothics and romances.

One day she knew she could write a better romance than what she was reading, and thus began her career as a writer. For several years she wrote articles and poetry, and a novel that didn't sell. Then she completed a Gothic, *Secret of Mirror House,* which Fawcett published in 1970.

Patricia is best known for her historical romances written under the pseudonym Jennifer Blake (a favorite first name plus her grandmother's maiden name), but her early books were written under her married name, Patricia Maxwell, and her own maiden name, Patricia Ponder. She also wrote one novel in collaboration with a friend under the pseudonym Elizabeth Trehearne. Besides historicals, Patricia has written contemporary romances for Signet under the pseudonym Maxine Patrick.

Historicals, however, remain her first love, particularly the pre-Civil War period in the South. "You can do so much more in a period novel," she notes. She's seen a significant change in the styles of historicals since she began writing in the genre, and has adapted her writing accordingly. "When I first started writing romances," she says, "rape was a large part of historicals. Now that's changed. I write in a more sensuous style, with less violence."

She particularly enjoys the research involved in historicals, which includes reading other historical novels. "I do a lot of reading to make certain I'm not copying someone else or coming up with the same idea," Patricia says.

Patricia and her family make their home in Quitman, in northern Louisiana, about ninety miles southeast of Shreveport. She has her own office and library as well as a word processor, and she no longer has to work out of a bedroom corner.

"I treat my writing as a job," she says. "I start around 8:30 to 9 in the morning and go to 3 in the afternoon, although it depends on deadlines. If I'm on one, my hours stretch and there's no telling how late I'll work!" By writing seven to ten pages a day, she completes a historical in about six months.

For leisure diversions, Patricia enjoys gardening, shopping for antiques, trying out new restaurants and traveling.

PARRIS AFTON BONDS

"The desire to write is born with you," says Parris Afton Bonds, who speaks from experience. At age six, she penned her first story, an adventure tale entitled "The Blackhawk Raiders." Although only three chapters and three pages long—one page per chapter—it reflected Parris' fertile imagination and her innate ability to spin a good yarn. It was an ability that later would enable her to write best-selling and award-winning romantic novels.

Parris, a slender, attractive woman who speaks with a soft Southwestern drawl, was named after the city where her mother says she was conceived—Parris, Kentucky. She was born in Tampa, Florida on July 21, 1944, and at an early age she developed a keen interest in westerns and adventure novels, such as those written by Zane Grey and Frank Yerby. "I also read men's action magazines because there were so few romances for women," recalls Parris. "I liked to read them for the love scenes."

One of her favorite historical novels was Kathleen Winsor's *Forever Amber,* the story of an English peasant girl who seduces a succession of aristocrats, including the king of England, to improve her station in life. Such sexual behavior seemed shocking in the days of Parris' childhood, and because *Forever Amber* was frowned upon as a scandalous book, she hid it under her mattress and read it under the covers at night.

Parris began her serious writing career as a nonfiction free-lancer in Mexico, where she lived for several years with her husband, Ted, and where two of her five sons were born. She wrote articles for newspapers and magazines, and for very low pay. "I think I sold about ten manuscripts altogether and made about $435, but the writing experience was incredible," says Parris, who did not attend college or have any formal training as a writer.

After nonfiction, the next step was a fiction novel. "I always wanted to write a book," says Parris, voicing the dream of so many aspiring novelists. In 1976, after her family moved to Texas, she pursued her goal by writing *Sweet Golden Sun.* It sold the first time out and was published in 1978 by Fawcett/Popular Library. She sold two more books to the same publisher, *Savage Enchantment* and *The Flash of the Firefly,* before an agent began handling her material.

Parris favors historical settings in the Southwest, where she can create strong, assertive pioneer-stock women. Her ideas for plots come from many different sources. For example, a Marty Robbins song, "El Paso," provided the inspiration for *Sweet Golden Sun.* She writes to please herself and has a hard time releasing her characters when a book is finished. "I usually cry," she confesses.

Parris and her family now live in Hobbs, New Mexico, and with five boys around the household, you'd think the time and energy to write would be hard to come by. While Parris acknowledges that her writing habits are "erratic," she credits Ted and her sons with making extra efforts to give her the time she needs. A word processor helps speed the progress of a novel.

Parris believes strongly in making use of God-given talent and in pursuing personal goals. "You have to make time to do what you want to do," she says. "As for success, I believe a lot of it is luck. If you believe in the roll of the dice, and if you have enough money to stay at the tables, then you'll eventually win."

Parris has accomplished many of her goals: she's a published novelist; one of her books, *Deep Purple* (Fawcett), has appeared on a best-seller list (Waldenbooks); she's won awards, regional and national, for *Dust Devil* and *Made For Each Other*; and she's been published in a foreign language, with the Italian edition of *Dust Devil.* Among her future goals are writing a

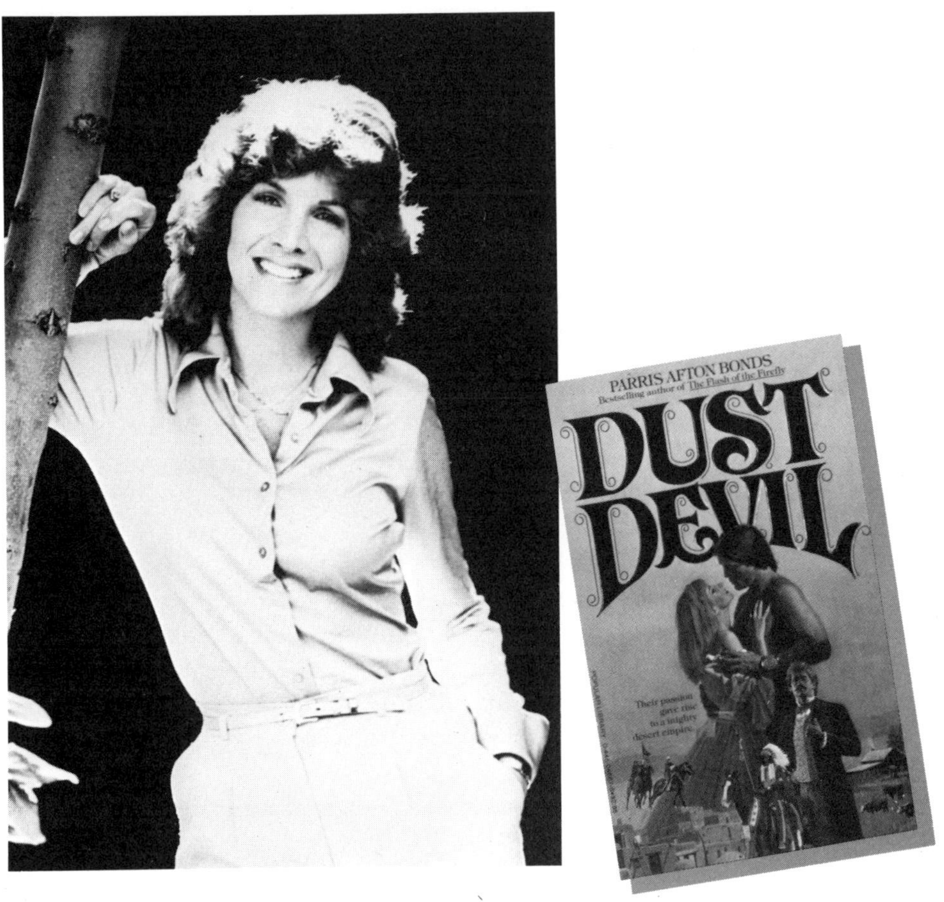

screenplay and making a movie ("I'd like to show Robert Redford how to kiss"). Knowing Parris, with her ability and determination, she'll have no trouble achieving those goals.

REBECCA BRANDEWYNE

Her horoscope once predicted success in publishing. Whether it was fate, her considerable talent or her keen promotion savvy—or a combination of all three—Rebecca Brandewyne has indeed achieved glamorous success as an author. Her Gothic-tinged historical romances, such as *No Gentle Love* and *Forever My Love* (both Warner), have made her one of the youngest published authors in the romance field.

Born on March 4, 1955 in Wichita, Kansas, Rebecca Wadsworth (her given name) grew up reading romances, particularly Gothics. "Mary Stewart was and is my favorite author," says Rebecca. "I also read a lot of historical biographies; I loved true stories about kings and queens. When I decided to go into writing, I wanted to combine those elements and throw in some sex. What I came up with was a historical romance. At the time I didn't know it, but twenty million other women came up with the same thing!"

Rebecca's first novel, *No Gentle Love,* was published (after six rewrites) in 1981, when she was 26. She chose her own pseudonym for its romantic and memorable sound and then adopted it legally. She put together her own promotion plan for the book, and it proved to be a key ingredient in her success.

Knowledgeable in public relations, she developed a press kit and a mailing list and set up a promotion tour—all on her own "shoestring budget." Her determined campaigning helped her book to sell out the book's first printing of 105,000 copies in one month and led to a $25,000 budget put up by Warner for her to use to promote her second novel, *Forever My Love*. Her third novel, *Love, Cherish Me* (Warner), was backed by a $50,000 promotion campaign.

The years preceding Rebecca's writing debut were characterized by a streak of independence that inspired her to make it on her own. She is not, she explains, a nine-to-fiver.

Originally, Rebecca wanted to be a dancer, but her mother discouraged her from taking ballet lessons. She struggled through public school but was a superachiever at Wichita State University, graduating with a bachelor's degree cum laude in journalism (testimony to her acumen is her membership in MENSA). She also earned a master's degree in communications. Following school, she held secretarial posts and free-lanced as a writer in public relations, advertising and journalism. In addition, she taught an interpersonal communications class at her alma mater.

Rebecca opted to stay in Wichita, where she enjoys a single life, and has pursued her interest in dance with ballet lessons and belly dancing. She plans to combine both writing and dancing interests with a novel about a belly dancer.

Her books have long, complex plots with Gothic overtones, because that's what she enjoys reading.

"I'm a very fast reader, and I like to read long books," says Rebecca. "I can go through seven Harlequins in one evening. When I buy a book, it's seldom less than 400 pages long, because I read so fast."

Rebecca's goals as a writer are to explore other genres, such as science fiction, and to produce a classic. "I think every writer would like to do a classic," she observes. "A classic something like Jane Austen wrote, that people will remember. Margaret Mitchell only wrote one book in her life, but what a book! That's what I'd like, for people to remember me and my name to live on for something that I wrote."

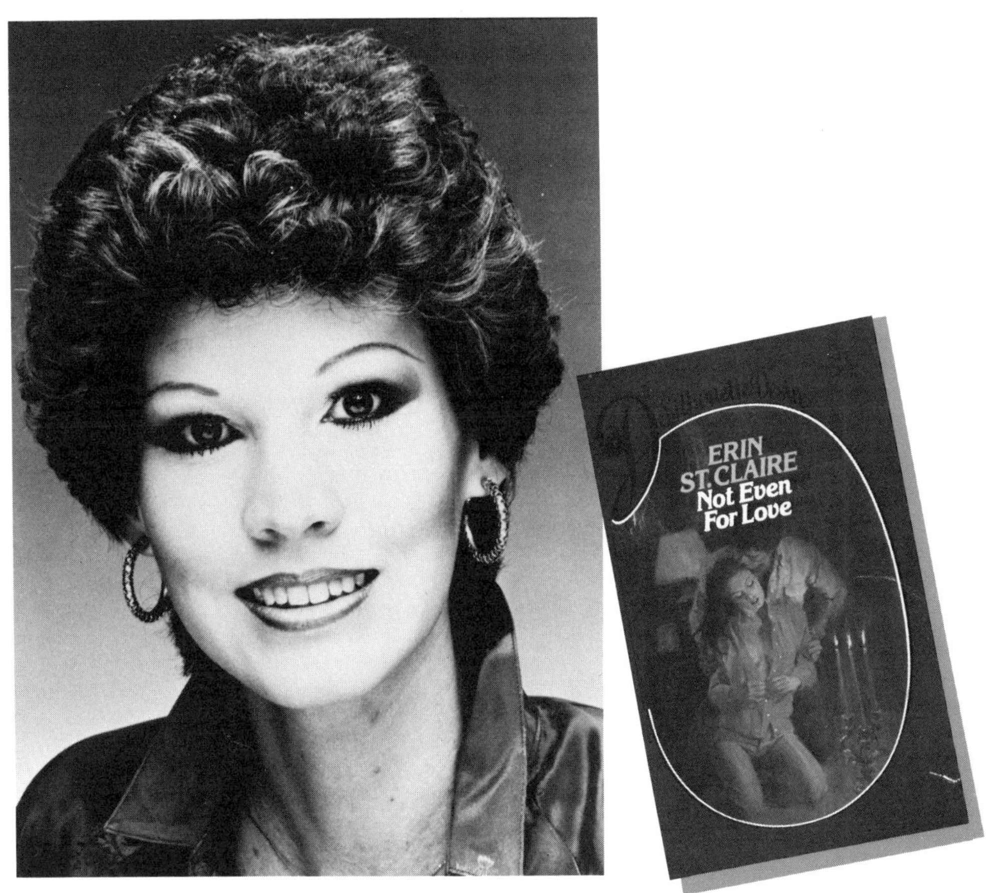

SANDRA BROWN

"I'm a pure, dyed-in-the-wool, unrelenting romantic," says Sandra Brown about herself. Sandra likes women to be ladies, men to be gentlemen, the sexual sparks to fly between them and marriage to cement their relationship. She writes what she likes, and evidently a good many other women like the same things, for Sandra's books are published in almost every major romance line on the market. In her first two years as a writer, she published or contracted for twenty novels.

Readers know her as Rachel Ryan for Dell Candlelight Ecstasy; Laura Jordan for Richard Gallen; Erin St. Claire for Silhouette Desire; and herself, Sandra Brown, for Harlequin's North American line, Jove's Second Chance At Love and Bantam's Loveswept. Two of her pseudonyms, Laura Jordan and Erin St. Claire, popped off the top of her head; Rachel Ryan combines the first names of her two children.

Sandra is a personable native Texan, who was born on March 12, 1948 in Waco and grew up in Fort Worth with Southern-lady manners. Today she lives in Arlington, which lies between Fort Worth and Dallas, with her husband, Michael, and children. "It never occurred to me that someday I'd be doing this," she says of her full-time writing career, "but I've probably been preparing my whole life for it. I've always been a real wool gatherer—it just never occurred to me to write the stories down."

Her father was a journalist. "I grew up with an appreciation of the written word," Sandra says. "Books were a very important part of our household; we were all bookworms." She read Nancy Drew and a lot of romance-laced historical, adventure or suspense novels by Thomas Costain, Frank Slaughter, Frank Yerby, Victoria Holt and others.

She married young, at twenty, and had a series of what she calls "mini-careers" that gave her excellent experience and preparation for writing. She worked in summer stock and as a fashion model, a cosmetologist and a local television personality, a job that included doing features for *P.M. Magazine.* Michael is a professional speaker for seminars, conventions and industrial films.

When she grew tired of television, Michael suggested she pursue the writing she'd always wanted to do but had always put off. She met author Parris Afton Bonds, who explained the popularity of romances and urged her to try the genre. "I'd never even read a Harlequin," Sandra says. "I went to the bookstore and bought about twelve romances. As I read them, a story I had in my head began to expand until I thought I had a pretty good idea for a novel."

Her first try at romances never sold, however, but her second and third, *Love's Encore* and *Love Beyond Reason,* sold to Dell Candlelight Ecstasy in 1980. Although she did a historical, *Hidden Fires,* for Gallen, she has concentrated on the contemporary subcategory. Among her other contemporaries are *The Silken Web* (Gallen) and *Eloquent Silence* (Ecstasy).

Sandra believes firmly in one-to-one relationships, abhors forced or violent sex and likes to see strong but sensitive men grow and change along with the heroines. "I like to see a man evolve through the heroine's love," she says. "If he's been hurt or disillusioned with life, she takes that one little thread in his heart and brings him around."

While she has old-fashioned values, Sandra still enjoys sensual, sexy books, ones that "get the heartbeat going, the palms perspiring and make the throat dry. I try to give that to my readers, build up the tension so that they're just screaming for the hero and heroine to get into bed together," she explains.

Sandra believes readers want to recapture some of the mystery of romance that's been lost in the last tumultuous decade or so. Readers, it appears, agree with her.

CANDACE CAMP

Candace Camp seemed headed for a career in law, but romance intervened. It was not her own romance, though she is happily married and the mother of a baby girl, but romantic fiction that put an early end to Candace's law aspirations. Her success as a novelist demanded more and more of her time, until she quit her job as a lawyer in Paris, Texas to write full time.

"I enjoy writing much, much more than law, although sometimes I miss the business environment," says Candace, whom readers know as Kristin James (Gallen/Pocket Books, Silhouette), Sharon Stephens (Tapestry) and Lisa Gregory (Jove). "But now I can set my own hours, and I enjoy being able to work by myself. I didn't really fit into the corporate mold—I like to make my own decisions."

Candace was born on May 23, 1949 in Amarillo, Texas to parents who were in the newspaper business; her mother was a journalist and her father was the business manager of the *Amarillo Globe-News.* Neither of them was surprised that their daughter showed an early inclination towards writing. Although she loved to make up stories, Candace seldom finished her tales—until much later in life.

After college (West Texas State University), Candace taught junior high school English and history and then went to work for a bank. Her exposure to lawyers at the bank plus the influence of her lawyer brother motivated her to enter law school.

"In a way, writing always seemed like a dream to me," explains Candace. "It was my hobby and my release, but I felt like I needed a 'real' job, and law was a good field for a woman. I worked with a lot of lawyers at the bank, and I thought if they could do it, so could I."

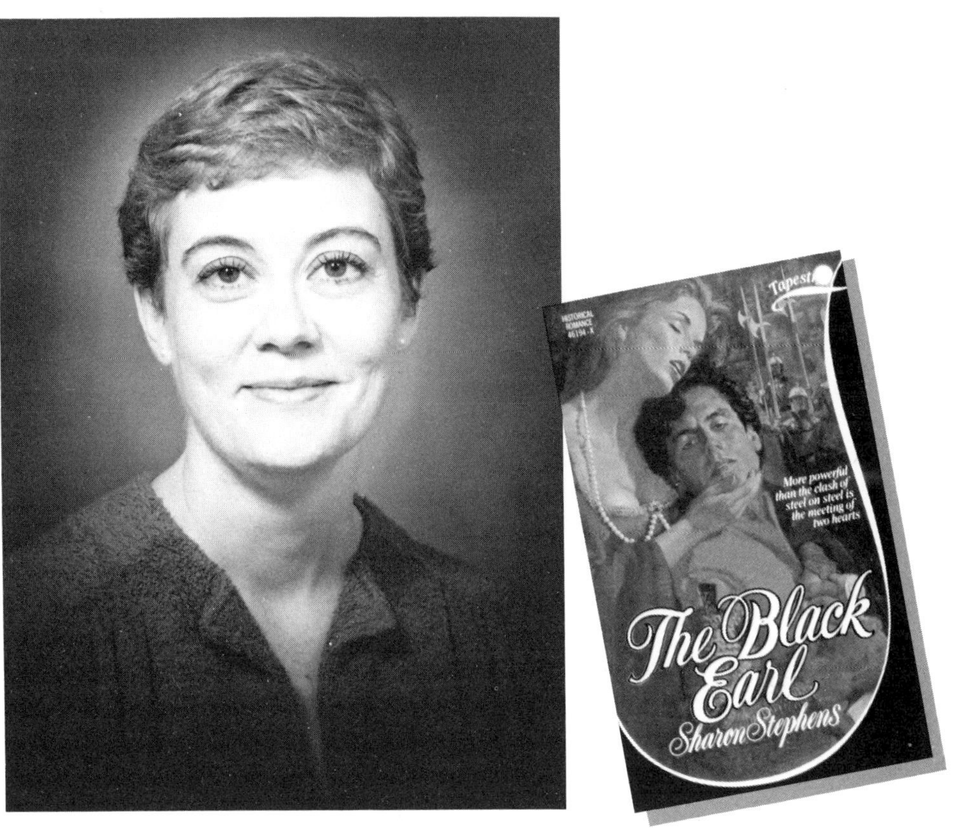

Law school proved to be tough, but from the experience Candace learned discipline and organization that has benefitted her as a writer. For the first time, she finished a piece of fiction. And then she sold it.

She began her first historical romance, *Bonds of Love*, during her initial year of law school, after reading Kathleen Woodiwiss' *The Flame and the Flower.* That novel inspired her to try one herself. Avon turned it down, but Jove bought it, the sale coming after Candace had graduated and moved to Paris to take a job as a lawyer. The sale, says Candace, "absolutely thrilled me. The only other thing I can compare it to is the birth of my daughter."

When Jove bought her second historical romance, *The Rainbow Season,* Candace realized she couldn't write and work full time, too; so she quit her job and hung out her own shingle as a part-time lawyer. Eventually, she also gave that up, though she is still a member of the Texas Bar Association.

The same year that *The Rainbow Season* was published, 1979, Candace married Pete Hopcus, a marriage and family therapist. Their daughter was born in 1981.

Although Candace began her writing career with historicals, she produced contemporary romances for Gallen and is now concentrating on contemporaries for Silhouette. Candace says that it's an asset to be able to work in both subcategories and that each has its own appeal: historicals tend to be larger than life and more melodramatic, while contemporaries offer more possibilities and flexibility in plots and character development.

Candace uses a word processor ("I love machines") and works around the baby's naps or hours with the sitter. She can produce a novel in about four months. Her writing and family activities take up most of her time. When time permits, she enjoys reading romantic suspense novels; Mary Stewart is one of her favorite authors.

She'd like to write romantic suspense sometime in the future as well as a longer romantic saga. Writing, Candace says, has changed her life. "It allows me to get paid for doing what I like to do—daydream."

BARBARA CARTLAND

Barbara Cartland, named the best-selling author in the world by the *Guinness Book of World Records*, is more than an author—she's a phenomenon unto herself. The list of the significant accomplishments of this remarkable lady would be enough to fill a volume of considerable size.

Born into English aristocracy on July 9, 1901 (she is a Dame of Grace of St. John of Jerusalem and step-grandmother of Princess Diana), Barbara has led a full and glamorous life as a novelist, historian, playwright, lecturer, political speaker and television personality. Her 350-plus books have sold 350 million copies around the world.

She's best known for her chaste and idealistic historical romance novels in which the heroine *never* surrenders her virginity before marriage, books that have earned her the title of High Priestess of Love. She's also authored dozens of books on other topics as well, including philosophy, history, biography, autobiography, verse, cooking, decorating and general interest (*Saturday Review* in 1981 named her the second most successful living author in the world, behind Harold Robbins). She's written plays for the stage and radio, and a radio operetta, and has sung love songs for a record, *An Album of Love Songs*, with the Royal Philharmonic Orchestra. Her novel *The Flame Is Love* was recently made into a film. *Barbara Cartland Romances*, a book of cartoons, is published in the United States and Britain, and her romantic cartoon strip appears in seventy-five newspapers in America and other parts of the world. Her name appears on a line of perfume, fabrics and home-decorating items. For the latter she was named "Woman of Achievement" in 1981 by the National Home Fashions league, an American organization.

In addition, Barbara has appeared on some of the most prestigious television talk and feature shows the world over, usually dressed in her signature color, pink. Pink, she says, is a "warm and happy" color, much preferable to beiges, which "make a woman look like a baked potato."

It's not surprising to wonder where Barbara, who has just entered her eighties, gets the enormous amount of energy to do all these things. A strong believer in self-discipline, she follows a health-conscious regimen of work, diet and sleep habits, supplemented with more than seventy vitamin pills a day. (Her interest in vitamin therapy led her to found the British National Association for Health, of which she is president).

Barbara's day at her large mansion at Camfield Place begins early, with breakfast between 8 and 9 a.m. She dictates or writes between 6,000 and 9,000 words during the course of the day, an output that has enabled her to break the world writing records for eight years running, with twenty to twenty-four books a year.

She has been a widow since 1963, when her second husband, Hugh McCorquodale, died after twenty-seven years of marriage (the couple had two sons). Her first marriage, to Hugh's cousin, Alexander McCorquodale, was dissolved.

Barbara is quite outspoken on the subject of virginity before marriage. Many may think her romances hopelessly sweet and old-fashioned, but she points to her incredible sales as proof that women want ideal, pure and romantic love.

"I was brought up in the twenties when we were very pure and innocent," says Barbara. "Although I realize, of course, that people today go to bed without being married, I do not think that is very romantic."

Social pressure to indulge in easy sex can be damaging to a young woman's personality, believes Barbara, and she is relentless in her crusade for a return to a sterner, fundamental morality.

"The romance that I write is just as true to life as the kitchen sink," she says. "We all reach for the stars, and although we may not touch them, we try."

JAYNE CASTLE

Jayne Castle wrote her first romance in 1973—trouble was, nobody in publishing was turning out her kind of contemporary romance. "Not to spec" came back rejection after rejection for six years, long enough for less determined writers to throw in the towel. Then the romance market expanded. Contemporary romances became bolder and more sensual, with more independent-minded heroines, and Jayne suddenly had no trouble finding a receptive market for her work. Today her category romances, written for Dell Candlelight Ecstasy under Jayne Castle (her maiden name), or for Silhouette under the pseudonym Stephanie James, are sure-fire sellers. Futhermore, she has written the important introductory titles for two new lines.

Jayne is adept at giving characters and plots a different twist that makes them stand out, and she admits regularly breaking whatever "rules" prevail in the genre. She treats her men and women more as equals and imbues them with a sense of humor that shows in sparkling dialogue.

Jayne, born on March 28, 1948 in San Diego, never aspired to be a writer as a child. She did love books and reading, however, devouring adventure and espionage stories and science fiction. As a teenager, she discovered E.M. Hull's steamy and shocking (for 1921, the year it was published) *The Sheik*. She later went on to read Gothics and Harlequins, although she thought the English-inspired heroes of the latter were too dark and too perfect and the women too submissive.

"I think more Americans see romance as in the style of the old Spencer Tracy-Katharine Hepburn films—the classic, feisty battle of the sexes," says Jayne. "Sometimes the hero comes out on top, sometimes the heroine does, but the heroine always holds her own in the long run."

Jayne also believes that the vulnerability created by flaws and imperfections (either in body or personality) makes characters more appealing and endearing. Consequently, her women are not classically beautiful, and her men don't fall into what she calls the "Greeks and sheiks" category.

One of the more unusual imperfections to surface in the romance genre was her hero in *Gentle Pirate*, one of Dell's introductory Candlelight Ecstasy Romance titles, published in 1980. A Vietnam veteran, this man has a hook instead of one hand, but it doesn't prevent him from coming across as sensual, sexy and appealing to the heroine—and the readers.

Blessed with a vivid and fertile imagination, Jayne weaves her characters out of whole cloth, seldom drawing on real life people for models. She's used a number of corporate settings for her romances, including *Corporate Affair*, the introductory title for Silhouette's Desire line launched in 1982. She gets many ideas from the *Wall Street Journal*. "I think the intrigue that goes on in the corporate world hasn't been sufficiently tapped," says Jayne. "It's a very rich source for plots, and it's a very modern way to get characters together."

Before turning to writing romances full time, Jayne worked as a librarian. She holds a bachelor's degree in history and a master's degree in librarianship. She earned her master's degree in 1971, the same year she and her husband, Frank, eloped—romantically!—to Canada. Frank's work as an engineer has taken them to live in a variety of places, including the northwestern and southeastern parts of the continental United States and the Virgin Islands. They now live in San Francisco, California but would like to return to the cool and beautiful Pacific Northwest someday.

As a writer, Jayne wants to stay with romantic fiction but would like to stretch herself with longer books that include more adventure—midlist romantic novels that are neither category nor mainstream. "I never started out to be a writer," she says, reflecting on her evolution from a reader and keeper of words to a writer of them. "I was quite content to be a librarian. I just wanted to tell romantic stories—my way!"

ELAINE RACO CHASE

Elaine Raco Chase has a no-nonsense, call-'em-as-I-see-'em way of looking at life, mixed liberally with a sense of humor. Her outspokenness has occasionally landed her in trouble—like the time she almost blew a federal drug bust—but it was instrumental in launching her writing career. It got her *noticed.*

Elaine (Raco is her maiden name, Chase her married name) is well known to romance fans as the author of such Dell Candlelight Ecstasy titles as *Double Occupancy* and *Designing Woman.* Her books also include six titles for Silhouette's Desire line and *Best Laid Plans* for Avon's Looking For Mr. Right line. She writes in a light, entertaining style about strong, independent women.

But let's go back to Elaine B.R.—Before Romance. Born August 31, 1949 in Schenectady, New York, she devoured mysteries as a child, graduating from Nancy Drew to Mickey Spillane by age 12. After business college, she worked as a computer operator at a hometown

TV station. In 1969, she married Gary Chase, now a video sales consultant and design engineer. They adopted a daughter and then had a son of their own.

Elaine moved from computers to copywriting with a job at an ad agency in Albany, where she loved the demands of writing thirty-second sells. But it was a journalism class that spawned the desire to write a novel. "I dug out Gary's portable and started writing a romance," Elaine says. "I can't tell you why it was a romance—I didn't read them, I'd always read mysteries."

When she finished *Rules of the Game,* she sent it to Harlequin. "Like nearly everyone else in this business, I have a Harlequin rejection," she laughs.

Elaine joined the International Women's Writing Guild and attended its annual conference at Skidmore College in Saratoga Springs, New York in 1978. Most of the participants, many of whom held graduate degrees, talked about their serious novels and poetry. "When I said I wrote romances, they all burst into laughter," recalls Elaine. "I said wait a minute, you can all keep writing your poetry, but romance is the only thing that's selling."

New York literary agent Denise Marcil approached Elaine later. "She asked me if I wrote the same way I talked, and I said, 'Yes, unfortunately!' " Denise sold her work to Dell, and Elaine was on her way.

Her family was skeptical at first. "Now they'd like to chain me to my word processor," jokes Elaine, who works out of their home in Ormand Beach, Florida, where they've lived for several years. She also teaches a creative writing class.

Still a mystery fan, Elaine has outlined six books for a series about an insurance investigator that she hopes to market. She would also like to write a longer suspense novel or mainstream fiction. Her fertile imagination keeps her well supplied with ideas for plots and characters.

Elaine hasn't traveled much, claiming she gets into enough trouble at home. She's crashed her car, fallen down steps, breaking both feet, and fought off a mugger. And she once stumbled onto a cocaine stakeout.

That incident occurred one night when she and Gary noticed a strange car parked in a neighbor's driveway. Seeing the occupants had shotguns, Elaine got out her Mace, pulled up her Chevette behind them and demanded to know what was going on. When the men showed their badges identifying them as federal agents, she scoffed, "You can get those things anywhere." Then she called the sheriff.

The stakeout was legitimate, Elaine soon learned, and fortunately, it wasn't blown; arrests were later made in a $2 million drug bust. Sounds like an adventure you might read in a book. . . .

VIRGINIA COFFMAN

One day during a college English class, a distracted Virginia Coffman sat composing a historical novel instead of paying attention to the professor. A classmate, Kathleen Winsor, leaned over and warned, "That'll get you nowhere!" Famous last words, for Kathleen eventually wrote best-selling historicals, such as *Forever Amber,* and Virginia went on to become Queen of the Gothics.

Virginia now has some sixty-nine books to her credit, quite a track record for a lady who didn't see her first novel published until she was nearly forty years old. She specializes in mystery, horror, eerie settings and fiendish villains and is the author largely responsible for setting off the Gothics craze of the 1960s.

She's been fascinated with Gothic stories since childhood. "I was born in San Francisco

[July 30, 1914], surrounded by the most Gothic of architecture, and Gothic childhood games which my writer-sister [Donnie] and I invented to scare our friends," recalls Virginia. "I spent night after night buried in romantic literature and thrillers of past centuries."

Her first work of fiction, however, was an "epic" of one and a half pages on the U.S. Cavalry versus Indians, penned at age seven. Later, she was a high school journalist and actress.

"My adult life was spent in Hollywood, first as a secretary during the spectacular—and peculiar—Howard Hughes regime at RKO and then at a small studio where I had the distinction of buying the daily coffee break refreshment for a man I now hear called the 'richest man in America,'" says Virginia. (His identity shall remain undisclosed.) She also worked for David O. Selznick, Harry Cohn and Hal Roach. She eventually moved from secretarial work to script editing, which actually involved writing without screen credit, she says.

She spent nine of her twelve years in Hollywood working in her spare time on *Moura*, her first book, which was published by Crown in 1959. *Moura* helped revive the popularity of the classic Gothic theme. Set in the early nineteenth century in France, it concerns an apparently wicked uncle, an evil housekeeper and a sweet young girl. Typical of Gothics, *Moura* has a surprise ending, only this one is a double whammy: the sixteen-year-old "heroine" is really the villain, the "wicked" uncle the good guy. The ending was intended as a little joke, an amusing play on the classic Gothic theme, according to Virginia. Although the book was enormously successful, no one seemed to get the joke. She still chuckles at the recollection of one publisher who rejected the manuscript because it was "so wild and preposterous, it's positively Gothic."

Virginia's second book, *Affair at Aklai*, was published in 1960. Then came a long dry spell before three sales enabled her to become a full-time writer in 1965.

Dozens of books later, Virginia is still writing from her home in Boise. Her more recent novels, which are not Gothics, are set in the late nineteenth and twentieth centuries. She often works with the television set on and particularly enjoys afternoon soap operas, such as *One Life to Live*, *Days of Our Lives* and *All My Children*.

Virginia, who is still single, loves to travel and gleans many of her story ideas from her travels abroad. She always travels to Europe by ship ("Flying is for the birds") and has made 22 Atlantic crossings. Paris is her "all-time favorite" romantic city. She prefers to travel alone because she meets more interesting people that way—people who may wind up incorporated into her books as her newest characters.

Noting that few women writers are able to support themselves solely on their writing, Virginia is proud of the fact that she's been able to do just that. "Especially since my father never believed I could do it!" she says.

CATHERINE COULTER

If not for Catherine Coulter, would the pristine Regencies ever have gotten sexy? There were already some stirrings toward more realism, but somebody had to actually start the trend—and that's just what Catherine Coulter did in 1979 with her second Regency, *The Rebel Bride* (NAL/Signet). The hero, Julien, forces himself on his wife, Kate, not realizing that her refusals of him stem from her rape as a child, and not a desire to thwart him.

It was a risk to publish a Regency with—gasp!—sex, but Catherine's editor, Hilary Ross, was willing to try. The risk paid off, for the book has been enormously successful and has set a whole new trend in sensual Regencies.

"It did add a new dimension," Catherine says, rather modestly. "Sex, after all, is an integral part of human experience. Why ignore it and lock the reader out of the bedroom?"

A native of Texas, Catherine earned a bachelor's degree in French literature and European history and a master's degree in French and psychology. She has worked as a gymnastics instructor, an English instructor in Japan and a management consultant in both Europe and the United States. Today, she is a telecommunications manager with an insurance services organization in San Francisco, where she has lived since 1979 with her husband, Anton, who is a doctor and an assistant professor at the University of California at San Francisco.

Catherine began her writing career the way many writers have—reading a great deal and feeling that she could do better. The result was her first Regency, *The Autumn Countess* (NAL/Signet, 1978). "I grew up with Georgette Heyer," she says, "and since I have always found the Napoleonic era and Regency England fascinating, it seemed the only place to start."

In the late 1970s, while her husband was immersed in medical studies, Catherine was reading ten to twenty books a week. When she decided to write a Regency, she and Anton devised a plot. "There were three other plots, three books I had worked out in my head at the time," she says, "but I was hesitant to use them." She wrote *The Autumn Countess* in six months and gave it to a friend at William Morrow Publishing Company, who referred her to a free-lance editor, who in turn recommended it be sent to yet another publisher. First on the list was NAL and Hilary Ross. "Five days later," Catherine recalls, "Hilary called me up for lunch and offered me a three-book contract. I'll never forget how I just stared at her! I was very fortunate—there was no starving in a garret."

"*The Autumn Countess*," Catherine smiles, "had many of the problems of a first novel. I wrote it in first person and adverbed it to death! But," she adds with a bigger smile, "it had a nifty plot that saved it." To date, Catherine has written seven Regencies, the seventh, *An*

Intimate Deception (NAL/Signet), published in April 1983.

Her first long historical, *Devil's Embrace* (NAL/Signet, 1982), was praised by both reviewers and readers, although some took exception to a violent rape scene. The reaction surprised Catherine. She thinks rape doesn't belong in a contemporary romance and strongly objects to it in real life, but she doesn't believe it was out of place in a historical. The violence and sheer horror of the rape was not minimized or "romanticized." "It was," she says, "a necessary step in the plot to further the relationship of the hero and heroine, to add to the readers' understanding of their characters. However," she adds, "I have myself, as a reader of long historicals, gotten quite tired of the heroine who goes from rape to rape, stands up and dusts herself off, until the next time. I will not use any more violent rapes in my future long historicals. But that's not to say," she says, eyes twinkling, "that I will rule out forced seductions by the hero."

Catherine's Regencies take her an average of six months to complete. A long historical takes nine months. Using a computer, she writes from 5:30 to 7 A.M. weekdays before going to work and several hours on weekend mornings. Besides romances, she is considering writing a modern-day medical thriller with Anton.

Catherine feels that "romances should above all be excellent entertainment. Most people, myself included, live reality, after all. They don't want to be immersed in the same problems in their reading, not in a romance novel."

TOM AND SHARON CURTIS

"Our books are a crystallization of the best in us and in our marriage," say Tom and Sharon Curtis, a Wisconsin husband and wife writing team readers recognize as Laura London (Dell historicals and Candlelight Regencies) and Robin James (Jove's Second Chance At Love and To Have And To Hold). It's not unusual for two or more persons to collaborate on a novel, but husband and wife writing teams in the female-oriented romance genre are a rarity. Tom and Sharon are able to blend the emotions and viewpoints of both sexes so that all their characters, male and female alike, are appealing and sympathetic. Those qualities helped make *The Golden Touch*, a Second Chance At Love, an instant classic upon its publication in 1982.

Their close collaboration involves drawing up a synopsis and outline and writing three drafts. The first draft is composed together, Tom at the keyboard of their electronic typewriter and Sharon seated nearby in an easy chair. Sharon reworks the draft alone and then gives it to Tom for his revisions. "We try very hard to write so that people will never suspect the book was written by two people," says Tom. He describes their collaboration as "an anvil and hammer with sparks flying, fire and red-hot going." When they're at an impasse over differences, they often turn to a close friend for arbitration.

Collaboration on sensual scenes was awkward and embarrassing at first, Sharon says. "We stammered around a lot. Actually," she adds with a laugh, "we're pretty shameless!"

Both Tom and Sharon have varied and interesting backgrounds that serve them well as writers. Tom, born on November 11, 1952 in Antigo, Wisconsin (he grew up in Darlington), is a guitar player and was once a member of a rock band. He also worked as a TV journalist, and now is a truck driver, hauling hazardous chemicals, such as chlorine gas, all over the country in an eighteen wheeler. Sharon was born on March 6, 1951 in Dahran, Saudi Arabia to parents who worked for an oil company, Aramoco. She lived in Canada, the Canary Islands, Pakistan and Iran (Ankara and Tehran) before settling back in the United States in Madison, Wisconsin, where she and Tom met at a party in 1969. They were married the same year, and the birth of their son soon followed. A daughter was born eight years later.

Both attended college, read Jane Austen and became acquainted with Georgette Heyer Regencies. "We saw a lot of Regencies on the bookstands," says Tom. "We thought we could write a good one."

College became a financial hardship, and Tom and Sharon had to drop out. Sharon became a beautician but wanted to try writing; journalism left Tom feeling unsatisfied. "I wanted to do just writing," he explains. "Journalism seemed like a compromise. Then I got an itch to drive a truck. I wanted to write, but I hadn't experienced any real life." The couple moved to Greendale, a suburb of Milwaukee, where they live today.

Their first Regency, *A Heart Too Proud* (Dell), was published in 1978, and Sharon quit her job to write full time. "I was the success story of the beauty shop," she says. They wrote four more Regencies, all more sensual than Heyer-type novels, and a longer historical for Dell. Then they turned to contemporary romances, writing for Jove and Bantam (Loveswept). In addition, Tom writes mainstream fiction.

Their college friends thought they were crazy to write romances, but Tom's blue-collar peers have never poked fun at it. "I met guys on the road who've heard about me on the news," says Tom. "I was nervous about getting publicity. But the guys' wives all went out and bought our books, and I haven't gotten any ribbing in six years."

"Writing about love is fun," says Sharon. "Romances have a real optimism, a faith in human nature. People want that."

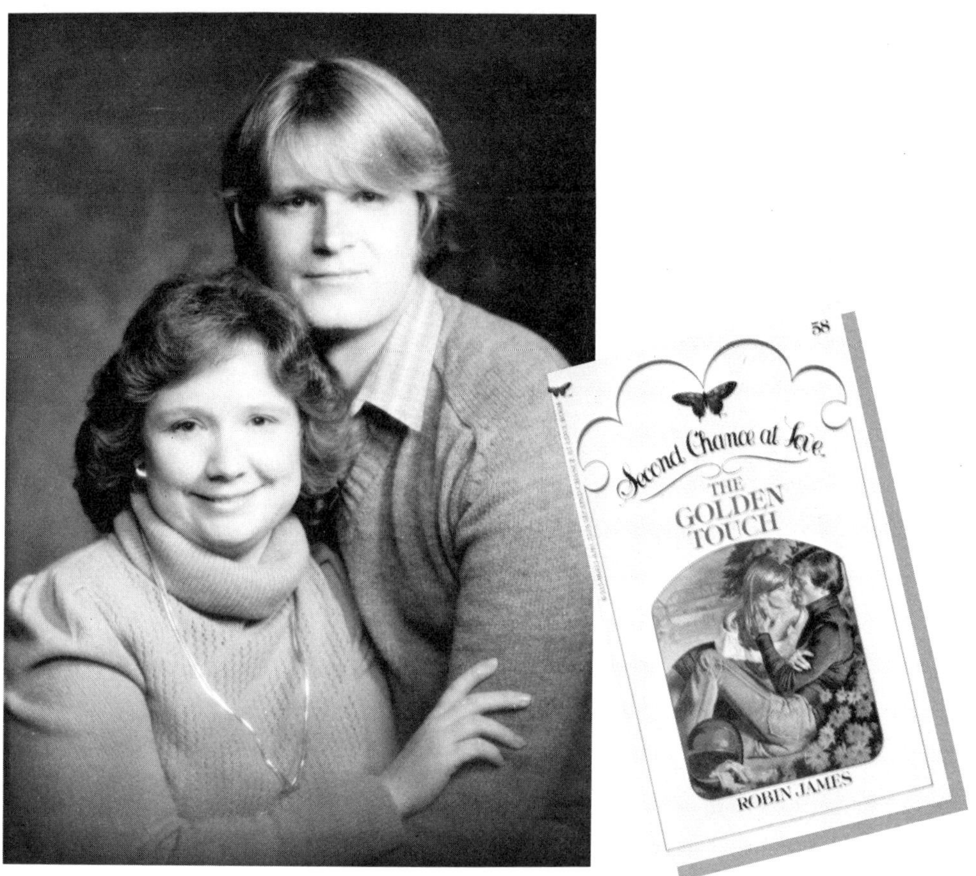

JANET DAILEY

Her incredible success has been heady, but despite the riches and the fame, Janet Dailey has managed to keep her feet firmly planted on the earth. The daughter of an Iowa farmer, she still keeps farmer's hours, arising at 4 A.M. most days to work ten to twelve hours on her latest romance. The result, in a remarkably few short years, is some seventy-six novels completed and more than 90 million copies in print in seventeen languages, making Janet America's leading romance author and the fifth most successful living author in the world.

Despite her seven-figure annual income, Janet still comes across as a down-home midwestern girl, as traditional and American as apple pie. She says she resembles the heroines of her longer, more recent novels—such as *Night Way* and *This Calder Sky* (both Pocket Books)—independent women "patterned after a rugged individualism that made this country what it is."

Born on May 21, 1944, Janet grew up a tomboy and a voracious reader in Early, Iowa. By the fifth grade, she knew she wanted to be a novelist—trouble was, she didn't know just what *kind* of novels.

After high school she moved to Omaha to attend secretarial school. She met her future husband, Bill, by chance on the street, and it was instant mutual attraction. She started work as secretary at his construction and land development company, and the attraction soon blossomed into love. "We still argue over who proposed to whom, probably because it was a mutual decision," Janet says. "We simply closed the office one noon and got married, then went back to work for the rest of the afternoon."

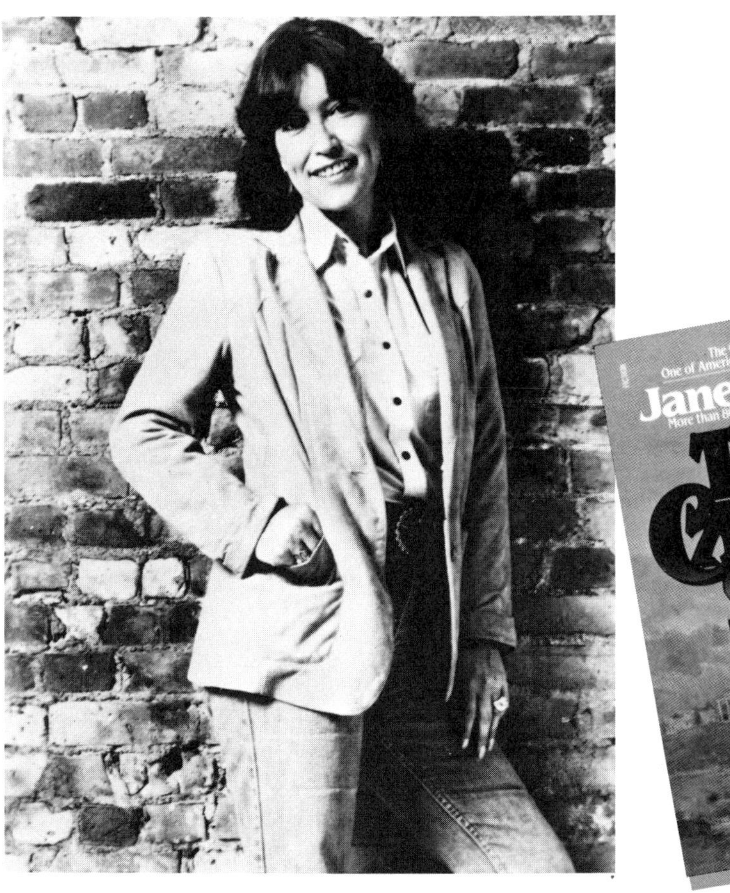

They devoted the next dozen years to building up Bill's business. Meanwhile, Janet discovered Harlequin romances and knew she'd finally found the kind of books she wanted to write. "I felt a complete identification with the books and knew there was a natural link," she explains. "I kept coming up with ideas for plots."

When Bill was forty-five and Janet thirty, they sold their business to travel around the country in a thirty-three-foot Silver Streak trailer. Janet's constant assertions that she could write better romances finally induced Bill to tell her to fish or cut bait. Characteristically, Janet took up the challenge. *No Quarter Asked* was purchased by Harlequin—without revisions.

Since that book's publication in 1976, Janet's rise has been a meteoric one. The early retirement was cut short, and now she and Bill oversee a burgeoning business empire. Janet can turn out a novel in anywhere from eight to forty-five days; Bill assists her with research and manages their business affairs. They live in a fifteen-room lakeshore home near Branson, Missouri. For their swimming pool, Bill had tiles custom-designed with Janet's book covers.

Janet wrote fifty-four Harlequin novels before signing with Silhouette; her longer books are published by Pocket Books, which also produces a biannual newsletter on her for some 33,000 fans. She's temporarily lived in and set a book in every state in the union, which has earned her a place in the *Guinness Book of World Records.*

Meanwhile, new deals keep coming thick and fast. The Daileys' Ramblin' Productions has television, radio and record interests; Wildwood, U.S.A. is a proposed country music theme park near Branson; and the Dailey Institute is an educational subsidiary that offers business seminars and information services.

What's ahead? Television ventures, perhaps, and more books. Their goal is to make Janet the top-selling author in the world, ahead of Harold Robbins, Barbara Cartland, Irving Wallace and Louis L'Amour. Janet's fans seem more than willing to help her get there, a special rapport she's proud of. "I know how my readers think, how they feel, because I've actually lived with them," she says.

JUDE DEVERAUX

She chose her pseudonym, Jude Deveraux, because she thought her real name, Jude Gilliam White, was "pretty boring." And while she insists she's just everyday folk, Jude Deveraux is anything but dull. She's a talented writer of historical romances, most noted for her medieval settings, and she may be the only writer who researches her novels by making doll-sized period costumes and building model villages. What's more, she's a sensitive person who emotes easily, crying when she's happy, sobbing over her galleys when she's not and feeling genuinely distressed when her characters are in a tough spot.

Jude has always been a history buff, tracing her own roots to Appalachia and her ancestors' arrival in America to Pilgrim and Revolutionary War times. She was born on September 20, 1947 in Louisville, Kentucky and spent part of her childhood on a farm in Fairdale. She studied art in college, where she met her husband, Claude White. After her graduation in 1970, they married and immediately moved to Santa Fe, New Mexico, where Claude started his own business as a home designer and builder. Jude taught elementary school and remedial reading until writing changed her life.

She wrote her first novel, *The Enchanted Land*, because she was dissatisfied with many

historicals on the market. "I wrote half of it in a passion and then got scared I was getting in over my head," Jude says. "Lowly school teachers didn't write books." But the novel haunted her, and two years later she finished it—but mailed it to Avon Books only at Claude's insistence.

"I knew my whole life was going to depend on whether or not it was accepted," Jude says. "I got sick and went to bed for three days." Much to her joy and amazement, Avon bought it within a month. She was so excited she tripped on her steps and bloodied both knees.

She wrote her second book, *Black Lyon*, out of fear that she was only a one-book author. She needn't have worried. She now has a dozen or so books out or under contract; she has more than 3.5 million copies in print. Her popularity has spread rapidly with such titles as *The Velvet Promise* (Gallen/Pocket Books) and *Highland Velvet* (Pocket). She is working on a three-book "Virginia saga" with a plantation setting during the 1700s, as well other novels set during frontier times in the American West.

Jude's interest in costume history began with *Black Lyon*, a medieval novel. Before writing, she designs doll costumes, shopping carefully for fabric with small enough print and weave. "If I find a print I like in a fabric store, I cry," says Jude.

She studies museum costume exhibits and has amassed a library of books, slides and drawings on the subject. She's even joined the Costume Society of America. She spends about sixty hours sewing the outfits, and several hundred more hours constructing model villages and castles from kits. It all gives her a clearer picture of the time period she's writing about, she says.

To accommodate her writing, her growing library and files and her dolls and models, Jude has expanded—from an office in her home to the entire house next door, which she and Claude purchased. Incredibly, she writes everything in longhand, averaging 3,500 words a day—and seldom rewrites a sentence. "I don't even own a typewriter," Jude says with a chuckle. "I write faster than most people can type, and it's very legible." All that handwriting can put a cramp in one's muscles, however, and Jude lifts weights to alleviate strain.

When the galleys come, it's a trying moment of truth for Jude. "I cry and tell Claude it's so awful I can't allow it to be published," she confesses. But the moment passes, the book is published—and then the praise starts coming in.

ROBERTA GELLIS

Little girls often become enchanted with tales of castles, fair damsels in distress and knights in shining armor. As a child, and through her adult years, Roberta Gellis loved to read such stories. Although her fascination with medieval history has never lessened, her outlook on this period has changed.

"As I grew older and read more, I discovered that the armor didn't shine, but was full of rust and blood," says Roberta. "And *everyone* back then was full of fleas—baths were a luxury, you see. It wasn't as pretty as the fairy tales, but it was ever so much more interesting!"

Roberta's childhood interest later turned into a serious study of history and literature. Today she is so thoroughly knowledgeable about her two favorite periods—medieval and Napoleonic—that she can relate intimate anecdotes about famous persons as though they were her close friends or next door neighbors. "If there's one thing readers get from my books, it's a sense of history," says Roberta, who brings the past to vivid life in such novels as *The Roselynde Chronicles* (Playboy Press) and *The Heiress Series* (Dell). "I'm intrigued by the interaction of people and their society. I try to give readers an understanding not only of the political events

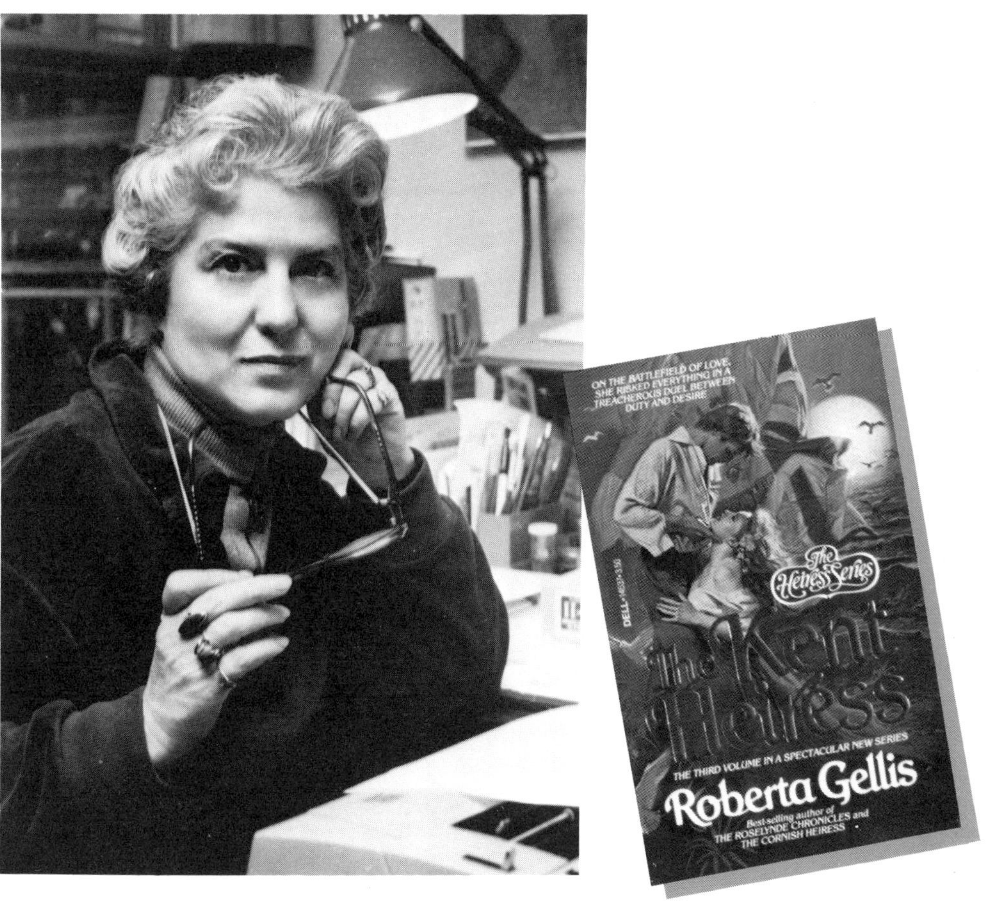

that took place, but people's reactions to them. I try to portray the way they really lived. I don't shirk from unpleasant facts of life," she adds, referring to the terrible sanitary conditions during the Middle Ages.

To tell her stories in such realistic detail, Roberta devotes a great deal of time to meticulous research, including the reading of original historical documents she finds in libraries and museums. She reads French, German and some Spanish as well as enough Latin and Greek to decipher inscriptions. Middle English, which often reads like a foreign language itself, is a snap for her—she grew up reading stories about King Arthur written in it ("I swear that's why I still can't spell," she says with one of her engaging chuckles).

Besides history and literature, Roberta is well versed in science and holds degrees in chemistry and biochemistry. Considering her upbringing, those diverse interests are no surprise. She was born on September 27, 1927 to a mother who was a Greek and Latin scholar and a father who was a well-known chemist. After graduating from college, she worked as a science editor, microbiologist and free-lance editor, meanwhile earning a master's degree in her second love, medieval literature. She finished courses for a doctorate in the subject but chose not to write a thesis because she did not intend to teach.

Roberta works at home in Roslyn Heights, New York, where she and her husband, Charles, have lived since 1957. A son, Mark, is in college. When she isn't working on a novel or speaking to a writer's group, Roberta free-lance edits scientific books. She's a voracious reader of histories, biographies and science fiction. She doesn't like to read contemporary romances—they're "too simplistic"—and shuns historical novels because she fears subliminal plagiarism.

While some may consider her prolific—she's written more than sixteen books since 1975—Roberta claims she is a slow writer. She once wrote everything in longhand with fountain pens, but now she uses a word processor. She carries her work with her everywhere she goes, jotting down notes and passages whenever an idea strikes.

"My characters are very real to me, though I don't identify with them," Roberta says. "I know some authors sublimate their own desires in their characters, but I can't say that I do. But my characters are very real friends who tell me everything, whose feelings I know and understand, as if I were part of them." Her understanding of her characters and her extensive historical knowledge have helped to make Roberta a very popular romance novelist.

BROOKE HASTINGS

The discovery of romances was accidental for Deborah Gordon, but it proved to be a fateful one: so inspired was she that she wrote and published eight novels, all Silhouettes, between 1980 and 1982. Now a full-time writer, Deborah is busy on more novels, thanks to a multiple-book contract with Silhouette. She writes exclusively under the pen name Brooke Hastings, her middle name and her father's name.

Until the late 1970s, Deborah never thought of becoming a fiction author. She had a varied background in such areas as academic research, educational books and filmstrips, political science and consulting, but she'd never written any fiction since her short-story days in high school. Her discovery of Harlequins changed all that.

Born on May 31, 1946 in New York City, Deborah grew up in suburban Yorktown Heights,

learning to play the violin. She graduated from Brandeis University in Massachusetts, Phi Beta Kappa, with a major in political science and additional emphasis on Russian studies. While in school, she married Dave Gordon, now an education administrator for the state of California. The couple later had two children.

Her liberal arts background led her to an assortment of employers, including the Center for Research and Education in Civil Liberties at Columbia University and the Book and Educational Division (now defunct) of the *New York Times*. Following a move to Sacramento, California, where she and her family live today, she worked as a secretary for an insurance company and an analyst for a consulting firm. All of it was great grist, as they say in the writing biz, and Deborah later used some of her experiences in her novels.

It was her involvement in volunteer community work that led Deborah to romances. She collected used books for an organization's sale and started reading the Harlequins that piled up in her garage. Stories by authors such as Charlotte Lamb and Mary Wibberly hooked her immediately.

"They were the most marvelous escape and entertainment," Deborah recalls. "For a couple of hours, they took you away to another world that relaxed you. And at the end, you always felt happy and calm. I had two little kids who were not conducive to calm, and I was going through personal problems at the time."

Deborah quickly wrote two romances and started a third, meanwhile going back to work full time. Her first novel, *Playing for Keeps*, was turned down by Harlequin, but Silhouette snapped it up along with her second, *Innocent Fire*, and all her subsequent novels.

"When I sold the first two, I quit my job within weeks," Deborah says. "With the advances, I was doing just as well as I would have been working for the next nine months—so it was ridiculous for me not to try to make it full time as a writer." She adds, "It's scary to give up the security of a regular paycheck, especially when you need the money. I'm a conservative person, and it wasn't easy to do."

Her worries proved unfounded, however, and today she's still enjoying and profiting from her new career. Besides work and family, Deborah reads a great deal, especially newspapers and magazines for story ideas. She intends to become more involved in writer's groups, such as Romance Writers of America.

Deborah prefers contemporary novels—historical women are too limited in their options, she says—and welcomes the acceptance of more adventure in plots. Asked about her future goals, Deborah replies, "I used to worry a lot about that, what I was going to be doing in five years, but I don't anymore. I think I'd like to try mainstream fiction, but I'm very happy with what I'm doing. I just take it as it comes and try to make every book a good one."

PATRICIA MATTHEWS

"I was always a want-to-be writer," says Patricia (Patty) Matthews, who successfully transformed her childhood dreams into a string of best-selling historical romances, as well as publishing novels in other categories. "I was a bookworm as a kid and I had a rich fantasy life. I put on plays and I wrote poetry. I always wanted to write a book, but it never dawned on me that I could do it myself."

Patty, a native Californian born on July 1, 1927, was an adult before she realized she *could* do it herself. She attended a college creative writing class that gave her the self-confidence she needed to start turning out serious poetry and science fiction short stories. Some of the poems were sold for a dollar apiece to a newspaper poetry column; her first short-story sale was a

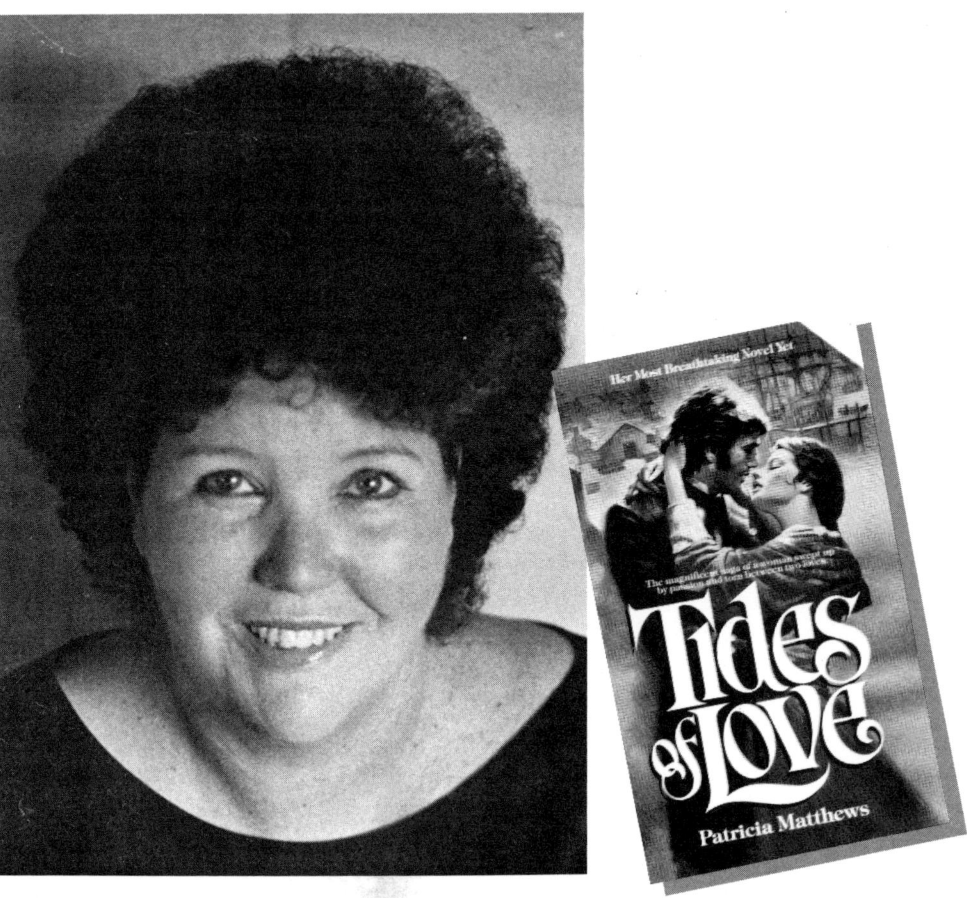

fantasy piece to a men's magazine. Her first novel, science fiction, was sold around 1960, without an agent, for the modest sum of $500.

Patty believes strongly in writing groups, which have proved to be important to her writing career. She helped form one for struggling writers in California and benefitted from the critiquing and mutual support. And it was through a writing group that she met Clayton Matthews, who later became her collaborator and second husband. Since their marriage in 1971, the pair has teamed to write Gothics, mysteries, juvenile fiction and sagas, as well as writing individually. One of their recent major collaborations was *Empire* (Bantam), a saga set in the Alaskan frontier.

Patty entered the historical romance field in the mid-1970s at the suggestion of her agent. "I've always been fond of history," says Patty. "I'm a frustrated social anthropologist. I thought a romance might be fun." She set her first romance, *Love's Avenging Heart* (Pinnacle), in Williamsburg, Virginia, because her interest in that colonial community had just been piqued by a trip there. The book, published in 1977 by Pinnacle, sold more than 1 million copies, enabling Patty to quit her job and become a full-time writer. Her next eleven historicals published by Pinnacle (her other books are published by Bantam), all sold more than 1 million copies each, proving that Patty indeed has the knack for weaving a compelling tale.

"I want to entertain and inform," says Patty. "The history in my books must be accurate, with the fiction story played in front of it. I like to use real people, such as Stephen Crane, Clara Bow and Teddy Roosevelt, as bit players—they add a feeling of the time period. Readers enjoy getting history painlessly."

Patty likes to create strong heroines. Her leading ladies, she notes, "don't stamp their little feet or toss their curls or pound their fists on chests." Another trademark of her novels is the villain. "I always have a strong villain—I learned that from Dickens," she says. "My villains are really *rotten*. Some have a few redeeming qualities, but most are rotten to the core. And they always have to get it in the end, because people want to see justice prevail. Readers love to hate the villains."

Patty's writing habits vary. While Clayton is an early-morning worker, she concentrates on getting a steady amount of work done at varying hours, averaging five typed pages a day. "My first drafts look like they were typed by three chimpanzees, because I don't worry about spelling or typos," she says with a laugh. A new word processor now makes revisions and corrections easier and faster.

Patty and Clayton live in Los Angeles in a beautiful hillside home with a stunning view of the city. Patty plans to continue her winning streak in historical romances, with goals to author more mainstream and fantasy fiction as well.

ALICE MORGAN

Alice Morgan just may be redefining the word "sensual." Her contemporary category romances are so steamy she's even been asked on occasion to "tone it down"—even though "sexy" and "sensual" are the bywords of today's romantic fiction. For Alice, sexier romances are better. They're definitely more fun to write, she says, and writing them is still a new career for this former policewoman.

"I read about 3,000 romances over a three- to four-year period before I wrote my first word," says Alice, noting that her reading preference runs to contemporary "category" novels. "I thought romances needed to be sexier by going *beyond* the bedroom door. There was plenty of this in romance books filled with bed hopping, but I wanted to see it in books committed to a monogamous relationship. I adore sensual men, but only ones faithful to one woman after they fall in love."

The desire to write a romance "just hit me out of the blue," she says. She'd never written a book before, never even considered being a writer, but her new career suits her well. Dell Candlelight Ecstasy published her first three novels, *Masquerade of Love, Sands of Malibu* and *Mysterious Surrogate,* all in 1982, and Alice quickly gained a following. Two more of her books were purchased by Harlequin for its North American line.

Alice, who has spent all but a few months of her life in her native California, was born on July 6, 1933 in Long Beach. She married her high school sweetheart, Bill, right after graduation, in what turned out to be a tragicomic ceremony. Lacking funds for a honeymoon, the young bride-to-be wrote to a Los Angeles television producer asking to be featured on *Wedding Bells,* a show in which couples were married on the air and sent off on an expense-paid honeymoon.

Alice and Bill were accepted, but Bill was injured in an automobile accident on the way to the studio altar. Suffering a concussion, he was taken to a hospital. But the TV staff, not to be done in by a no-show, held the wedding ceremony in the hospital's surgery room. "The only thing I didn't get was the honeymoon, and it serves me right for being so greedy," says Alice with a laugh. A son and a daughter were later born in the same surgery room.

Bill joined the Los Angeles Police Department as a patrolman in the juvenile division, and after their daughter was born, Alice joined the same division as a patrolwoman. Both of them worked a great deal in the juvenile jail. "It was a very exciting, interesting career for a woman to have," Alice observes. "This was back in the 1950s and things were so much different for women—they were more limited in their work."

After five years on the force, Alice sustained a back injury in a scuffle with a female prisoner who objected to being searched, and she had to retire from duty. But her police

experience has given her a rich mine of material for her novels; for example, her heroine in *Sands of Malibu* is a policewoman, an occupation Alice had not seen before in category romances.

Her success as a romance author has significantly changed her and Bill's life style. To accommodate her writing, they moved from a time-consuming citrus ranch in Oroville to a house on the beach in Fort Bragg. In their leisure time, they enjoy beachcombing and hiking along the beach or in the nearby redwood forests. And they've been able to do more traveling.

"I like to write sensuous novels," says Alice. "I feel I've made my hero more sensual than average, because he falls in love with the heroine the moment he sees her, and the reader is aware of it. Most books you have to wait until the last page to realize how strong his feelings are."

LAURA PARKER

"I was a closet writer," laughs Laura Parker in reminiscing about her first novel, a historical romance. "I didn't tell a soul what I was doing, because I thought ordinary people didn't write. My husband was the only one who knew what I was doing." Several years later, when the fruits of her secret labor were purchased by Dell, Laura excitedly called friends and relatives with the news. "What book?" they responded in amazement. "We didn't know you'd written one!"

Her novel, *Silks and Sabers* (1980), had a 200,000-copy first printing and hit B. Dalton's Top 40 list. For Laura, who'd always intended to pursue a science career, it marked the beginning of a writing career instead.

Born on September 18, 1948 in Fort Worth, Texas, Laura grew up in Pine Bluff, Arkansas.

She met and married her husband, Chris Castoro (Parker is her maiden name), in college in Washington, D.C., where she was studying microbiology. The couple moved to Texas, and childrearing terminated Laura's college studies. "Otherwise, I'd probably be working in a lab somewhere right now," she says.

After three children and some moves—the family settled in Plano, Texas, near Dallas—Laura was feeling tied down and frustrated.

"When I was pregnant with my third child and feeling sorry for myself, a neighbor came over one day with a whole sack full of romances," says Laura. She read books by Daphne duMaurier, Mary Stewart and Kathleen E. Woodiwiss, among others, and found they were a terrific fantasy escape. "*The Flame and the Flower* [Woodiwiss] stuck in my mind. I didn't know books like that were being written. But even though I enjoyed it very much, the heroine was such a frightened, timid thing. I kept thinking, wouldn't it be neat if the heroine could take care of herself and save the hero for a change?

"I'd been reading a lot of books by Raphael Sabatini, and I decided it would be fun to write about a heroine with the spirit of a cavalier and who could handle a sword as well as Scaramouche. I wrote about fifty pages and got hooked on finishing it."

Finishing it took about a year and a half, and then, at the urging of a writer she met at a writer's conference, Laura sent her manuscript to Dell. After the success of her first book, Dell contracted for two sagas, *Jim Bridger: Mountain Man* and *Kit Carson: Trapper King,* as well as one book in a historical series on Australia. *Free Woman* (1983) appears under Dell's chosen

pseudonym, Terry Nelsen Bonner, shared by all the writers who've contributed to the series.

Like other historical writers who've seen their market wane as contemporaries have increased, Laura is making the crossover to modern times. In *Til Love Is Enough,* to be published as one of Avon Books' Finding Mr. Right series, two appealing suitors pursue and bed the heroine (but only one wins her in the last chapter).

Laura is maintaining her presence in the historical market with *Emerald and Sapphire,* a title for Pocket Books' Tapestry line, which debuted in October 1982.

Laura puts in a full day at her writing career, working with her word processor in an office at home, often while classical music plays in the background. "I work at writing at least eight hours a day," she says, "and that doesn't include the time I spend thinking about it while I'm washing the dishes or setting the table!" What little free time she has is usually devoted to family activities or reading.

"I'm thrilled to be doing what I'm doing," says Laura, adding that one of her goals is to write and publish midlist fiction in addition to romances.

ROSEMARY ROGERS

Rosemary Rogers is one of the few romance authors who looks and lives like one of her heroines. Slender, glamorous, a lover of champagne, nightlife and first-class travel, she's the envy of many of her fans and associates. Although she enjoyed a comfortable childhood—she was born in 1933 in Ceylon to parents who owned private boarding schools—she had her share of tough times as an adult before her first novel, *Sweet Savage Love,* earned her fame and fortune.

Two broken marriages left Rosemary with four children to support, which wasn't easy on the secretary's salary she was earning in Fairfield, California. She'd always been an artful storyteller as a child, and so she turned to writing as a possible way to earn more money. But her manuscript for *Sweet Savage Love* languished in a drawer until Rosemary noticed the success of Kathleen E. Woodiwiss' first novel, *The Flame and the Flower,* published by Avon Books in 1972. She sent her manuscript to Avon. A practitioner of positive thinking and yoga, Rosemary "imaged" a best-seller, and sure enough, it happened. Avon published *Sweet Savage Love* in 1974 as a "Spectacular" with a large advertising and promotion budget. All of Rosemary's novels published since then, both historical and contemporary, have enjoyed best-seller status. She has some thirty million copies in print and translations in eleven foreign languages.

Rosemary, who still lives in California and keeps an apartment in Manhattan, is a firm believer in the benefits of positive mind power. "You can use your mind to do and achieve things," she asserts. "Mind power also provides inner peace—it helps you stay calm. I don't go around screaming or throwing tantrums, like some people do when they get uptight. I meditate and get inner peace so that I can deal with problems instead of going off the deep end. I don't think you can achieve anything by worrying—it wastes a lot of energy."

When Rosemary is writing a novel, she prefers to work in the afternoon and evenings, scattering her notes and manuscript pages all around her. "Sometimes I write for twenty-four hours at a stretch," she says. "I get up in the afternoon and stay up all night—that's the way my time clock works. I get very energetic at night."

Her irregular habits and hours, she says, are suitable to her single status, which she is determined to keep. "I don't think anyone could stand to live with me because I'm so independent," she says. "My hours are absolutely *weird.* I stay in bed all afternoon sometimes.

If I don't feel like eating, I fast. And when I want to travel, I can take off for someplace at a moment's notice."

Rosemary is a music lover, enjoying the full gamut from disco to opera. She likes to play classical music by Wagner while she writes, and when she's in New York during the opera season, she can be seen at the Metropolitan Opera.

Cooking, she says, is her therapy. "Sometimes when I get a little uptight, I cook. My family usually laughs at me because I never seem to be able to cook in small quantities. I cook in huge quantities and put them in Ziploc bags in the freezer. They always ask if it's safe to open the freezer, because the bags are always falling out."

Rosemary feels very strongly about her family—she's a grandmother now and has adopted a niece—and about being honest and "upfront" with all people. She confesses she was in love with her first fictional hero, Steve Morgan, whom she created for *Sweet Savage Love* and its sequel, *Dark Fires*. *Sweet Savage Love* was a story that percolated in the back of her mind for years before it finally emerged as a published novel. "Would you believe I was writing that on and off since I was twelve years old?" she asks, chuckling in amazement at the idea.

MAURA SEGER

In 1981 Maura Seger was working full time as a free-lance advertising copywriter and had no books published. By the end of 1982, her first romance was published (it sold out its first printing within a month), she had at least ten more books under contract and she was already being talked about as a leading writer of the "new historical." She folded her copywriting business, bought a word processor, adopted four pseudonyms and plunged headlong and full speed into romance.

Whew! Not bad for a start, even though the transition was not without its worries. Leaving a successful business and becoming a fiction writer was, says Maura, "probably the scariest thing I've ever done. Beyond the straightforward financial concerns, I knew I risked shattering a dream I had nourished since childhood. It was very frightening to finally put myself on the line like that, but the rewards have been enormous."

Enormous, indeed. Maura's first published novel, *Defiant Love*, was one of two introductory titles for Pocket Books' Tapestry Romance line in October 1982. It hit both the B. Dalton and Waldenbooks best-seller list, sold out its first printing of 265,000 copies and went back to press. It's a sensual, one-man-one-woman novel that, unlike most historicals, has no violent sex. And it's prototypical of more "gentle persuasion" historicals to come.

Sexual violence is "enormously offensive," says Maura, adding that she prefers strong but tender and loving heroes and heroines.

Beginning in 1983, romance readers will see Maura's novels often on the bookshelves. Several Tapestry historicals, including *Rebellious Love, Forbidden Love* and *Another Season*, and a Silhouette Special Edition, *Freedom to Love*, will appear under her own name. Under the pseudonyms Anne Michaels (the first names of Maura's mother and husband), Sara Jennings, Laurel Winslow and Jenny Bates, she will write for NAL/Signet (Regency), Dell Candlelight Ecstasy, Avon's Finding Mr. Right, Jove's Second Chance At Love and Jove's To Have And To Hold.

To keep up with deadline demands, Maura purchased an Apple III word processor, which she christened Agatha, after Agatha Christie, who often was inspired while eating apples. Agatha resides in Maura's office at home in Stamford, Connecticut.

Although Maura always wanted to be a fiction writer, it was only recently that she discovered romances. Born September 16, 1951 in New York City, she graduated from college with a degree in history and economics and went to work for McGraw-Hill in direct-mail advertising.

Her sole try at fiction writing was a historical novel she wrote in college. "It deservedly went into oblivion," she laughs. She was, however, able to dust it off ten years later and use parts of it in *Defiant Love*.

At McGraw-Hill, she met Michael Seger in 1975, and the two were engaged and married in a whirlwind courtship. They later moved to Stamford, where Maura set up her free-lance business. Michael is now a manager at Playtex International.

It was a free Silhouette Romance attached to a bottle of Ivory liquid soap that piqued Maura's interest in romances in 1980. She spent about a year reading several hundred of them before making her own contribution to the field.

The idea for *Defiant Love* was born almost out of desperation, a daydreaming excursion to escape the drudgery of cleaning out the bathtub. "Proving, if nothing else," says Maura, "that breaking down and cleaning the house can have its own reward."

BERTRICE SMALL

If Bertrice Small could design her own bumper sticker for her car, it wouldn't read, "I'd rather be sailing" or "I'd rather be dancing." It would read, "I'd rather be working." And most days, that's exactly what you can find this energetic author of historical romances doing: working away on her latest manuscript.

"I don't really have leisure time," says dark-haired, ebullient Bertrice, whose appropriate nickname is Sunny. "I like what I do. But I take Sundays off because my family insists, and to me, my family is all."

Born December 9, 1937 in Manhattan, Bertrice has always made up colorful stories as an outlet for her vivid imagination. Her characters take on a life of their own, coming to stay for a time at the Small household in Southold, Long Island. "I think writers of historical fiction are basically half mad," says Bertrice with a laugh. "They have to be in order to come up with the things they do! I think they have contact with something that is not of this plane of awareness."

Whatever special gift or insight that is, it showed in Bertrice's first novel, *The Kadin*, which she spent several years researching, writing and revising before Avon Books published it in 1978. As one of a coterie of Avon romance authors known facetiously as "the Avon ladies," her fortunes as a novelist began to rise. Her success was fortuitous, for her husband, George, a commercial photographer, was experiencing difficulty in his career. As her writing began to demand more of Bertrice's time, they agreed to switch roles, and George now looks after the household, their son, Thomas David, and some of Bertrice's business affairs.

It's hard to believe that this outgoing lady could have any fears or phobias, but early in her marriage, Bertrice suffered from agoraphobia, which is fear of open spaces. Happily, she overcame the phobia and now travels to promote her books. She no longer flies on airplanes, however, having decided on her fortieth birthday that she was entitled to quit doing a few things she especially disliked, and air travel was one of them.

Bertrice now works in an office in Southold village instead of at home. "It's impossible for me to work at home," she explains. "If I do, I revert to type—I make jam, work in the garden, put up wallpaper." She once wrote everything out in longhand, then graduated to a typewriter and has been considering getting a word processor. Typically, her utensils have names. "My current typewriter is Rachel and my previous one was Rebecca," she says. "I had

one in between that had a man's name, and he was a lemon from the word go. It was very strange, because I never have any problems with men. But this typewriter was such a lemon, I can't even remember his name!"

Her chief hobby is gardening, which she approaches with the same vigor as her writing. "I love to get out in the dirt and dig. It's a nice release," Bertrice says. "I never wear gloves. One of the reasons I like gardening is flowers never talk back, and sometimes I need that."

Bertrice is a voracious reader of biographies and history, a keen interest she has had since her college days. She intends to keep writing as many years as she can, building on the best-selling success she achieved with her Ballantine books, *Skye O'Malley* and *Unconquered*. Her basic approach to life, she says, is to never say *never*. "Life is too mercurial," she observes. "It can play funny tricks on you, and you don't want to get yourself boxed into a corner." That's something Bertrice undoubtedly will never have to worry about.

ELIZABETH NEFF WALKER

A desire to write that never quite found the right outlet and then lay dormant for several years suddenly blossomed again for Elizabeth Neff Walker with the discovery of Georgette Heyer Regencies.

The year was 1978 and Neff (her nickname), who'd earlier lived in London for two years, quickly became engrossed in an England of time past. "I was introduced to Regencies by a friend," recalls Neff. "I read all the Georgette Heyers and when I ran out I noticed that Fawcett had a line [Coventry]. I started reading Joan Smith and other authors, and within two months I knew I wanted to write one."

The surge of creativity resulted in six Regencies—and sales. In fact, her first sale comprised two books, to different publishers. "I was thrilled," says Neff. "When you start writing you always think you'd like to get published, but you know how hard it is to get your foot in the door, so you try to keep your expectations within reason. So, to hear that two editors wanted my books was a big thrill."

Neff rode the Regency boom for several years, writing thirteen of them between 1978 and 1982. She's written under the names Elizabeth Walker (her maiden name) for Fawcett and Dell and Laura Matthews (the first names of her daughter and son) for Warner Books. Some of her noteworthy titles are *Alicia* (Dell), *Aim of a Lady* (Warner Books) and *The Lady Next Door* (Fawcett).

But Regencies began to dwindle in the marketplace, and Neff made the crossover to contemporary romances, specifically Avon Books' Finding Mr. Right line, scheduled to debut in 1983. Neff wrote the line's introductory title, *Paper Tiger*, as well as *A Program For Love* (tentative title).

Neff likes the concept of the Mr. Right line: the heroine chooses between two men in her life. She may be sexually involved with both men before she makes her choice, a new twist to category romances that previously have limited the heroine sexually to one man.

Neff still plans to write Regencies as much as the market will allow, keeping her Laura Matthews name for that subcategory and Elizabeth Neff Walker for contemporaries. She is also working on two midlist books, more serious and complicated than most books in the romance genre.

All this writing is a release of creative energy that had simmered inside of Neff since high school. She was born on August 12, 1944 in Pleasant Hills, a suburb of Pittsburgh. For years as a teenager and then an adult, she tried her hand at short stories but sold only one. "They were mostly autobiographical," she says.

After college, Neff headed west and fell in love with San Francisco, where she settled and worked in a variety of clerical jobs. She married her husband, Paul, an architect, in 1966. The couple spent a fascinating two years living in London, giving Neff a perfect background for her later Regency writing. She and Paul returned to San Francisco, where they live now in the fashionable upper Haight-Ashbury district.

Neff enjoys writing romances and has found the switch in time periods and styles easier than she first thought. "I quite enjoy contemporaries," she says. "I didn't think I was going to like it—I had so much fun doing the research for the Regencies."

The sensuality of contemporaries is not new to her—she'd written some sensual scenes for some of her Warner Regencies, and she likes romances to have sensuous detail—but she feels strongly about heroines retaining their own identity and not losing themselves in a man.

Neff also strives for wit and humor in all her novels. "Almost nothing is as enjoyable as a good laugh," she says. "If you can write an amusing book, you've got a winner."

LINDA WISDOM

What she terms her "overactive imagination" and a keen interest in books helped propel Linda Wisdom to her writing career, although it wasn't until she was fired from a job that she turned to writing full time. It was a traumatic lemon of a moment that soon yielded a sweet lemonade, for writing is what Linda does best, as her success as an author of contemporary romances shows.

As many other budding young writers have done, Linda concocted and wrote stories as a child, drawing on her friends for character and plot ideas. A native Californian, born on April 18, 1950 in Santa Monica, she studied journalism in high school and college. She did not pursue a career as a journalist, however, choosing instead secretarial and word-processing work. Her last job was as manager of an employment agency, where she had personal differences with her boss.

Linda has long enjoyed reading Harlequins and historical romances, and the books influenced her to try writing romances herself. She used her experience in a ballet class as background for her first romance and sent the manuscript to Harlequin; when it was rejected, she enrolled in a creative writing class to learn more about technique. On her second try, to Silhouette, Linda was successful, and *Dancer in the Shadows* appeared as a Silhouette Romance in December 1980. More contracts with Silhouette followed, resulting in more than seven Silhouette Romances and Special Editions, such as *Fourteen Karat Beauty, Bright Tomorrow* and *A Man with Doubts.*

Movies have provided a lot of inspiration to Linda, an avid cinema fan with an extensive library of films for her videocassette recorder at home. "Harrison Ford is it for me," she confesses. "I'd like to kidnap him and take him away!" She's watched such Harrison Ford films as *Star Wars, The Empire Strikes Back* and *Raiders of the Lost Ark* more than a dozen times each.

She also uses movies for ideas for love scenes. The fiery seduction between Frank Langella and Kate Nelligan in the recent version of *Dracula* is one of her favorites.

Linda, who lives in Fountain Valley, California with her husband, Bob, an accountant

(they were married in 1971 and have no children), keeps irregular writing hours but prefers late afternoons and evenings. When ideas flash in the middle of the night, Linda jots down notes at the bedside with a flashlight and pen. With the exception of two years in Boston, she has lived in California all her life and prefers the warm, sunny climate that enables her to spend summer afternoons sunbathing by her pool, building up a dark tan to compliment her strawberry blonde hair.

She works her first draft in longhand. Like many other writers who want to boost their productivity, however, she may soon switch to a word processor. A pet cockatiel, Shadow, keeps her company while she works. "Shadow is not happy unless he sits on my shoulder while I write," says Linda. "He talks to me. He can say, 'Silhouette, give me a kiss, pretty boy, hello Shadow' and 'hello Terry'—that's my mother's cockatiel. In his own way, he's great company. I can't work in total silence—I put on records or have the TV going."

For relaxation, Linda swims, does needlepoint and paints plaster figures and plaques. She also collects unicorn pictures, jewelry and knicknacks.

Linda enjoys creating romance stories for the many people who enjoy reading them. "Romances are part reality and part fantasy," she says. "Readers want to lose themselves in them and forget about their troubles. I like to make other people feel good."

KATHLEEN E. WOODIWISS

The woman who set romantic fiction publishing on its ear in 1972 is a shy person who shuns publicity in favor of a quiet life with her family in Princeton, Minnesota. Yet her first four books—all epic historical romances published by Avon Books—have an astounding 15 million copies in print. Thousands of romance readers name her as

their favorite author, and numerous romance authors cite her as their inspiration. She's credited with starting the romantic fiction revolution—with scarcely a press interview or publicity tour.

What Kathleen did by writing *The Flame and the Flower* in the early 1970s may not seem so remarkable now, in light of a $450 to $500 million publishing industry that serves up more than 100 romance novels a month. But the book, a sensual one-man-one-woman romance told from the heroine's point of view, established the predominant pattern for paperback best-seller romances for at least a decade to follow.

What's even more remarkable, Kathleen's trend-setting novel was a slush pile discovery. Thousands upon thousands of unsolicited manuscripts from unknown and would-be writers arrive each month at publishing houses, are condemned to sit on the slush piles and then die unceremoniously. But Kathleen's fat manuscript hooked the attention of Nancy Coffey, then an editor at Avon (now editor in chief of The Berkley Group), who could hardly put it down. Nancy not only lobbied for publishing the novel, but was also able to bring it out as the lead title. *The Flame and the Flower* sold 3.5 million copies.

Between 1972 and 1979, three more of her historicals appeared, set in various time periods and always with lovers faithful to each other. *The Wolf and the Dove*, *Shanna* and *Ashes in the Wind* were all multimillion-copy best-sellers.

"Kathleen possesses a very strong story-telling ability," says Nancy Coffey. "That's what kept me turning the pages. She also cares about her characters, and you have to have that caring for the novel to really come alive. She writes at her own pace and won't deliver her manuscript until she's satisfied with it. And the editor rarely has to do anything to it."

Kathleen did make some publicity appearances and do a promotion tour. "Then we realized that we didn't have to do that to sell her books, and she didn't enjoy it," says Nancy.

In 1982 Avon published her fifth novel, *A Rose in Winter,* with a 1-million-copy first printing, which quickly became a best-seller. In a break with her reclusive habits, Kathleen, Avon's best-selling historical novelist in Canada, made her first-ever trip to Toronto to publicize her book with media appearances and autograph parties.

When she's not writing, Kathleen, a native of Louisiana and a born-again Christian, prefers to spend time with her family, her husband, Ross, now retired from the Air Force, and their three sons. Horses are her relaxation, twenty-five thoroughbred Morgans trained for show around the country.

Her first career was as a fashion model in Japan, where Ross was stationed shortly after their marriage. Then she devoted herself to raising their sons. She decided to write a book when she ran out of the sort of novels she liked to read. In addition to encouraging her, Ross contributed a poem that became the prologue to *The Flame and the Flower.*

Kathleen now composes on a word processor, which she finds a great boon to her writing. In fact, she sometimes gets so carried away that she burns the roast while lost in thought in another century.

"To many of her fans, Woodiwiss is easily the best, most meaningful writer they have ever read," observes King News Service. Perhaps one reason is the thread of faithfulness that runs through all her stories, a sentiment she embodies in her own life. "Marriage is a very important thing to me," Kathleen says. "I just can't imagine it any other way!"

Secrets and the stories behind the stories . . . names and identities revealed . . . what *really* happens when your manuscript lands on an editor's desk . . . and lots of advice, from breaking into the romance market to picking an agent to staying happily married once you're famous. . . .

CHAPTER ONE
Also Known As

Pseudonyms—nearly every writer in romance has one, or more. For some, they're a mask to hide behind; for others, a contractual necessity; and for still others a burden they'd like to shed.

Pseudonyms are nothing new in the writing business. In centuries past, when it wasn't acceptable for women to write, female authors assumed male identities, such as George Sand (Amandine Aurore Lucie Dupin) and George Eliot (Mary Ann Evans). Even today, women use male pseudonyms for novels in traditional male fields, such as westerns, adventures and spy thrillers.

Famous writers have used pen names; Charles Dickens, for example, used the name Boz. And we know many famous writers by their pseudonyms rather than their real names: Stendhal, who was Marie-Henri Beyle; Lewis Carroll, who was Charles Dodgson; Voltaire, who was Francois-Marie Arouet; Mark Twain, who was Samuel Clemens. Ellery Queen was the famous pseudonym for two mystery writers: Manfred B. Lee and Frederic Dannay.

It's not unusual for established authors to use a pseudonym when they try something different, say switching from westerns to science fiction, to avoid disappointing established fans. "It's a time-honored tradition in publishing to write under different names for different audiences," says Carolyn Nichols, senior editor of Bantam's Loveswept line.

Publishers and book packagers sometimes use pseudonyms for series, thus giving customers the impression that one or two writers are responsible for works actually created by many writers—dozens in some cases. The late Harriet Stratemeyer packaged such popular young adult series as Tom Swift Jr., Nancy Drew, The Hardy Boys and The Bobbsey Twins this way. Romance writer Laura Parker (real name: Laura Castoro) was one of several writers contributing to a Dell historical series on Australia. All of the novels in the series, including Laura's (*Free Woman*), appear under the single pseudonym of Terry Nelson Bonner.

Writers are constantly admonished by their colleagues to "save" their real names for their "serious" books. If you must break into publishing by writing westerns, science fiction or—horrors—*romances*, for heaven's sakes use a pseudonym. Then, when you finally write the Great American Novel that will leap to the top of the *New York Times Book Review* bestseller list and win the Pulitzer Prize, you can be famous under your own name. The assumed identities for all those pulp novels that fed you and paid your rent for so many years can be retired to the closet—where they belong.

But the brisk sales of romances have brought a lot of publicity to the genre, which in turn has focused attention on the writers. Many of these writers have become well known by their pseudonyms, rather than their real names, often to their dismay.

Writer identities are further fractured by the use of multiple pseudonyms, one for each publisher, instead of one name for the entire romance genre. The pseudonyms are often required by publishers for competitive reasons.

The practice of required pseudonyms for romances had its beginnings in the 1960s and 1970s, when Gothics and historical romances were very popular. Some authors wrote under their own names, while others who considered themselves too "serious" for the genre wanted pseudonyms. Willing or not, many were required to use pen names by editors who were striving for effect. "I was named by an editor who thought 'Diana Haviland' sounded romantic," says Diana, who in real life is Florence Hershman. Told she had to have a pseudonym, she suggested several, which were rejected in favor of the name she still uses today.

Laura Parker's pen name was created when a Dell editor told her that her own last name, Castoro, might be too difficult to pronounce and remember. "I suggested Parker, my maiden name," Laura says, "and she said fine."

Some writers, however, were able to establish themselves on their own names, and they remain some of the biggest stars in the genre: Kathleen Woodiwiss, Janet Dailey, Bertrice Small, Rosemary Rogers, Shirlee Busbee, Roberta Gellis, Parris Afton Bonds, Patricia Matthews, Virginia Coffman, to name just a few.

Aliases are automatically required for men and collaborators. No one in publishing seems to like the idea of male or multiple names on a romance cover. "I wasn't crazy about writing under a woman's name," says Morris Hershman, aka Janet Templeton, Evelyn Bond, Jessica Wilcox and Sarah Roffman. "The publishers think this type of book would naturally be written by a woman. There's a feeling that it wouldn't sell otherwise."

Tom Huff, who'd used the female pseudonyms Edwina Marlow and Beatrice Parker for Gothics and Regencies, was given his most famous alias, Jennifer Wilde, by a Warner Books editor. "*Love's Tender Fury* by Tom Huff does not have the cachet that *Love's Tender Fury* by Jennifer Wilde does," acknowledges Tom. Another male writer, Michael Hinkemeyer, was christened Vanessa Royall by Dell.

A few well-known pseudonyms for collaborators include Fern Michaels (Roberta Anderson and Mary Kuczir), Robin James and Laura London (Tom and Sharon Curtis), Diana Morgan (Irene Goodman and Alex Kamaroff), Linda Trent (Linda and Dan Trent) and Day Taylor (Sharon Salvato and Cornelia Parkinson).

Writers of contemporary romances are most often required to use pseudonyms. In many cases, the publisher not only insists on a pseudonym but retains ownership of it, so that an author writing for different lines has to use a new name for each line. Hard-nosed business reasons are behind this practice.

Harlequin romances, which monopolized the market until the 1980s, seemed to sell in about the same quantities regardless of author, and American publishers strived to imitate Harlequin's brand-name success. "We had no trained pool of our own talent," says Carolyn Nichols, who was senior editor of Jove's Second Chance At Love when the American contemporary romance industry was taking shape. "Very quickly we [editors] had to educate ourselves and our authors. So we did two things—we wrote extensive guidelines and instituted the pseudonym. One of the reasons I myself required pseudonyms [for Second Chance At Love] was that I was trying to bring authors over from other subcategories, such as Gothics and Regencies, and I didn't want to confuse the audiences."

While a few contemporary writers have started with their own names, still fewer have managed to hang onto them when switching lines, even if they're well-known, due to exclusion clauses in their contracts. Elaine Raco Chase is perhaps one of a handful who writes for several lines under the same, and her own, name. She started with Dell Candlelight Ecstasy and now also writes for Silhouette and Finding Mr. Right. "I don't want to write anything I can't put my own name on," Elaine says.

Author David Wind, best known as Monica Barrie as well as Jennifer Dalton and Marilyn Davidson, has unusual contract terms that allow him to retain limited use of two of his pen names (Marilyn Davidson is used for only one publisher: New American Library). David can switch Monica Barrie and Jennifer Dalton from line to line, as long as it's not for books of the same length. That is, he's precluded from writing short contemporary romances for two different publishers under Monica Barrie, for example, but he can write short books for one and longer books for another. It all depends on the word count.

If you're a famous writer with a track record and a tough agent, you've got leverage. Other less established writers have little leverage, and unpublished writers who want to break in have none. "We require exclusive pseudonyms," says Robin Grunder, editor of Rapture Romances. "We don't want to see a name built up and then have the author move to another house." If a publisher owns the name, it can be used no matter who is writing the books, even long after the original author may have left.

Publisher ownership of pseudonyms is disadvantageous for writers. It's a name-recognition business, and a prolific author who writes for several lines can't build a following on a single name identity. Established audiences help boost the earning power of authors. Having to use multiple pseudonyms means they often compete against themselves. Even though dedicated fans make an effort to keep track of the aliases of their favorite authors, casual and impulse buyers may not. Readers more and more are buying according to author rather than by brand line or cover appeal. A familiar name can clinch a book sale, whereas a popular author's new and little-known pseudonym may not.

Carolyn Nichols thinks it's time to get away from the pseudonym, particularly the multiple pseudonym, game. "That's not the way authors build a career," she says. "I'm certain that in a limited number of cases there's always going to be a need for a pseudonym. But I think you're going to see the industry change, and I hope Bantam is going to be the trendsetter."

All Loveswept authors are being published under their real names. In addition, they'll be promoted on the inside covers with their photos and a short biography. For many, that's a welcome opportunity for some real name recognition.

ALTER EGOS

Using a pseudonym is customary in the romance genre, and many authors are known better by their assumed identities than their real ones. Some authors have only one or two pen names; others have collected several, one for each type or line of romances. Below is a list of authors and their pseudonyms, compiled with the help of Kathryn Falk, publisher of *Romantic Times:*

AUTHOR'S NAME	PSEUDONYMS
Bancroft, Iris	Iris Brent Andrea Layton
Brown, Sandra	Laura Jordan Erin St. Claire Rachel Ryan
Browning, Dixie	Zoe Dozier
Camp, Candace	Kristin James Lisa Gregory Sharon Stephens
Castoro, Laura	Laura Parker
Chesney, Marion	Jennie Tremaine Helen Crampton Ann Fairfax Charlotte Ward
Coffman, Virginia	Jeanne Duval
Curtis, Tom & Sharon	Robin James Laura London
Delinksy, Barbara	Bonnie Drake Billie Douglass
Dial, Joan	Amanda York Katherine Kent
Eliott, Nancy	Ellen Langtry
Garlock, Dorothy	Johanna Phillips Dorothy Phillips
Gordon, Deborah	Brooke Hastings
Guntrum, Suzanne	Suzanne Simmons Suzanne Simms
Hershman, Florence	Diana Haviland
Hershman, Morris	Janet Templeton Evelyn Bond Jessica Wilcox Sarah Roffman
Hibbert, Eleanor	Victoria Holt Jean Plaidy Philippa Carr
Himrod, Brenda	Megan Lane

AUTHOR'S NAME	PSEUDONYMS
Hines, Jean	Valerie Sherwood Rosamund Royal
Hinkemeyer, Michael	Vanessa Royall
Hold, Joan M.	Amii Lorin
Holland, Sheila	Charlotte Lamb Laura Hardy Sheila Lancaster Victoria Woolf Sheila Coates
Huff, Tom	Jennifer Wilde Beatrice Parker Edwina Marlow
Kamian, Marcia	Marcia Rose
Krentz, Jayne	Jayne Castle Stephanie James Jayne Bentley Jayne Roberts
Lee, Elsie	Elsie Cromwell Jane Gordon Lee Sheridan
Leigh, Roberta	Rachel Lindsay Rozella Lake
Maxwell, Patricia	Jennifer Blake Patricia Ponder Elizabeth Trehearne Maxine Patrick
McCue, Noelle Berry	Nicole Monet
Mittermeyer, Helen	Ann Cristy Hayton Monteith
Neggers, Carla	Amalia James
Pearl, Jack	Stephanie Blake
Preston, Fayrene	Jaelyn Conlee
Roberts, Janet Louise	Janette Radcliffe Louisa Bronte Rebecca Danton
Rogers, Rosemary	Marina Mayson

AUTHOR'S NAME	PSEUDONYMS
Saunders, Jean	Jean Innes Rowena Summers Sally Blake
Sederguest, Mary	Katherine Granger Katherine Ransom
Seger, Maura	Anne Michaels Sara Jennings Laurel Winslow Jenny Bates
Stevenson, Florence	Zabrina Faire Lucia Curzon
Strother, Pat Wallace	Vivian Lord Patricia Cloud Pat Wallace
Townsend, Tom	Tammie Lee
Vandergriff, Aola	Kitt Brown Jacqueline Gibson Jacqueline LaTourette
Walker, Elizabeth Neff	Laura Matthews
White, Jude Gilliam	Jude Deveraux
Williams, Jean	Megan Castell Jeanne Crecy Jeanne Foster Dierdre Rowan Megan Stuart Kristin Michaels
Wind, David	Monica Barrie Jennifer Dalton Marilyn Davidson
Wright, Cynthia	Devon Lindsay

CHOOSING AN ALIAS

When an author must use a pseudonym, how does she or her select one? Go through the phone book?

Usually not. Romance pseudonyms are almost always names in the writer's family. Or they're concocted for their appropriately romantic and hopefully memorable sound.

Maiden names are commonly used, as are the first names of children, such as Rachel Ryan (Sandra Brown's son and daughter), or Lisa Gregory and Kristin James (Candace Camp's nieces and nephews). A mother's or grandmother's maiden name may also be used; Patricia Maxwell took her grandmother's maiden name, Blake, and combined it with Jennifer, a name that had always been a favorite of hers. While Patricia has other pseudonyms, she's best known as Jennifer Blake. Maura Seger uses the first names of her mother and husband for one of her pseudonyms: Anne Michaels.

Once family names have been used, an author must turn elsewhere for a nom de plume. One author went so far as to legally adopt her pen name. Rebecca Wadsworth replaced her last name with Brandewyne because she liked the sound of it and it started with a "B," thus guaranteeing her a high place on a bookshelf. Brandewyne is one of the first names a browsing customer is likely to spot.

WOULD KEN FOLLETT WRITE A ROMANCE?

There's a romance editor who has a secret dream: somehow convince best-selling thriller author Ken Follett to write a love story—under a pseudonym, of course. Here's why.

"I thought the end of *The Eye of the Needle,* which involves a woman, was so beautifully and carefully done from a woman's point of view," says the editor, who shall remain anonymous (at this writer's discretion). "He's one of the few men I've ever seen able to write that superbly for a woman reader. It's one of my fondest dreams that one day I could convince Mr. Follett to write a woman's book—a romance.

"Naturally, if you could get someone like him to do that, you wouldn't put his real name on it, for the reason that his millions of fans, expecting to pick up a super spy thriller and finding a love story instead, would be angry."

But under a pseudonym, there would be those millions of romance readers looking for a super love story. . . .

IX. TRUE CONFESSIONS

Despite those feminine names on the cover of every romance, not every romance author is a woman. Yes, some of them are indeed men, but most of them stay in hiding, either under pain of death in their contracts or due to acute embarrassment. They'd rather be caught eating quiche.

There shouldn't be anything unmanly, however, about writing romances. In fact, they're darn hard for a man to do well, and men who are successful at it deserve a special pat on the back for their understanding of women; it's men's lack of understanding of women that helps make romances so popular in the first place. And there's definitely nothing unmanly about banking a hefty royalty check.

Estimates of the number of men successfully writing romances vary greatly. Author Tom Huff, better known as Jennifer Wilde, believes 40 percent of all romance writers are men. Vivian Stephens, senior editor of Harlequin American Romances, places the figure at 20 percent. Silhouette Books editors say they have "a few" men, less than half a dozen, out of 185 or so writers (Silhouette contracts stipulate that male writers keep their identities secret). Robin Grunder, editor of New American Library's Rapture Romances, figures she has "five or six" men among fifty writers.

Carolyn Nichols, senior editor of Bantam's Loveswept line, says she has no male writers, having tried and failed with several of them.

Regardless of how many male romance authors really exist, one thing is certain: there are many, many more men who would like to write and sell romances. The lure of the cash register is a powerful one.

But writing a romance is not as easy as it looks, especially for a man. They may understand the skeletal framework of the novels, but they often miss the heart and soul—the emotion that's so important to a woman. "Romance is a woman's fantasy, which is different from a man's fantasy," says Robin. "A lot of men either don't understand the fantasy or they just try to copy someone else's style, and it shows."

"You have to have a gift for flowery language, and you have to put a lot of passion in scenes where the hero and heroine are in conflict or in bed," according to Michael Hinkemeyer, who writes historical romances as Vanessa Royall. "It has to be done with more fever than most men would write."

Good point. Men do face two significant obstacles in trying to write romance from a female viewpoint: sexual and sensual description.

"Male and female fantasies are very different, and male and female descriptions of them are different," asserts Karen Solem, vice president and editor in chief of Silhouette Books. "Men are much more graphic and mechanical."

Leslie Wainger, Silhouette editor, adds, "Men write sex scenes, not love scenes. It's something in their tone that's very matter of fact. They don't get the emotion that a woman feels. It's hard to explain, but easy to recognize."

The graphic nature of male fantasies has enabled men to be more successful with bodice ripper historicals and blockbuster sagas than with short contemporary romances. Historicals and sagas tend to have more adventure and more violent sex, including rape. Karen says, "In many of the stories either edited or written by men, rape is seen as nothing wrong. But rape is not a pleasant experience for any woman, and it's never portrayed that way in a book written by a woman."

Not all men automatically put rape in their books. "It's offensive to me," comments Michael, who keeps rape out of his historicals.

Longer historicals, sagas and mainstream novels are also easier for men to write than are romances, because, notes Carolyn, "they are written from broader canvases, from shifting points of view or from the omniscient third person. But these contemporary romances are intimate little pieces, and they're written more or less from the heroine's point of view."

And neither the heroine nor the reader is interested in getting undressed a lot. Some terrific love scenes, sure, but the emphasis is on emotion. Women become immersed in the emotion of falling in love and in loving; men are more concerned with sexual technique.

Men often don't realize how critical women are of their own bodies and appearances. Even if a woman is attractive—as all romance heroines are—she still casts a harsh eye upon herself, usually wishing that this or that were different. A male-created heroine often admires herself too much.

So much for sex and bodies. The second stumbling block men encounter in writing romances is sensual description, which is not limited to sexual description but involves all senses in all things. Women notice details, such as colors, textures and smells, but it's a subtle awareness. "I believe this is part of nurture, not nature," says Carolyn. "Culture teaches such things differently to men and women. A woman generally has been taught to be more aware of her surroundings, but it's unconscious."

Male writers, once they become attuned to this awareness difference, still have a difficult time grasping the subtlety of it. They tend to describe things too pointedly and to excess.

Many aspiring male romance writers are professional writers in other fields and are attracted to romances because of the demand, the money and the deceptively simple appearance of them. Why not knock out a few and cash in? However, the editors universally insist that previous experience as a writer doesn't guarantee success in the romance field. The best writers, in fact, are readers who've read hundreds of romances and love the fantasy and have something to add to it—and most of them have never written a book before. "I don't see how it would be possible to turn out a great romance if they're just working for big bucks and we're just any old editors," Carolyn contends.

Nevertheless, male romance writer Tom Townsend (aka Tammie Lee) says: "I fail to see any real discrimination against men in the business, although I doubt if we are likely to see male bylines on romance novels for some time to come. That, however, is the publishing business."

Let's meet a few male romance authors who've overcome the obstacles and won against the odds:

MONICA BARRIE

When Richard Gallen Books published *Invitation Only* by Monica Barrie in March 1982, the book was hailed by romance reviewers and sold well in the stores. Much to everyone's astonishment, the author turned out to be a man—David Wind.

The fact that he can write so well from a woman's viewpoint doesn't surprise David. "It's a writer's job to write from the character's point of view," he says. "I have always had good empathy and a lot of friendships with women. I would never try to write in the first person from a woman's standpoint, but I can put myself in a woman's place."

David believes that basically men and women really do not think and feel differently—they're just conditioned by culture to think and act in certain ways. He uses both male and female points of view in his romances. David also credits his wife, Bonnie, with helping him stay on the right track with his female heroines. "She does a lot of my pre-editing," he says.

By the end of 1982, David had signed enough contracts for novels to begin writing full time. It took him six years to get there, and the woman who gave him his first break was Star Helmer, formerly editor in chief of Richard Gallen and now editorial director of Harlequin's Superromance line.

From the time he was a teenager and was reading 200 to 300 books a year, David knew he wanted to write, but he had a varied career before he reached his goal. He was born in New York City on February 29, 1944 and spent his adolescence in Hollywood, Florida. He studied law and then went to work for Playboy as an assistant general manager of the Playboy Club in Chicago.

He served briefly in the U.S. Army Signal Corps, went back to work for Playboy in Chicago and later became an advertising account executive. Following that, he moved back to New York and became a hairdresser, establishing his own salon in Manhattan. Today, he and Bonnie, a social worker in gerontology, live in Pomona, New York with David's son from his first marriage.

His first two novels (both suspense) went unpublished, and David says he wasted two years taking his first manuscript from agent to agent. Star was a salon client of his, and one day he asked her to read his manuscripts and tell him what was wrong with them.

She told him she liked his writing, gave him a stack of romances and asked him to read them and see if he was interested in writing from a woman's point of view. David did an outline for a historical, *Whispers of Destiny*, and a week later Star bought it.

That historical was published after *Invitation Only*, a contemporary romance. David says, "From those two books, I was able to get more contracts," with Silhouette, New American Library and Gallen. Among his 1983 releases were *Cry Mercy, Cry Love* (Silhouette Special Edition); *Island of Desire* (Silhouette Intimate Moments); and, under another pseudonym, Jennifer Dalton, *Run on the Wind* (Gallen/Dell). He's also sold a mainstream historical novel to Pocket Books, scheduled to be published in 1984–85 under his own name.

David's best-known pseudonym, Monica Barrie, appears on his contemporary romances for Gallen and Silhouette; Jennifer Dalton is used for historical romances; and Marilyn Davidson for New American Library. "I picked them for the way they sound," David says. "I wasn't looking for exotic pseudonyms." Marilyn Davidson is a combination of his wife's middle name and his name with "son" added.

David doesn't mind acknowledging he writes in a female-dominated field. "It's usually writers who are ashamed of what they're doing who don't want their pseudonyms revealed," he says. "I'm not, because I like to entertain people. Writing romances hasn't stopped me from selling mainstream. Even so, I plan on staying with romances—I enjoy them."

TAMMIE LEE

Is it possible for a soldier of fortune, adventurer and bodyguard to find happiness and success writing romances? Certainly—just ask Tom Townsend, otherwise known to romance readers as Tammie Lee.

Tom's biography sounds like that of a swashbuckling romantic hero, and his colorful background has proved to be a plus in writing fiction. A native of Waukegan, Illinois (born January 6, 1944), he spent six years in the U.S. Army after high school and was discharged with the rank of first lieutenant. Since then, he's worked at what he terms "oddball occupations," including being a foreign military adviser in Central America, a bodyguard, a truck driver, a sailor and a yacht captain.

In the early 1970s, he lived aboard his own sailboat and worked as a yacht delivery captain in the Gulf of Mexico and the Caribbean. In 1976–77, he worked as a first mate on a square-rigged sailing ship; after that, he owned and operated a sailing school and taught celestial navigation. He also worked as a captain of yachts for a Texas oil company and as feature editor for a boating magazine.

Tom began free-lance writing in 1970, selling some 300 magazine articles to date, mostly to treasure and boating magazines, plus articles on UFOs and psychic phenomena. Today he concentrates on books and lives with his wife, Janet, and teenage daughter on a small ranch in Kemah, Texas, south of Houston.

"My first interest in romance was admittedly economic," Tom says candidly. "I have always had to write for money and have always tried to write what is selling. However, love is undoubtedly the greatest driving force in the universe and is therefore an essential part of most all fiction."

His first romance, a historical, was published in April 1983 by Zebra Books as part of its Leather And Lace series. *Texas Wild Flower*

is the story of Madeline Regaud, wife of pirate Jean Lafitte of Galveston Island. Tom, who likes a fast-paced book with lots of adventure, lets his heroine take part in the action and battles.

"Historical romance is easier for me to write than contemporary romance because it allows for more action and subplotting. Most historicals contain relatively large elements of adventure and at least some violence, both of which have long been cornerstones of American literature. It is perhaps harder for a man to build a good story strictly on character interaction."

His pseudonym "is as close as I can get to my own name. Lee is my middle name, and Tammie substitutes for Tommy."

Tom has written other books: one mainstream novel, *The Last Gray Wolf* (Larksdale Press); and three nonfiction books, *Texas Treasure Coast* (Eaken Press) and *Researching for Modern Fiction* and *Care and Feeding of Fictional Characters* (both Larksdale).

He says he doesn't think it is true that women generally don't like to read romances written by men. "I have been told by publishers that women do not like to think that a man knows enough about them to write from their point of view. Speaking for myself, I can only say that I have been very interested in women since I was twelve years old. They have caused me more trouble and more pleasure than any other single factor in my entire life. I make no pretense of understanding them, but they have been a subject of considerable study for me for many years.

"I believe that a good writer can write from almost any point of view," Tom continues. "The creation of any fictional character requires a considerable amount of projection into that character no matter what sex is involved.

"It's unfortunate," adds Tom, "that authors today are forced to classify all fiction under some specific category. This stifles an author's creativity and eliminates from the market some of the best novels simply because they do not meet any major publisher's guidelines."

VANESSA ROYALL

Historical romance author Michael Hinkemeyer has a clear picture of the imaginary woman who is his pseudonym—Vanessa Royall: "I see Vanessa as thirty-two, brunette and fiery, has some dark secrets in her past, and dumps men right and left. Mean!" he adds with a laugh.

Michael, who also writes suspense novels under his own name, doesn't mind being Vanessa Royall, because the female alias has brought him a lot of publicity and exposure he might not have received in the suspense genre. "I'm jealous that Vanessa is doing better than I am," he jokes.

As Vanessa, Michael has written five historical romances, all published by Dell. His first, which appeared in 1978, was *Flames of Desire*. It was followed by *Come Faith, Come Fire*, *Firebrand's Woman*, *Wild Wind Westward* and *Seize the Dawn*. "When I started writing historicals, I didn't suspect that I would be using a pseudonym," he says. "Dell chose the name for me. It didn't bother me, but I wondered why." The explanation that women would be more likely to buy a romance written by a woman made sense to him, though today it doesn't seem as important.

Michael worked in academia before turning to writing full time. He was born in 1940 in St. Cloud, Minnesota and was raised on a farm outside of town. He earned a bachelor's degree in history and then joined the Army, which sent him to Germany as a quartermaster.

It was in Germany that he became acquainted with historical romances. "I knew a girl who was reading a book that looked pretty trashy—I thought I knew all about great literature—but I picked it up and read it, and it was a real grabber all the way through. It was Kathleen Winsor's *Forever Amber*. It was the only book I'd ever read like that other than *Gone with the Wind*."

While *Forever Amber* was interesting, more than a decade passed before Michael thought much about historical romances again. Mean-

while, he returned to the States, earned a master's degree in history and a PhD in education at Northwestern University and taught at high school and college. In 1971, he moved to New York to teach at Queens College, where he stayed until 1976, when he began writing full time. Today Michael lives in Manhasset on Long Island with his wife, Arlene—a former teacher and textbook editor and now president of the local chapter of the League of Women Voters—and son and daughter.

His first suspense novel, *The Dark Below,* was published in 1974 by Fawcett. Michael wrote three more suspense novels before his agent suggested he try historical romances, which were selling well in the marketplace. Then Michael recalled *Forever Amber* and decided to give it a go. "I thoroughly enjoyed writing it," he says of *Flames of Desire*. "I wrote it in about three months—it just came roaring out." Michael adds, "I was quite pleased [with its success] because it meant I knew something about love." He continues to write suspense novels as well as historicals.

From the beginning, his male identity was no secret, and Michael was encouraged to do interviews. Asked if he received much negative reaction, he responded, "I lift weights and I'm a pretty strong guy, so they probably keep their mouths shut." He adds, "There were a few signs of surprise from my ex-colleagues in the university business. They don't read anything but tedious tracts, and they were surprised that I was writing popular fiction—they thought I was more serious than that."

Michael, all of whose historicals have sold well, is surprised at the continuing strength of the historical romance market as a whole. "Essentially, it's the same story over and over, even though the settings and characters change. And it's been done for about the last ten years."

Michael uses both male and female viewpoints in his romances. He says that for the heroine it's a matter of knowing her, knowing what she would do in a situation and how she would react. "But the man has to enjoy it, too," he says.

JENNIFER WILDE

The name Jennifer Wilde conjures up an image of an exotic, feline female—perhaps one with porcelain skin, a thick mane of shiny red hair and pouty, sensuous lips. In reality, the person behind that sexy name is a man: Tom Huff, a tall and imposing Texan with graying hair, dark spectacles and a soft-spoken, pleasant manner.

Tom was christened Jennifer Wilde by Warner Books in 1976 with the publication of *Love's Tender Fury*, part of Warner's line of historical romances. "It was felt then by many in the publishing business that women wouldn't buy romances written by men," explains Tom. "They [Warner] thought 'Jennifer' sounded very aristocratic, and they wanted a last name to go with it that would bring to mind all those wonderful movies with Maureen O'Hara and Cornel Wilde."

Tom has written and published other novels under his own name, but it's been as Jennifer Wilde that he has achieved best-sellerdom. In addition to *Love's Tender Fury*—which has had forty-one printings with over 3 million copies in print—*Dare to Love* and *Love Me, Marietta* have been blockbuster historical romance titles.

Tom readily admits that there's never really been any secret about the true identity of Jennifer Wilde. Although he shies away from publicity, he's always acknowledged his "alter ego."

Born on January 8, 1940 in Fort Worth, Texas, Tom did a stint in the Army and then taught high school English for four years before he sold his first novel. He quit to write full time, nine years elapsed before he achieved fame as Jennifer Wilde. Tom still writes under his own name as well as other pseudonyms and has penned twenty-three mysteries, Gothics, Regencies and contemporary mainstream novels.

Although he's lived in glamorous cities, such as New York and London, Tom prefers Fort Worth, with its relaxed, folksy ambience. He lives in a brick, three-story, octagon-shaped house he describes as "Dragonwood Castle," which he shares with his mother, Beatrice. A carpentry buff, he renovated the house himself. It includes a swimming pool and spa, and it's filled with books—some 25,000 of them.

IX. TRUE CONFESSIONS

"When I'm working, I'm extremely disciplined," Says Tom. "I let nothing interfere. I don't have a phone in my study and I do virtually no socializing. I'm really a social creature—I like the opera, theater, traveling and being with good friends like Rosie [Rosemary Rogers]—but when I'm working, I have very little time for those activities."

Tom's work habits vary. Once he preferred to arise around noon and work all night long, typing away on his manual typewriter. Now he likes to get up around 10 A.M., swim a mile and then work in three or so stretches until the early hours of the morning. Since he isn't married, he doesn't have to worry about family distractions and schedules.

Tom says his outlook on life is very old-fashioned. "I think we should love one another and do unto others as we want them to do unto us," he says. "I'm a very amiable, easy-going person. I think people around the world should have more compassion, more laughter and more levity. People who do not take themselves seriously do not throw bombs and take others hostage, and they don't kill each other."

Tom plans to continue writing books under both his own name and that of his famous alter ego. "I want to write very good books that others will enjoy," he says. "I like bringing that kind of pleasure to people."

IX. TRUE CONFESSIONS

Success as a romance writer isn't all hearts and flowers, swimming pools and a Mercedes in the driveway. The success comes with its own peculiar problems, especially for the spouse. Most romance writers are women, and their husbands—well, those male egos can take a beating when the Little Woman starts raking in money and basking in fame. No longer is he the chief breadwinner and dominant marriage partner. Instead, the romance-husband can find himself doing the laundry and feeding the kids while his wife composes best-sellers and grants press interviews.

But take heart, all you bewildered husbands, overwhelmed by royalties and dirty dishes. There *is* a way to stay happily married and preserve your ego. Take it from one who knows from experience, George Small. George is married to Bertrice Small, best-selling writer of sexy historical romances, and he's learned a few things the hard way. He's come through his trials by fire with his sense of humor and marvelous wit intact, and he willingly shares his insight with fellow romance-husbands.

George was once making good money as a top-notch commercial photographer. But during the 1970s, due largely to a business deal that went sour, George found himself without work and clients. Meanwhile, there was a wife, a son and an expensive Manhattan apartment to support. "I began working in catalog studios where cockroaches walked over my feet while I photographed bad towels," relates George. "It was a terrible comedown—and I wasn't making any money."

Bertrice, meanwhile, was laboring over her first novel, *The Kadin*. It was published by Avon Books in 1978, and her star as a writer began to rise.

Since she had the better deal going, Bertrice and George decided to combine their efforts on her new career. They moved from Manhattan to Southold, on the eastern end of Long Island, and George concentrated on running the household and making it as easy as possible for Bertrice to write. "That didn't mean I was going to like everything I had to do," says George. "I hate housework!"

But George did it as part of the marriage partnership. He also plays chauffeur—Bertrice doesn't drive—and keeps her business records. They split the cooking. For a while, he ran a gift shop, The Fat Cat, where he also made and repaired clocks, but that became too time-consuming and the shop was converted to an office for Bertrice.

George understands how a romance-husband can react to his wife's success as a writer: "He feels deserted. Suddenly, his wife is engaged in an occupation which he's locked out of—he has no knowledge of it, so he can't even criticize it. He may have struggled all of his life and not made much of a success or much money, and now his wife writes a few books, sends them away and the tooth fairy dumps a pot of gold on the doorstep. She's making more money in a month than he can make in a year! This is ego-destroying."

George warns husbands that there are subtle dangers in coming to grips with this situation. Men still have a tendency to hold their emotions inside, he says, and when their wives ask them to help out around the house, they say "sure" and swallow their resentment. But this pent-up resentment has ways of popping out—the husband subconsciously undercuts the wife. He mismanages her affairs, makes it difficult or impossible for her to write, criticizes her work, downgrades her in public or makes a fool of himself with her agent or publisher.

Don't be such a jerk, admonishes George, because it's self-defeating. Instead, pitch in and help your wife, because her success will be *your* success. "No man ever made it to the top without a woman behind him picking up the slack," reminds George. "It's no longer the Me Generation, it's the *Us* Generation."

Your wife's earnings are the family's earnings, he points out. "If you feel embarrassed about living on your wife's money, blush all the way to the bank. If you feel a deep-seated resentment, buy yourself a Ferrari—it saves a lot of money on psychiatrist bills." It's also important, he adds, for a husband to have some pursuit that is exclusively his own.

Sometimes a husband may try to regain control of a relationship by becoming his wife's business manager. Or she may suggest it herself, sensing his wounded pride and feeling sorry for him. This can be a serious mistake, says George. A husband inexperienced in such matters can lose his wife's money faster than she can make it. Leave the heavy business affairs to the experts—agents, accountants, lawyers and tax advisers. However, adds George, both husband and wife should understand enough about publishing and investments to know whether or not the experts are doing a good job. Check professional references, he stresses.

George has three basic "don'ts" for romance-husbands:

1. "Don't negotiate with the publisher yourself unless you have the mentality of an Arab street merchant and six degrees in contract law. It's not a game for amateurs and they will take your bloody pants off if you don't know what you're doing.

2. "Don't tempt God or the IRS. Do not invest your wife's money yourself or set up tax shelters unless you're an investment expert—the Wolf of Wall Street. Even experts can't always predict the stock market. It's a game for people who watch the Big Board twenty-four hours a day.

3. "Don't tell your wife how to write books. If she asks for your opinion or criticism, try to be honest; if she doesn't, leave her alone. If you can write a book yourself, write it. If not, keep your mouth shut—she's making the money and you're not."

George also has a little advice for the wife who is a romance writer. Your husband, he says, probably considers his efforts to be a sacrifice and wants to be recognized for performing noble acts of unselfishness. If he helps out around the house, don't reduce him to "coolie status" by barking commands and criticizing how he does things. "You can't crush his dignity and have him come up smiling," says George. "A man at all costs must retain his dignity."

Bertrice and George Small

IX. TRUE CONFESSIONS

Romances, once scorned as a lowly form of fiction unworthy of many a writer, have gained a new respect. The market has become so large and lucrative that many writers and would-be writers want to cash in on the action. In a time when it's tough to sell fiction of any kind unless you're a big name, romances offer a virtual certainty of financial reward for beginners as well as stars.

The numbers are enticing. An estimated 150 romance titles are published in the United States every month. Advances for brand-name contemporary romances, the largest segment of the romance market, range from about $3,000 to $10,000, depending on the publisher, the length of the book and the track record of the author (big names can earn more). The printings run from about 150,000 to 350,000 copies; even with modest royalty rates and low cover prices ($1.75 to $2.50), an average contemporary romance can earn an unknown writer thousands of dollars. Leading writers easily earn six figures a year. So, why starve trying to write "literature" when a commercially successful romance can put steaks and champagne on the table?

With all this attention, however, has come stiff competition among established and aspiring writers, as well as pickier editors. Until the early 1980s, before media publicity exposed how lucrative the market was, it was much easier for newcomers to break in. Now more and more people are trying their hand at romance writing, encouraged by news stories about women who one day threw down the romances they were reading and said, "I can do better than that!" and did.

Newcomers, however, no longer have virgin territory to work over. Established authors already have loyal customers, who are showing increasing tendencies to stick with familiar and favorite names. The sheer numbers of nearly lookalike covers sitting on the shelves each month make it difficult for one name to stand out. "Readers give a book about twenty pages," says author Elaine Raco Chase. "If you haven't grabbed them by then, they take your book to a used bookstore and get somebody else." She says reviewers give a book about sixty pages.

Building name recognition isn't easy, even if you have published several books. Publicity, especially for writers of brand-name romances, comes largely at the author's expense.

These obstacles, however, fail to deter thousands of aspiring romance writers, as evidenced by the attendance at dozens of writer's conferences and how-to seminars and classes held across the nation. Further evidence is the rising stacks of manuscripts that arrive each week, solicited or not, on the desks of editors.

Interestingly, most editors say the manuscripts that hit the mark are usually written by nonprofessional writers. That is, these women—and romance writers overwhelmingly are women—generally were not journalists, free-lance writers or authors of other books before they decided to write a romance. Many of them may have always had a yen to write—a little poetry, an article here and there—but had not turned to it as a profession. Invariably, however, they are avid *readers* of the genre, and they know very well what other fans want to read. Their manuscripts may require more editing than those of professional writers, but they have their fingers squarely on the pulse of a strong romantic heartbeat. They understand the feelings and emotions portrayed in and evoked by these novels. Most of all, they know the fantasies women have about their ideal men and love affairs. That doesn't mean that someone who hasn't read 300 romances can't successfully write one—it just means that those who are thoroughly familiar with the genre have a natural advantage.

Think you're ready to tackle writing a romance? Check your bookstore for writer's guides devoted exclusively to romances, but for a few quick tips, read on.

1. *Read before you write.* Remember the point that was just made about familiarity with the genre? Right. You can't write it well unless you know it, and to know it, you've got to read it. If articles in the press have led you to think that all romances are the same, with the same stereotyped characters and the same basic formula, you are wrong.

"No matter what a writer is writing, he or she has to know the market," says agent Denise Marcil. "I would say go out and read a hundred romances, and pick them from the different lines. Then study what the authors do, make notes and analyze."

If you're unfamiliar with the latest hot stuff, ask your bookstore proprietor for help. But *don't* content yourself with one or two titles and think you've got the genre down pat. There's considerable variation among the lines, and editors are constantly tinkering.

2. *Identify your target market.* Not all types of romances sell equally well. The romance market is segmented, and the popularity of segments seems to be cyclical. The largest and fastest growing segment—and therefore the best shot for a newcomer—is the brand-name sensual contemporary romance. Short books range from about 50,000 to 60,000 words; longer books of 75,000 words and up allow subplots, adventure and suspense. Each line has its own personality, and you'd be wise to check it out.

The popularity of historicals, which were very big in the 1970s, has dwindled, but they still hold a strong audience. The field, however, is dominated by established writers, and even some of them aren't selling as well as they did before the 1980s boom in contemporaries. Authors without track records face tough obstacles to breaking in. If you do give it a try, make sure your research is thorough and accurate—historical fans have an amazing accumulation of knowledge and they dislike inaccuracies.

Regencies, also very big in years past, dropped way down but have made a comeback, though not to the degree they were once popular. Regencies require a thorough knowledge of the period and the slang.

Young adult romances offer a large and steady market but require a familiarity and understanding of teen concerns and habits.

3. *Obtain tip sheets.* Once you've decided what type of romance you want to write, identify the appropriate publishers in the market segment and study a few more of their books. If you're targeting your manuscript for one of the brand-name category lines, such as Harlequin, Silhouette or Second Chance At Love, it's likely the publisher offers a tip sheet that tells what editors look for in plots, characters and sensuality.

Don't expect a tip sheet to be a formula road map that will practically write your story for you. There isn't any "formula" for writing romances anymore, only a format of a story about a man and woman falling in love, overcoming obstacles and pledging to get married in the end, told largely, if not exclusively, from the woman's point of view. At one time, tip sheets were quite detailed and rigid, even spelling out physical and personality traits of the characters, but now they're much more general, which gives writers more room to experiment. In general, the do's and don't's are helpful, and most experienced writers advise beginners to follow the guidelines. Experimentation, however, is often welcomed, and editors are always on the lookout for "fresh" angles.

4. *Get a book of names.* A what-shall-we-name-the-baby book costs only a few dollars and is well worth the investment, for names are most important in romances, and you'll refer to it again and again. Naturally, for period romances, names should reflect the particular era and nationality you're dealing with. Beyond that, look for something unusual or memorable that will help make your characters stand out—those who stand out will be remembered by readers. You don't, however, have to christen *every* character with an exotic name. A name

book is most helpful in uncovering little known or used names, and a good book will give national or ethnic origins and meanings. Using a name with a certain meaning, for example, could reinforce the personality of your character. Or perhaps you just need a name that sounds "romantic."

5. *Outline your plot and characters.* Work methods are a highly individual matter, but most writers find it essential to know where they're going with a book before they actually begin writing it. That doesn't preclude changing course in midstream—*anything* can happen as characters come alive and take off on their own. But you can't really make them come alive unless you're familiar with them and the situations and dilemmas which will confront them.

So, outline your plot, setting and time period (if the story takes place in the past; contemporaries take place in an undated "everlasting present"). Do profiles of your characters, including appearance, personality, ambitions, past experiences that may influence them during the course of the book, likes and dislikes etc. You get the picture.

Some writers prefer to do rough skeleton sketches of their characters, filling in details later as they write. But beginners are better off putting in more time up front on detailed descriptions in order to get a firm mental fix on the characters. The extra work will pay off later with more believable characters. You must know your people.

Editors these days want romance characters and plots to be "realistic," but remember that you are still dealing with a fantasy world, and some idealism is vital to your book. Furthermore, what constitutes "realism" is very subjective. It's *not* real life, which is too sobering and harsh for a romance novel.

"There's a fine line between realism and fantasy," cautions Alicia M. Condon, Silhouette senior editor. "The story must be real enough for the reader to sympathize with and get inside a character. Then let the fantasy take over."

In most contemporary romances, such contrivances as forced marriages, jealous, bitchy other women and misunderstandings that could be cleared up with a simple question are out. Also out, according to Ellen Edwards, senior editor of Jove's Second Chance At Love, are cliche interruptions of lovemaking, such as phone calls, knocks on the door, weeping, fainting and sudden sieges of conscience.

6. *Make your characters memorable.* Characters who stand out in some way will grab the attention of editors and readers. An unusual occupation, such as a female bush pilot, an unusual name, personality quirks or a unique appearance can make the difference between a dull character and an intriguing one. Physically flawless characters are no longer de rigueur—or even desirable. "Avoid sleek flanks, rippling chest muscles, tight thighs and washboard stomachs," counsels a Harlequin editor. "Tell something about the characters' backgrounds. Too often we get the feeling the characters were found under a cabbage leaf only seconds before the plot begins."

You may wonder how it's possible to keep coming up with something unique and memorable with hundreds of new characters appearing on the bookshelves each month. That, aspiring writer, is the job cut out for you.

7. *Emote!* Romances are sensual books, not just from a sexual standpoint but involving all the senses. The emotions and perceptions of the heroine are a key factor in romances and are described in ample detail. The reader wants to identify with the heroine and become swept up in her experiences, *feeling* every tender kiss, every caress, every throb of passion. "You have to want to be the heroine yourself," says Leslie Wainger, Silhouette editor. "Why you want this man keeps you going through the book." Even if your book has a subplot or some adventure, the romance and sexual tension between the heroine and hero is still the main focus, *never*

secondary. If she isn't with the hero, what is she thinking or feeling about him? Think about your own experiences falling head over heels in love—the romance occupied the center of your life.

Sex scenes can be passionate and sensual without being excessively explicit. An editor isn't going to buy your book because of a knockout sex scene, or scenes—the plot and characters have to be interesting first. Editors can always ask you to tone it down or spice it up.

8. *Make sure you have the right tone.* The only thing that will teach you the proper tone is extensive reading. Tone is a crucial element of many historicals, especially light-hearted Regencies, for diction changes over the course of time. "Tone is something a reader can pick up on right away," notes Barbara Dicks, executive editor of Ballantine's Crest Books.

Many editors appreciate and look for romances written with a sense of humor—characters who are capable of laughing at themselves and engaging in witty, sparkling dialogue. Some of the authors known for their skill with humor are Dixie Browning, Sandra Brown, Elaine Raco Chase and Tom and Sharon Curtis. But humor doesn't come naturally to everyone. Romances still sell without it, and writers who have difficulty with humor should avoid it rather than try to force it. "You can't have two people be flip with each other and then fall into bed and have adult sex," says Sandra. "It just doesn't jibe."

9. *Write every day.* A little bit of work done every day eventually adds up to a finished manuscript. Even if you write only an hour or two a day, it's important to establish the pattern and habit. Just as musicians, actors and singers practice their craft daily, so do writers. Practice leads to polish and improvement. Pick a time of day or evening when you are least likely to be interrupted. You can find time even if you hold down a full-time job. Author Catherine Coulter gets up two hours early on weekdays and writes before leaving for work; she also works a few hours each day on weekends. Between 1979 and 1982, she had seven Regencies and historicals published by NAL/Signet.

When you are in the habit of writing daily, you're less likely to succumb to that demon—writer's block. Techniques vary for overcoming writer's block. Some writers like to take a break and walk away from their project, while others keep writing something—anything—just to generate words until the block is broken. Experiment to find what works best for you.

10. *Submit your manuscript.* This may sound silly, but many a novice has worked diligently on a book only to quail when it came time to subject it to an editor's scrutiny. Think what a waste it would have been if Rosemary Rogers had let *Sweet Savage Love* die in a desk drawer (as it almost did) instead of sending it to Avon Books!

Romance editors treat the slush pile—unsolicited manuscripts—with some respect, and all submissions are read. What have you got to lose?

11. *Consider classes, writer's groups and agents.* At some point in your writing career, you're bound to consider at least one of these, if not all. If you've no previous experience as a writer, a creative writing class can teach you a lot about plot construction and character development, as well as help boost your self-confidence. Writer's groups, such as Romance Writers of America (RWA) or the Society of Romance Novelists (SRN), plug you into a network of writers and help keep you up to date on trends. Writing tends to be a lonely pursuit, and it's gratifying to get to know others who share your goals. (Note: you must have published romances to join SRN but not RWA.)

While you'll probably want to get an agent eventually, it's not necessary to have one in order to have your manuscripts read and considered for publication. Finding the right agent is not something you should undertake hastily; the relationship is a highly personal one, and it may take you a while to find someone with whom you click.

If a publisher offers you a contract for your unsolicited manuscript, it's a good idea to have an agent negotiate it. Contracts are full of legal mumbo jumbo and virtually inscrutable to the uninitiated.

How do you find an agent who's active in the romance field? Many agents attend romance conferences looking for new clients. Or you may get recommendations from people you know in your writing class or group. New York agent Steve Axelrod, of The Sterling Lord Agency, offers this advice: "The best way to get an agent is to write to one whom you know is active in the field and offer to send in what you have. Speaking for myself, I prefer to see a full manuscript rather than a partial, but I'd rather see a partial than a query. I can't imagine an agent taking someone on the basis of a query, but I could on a partial, if it's strong."

Agents frown on multiple submissions, so query one at a time. Some agents charge a nominal reading fee, regardless of whether they agree to represent you.

A GLOSSARY OF THE MOST OVERUSED EXPRESSIONS IN ROMANTIC FICTION

The well-read romance reader knows that certain expressions keep surfacing in book after book. Coming up with new ways to say the same things is a problem for writers and editors. "Freshness is a crucial element right now," confides one editor. But how many ways are there to describe seduction and lovemaking without sounding ridiculous? Therein lies the challenge. Nevertheless, a few expressions are overdue for replacements. The following examples were compiled expressly for *LoveLines* and not taken from any particular book.

TERM	EXAMPLE
arched	she arched her body against him
briefs	she wore white briefs
bruising	his lips covered hers in a bruising kiss
caught helplessly	she was caught helplessly against his massive chest
darkened	his eyes darkened with desire
full name	"You don't mean that, Jeremy Smith!"
greedy	his greedy mouth opened her lips and plundered the warm moistness within
ground out	"I won't," he ground out
growled	"You're gorgeous," he growled
hair-roughened	his hair-roughened chest
hoarsely	he whispered hoarsely
huskily	"I want you," he murmured huskily
little one	"I'll take care of you, little one," he promised
quirked	his mouth quirked up in a smile
nibbled	she nibbled his ear/throat/lips etc.
minx	"Come here, minx," he commanded
peaks of passion	they scaled new peaks of passion
plundered	see greedy
rasped	his voice rasped in her ear

rippled	his muscles rippled under taut skin
ruefully	she smiled ruefully
sculpted	she gazed at his sculpted features
steaming	she brought out steaming mugs of coffee
sumptuous	she wore a sumptuous blue silk ball gown
taut	see rippled
thickly	"Please go," she said thickly
thinned	his lips thinned in irritation
traced	his tongue traced the curve of her throat
traitorous	her traitorous lips responded to his kiss
unbidden	tears sprang unbidden to her eyes
warm moistness	see plundered

A FEW TIPS FOR THE FELLAS

For men who want to write romances, here's some advice from two successful male writers: Michael Hinkemeyer (Vanessa Royall) and David Wind (Monica Barrie). Women writers can benefit from their advice as well:

1. *Read the best women romance writers.* "Kathleen Woodiwiss, more than any other author, writes from a very feminine point of view," David says.
2. *Understand and appreciate sensuality.* "Read *My Secret Garden* by Nancy Friday for descriptions of female fantasies," advises Michael. He adds, "Hopefully, the writer will have had at least a couple of passionate relationships himself for a grounding in romance and passion."
3. *Don't overwhelm your characters with plot.* Men tend to put too much adventure in romances—remember, they're basically emotion books.
4. *Show your manuscript to a woman.* Select someone who's knowledgeable about either women's fiction or romances, and let her guide you on the female point of view.

WHAT TO EXPECT FROM AN AGENT

Happy day—you found an agent who wants to take you on as a client! But now what? Do you sign a contract? What services should you expect for the agent's commission of 10 to 15 percent? *LoveLines* asked agent Steve Axelrod of The Sterling Lord Agency in New York for some answers.

Many agents will ask you to sign an exclusive contract, which should be studied carefully before you commit yourself in writing. "Some agents want one, two, even three-year commitments, and no matter what happens to your relationship, they get to commission your work even though they're not selling it," says Steve. "Also, writers should be careful of any clause the agent puts into a contract that stipulates that the option book, for instance, is automatically commissioned whether or not they sell it personally. I think that's taking unfair advantage of an author."

A contract should have a termination clause that allows either party to dissolve the relationship upon notification and that stipulates any manuscripts presented for sale after termination of the relationship—even if they were written while the contract was in effect—are not commissionable. Thirty days' notice is reasonable, although some agents ask for ninety days.

You should also know what expenses, if any, will be considered extraordinary, that is, billed to you, such as photocopying expenses, copyright fees and long-distance phone calls. These vary by agent.

It's a good idea to have a lawyer review an author/agent contract before signing it, but be aware that many lawyers aren't familiar with publishing and those who are charge high fees, up to $120 an hour.

Once you're satisfied with your own contract, trust your agent concerning any publishing contract presented to you.

♥ IX. TRUE CONFESSIONS ♥

"Authors can expect their agent to read their material reasonably promptly and to give them an evaluation of its market prospects," says Steve. "If prospects aren't good, they can expect advice. Once the agent is satisfied with the marketability of a manuscript, he or she should take it to market with vigor and enthusiasm. It isn't good to have an agent serving the same function as a mailroom, just trafficking things.

"One of the most important things an agent does is help an author shape a career rather than make single sales," Steve continues. "That's less important to someone who's trying to get their first book published than it is to someone who's had several published and now has several paths open to them." Such an author may need help in deciding whether to work exclusively for one romance publisher or play the field, or whether to sell to a publisher who offers higher royalties but has smaller press runs than one who offers the opposite. "What is in your best interests, both short and long term, is vital," says Steve. And that's where an agent can often help the most.

IX. TRUE CONFESSIONS

You wrote, rewrote and polished your romance; neatly typed and packaged the manuscript; and sent it off to the Great Unknown—the slush pile of unsolicited manuscripts at a publishing house. Even though it is unsolicited, you know it will be read—the editors all promise that they read the slush pile, because some of their greatest discoveries have come in over the transom. Right?

So you sit back and wait to hear your fate, but niggling doubts cloud your mind. What if they really *don't* read the slush pile? What if they only read the first five pages, not knowing your truly great stuff is at the end of the first chapter? For all you know, now that your manuscript has vanished into some mysterious editorial maw, some junior assistant is laughing hysterically over your prose and spilling coffee on your meticulously typed pages.

What *really* happens to your manuscript once it lands in a publisher's office? And if it's sold, how long does it take to be published in book form?

Assuming that your manuscript is not obviously unsuitable—a graphic sex fantasy, for example, or handwritten, or typed on hot pink paper and decorated with smiley faces—it's read, more than once, even if it's rejected. There are no "tricks," says Karen Solem, vice president and editor in chief of Silhouette Books. Some authors think that unless their manuscript comes back dog-eared, stained and with pages upside down or out of order, no editorial eyes have been set upon it. Karen asserts that this is not the case; manuscripts are sent back in the condition in which they are received, in original containers if possible. "Our business is built on unsolicited manuscripts. Most of the Silhouette authors have come out of unsolicited, so I feel a great responsibility to it," she says.

All romance publishers use free-lance readers to some extent, depending on the volume of manuscripts they receive. Some may have only three or four readers, while Silhouette, which receives 400 to 600 manuscripts a month, uses "a small army," as Karen describes them. The free-lancers are carefully selected and trusted for their judgments, but they never have the one and only say on a manuscript. Everything is double-checked.

The first reading of a manuscript is done by either a free-lancer or someone in-house. At Silhouette, everything is sent outside first. "We try to have everything read at least once outside of the house," says Karen, "maybe even twice, before it comes inside. Our feeling is, as many people as possible should read and like a book. We have to appeal to such a broad audience that the more readings, the better. If I can get ten positive responses to a book, then it's pretty good."

Manuscript readers write a report and recommend whether the manuscript should be rejected or given another reading. Plots are summarized, flaws pointed out and perhaps suggestions made for fixing them. If the report is negative, an editor double-checks to make sure the analysis is on target. If it is, the rejected manuscript is returned.

"Someone reads every word of everything," says Carolyn Nichols, senior editor of Bantam's Loveswept line. "Sometimes that someone is me. If not, and the manuscript is to be returned, I at least read some of it before it goes back."

Too often, according to Carolyn, beginners bog down their stories with too much background in the first few chapters. "They think the reader has to know everything about this character right away—where she was born, where she went to school, the ice cream flavor she preferred at age five. They don't realize that in reading other books, they learned background in the course of the story.

"I give them a break and wade through all that stuff to see if they've really got it," Carolyn says. "A lot of writers don't get their stories started until chapters three, four or even five. And then they might really have a good story." Manuscripts that look promising go through two or three more readings, and at Silhouette, sometimes as many as six or eight. Those that survive are purchased.

The odds of selling an unsolicited romance manuscript are formidable but not frightening. Every publisher receives, on the average, at least 200 or more manuscripts a month and can buy one in twenty-five or thirty. Submissions from agents fare better because agents have already screened the best that they receive.

"Agents get their material read earlier and get a faster answer," acknowledges Carolyn, "but we try to be evenhanded. The shelves where the manuscripts are placed are marked with their time of arrival. I don't go on to the next month's agented material until I've finished all that arrived in one particular month."

Sometimes editors will ask an author to make revisions before a contract is issued. If the submission is a partial, that it, several chapters and a synopsis, they may ask for the complete manuscript before committing themselves, especially if the author is unpublished. The editors want to be certain the writer can sustain the plot and tension to the end.

Once the finished manuscript is purchased, it still may be another year or so before the book actually comes out, because editors buy well in advance. There is also much production work to be completed: the cover designed, the title chosen (if it is to be different than the author's), the jacket blurb written, the manuscript typeset into galleys, the galleys proofread, mechanicals made from the galleys and the book printed, bound and distributed.

It may be even longer before you see any royalties from your book. Royalty checks are issued twice a year, in the spring and fall, and your book must earn out its advance before you begin receiving royalties. Unlike other categories of genre fiction or mainstream fiction, the average beginning romance author stands a good chance of making money beyond the advance—at least a few thousand, maybe a lot more. Harlequin claims the average Superromance author earns about $40,000 over a two-year period. That's not bad and definitely worth a little wait.

X. FOR LOVE AND MONEY

Browsing through a book in a bookstore is like seeing the tip of an iceberg—there is much more to the book than meets the eye. Before a romance or a line of romances is introduced in the stores, months of work precede it, usually involving the editorial, art, sales, advertising and publicity departments of a publishing company. The end results are scrutinized by bookstore buyers and then set out on the racks to live or die. Many books are as perishable as fresh fruit or vegetables—if they haven't sold within a few weeks, out they go. To help keep their books alive as long as possible, some authors take to the publicity road, and publishers spend considerable sums on advertising.

CHAPTER ONE
Birth Of A Love Line

Romances are a rich business, and the powerful lure of money has drawn more and more publishers into the marketplace, especially with a brand-name line. "We couldn't afford *not* to be in it," explains one marketing manager. The profits can be substantial, but the competition is fierce; consequently, money and time are invested on market research, development of an editorial format and strategies for "positioning," that is, identifying the line's potential audience and determining how it will be advertised and promoted against the competition.

Let's take a look at some of the planning and thinking behind three diverse lines launched in 1982 and 1983: Pocket Books' Tapestry Romance, Avon Books' Finding Mr. Right and New American Library's Rapture Romance. Each line is intended for a different segment of the market: Tapestry for brand-name historicals; Mr. Right for longer, sophisticated contemporaries; and Rapture for short and sexy contemporaries.

The Fastest Launch In History?

The idea for Tapestry Romance began to take hold around March or April 1982. A very short time later, October 1, the first two introductory titles were on the bookstore shelves. In that pressured time period, a name and editorial format were chosen, a cover format designed, twenty-four manuscripts purchased, promotion and advertising campaigns developed and a marketing plan put into action—not to mention that the first two books had to be edited, typeset, proofed, printed, bound and distributed. "All the departments go into high gear at the same time in a launch," says Kate Duffy, senior editor of Tapestry. "Editorial doesn't lead—it contributes. It's all a team effort."

Kate Duffy

Although Pocket Books committed one of the largest advertising and promotion budgets in its history to the launch of Tapestry ($500,000 to $700,000), it did no preliminary market research. It didn't have to. The division of Simon & Schuster had published and distributed Richard Gallen's historical and contemporary romances, and when Gallen and Pocket terminated their arrangement, some slots were opened on Pocket Books' publishing schedule.

"Silhouette [also a Simon & Schuster division] had the contemporary romance market very well covered," notes Kate. "People were saying the historical market was dead because of the boom in contemporaries, but as an historical reader myself, I didn't believe that. I think one of the reasons why historicals started to die was because they became too violent. I felt there had to be a crossover in readership between contemporaries and historicals, that many of the people reading contemporaries would also read historicals if they could find books they liked."

There were obstacles, however, to starting a line of historicals, not the least of which was the state of the market. There were production costs to consider that would affect the length and retail price of the books. Most historicals are thick books of about 350 to 450 pages, about 100,000 to 125,000 words long, with retail prices of $2.95 and up—mostly up. (Most brand-name contemporary romances, on the other hand, cost $1.95 for 50,000 to 60,000 words, and $2.25 to $2.50 for slightly longer books.) In a dwindling historical market, only a big-name author can draw enough sales to justify the production costs and a higher retail price. The Pocket Books marketing staff felt that $2.50 was the maximum retail price that could be charged for a new line of historicals.

That meant shorter books—not necessarily a disadvantage, for, as Kate points out, long historicals usually draw out the plots with lengthy separations between hero and heroine, forcing reader attention onto a subplot and reducing the sexual tension. In a shorter format, that plot device could be avoided.

"Taking all these things into consideration, we came up with a program for two romances a month, 85,000 words (about 310 pages), basically one-man-one-woman stories," Kate says. The plots would emphasize sensual romance and relationships, not the bodice ripping or violent sex found in other historical romances. Press runs were set at an average of 200,000 copies per title.

The name Tapestry was suggested by Pocket Books' then publicity manager, Joan Schulhafer, and derives from the huge tapestries medieval women used to weave to record stories. The name struck Kate as perfect, but it still took a bit of lobbying to convince others to approve it, including Pocket Books president Ron Busch.

The crunch for Kate and her associate editor, Liza Hatcher Dawson, came in trying to round up a year's worth of manuscripts in short order. The problem: no short historicals to be had quickly. Calls went out to agents and writers. "I have the world's biggest Rolodex and the fastest dialing fingers in the business," laughs Kate. Mission was accomplished in three to four months. "It must have been like giving birth. In retrospect, it doesn't seem as painful as I thought it was at the time. I remember going home one night and sobbing over a manuscript, thinking, 'There are no Tapestry manuscripts out there.'"

She received a partial manuscript from author Maura Seger for *Defiant Love* and decided she wanted it as an introductory title. "Maura had to type like a little demon to get it finished in time," she says. The second introductory title was *Marielle* by Ena Halliday.

But getting the manuscripts ready for publication was only part of the job for editorial. Kate also worked on publicity, including hosting a party at the 1982 Romance Writers of America conference in Long Beach, California and undertaking a two-week promotion tour of press interviews and meetings with jobbers (wholesale book distributors) and retail booksellers. Meanwhile, the publicity department prepared and sent out press kits and press releases, the advertising department scheduled print and television ads (most of the $500,000 to $700,000 launch budget was earmarked for advertising) and sales representatives made presentations at Pocket Books accounts. "They really sold it," says Kate of the sales force. "They went in and made people believers."

To help make the consumer a believer, Tapestry Romances were tagged, pointed to and displayed by various point-of-purchase materials, and backed by a double-your-money-back guarantee. All a dissatisfied customer had to do was return her Tapestry to Pocket Books with a note explaining why she didn't like it.

Tapestry
HISTORICAL
ROMANCE
45962-7
$2.50
In the darkness of a French dungeon, love lit a torch to burn forever!
Marielle
Ena Halliday

HISTORICAL ROMANCE
45963-5
$2.50

Tapestry

Defiant Love

For Brenna to be won, she would have to be wooed.

Maura Seger

To further attract attention, Pocket devised a consumer drawing to give away the original cover art for *Defiant Love*: an oil painting by Harry Bennett valued at $7,000.

Promotion, advertising and market research can get the ball rolling, but in the long run it's the quality of the books that makes or breaks a line. "Your instincts and your experience are the only things you can count on," says Kate. "I will not call my books 'products'—it's not like I was selling soap or umbrellas. In this economy, there are no trends. Quality sells."

Founding Mr. Right

A brand-name romance series that offers the sophistication and "bigness" of lead women's fiction—that's Finding Mr. Right, packaged by New York literary agents Denise Marcil and Meredith Bernstein and published by Avon Books.

The series, launched in February 1983 with *Paper Tiger* by Elizabeth Neff Walker, features one title a month, about 75,000 words. It's aimed at an up-scale audience that likes contemporary romances a la Helen Van Slyke and Danielle Steel, yet its brand-name emphasizes the line rather than any single author.

"The only way to sell romances in the paperback industry is to have a line," explains Denise. "The publisher has to have a clear way to market it. The whole key in paperback marketing is getting the wholesalers and distributors to buy the books. Most sales are through distributors, not bookstores. And all they care about is filling a slot with something that's identifiable. That's why there's no midlist fiction anymore—an individual book won't sell, but a brand-name line will. With a line, the readers know basically what the books are like, and they know the authors and the quality."

As packagers, Denise and Meredith developed the concept for Finding Mr. Right, a business plan and marketing projections, and sold the idea to Avon Books. Denise and Meredith select all the authors, buy the manuscripts and do all the editing. They deliver the edited copy to Avon, which produces and distributes the books.

Denise says they got the idea for the line from the continual requests they heard from editors for "big" contemporary romances. "That's what they were asking for, but what was selling was the identifiable package out on the shelves month after month—the Silhouettes and the Ecstasies," says Denise. "We decided to take what the editors wanted, the sexiness and sophistication of the big women's fiction books and put that in the identifiable package of the successful category romance."

Denise and Meredith began work on their idea in June 1981, developing story lines from outlines solicited from some of their authors. They then researched the packaging and business aspects—how the books would be positioned in the marketplace, estimates of the number of copies per title that would be sold, retail prices and suggestions for cover art. They wrapped up their contract with Avon by the end of January 1982.

Two names initially were proposed for the line: Looking For Mr. Right and Finding Mr. Right. Avon chose the latter, which sounded more optimistic.

"Historicals have always been Avon's strength, and this [Finding Mr. Right] is a small component in a very successful program," says editorial director Page Cuddy. "This seemed like a good entry in the contemporary field, for slightly more sophisticated readers who don't consider themselves part of the core romance audience. There aren't any more white horses. That whole notion appealed to me, that when you get older, you're confronted with less than a perfect reality and you do have to make some choices."

At one book a month, Finding Mr. Right is more a series than a line, according to Page, who approves all plot ideas. "One book a month seemed like a proper number," she says.

Meredith Bernstein and Denise Marcil

Denise points out that the length of Mr. Right books will allow subplots and more character development. As for the theme—Finding Mr. Right—"we had to come up with something that would be unique in an overcrowded market. There isn't one hero, but two, and the question is, how do you find the man who's right for you? They're not like other category romances in which one man is the red herring, obviously inappropriate from the beginning. The men in our books are both likable and appealing, but they have flaws—they're human beings. The heroine isn't perfect either. The suspense that keeps the reader turning the pages is, which one will she choose at the end? The reader doesn't know until the heroine knows.

"The heroine," Denise continues, "goes through a marvelous self-exploration deciding which man is appropriate for her. In some cases, it'll be a man who's wealthier and more successful than the other, but in some cases, she'll choose the other man because money isn't important to her. The books aren't predictable. Our writers have to make her choice believable and sympathetic."

Part of the package is a guarantee that every Mr. Right author has a track record. Besides Elizabeth, other authors include Jo Calloway, Elaine Raco Chase, Maura Seger, Laura Parker and Carla Neggers.

The covers of Finding Mr. Right are photographic rather than illustrated, with fresh, modern type. "We wanted an effect like the classy ads of men and women having a good time," Denise says. "We wanted to get away from the category look. These books are more like lead titles." Adds Page, "We wanted an upbeat, contemporary look—everybody looks like they're having a good time."

The covers, according to Avon art director Matt Tepper, evoke the feeling someone would

Page Cuddy and Tom Stanley

get when they open to a spread in *Glamour* or *Cosmopolitan* magazines.

The design should appeal to a broad age range of readers, Matt adds. "The models are appealing," he says. "An older woman looks at them and is reminded of her youth. An eighteen- or nineteen-year-old looks at them and can't wait until she's twenty-four, when she'll be dressing like that and going out with men like that." And there's the age group in between, which has immediate identification."

Originally, "Mr. Right" was going to have his face hidden. "I thought that was silly," says Matt. The male model's face isn't hidden, but it's not a "main stare" either.

Denise and Meredith will also package a line of romantic suspense novels for Avon, to be launched in late 1983 or 1984. The books will have Mary Stewart suspense with Dell Candlelight Ecstasy-type sensuality, and they will have brand-name identification. "I think romantic suspense is going to make a big comeback," says Denise, who receives more than 1,000 queries a year from authors, many of whom want to write romantic suspense. She points out that authors are also readers.

Denise and Meredith believe the two niches they're seeking in contemporary romances will flourish while other category lines face consumer overload. The brand-name contemporary romance isn't going to disappear, but glutted segments of the market will burn out, just as did Gothics, historicals and Regencies. "That's what happened to the sweet contemporary romances," according to Denise. "Everyone started doing them and all of a sudden they died, and nobody's buying them anymore. The same thing will happen to the sensual romances."

Room For Another

The sensual contemporary romance that's part of a brand-name line is the biggest and fastest-growing segment of the paperback market. It's also where the heaviest competition is among publishers, something that hasn't deterred New American Library from making a bid for consumer dollars with Rapture Romance, launched in January 1983.

"Our plots are stronger, the characters more realistic, and the love stories more satisfying," states editor Robin Grunder of the 50,000 to 60,000-word novels. "There's still room in the market for that kind of book, because I don't think any line has achieved the consistently good romance." She says the typical Rapture Romance "illustrates the theme of finding, not the perfect man, as if there *were* a perfect man, but the perfect man for you."

Robin Grunder

Rapture marks NAL's major entry into the contemporary brand-name field. Under its Signet imprint, the publisher has established a strong presence in historicals and Regencies. Also under Signet, NAL has published a series of contemporary romances called Adventures in Love. Under consideration is another contemporary line featuring older heroines.

Planning for Rapture, based on market research, began in late 1981. Silhouette had considered the name "Rapture," but editors there said it didn't test well. But it tested well for NAL in house and in focus groups, and seemed to capture the essence of the new line. "It best expresses the emotion of being swept beyond yourself by the strength of the most powerful of emotions—love," observes Robin.

Work began on press kits, promotional materials and a logo and design theme. The decision was made to use a double "R" for the logo, rather than the Signet logo, to further strengthen the name identification of the line. "It has continuity with our regular Signet logo, but it's all a little more delicate," notes art director Jim Plumeri.

The covers feature a bold wave of deep, eye-catching magenta, accented with red. The "undulating wave of passion" plus the illustrations that depict passionately aroused couples combine to communicate subliminal sexual messages, according to Jim. "We wanted the cover to be as distinctive as possible to combat other lines who have heavy consumer advertising budgets. Within the illustrations, we wanted to show that this was a sexier product than other romances. We're playing directly against Desire [Silhouette] and Candlelight Ecstasy [Dell]."

Magenta was Jim's choice of dominant color right from the start. "I wanted a color that would work with everything else," he says, adding that magenta is more evocative of passion than red, which is also used for anger. The authors' names are positioned more prominently than the book titles, because research has shown that consumers are buying more by author name than anything else.

Authors, however, are required to have pseudonyms used exclusively for Rapture. The reason is competition. Any reader following built on a Rapture name can't benefit another publisher.

Robin's background in romances was in Regencies, and she freely acknowledges that she used to turn her nose up in disdain at short brand-name contemporaries. "Not for me the helpless heroine, the obnoxious hero, and the kiss on the last page," she says of her mistaken impression of that type of book. "But when I read my first one and saw the state of the art, I knew that creating a line for today's reader was going to be nothing but fun."

Her first task—extensive reading of the competition. "I bought a shopping bag full of romances—I got some strange looks when I walked out of Barnes & Noble—and took them on a weekend ski vacation," Robin recalls. "From reading them I got a feeling for the state of the art and what was selling well. Sensuality is the smart place to be." Somehow, she also managed to get in some skiing.

Robin created a tip sheet for writers, which she says "really crystallizes what we want." That means strong, successful, active characters—no stereotypes, please—realistic conflicts—no cliche contrivances—and the development of a warm, passionate, sensual relationship. "In many romances, it just doesn't make sense that the characters bitch and moan at each other the whole way through until the last page, and then they suddenly decide to get married. How can anybody understand how they could possibly like each other, except for their physical attraction?"

Once Robin knew what she was looking for, her next challenge was to recruit the right authors. She attended many romance conferences and talked to many more agents. Although there are thousands of aspiring romance writers wanting, even dying, to get published, there is a very small pool of fine writers, and the competition for them is intense, Robin says. "If all I wanted to do was fill the line, I could be booked into 1986 by tomorrow."

Leading off the launch were *Love So Fearful* by Nina Coombs, *River of Love* by Lisa McConnell, *Lover's Lair* by Jeanette Ernest and *Welcome Intruder* by Charlotte Wisely. As part of the launch promotion, *Love So Fearful* was given away to 1,000 readers.

While realism is desired in today's contemporary romance, the fantasy element shouldn't be lost, notes Robin. "The point of these books is not having depressing real-life problems but in getting married and living happily ever after. These books have a tremendous appeal. I don't think romance is going to die, ever."

RAPTURE ROMANCE • 451-AJ2065 • $1.95 RR

NINA COOMBS

PASSION'S DOMAIN

RAPTURE ROMANCE #6

RAPTURE ROMANCE • 451-AJ2003 • $1.95 RR

NINA COOMBS

LOVE SO FEARFUL

RAPTURE ROMANCE #1

X. FOR LOVE AND MONEY

The faithful romance reader knows that in the long run it's what's between the covers of a book that attracts her—nothing more, nothing less. Despite this conventional wisdom, publishers of romance novels spend millions upon millions of dollars annually to try to attract and hold romance readers.

Romance novels are the most heavily advertised and promoted books in the publishing industry. While it's not uncommon for a major publisher to sink $50,000 to $150,000 to promote a single title by a heavyweight writer, romance publishers spend more than the rest of the industry spends as a whole. In 1982, Silhouette Books budgeted $22 million for advertising; Harlequin spent more than $15 million—and budgeted more than $20 million for 1983—Dell put up more than $1 million for Candlelight Ecstasy; and Pocket Books launched Tapestry Romances with $500,000 to $700,000, the largest campaign in its history. Those are the largest, but by no means all, of the numbers.

Not all romance publishers spend big bucks on their books, yet collectively the sums are enormous. The money is spent on network and cable television ads, radio spots, print ads in consumer and trade magazines and all sorts of snappy ways to attract the attention of the customer: contests, T-shirts, bookmarks, giveaways (get a free romance when you buy a box of plastic garbage bags), notepads and more. Inside the store, books are often highlighted by shelf tags, signs, special "romance center" shelves and racks, and "dumps," cardboard displays to set either on the floor or at the check-out counter near the cash register—which rings steadily with romance sales.

Romance publishers aren't the only ones promoting their merchandise—booksellers and manufacturers of display racks are realizing the profits as well. Special racks not only increase book sales but make money for manufacturing firms, and as romance sales have neared the 50 percent mark of all paperbacks sold, bookstores, supermarkets and drugstores have reorganized their space to accommodate more of the books. Waldenbooks, the nation's largest chain of bookstores, created a Romance Book Club in November 1982. The club entitles members to free books with certain purchases, discounts on consumer goods in a *Bonus Boutique* mail catalog and a free romance newsletter; 30,000 persons signed up in the first two months. B. Dalton Bookseller, the nation's second-largest chain, matched the free book offer and created a Romance Pick of the Week special display for selected titles.

If romance traffic is particularly good at a bookstore, someone on the sales staff may start specializing in the genre to advise and help customers make selections. "If the customer gets encouraging feedback from our booksellers, she'll keep coming back for guidance and advice," says Ofelia, president of the Waldenbooks Romance Book Club. "Some of them spend $60 a month, and they'll go where they feel comfortable buying romances. We have loyal customers who keep coming back to stores where we have a romance expert on the staff, who takes time to know the books and promote them with the clientele."

All this effort on the part of so many is made just to attract you, the customer. It's an effort that's warranted, of course. High numbers are at stake: romance readers spend hundreds of millions of dollars a year on their favorite books—some estimates go as high as $450—$500 million. As a result the marketplace has become very crowded since 1980.

"The romance market is important for any bookstore because of the repeat audience," says Kay M. Marcotte, buyer for Waldenbooks, which has 810 stores across the nation. "The romance reader comes back every month to make purchases, and the industry has grown phenomenally in the last few years compared to other categories, and is still growing."

"The market really took off around the end of 1981," says Julie Arthur-Sherman, buyer for

You'll Love
Waldenbooks
Romance
Book Club
Buy 6-
Get I Free
Ask booksellers
for details
Waldenbooks
Romance
New in Romance
Romance
Romance
New in Romance
Silhouette Romances
Silhouette Romances
Second Chance at Love
A Candlelight Romance
Harlequin Books.
Harlequin Books.
Harlequin Books.
Romance
Romance Center
RAPTURE ROMANCE
RR

B. Dalton Bookseller. "The brand-name series have exploded, and the rest of the market has shown a nice, steady increase." For B. Dalton, with nearly 670 stores throughout the country, romance sales overall increased 46 percent from 1981 to 1982, while the fast-growing brand-name contemporary segment of the market jumped 98 percent, according to Julie.

It's in this portion of the romance market—the brand-name lines—that publishers spend the most money and make the most effort to snare sales and customer loyalty. Harlequin tells you that nothing will touch your heart quite like one of its books and that the "romantic heroines" and "irresistible men" in American Romances will "boldly face confusing challenges"; Silhouette tells you it's ready for your own special time; Dell Candlelight Ecstasy proclaims, "That's Ecstasy!"; New American Library promises to turn romance—and consequently merchandising and sales—into "sheer rapture" with Rapture Romances.

There are sweepstakes for original cover art (Tapestry Romances) and romantic trips (Rapture and Avon's Finding Mr. Right). "Take you and your Mr. Right to Hawaii" enticed customers to try Avon's new contemporary series; in addition, the publisher sent out 20,000 advance copies of the launch title, *Paper Tiger* by Elizabeth Neff Walker, to major sales accounts and sold Mr. Right T-shirts at cost to readers in a mail promotion. The shirts came in two versions: "I Found Mr. Right" for women and "Mr. Right" for men.

In addition, there are giveaways galore—bookmarks, free books when you purchase others, free books when you join a romance book club.

Such heavy artillery doesn't always help. In 1982, Bantam Books, for example, invested seven figures—in what was termed "the largest and most intensive marketing commitment in the company's history"—in a line that only survived several months—Circle Of Love. The wholesome books were aimed at a market that had shifted away toward sexier books before Circle Of Love was launched—but that's the breaks of the business. Bantam bounced back with a sexier line, Loveswept, in 1983, although the new line was not backed by an expensive advertising campaign. Instead, Bantam printed and distributed free of charge 250,000 copies of a Loveswept "sampler," the first chapters of the first six titles plus information on the authors. The sampler was intended to pique the curiosity of potential customers.

There was a time when romance lines could be launched with no or little fanfare and grab a hold in the market. Dell Candlelight Ecstasy did in 1980, and so did Jove's Second Chance At Love in 1981. But that was back when the competition wasn't so intense and the market wasn't so crowded. Nevertheless, says Carolyn Nichols, senior editor of Loveswept, that doesn't preclude a new line from succeeding even though it isn't heavily advertised. "I think you have to look at the Second Chance At Love and Ecstasy success stories as a model," she says. "Those lines succeeded without one penny of advertising, on the basis of the content of the books alone. You can hype the public all you want—you can put $15 million into television advertising—and it's going to do absolutely no good, except the first time the consumer buys a book. But they're not going to come back to you, no matter how glorious your ads are, unless you deliver the story.

"I'm a firm believer in letting the books sell themselves, in putting any promotion money into good, strong sales efforts, making sure the books are in the right places," Carolyn states. "Let the books start off slowly and not sell 300,000 copies each. We're ready to stand the test of the consumer, which is the only test that counts."

X. FOR LOVE AND MONEY

CHAPTER THREE
Filling The Shelves

When you stop by your favorite store to check out the latest romance titles, do you ever wonder what prompts you to pick up one book and pass on another? The author's name is always important—you look for your favorites—but what if you don't know the author? Do you judge a book by its cover illustration, its title or the teasing jacket copy on the back? Different people have different criteria for judging a book, but booksellers invest a lot of time trying to anticipate what most readers will buy most of the time. "I let my customers decide for me what I'm going to keep buying," notes Julie Arthur-Sherman, buyer for B. Dalton Bookseller, the nation's second-largest bookstore chain with nearly 670 stores. Once an author or a line of romances establishes a sales track record, buyers use that as a guide for determining how many copies to buy of the newest titles.

However, many times the author is unknown or the line is new, and there is no track record to consult. Then the book has to pass the acid test of a book buyer, who only has so much space to fill, so much money to spend—and a lot of books to choose from. "We're second guessing a lot, because the customer can sometimes be very discriminating," says Kay M. Marcotte, buyer for Waldenbooks, the nation's largest bookstore chain with 810 stores. "There's a network of communication among the romance readers. If a book is good, it takes off; if it isn't, it just sits there."

Kay M. Marcotte

Most stores that have heavy romance sales try to give a shot to as many new titles as possible each month—that's 150 or more new titles, including the brand-name lines, which each issue a set number of books. "Usually we try something of everything that would remotely appeal to the romance reader," says Vivien Lee Jennings, president of the six-store Rainy Day Books chain in Fairway, Kansas, for which romances constitute about 50 percent of the total business. Vivien adds that she will pass on books that sound unhappy or "hard road," that is, filled with trials and tribulations.

Major bookstore chains also buy as many different titles as they can, although some stores may receive titles that others in the chain don't. It all depends on each store's size and volume of romance sales. Smaller bookstores, supermarkets and drugstores with more limited space for book racks have to be choosier. Some books make it, others don't.

Each month, sales representatives for the publishers present new titles to book buyers. Kay Marcotte, for example, buys about 130 romance titles every month, which include such brand-name lines as Harlequin. Julie Arthur-Sherman buys between seventy to eighty-five titles. Brand-name lines, which publish a set number of titles every month, are bought in groups, and titles are not judged individually.

All other books are judged on an individual basis. The first and foremost consideration is the author's name—well-known authors are bought automatically, as are lesser-known authors who have established sales records with previous books.

The second most important factor in judging a book is what buyers call the "package"—the cover art, the copy on the back of the jacket, the number of pages and the price. Romance readers, while they buy many books every month, are still cost conscious and demand good value for their dollar. A slim book with a high cover price may be difficult to sell, no matter how good the cover or how intriguing the title and jacket copy. "If the author is unknown, I usually go by the package," says Kay. "If it's great, we'll usually give the book a shot."

"The cover is very important," Julie observes. "A sharp cover can attract a lot of attention—it can really make or break the book. Some publishers do better covers than others. Zebra Books, for example, does some wonderful things and they've had some good success with their romances. They take unknown authors, give them a good cover, a good price and a lot of pages, and it works. Avon Books also has been very successful."

Buyers also take into consideration the publisher's reputation in the romance field and the amount of advertising and promotion money, if any, that will be spent on a book. "I don't pass on very many books," Julie says. "If nothing else, I'll give my best romance stores a crack at a particular title."

Buyers don't expect every single copy of a book they order to sell; most expect to sell anywhere from 60 to 75 percent of the quantities purchased. "You don't want to cut it so thin on quantities that a customer walks in and finds the book gone," Julie says. A few books sell less than expected and the unsold copies are returned to the publishers, and some books sell out—they're called "clean sells," and everyone loves them, of course.

Since 1980, many brand-name lines of romances have entered the market; indeed, it's the largest and fastest growing part of the entire romance market. Most of them are contemporary romances, and many compete for the same readers. Book buyers usually give the new lines a chance to get established—two or three months. If sales are sluggish, fewer books are bought the next time around.

Although there are more romance writers in the southern, southwestern and western parts of the United States, according to Romance Writers of America, romance readers seem to be spread uniformly around the nation. Neither Julie nor Kay varies quantities strictly by geography. Individual stores with the largest romance trade, regardless of location, receive the most variety and quantities.

The job of the romance book buyers is likely to become tougher and tougher, however. With an increasing number of titles to choose from every month—some 150 titles a month in 1983, up from about 100 a month in 1982—romance readers can be more discriminating in their purchases. And many already are becoming so. "Readers are buying more selectively," confirms Vivien Lee Jennings. "What it's going to take to be successful from now on is books that are dynamite."

X. FOR LOVE AND MONEY

"If it's Tuesday, this must be Detroit," goes the saying about the rigors and grueling pace of author publicity tours. It's no exaggeration. A tight schedule of radio, TV, and newspaper interviews in a string of cities all over the map is exhausting and nerve wracking, and it's not uncommon for an author to wake up and not know what city she's in.

Nevertheless, most authors would kill for the chance to be nerve wracked and exhausted. Publishers, understandably, are quite choosy about whom they're going to spend promotion money on. And even though the romance genre is profitable and has received a great deal of press attention since about 1979, merely being a romance writer isn't enough to warrant a tour.

How do publishers decide which authors they're going to promote, and how do they build an image? What goes into a publicity tour? For answers, *LoveLines* turned to publicity expert Joan Schulhafer, formerly publicity manager of Pocket Books, who handled such stellar romance authors as Janet Dailey and Jude Deveraux, and now director of publicity and public relations for Silhouette Books.

"A lot of the surge in romance publicity can be tied directly to Janet [Dailey]," says Joan. "Her publicity was years in the making, and she was one of the big breakthroughs in showing the public what a big business romance is."

Janet's publicity began on a small scale during her years with Harlequin (she signed with Pocket Books in 1978 and then left Harlequin in 1979 to write exclusively for Pocket and Silhouette). She and her husband, Bill, did whatever promotion they could on their own, such as small shows and publications, and by 1980, Janet had built up a large following. That awareness base made it possible to go after national publicity markets, such as the *Today* and *Good Morning America* TV shows and *People* magazine.

Janet's big publicity breaks came in 1981, beginning with publication of *Night Way* (Pocket Books). She appeared on *20/20* and was guest of honor at the first Romance Writers of America conference in Houston. Magazine articles appeared, and Janet enjoyed a high profile for several months. The result: she moved out of the romance genre, where a big name author might sell up to 400,000 or 500,000 copies of a book, to the mass market audience, where best-sellers range into the millions of copies.

Janet doesn't have to hit the tour trail anymore, but to maintain momentum publicity efforts continue. They include special press kits with her photo printed on the covers, and a quarterly newsletter mailed free to over 40,000 fans all over the world.

It's easy to forget that a superstar like Janet once plugged her books in small, local and regional markets. But that's the way many authors are built up, explains Joan—start small and, when recognition is established, go for the big markets, a process that can take several years.

But it's not just any author who's selected for such mass media exposure. Authors who write for brand-name lines don't stand much of a chance of gaining national fame. They will receive limited publicity help, because the brand-name lines invest their advertising and promotion dollars on building up the name identification of the line. Otherwise, to qualify for major publicity treatment, authors must meet several criteria:

1. *Mass market potential.* Does the author have enough of an audience and the quality of writing to transcend a genre audience?

2. *Commitment.* Has the author signed a multiple-book contract with the publisher? "We're not going to make a whole lot of money on the first book, although it will do better because of publicity efforts," says Joan. "We're really building on the author's sales two, three, even four books down the road."

Joan Schulhafer

3. *Presentability.* It's a TV world we live in, so how is the author going to come across on the screen? What's her background? Does she have something interesting or provocative to say? "You need hooks," Joan says. "You have to have more to talk about than, 'I've written this book. . . .' " Jude's "hook," for example, is the miniature period costumes she sews for dolls as part of the research she does for her historical novels. "Once we break her in with that angle, we can have her talk about a lot of things," Joan adds.

The hook is crucial because of the great numbers of romance novelists seeking publicity and the resistance many interviewers have to novelists (nonfiction, on the other hand, provides meatier material for a talk show host).

Authors who pass the test get the grand treatment—video coaching, press kits and releases, all kinds of give-away goodies (known as collateral)—bookmarks, flyers, buttons and the like—and, of course, the publicity tour. Even more important, the books are distributed *everywhere,* so the public can't fail to see them. For Jude, Pocket Books also sent out 15,000 preview copies of *Highland Velvet* in 1982 to drum up advance enthusiasm. Preview editions are expensive; the last times Pocket had done that for an author was in 1979 with V.C. Andrews' *Flowers in the Attic* and in 1981 for Douglas Adams' *The Hitchhiker's Guide to the Galaxy.*

Hitting The Road

A publicity tour, even a modest one, is no small undertaking, requiring artful scheduling and coordination, infinite patience and lots of stamina. That's a polite way of saying that everybody involved tries not to tear out their hair before it's over. A lucky author has someone accompany her to worry about details, changes and shuttling around between appointments. Others less fortunate get a copy of a schedule, soon to be obsolete, and best wishes for success. They're not left to navigate completely alone, however, for sales reps and escorts in the field often assist.

An average eight-city tour can cost over $10,000. "At Pocket Books, we ask the sales reps in each city to help out, or sometimes we hire an escort, at $100 to $150 a day, to take care of things like getting the author to appointments and to the airport, making sure they're on time," says Joan. "Escorts are an added expense but well worth it, because it's hard enough on authors to be on the road. However," Joan notes, "if the budget is tight, it might be a matter of choosing between having escorts or doing an extra city."

Hotel accommodations are expensive, usually because the author has to stay in the heart of the city, where prices are higher.

The tour schedule is apt to change at any moment, and it's not uncommon for a publicist to send daily updates of revisions, additions and cancellations of interview appointments. In a single day, an author can bounce from one medium to another—newspaper, radio or TV—plus autograph signings at bookstores. "On one tour," commented a romance author, "the schedule was so tight there literally was no time to go to the bathroom. It's a good thing I had strong kidneys."

The tour schedule includes, besides times, any information that might be helpful to an author, such as what to expect (a hostile interview, a predictable one, a debate, questions from the audience etc.) as well as the names of other guests scheduled to appear on the same show. "Authors have horror stories about going on the air with a very serious nonfiction book in between the trained chimpanzee and the Julia Child look-alike from Oshkosh," Joan jokes.

Interviewers, most of whom have scant time to prepare, are given a few prep questions by the publicist in advance. Some use them, others don't.

Inexperienced authors are often coached on how to handle interviews, particularly hostile ones. Romance writers can expect to field such negative leading questions as, "How did a nice girl like you get mixed up in such a trashy business?" (These are usually posed by a man who's never seen the inside of a romance and goes home to his kung-fu novel.)

"Romance authors have to deal with a very volatile subject," Joan says. "They need to know how to agree with the interviewer while disagreeing at the same time."

Most receptive to romance authors are media in cities in the South, Southwest and Midwest, such as Atlanta, Dallas, Houston, Miami, Kansas City and Charlotte, North Carolina. Major markets, such as New York, Los Angeles, San Francisco and Chicago, are good, but tough for beginners to break into. The New England area seems to have a lower interest in romances than other parts of the nation, and authors are seldom sent there.

But all the touring, press kits, bookmarks and autograph signings in the world won't guarantee best-seller star status for an author. In the long run, it's word of mouth and repeat business at the cash register.

"You create a little bit of celebrity to help sell the books," says Joan. "You do what you can to get the word of mouth publicity going, but then the book has to stand on its own."

XI. PACKAGING THE GOODS

There's more than meets the eye in a romance cover. They're designed for maximum impact, communicating all kinds of messages about the contents. And if the cover illustration doesn't quite hook you, perhaps the teasing jacket copy will. Art directors, illustrators and editors tell how they make the most of the package that wraps around the romance.

CHAPTER ONE
The Arts Of Passion

The rise of the romance genre has given a whole new dimension to sexy book covers—sensuality from a feminine point of view. The key element in nearly every romance cover is the "clinch"—a man and a woman embracing. Although their poses and state of undress are often daring, the clinch is never portrayed in a purely sexual way, as it is for a men's adventure novel. Instead, it has a feeling of emotion, of love and of romance.

"I prefer to think of these books as love stories rather than romances," says illustrator Elaine Gignilliat. "Though many of the books I do are very sexy, they are never pornographic, because they're about two people falling deeply in love and making a lasting commitment." The covers reflect that commitment.

The romance cover has a short but interesting history, short because the genre is relatively young—it didn't coalesce until the early to mid-1970s. Not surprisingly, it began at Avon Books, where so many great historical romance authors got their start. And not surprisingly, it's been heavily influenced by women, for only a woman truly understands what strikes an emotional chord in another woman. As romances boomed in popularity and their contents and covers became sexier, "it became apparent that women have always had a deep, seething sexuality," says Barbara Bertoli, former art director of Avon and probably the most influential woman in the genre's art.

Back before historical romances made the best-selling scene in the 1970s, most books, including paperbacks, were written and packaged from a male point of view. "In the arts, men have constantly been interpreting us for ourselves," Barbara says. "Back in the 1940s, paperback covers were torrid no matter what their content—that's what gave paperbacks such a bad name. Eroticism was portrayed from a male standpoint. The covers were turning men on, but they weren't geared towards enticing women." One of the reasons why, according to Barbara, is that women's sexual expression was more repressed then.

XI. PACKAGING THE GOODS

The paperback "look" of the forties was created by illustrator James Avati, who portrayed panting men and women in "reasonably proper disarray," says Len Leone, art director of Bantam Books. Rooms with bare bulbs and rumpled beds were characteristic of his style.

Barbara Bertoli

Much later a different realism took hold, thanks largely to illustrator James Bama, whose work still influences illustrators and art directors today. Len, who used Bama, was influential in establishing the model for paperback design—lots of white space around centered spot art and type.

In the 1960s, Gothics became popular, and the covers all sported the same basic theme—a terror-stricken girl fleeing from a foreboding house or mansion, which had one lighted window upstairs, all done in dark, murky color. Most of those covers were "full bleeds," that is, the art was not contained in a spot but bled to the edges of the covers (sometimes to the back cover as well), and type was superimposed on the art.

In the 1970s, when romantic fiction began to take shape as a genre, the direction of cover art began to change again, and Barbara was the one who broke new ground. At the time, she was the only woman art director among ten or so publishing houses (she joined Avon in 1965, became art director in 1968 and left in 1981 to pursue her own water color painting). Barbara, along with former Avon editor Nancy Coffey (who discovered Kathleen E. Woodiwiss, Rosemary Rogers and other now-famous "Avon ladies"), created the distincitive "Avon look" of feminine, flowing art and type and passionate, vivid colors. Avon's romances, which catered to women from the inside out, proved to be bookstore bonanzas and spawned much imitation. In house, the sexy historicals were called "flaming thighs."

The cover art process evolved through trial and error; none of it was planned or scientific, says Barbara. "I was bored with the way covers looked. With Nancy it was like working hand in glove. Nancy is very sensual and intuitive, and that's the way I worked, too. We experimented a lot and we failed a lot, but we were very creative."

Experimentation was encouraged at Avon. While Barbara's first romance covers were reminiscent of Len's style at Bantam, eventually her own look evolved. "I don't like straight lines," she said. "I like curved lines. I'd curve space on the page—I wanted it used in an organic, female way." Typography was hand-lettered "to reflect the movement of the art, so that instead of looking pieced together, the lettering and the art came together in an organic whole." The result, Barbara says, "was a super-saturation of a subliminal erotic feeling in a female sense. The covers suggested what it really felt like to be in the arms of that wonderful hero, making the reader want what was happening on the cover to happen to her."

Barbara never read the books themselves. She would receive a reader's report summarizing the books. "Nancy and I would sit down and she would start talking about a book, and I would start visualizing," Barbara recalls. "I'd do thumbnail sketches and describe what I was seeing. Some of my fantasies were better than what was in the books." She researched magazines, paintings and photographs and then began designing the cover. "I guided the cover carefully to completion," she says. One of her fortes was the "significant romantic gesture."

She popularized the use of warm and hot colors on romance covers. Red-violet quickly became one of *the* romance colors when Barbara used it for one of Rosemary Rogers' novels, *Dark Fires* (1975).

Barbara's criteria for whether or not a cover was successful were, "Did it hit me in the gut? Was it poignant? I figured that if I swooned when I looked at it, someone else would, too. I thought I was a good sounding board for what other women were looking for."

One of her most successful covers, she says, was for Kathleen E. Woodiwiss' *Shanna* (1977). The illustration, done by H. Tom Hall, "just throbbed in the most delicious way," Barbara says. The background color is a rich orange; a flowered foreground is lush and warm; and there is a gesture—that "significant gesture"—between the man and woman. The man's face is not visible, but one gets the feeling he is holding tremendous power in check. "He looks as though he could crush her, yet he's very tender," Barbara says. "The woman is in a state of ecstasy."

Eventually Barbara wanted to do a romance cover showing total nudity. She commissioned Bob McGinnis to illustrate *Fires in Winter* by Johanna Lindsey (1980). Originally, the man's hands and arms were placed strategically across the naked woman, but Avon editors thought it went a bit too far and directed a slip to be painted on her. (Interestingly, two subsequent Johanna Lindsey novels published by Avon, *Glorious Angel* (1981) and *So Speaks the Heart* (1983), also illustrated by Bob McGinnis, feature naked men, their bodies cleverly shielded by the position of the woman, who is clothed.)

Barbara's feminine approach to romance art helped open many doors for other women in the field. "This is the greatest day for American women illustrators," says Len Leone. "They have a lock on the sensuality

Wicked
Loving
Lies

Captive
Bride

Lady
Vixen

of the romance cover, and they know how far to go. The men have been learning something from the women."

Barbara agrees. "I think the romance covers are all very good now," she says. "The male art directors are getting to be as good as the women."

CHAPTER TWO

Telling A Book By Its Cover

Scanning the racks of romances in a bookstore, you may think that all romance covers look the same—there's an illustration of a man and a woman in a passionate embrace, or "clinch"; the type is flowery or swirling; the colors lean toward vivid reds and pinks. Yet there's much more to romance covers than meets the eye. A good cover communicates to the customer on many different, often subliminal levels.

Most obviously, it tells her the book is a romance—she can see that in the passion and emotion flowing between the embracing couple, the warm colors, the frequent use of foliage and flowers, the fine detail. "It's the erotic nature of the art," says Avon Books art director Matt Tepper, in explaining what differentiates a romance cover from other types of fiction. "You know this is a woman's book and it's going to appeal totally to a woman's senses. It has passionate colors, like a lot of purples, lavenders and reds, strong type with a flow and femininity to it, and illustrations that are vivid, bold and daring."

Matt Tepper

Romance covers overwhelmingly feature illustrations rather than photographs, because illustrations evoke more fantasy. "Women thirty-five and older prefer art in the fantasy realm," says Milt Charles, vice president and art director of Pocket Books. "The looser the art, the more they like it. Younger women like it more precise. When you get down to teenagers, they like photographs."

The cover also obviously communicates the book's setting and time period. Small images of ships in the background indicate travel. Supporting characters, friends, rivals and villains may also be featured in the background, particularly if the illustration wraps from front to back.

Most importantly, however, the cover communicates the sensual and sexual level of the contents, telling the buyer whether the book is fairly tame or quite racy. This is a crucial signal, for buyers don't like to be unpleasantly surprised once they start reading. Someone who doesn't want a sexually explicit book will veer away from a racy cover. But someone who does and selects a book partly on the promise of the cover will feel cheated when she finds the contents don't live up to the packaging.

The cover represents the steaminess of the contents in a number of ways, chiefly in the body positions and clothing of the embracing couple. Pelvises, chests, legs and lips close together, and sensuous hand positions, such as the woman's hand placed aggressively on the man's thigh, indicate racy contents, according to illustrator Elaine Gignilliat. "If a man's hand touches very lightly around the girl's head, it might seem protective," she says. "But if it's more forcefully holding her face or turning it to him, it could show that he's forcing her to his will. If his hand is either below her waist, or above her waist and near her breast, it's naturally more suggestive than if his hand is at her waist."

Lots of bare skin suggests more sex, and a low-cut gown, even if correct as fashion in a particular historical era, accomplishes the same suggestive effect that was intended when it was originally designed, Elaine notes. "The way the woman touches the man also indicates sexuality. If she has her hand gently resting on his arm, it looks cooperative but proper, but if she's caressing him or exploring his body, that suggests she's aroused and interested."

Generally, the racier the book the more prone the couple is likely to be, although some electrifying things can be accomplished with upright couples. Illustrator Elaine Duillo pushed out the sexual frontiers a bit with her cover for Valerie Sherwood's *Bold Breathless Love* (Warner), which shows a kneeling couple on a beach and the man's hand lifting the woman's skirt high on her thigh. "Things hadn't been quite that leggy before," notes Lee Fishback, art director of Jove's Second Chance At Love.

Milt Charles

ast! The story that
llions of readers have
longed
for...

PURITY'S
SHAME

The fervor
that blazed across
the pages of PURITY'S
PASSION and PURITY'S
TASY now sweeps Purity to the
summate moment of her
r-crossed destiny. From
rench château to a
nsion on the Poto-
c, through the
ne-ridden slums
l reeking jails of
ency London to the
endors of a royal
onation, from the
ns of one lustful de-
ver to the next, she follows
dreams of undying love—
r seeking her beloved
rk Landless, who
ires her above
else in the
ld!

POCKET
82124
$1.95

POCKET
FICTION

Purity's
Shame
Janette
Seymour

0-671-82124-5-195

PRINTED IN U.S.A.

PURITY'S
SHAME

To the breathless peak of
soul-maddening rapture!

Janette Seymour

author of the bestseller PURITY'S ECSTASY

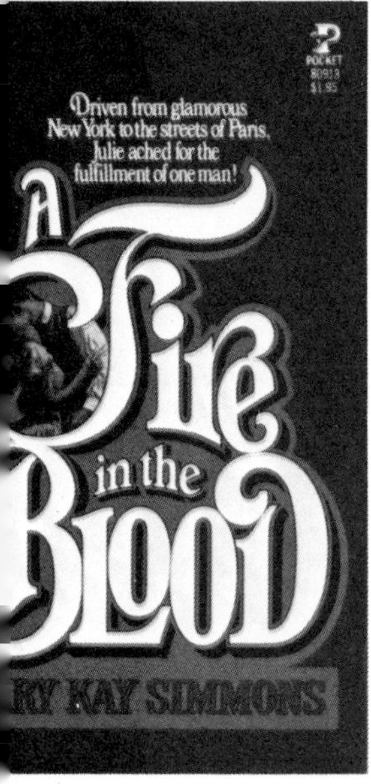

POCKET
80813
$1.95
Driven from glamorous
New York to the streets of Paris,
Julie ached for the
fulfillment of one man!
A Fire in the Blood
RY KAY SIMMONS

SIGNET•451-W7114•$1.50
THE SMUGGLER'S BRIDE
ROSALIND LAKER
LOVE AND TERROR—A SPELLBINDING NOVEL OF BEWITCHING ROMANCE AND BREATHLESS SUSPENSE...
"SUPERIOR!"—KIRKUS REVIEWS

RAPTURE ROMANCE•451-AJ2232•$1.95
JENNIFER DALE
TENDER RHAPSODY
RAPTURE ROMANCE
#7

62
Second Chance at Love
ON WINGS OF MAGIC
SUSANNA COLLINS

And covers for New American Library's Rapture Romances, a line of sensual contemporaries, show some sexually aggressive women, reaching inside a man's shirt or biting, not kissing, his earlobe. "You want involvement by both parties, not the woman in some orgasmic state with her eyes closed as he's looking at her," says Jim Plumeri, NAL art director.

No matter how sexy a book is, rarely does the embracing couple actually kiss. "The lovers become anonymous when their features are hidden, and their relationship seems only physical and impersonal," Elaine explains. "The reader wants to see the hero's and heroine's faces and know what they look like."

Passion can also be heightened by the heroine's hair. "If her hair is loose and flowing back, it conveys a sense of movement," says Matt. "It also shows some possibility of struggle, and you don't know if the heroine is coming on or being taken."

Sometimes the suggestion of sexuality can be more provocative than the portrayal of it. H. Tom Hall's cover for *My Lord Monleigh* (Avon) by Jan Cox Speas shows a man and a woman on a hillside who look as though they've just had some kind of passionate interlude.

More and more, however, the covers have gotten explicitly sexier as the books have gotten sexier. Before the passionate clinch became standard fare on romance covers—it came into vogue in the mid-1970s and was nearly universally established by the late 1970s—embraces were much cooler, if the man and woman touched at all, or the man was reduced to the background or eliminated (of course, a lot of the contents weren't all that racy either). Such covers often showed just a woman's face, with a motif from the story—ships or horses, for example. Others showed the woman in the foreground and a tiny hero far away in the background. "I call them munchkins," says Hilary Ross, senior editor of New American Library. "I got so tired of seeing little men on the covers."

A common pose for an embrace was the man standing behind the woman grasping her shoulders, or perhaps the two were face to face, but the clinch had all the heat of a 30-year marriage, a hi-honey-I'm-home squeeze. This wholesome look can still be found on tamer romances.

The one category of romance novels whose covers haven't changed much is the Regency. Most Regencies are comedies of manners and have little or no sex—it's only been since 1979 that they have contained any sex—and the covers reflect that. Traditionally, the man and woman didn't touch or barely touched. "Now they're sexier but still restrained and social-looking," says Hilary. Adds Jim Plumeri, "You can't get too carried away with Regencies."

"They have to have a romantic feeling and not be sexually explicit," says Barbara Dicks, former executive editor of Fawcett Crest Books. "Equally important is a careful rendering of the artifacts and clothes of the period."

The Search for Variety

The clinch, always the focus of attention, has its limitations. How many ways can you vary an embrace and stay within the genre's bounds of feminine appeal and sexual good taste—and still look different from all the other romances?

One approach, used occasionally in the past and now gaining more favor, is to show the woman in a dominant position. Milt Charles has used it, most notably for Richard Gallen contemporaries; illustrator Harry Bennett says one of his most successful covers, for the Tapestry historical (Pocket Books) *Kindred Spirits* by DeAnn Patrick, shows two couples with dominant women.

The role reversal seem to be readily accepted by romance readers, notes illustrator Gordon Johnson. "It conveys a certain frailty in men, that even though they want to be dominant, they have weaknesses," he says.

Nudity is another way to spice up a clinch. While no woman has ever been shown naked on a romance cover—former Avon art director Barbara Bertoli suggested the idea but was overruled—men have. Not fully naked, of course (something, usually the heroine, strategically blocks a full view) but nevertheless it's obvious that the man isn't wearing anything. This approach worked so well for two Johanna Lindsey novels, *Fire in Winter* and *Glorious Angel*, that it was repeated for her 1983 release, *So Speaks the Heart*. Illustrator Bob McGinnis did all three.

Nudity can be tricky, not only from a good taste standpoint, but from a sales standpoint. It may play in Manhattan, but will it play in Peoria? "If we think it's sensitive, we run it by the salesmen," says Lee Fishback. For *On Wings of Magic*, a Second Chance At Love romance by Susanna Collins, the cover shows a man and a woman in a Jacuzzi-type bath. The man is sitting on the edge of the bath, and the woman is rising out of the water. The cover: bubbles. "The salesmen liked it, but they were afraid they wouldn't be able to sell it," says Lee. "We needed more bubbles to confuse the issue a little. We did that one bubble by bubble." While the cover came off very successfully, at some point the bubbles would have lost their purpose, she notes. "Nudity is a lovely thing. If there had been too many bubbles, no one would have known they didn't have anything on—they could have been wearing swimsuits."

In the next bath scene Lee commissioned, for *Relentless Desire* by Sandra Brown, she had both man and woman in the water—not because of potential controversy, but for variety. "It reminded me of two missionaries in a pot," she chuckles.

Covers for brand-name contemporary romances have additional restrictions for art directors and illustrators seeking freshness and variety because several are published every month (and sit on the racks next to each other) and formats often limit the extent or position of the art. The illustration may have to be confined to an oval or circle, or it may have to work around type that is always in the same spot. Rapture Romance's vertical wave of magenta color on the front, for example, limits most clinches to vertical poses. "It's difficult to be different each time," acknowledges Jim Plumeri. "You hope through color, style and artists to pick up some nuances." Besides pose, each month's releases must have variety in color and setting, says Lee Fishback.

Format constraints notwithstanding, historicals offer more room for experimentation than contemporaries. "That's where you can play up the fantasy angle," says Matt Tepper. "The hardest covers to do are contemporary romances. They don't lend themselves as well to romantic poses or clothing."

Also, says Matt, more experimentation can be done with major authors, whose books are likely to sell well regardless of the cover. For example, the cover of Kathleen E. Woodiwiss' *A Rose in Winter*, done by H. Tom Hall, shows a man and woman, loosely garbed in flowing fabric, reaching to embrace rather than actually embracing. The cover originally was done for another book, then later seemed appropriate for Kathleen's 1982 release. It was even retouched to make it a little more chaste—the woman's breasts were covered up more.

The clinch, however, "will always be the mainstay of romances," Matt says. "There are some cases where one person on the cover might generate enough interest, but I think you'd always have to have a little clinch somewhere in the background." He cites the covers of two nonromance Avon books as examples of a possible new direction for romances. Both feature a woman on the cover and other characters and scenes from the story on the back: *A Green*

IT WAS TO BE AN UNOFFICIAL BETROTHAL. AND IT WOULD LAST ONLY FOR THE DURATION OF THE SEASON.
Cornelius often despaired of the behavior of his sister, Carrie and his ward, Bree. They shared a mischievous sense of humor, a breathtaking beauty and an uncanny ability to read each other's thoughts.
Responding to a threat against Bree, Cornelius enlists the help of two friends, Colin Traversham and Morgan Hawkscroft. His plan is simple. The gentlemen will become engaged to the ladies.
DeAnn Patrick
Tapestry
Kindred Spirits
DeAnn Patrick
There is a language only the heart can hear.
De Ann Patrick
Kindred Spirits
PRINTED IN U.S.A.

Tapestry

HISTORICAL
ROMANCE
46186 • 9

There is a
language only the
heart can hear.

DeAnn
Patrick

Kindred Spirits

Desire by Anton Myrer (cover by Vic Lavote) and *This Cruel Beauty* by Trevor-Meldal Johnsen (cover by Elaine Duillo). "There have got to be other ways to show romance," Matt says.

The Right Type and Other Innovations

In the mid-1970s, Barbara Bertoli, as art director of Avon Books, pioneered the use of flowing, feminine type that was hand-lettered and fit the overall design of the cover. Swashy type, as it is called, quickly became symbolic of romances. Barbara also put type in foil and embossed it, giving romance covers a tactile as well as visual appeal.

Milt Charles has also done some innovative things with type. "It's the key subliminal," he says. "You can pass by a book and still notice the type out of the corner of your eye. I try to have my own distinctive type. The more serious the book is, the straighter the type gets. The less swashes or decorative quality the less romantic. That's my little message to people out there, and they understand."

Milt has made some commanding uses of type with negative space (blank space) and die cuts. For *A Fire in the Blood* (Pocket Books) by Mary Kay Simmons, published in 1976, he made the entire cover typographic surrounded by negative space. A swirl in the type contains a small illustration of a clinch. The cover, he says, was his first major innovation in paperback cover art.

He introduced die cuts to paperback art in 1979 with V.C. Andrews' thriller *Flowers in the Attic* (Pocket) and, in the same year, introduced it to the romance genre with Janet Dailey's first novel for Pocket, *Touch the Wind*. The type is part of the die-cut design, and this style appeared on three subsequent Janet Dailey novels, all by Pocket: *The Rogue*, *Ride the Thunder*, and *Night Way*. Die cuts are used so often now that Milt says he uses them "only when necessary."

Milt's influence can also be seen in the use of large portraits and wraparound covers, which he first used in 1977 and 1978 for the Purity series (Pocket) by Janette Seymour.

Milt plans to use more strong typographic covers with lots of negative space. Set face out in bookstores against other romances, the typographic covers will be an eye-catching contrast, he says.

Color It Passionate

There's no doubt that warm colors—colors with red in them—work best for romances. You might think that gold foil would be warm, but copper foil, which has red in it, is better, observes Matt. Generally, the sexier the book the hotter the colors.

Brown, yellow and orange are seldom used for romances—people just don't respond well to those colors. "I don't use much brown or orange," says Lee, "they don't seem to work well romantically. However, anyone who's gifted can make a liar out of me, and I'm happy when they do." Oranges and browns do seem to fit sagas, says Gordon Johnson, because they give off an earthy glow.

There is disagreement over green. "Green should never be used at all, ever," says Milt Charles. "It doesn't work. It's cold and impassionate and a lot of people react negatively to it. If I'm going to have a lot of foliage or grass, I'll have the artist put it in the blue and lavender family."

Others feel that certain dark or vibrant greens are very successful. "It depends on the imagery and how the color is used," says Matt. "Certain greens can be warm and passionate. If you add copper to green, it livens it up."

Len Leone, art director of Bantam Books, uses green as well as a rainbow of colors for the Loveswept sensual contemporary line. "You rarely see green on major titles," he acknowledges, "but people buy by title and author, or the romantic idea of the book."

Wave Of The Future?

The styles and characteristics of romance art have filtered into other types of paperback novels. Art is more realisitic and more finely rendered with an eye for detail. There's more foil and embossing. The wave of the future for all paperbacks, says Len, will be in the sophistication of the packaging of the product—new ways to attract attention at the racks. Bantam is one publisher experimenting with paperbacks that look like hardcover books; the covers have a finished look and are much stiffer than paperbacks but not as stiff as hardcovers. Will that soon appear in romances? There are no plans at present, but perhaps that's somewhere in the future. Wait and see.

Leonard Leone

AVON 80630/$3.95

ROSEMARY ROGERS

SURRENDER TO LOVE

THE NEW, DARING
NOVEL OF LOVE AND DESIRE

THE POWER AND THE GLORY

Never underestimate the power of a book cover. Its influence on sales is tremendous, particularly if an author is unknown. "It's the showcase for the book," says illustrator Gordon Johnson. "If you have a prominent author and a good cover, it's a sure sale. Sometimes they're sleepers, and they sell because of the covers. It's an impulse buy, and if it looks cheap, customers aren't going to pick it up."

"You can't sell any book without a great cover, even if the author is really big," emphatically says Milt Charles, vice president and art director of Pocket Books. "Janet Dailey can be broken because of terrible covers. The sale can go down enormously because of a bad package—other people would like not to believe it's true, but it is. If anything goes wrong with a book, it's probably the cover."

For Janet's entry into the mass paperback market in 1979, the cover made all the difference, says Milt. Having built up an enormous following as a Harlequin author, Janet signed with Pocket Books (and later with Silhouette Books). But sales reps initially didn't get the big orders that were expected for her first novel for Pocket, *Touch the Wind*. "The sales reps came back with orders for something like 280,000 copies. In terms of mass distribution, that means the author will never make it. So I decided to do a different kind of cover, with the title outside and the illustration inside, a die-cut cover. They sold 570,000 copies of *Touch the Wind*, and now there's over a million out.

"Each Janet Dailey book that followed had that [die cut] look," Milt says. "They stand out in the stores because they're so simple—you can read the type from a mile away. I think this is the key factor in getting Janet Dailey into a million-copy best-seller."

But Milt altered the cover style for Janet's larger-size trade editions of her Calder series. "Janet Dailey is now a force on her own," he says. He's given her a more austere hard-cover look, with straighter type to indicate the "bigness" of the books.

While others feel that popular authors will carry sales on their names alone—"If you have a real hot author you can just put type on the cover," says Gordon—they acknowledge that good covers can further enhance sales. For heavies such as Rosemary Rogers and Kathleen E. Woodiwiss, Avon Books art director Matt Tepper says that "you could put them on a brown paper bag and still sell a million and a half copies. However, when we do a beautiful or unique cover, we hope to sell an additional half a million copies." Avon expected to sell 1.5 million copies of Rosemary Rogers' *Surrender to Love*, released in July 1982; instead, it sold more than 2.4 million by the end of the year. "I'd like to think it was the cover," Matt says, noting that significant changes were made in the illustration, type and design.

The art, originally done in an oval with small type, "was not worthy of someone like Rosemary Rogers," he says. Matt had the type enlarged and hand-lettered in copper foil, with Rosemary's name prominent at the top. The background was colored purple, and subliminals were added, such as a subtle heart shape in the background and exotic flowers in the foreground. The revised cover, says Matt, "is passionate, warm and fresh—it stands out. And the important thing is, everyone sees the name Rosemary Rogers."

FROM START TO FINISH

Designing a romance cover is no quick and easy task. It involves close coördination between art director, editor, illustrator and the sales department; research on the part of the illustrator; and a photographic shoot, as well as the actual rendering. Then, in many cases, the art director asks for changes. The entire process for a single cover (excluding brand-line romances, which have simpler covers than most other romances) can take anywhere from one to three months.

The cost goes into the thousands. Depending on the artist and the complexitiy of the job, the artists' fees can range from $1,200 to $3,200 for a single cover, and from about $2,700 to $5,000 for a wraparound cover (brand-line romance covers fetch anywhere from $1,000 to $1,700 or so). Add to that the artist's expenses and production costs. With all that money invested in a single book, naturally great care is taken to produce a quality cover that will appeal to the customer.

The art process begins when the art department receives a reader's report on the book or the manuscript itself from the editorial department. The reader's report gives details of the characters'

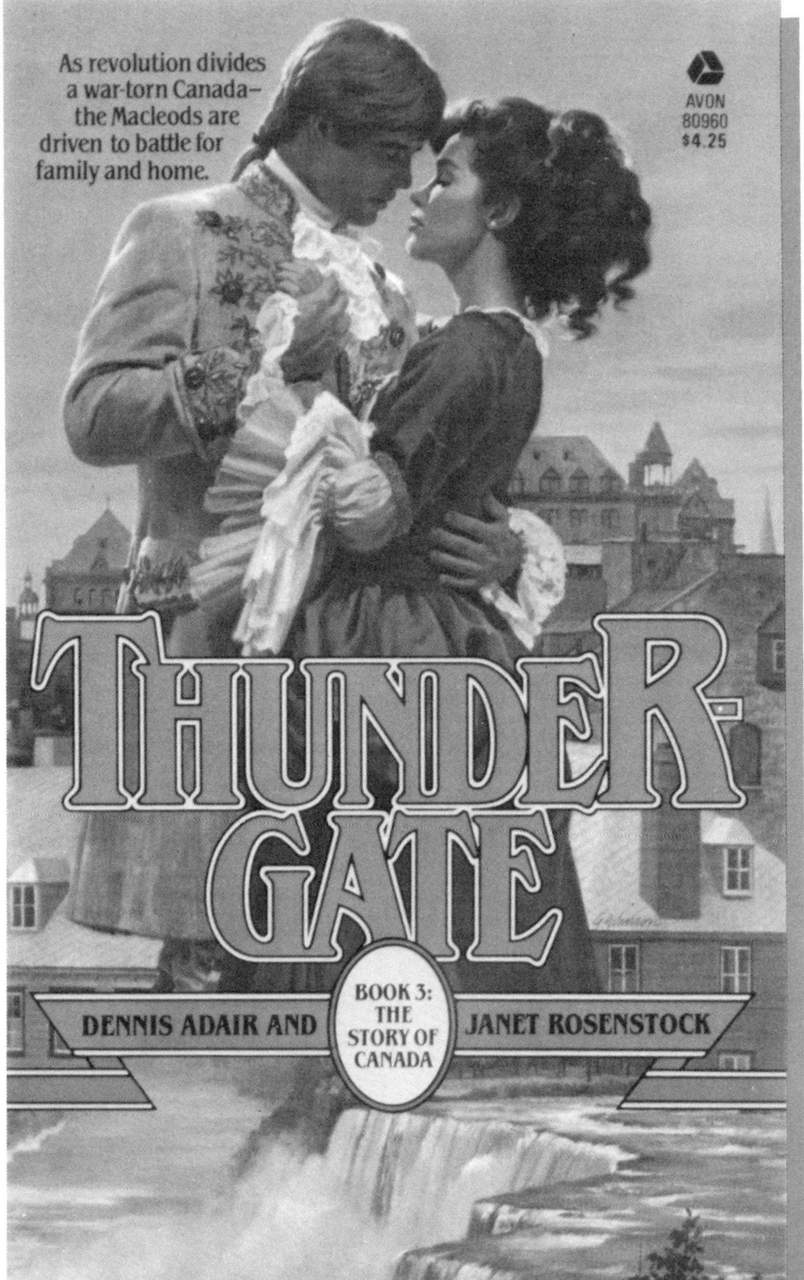

As revolution divides a war-torn Canada– the Macleods are driven to battle for family and home.
AVON
80960
$4.25
THUNDER-GATE
DENNIS ADAIR AND
BOOK 3: THE STORY OF CANADA
JANET ROSENSTOCK

Lee Fishback

appearances, some of their clothing, the setting and perhaps scenes from the book that would be possibilities for the cover.

The art and editorial departments meet and discuss ideas for the cover, then the art director commissions an illustrator. If a cover calls for certain period clothes, or for large portraits that demand good skin tone, the art director is likely to select someone who excels in that area and whom he or she knows. "It's important to get the right person for the job," stresses Matt Tepper, art director for Avon Books.

"I consider what type of scenes the artists like to do," says Lee Fishback, art director of Jove's Second Chance At Love. "Anything that can increase the artist's excitement helps."

The art director meets with the illustrator to discuss the project and give instructions, rough sketches or perhaps advertisement photos that capture a look or pose that is desired.

The illustrator does whatever research is needed for the setting, period and clothing, going through pictorial files in libraries and museums, books and magazines (most build up their own extensive files).

The illustrator does some preliminary sketches, either in pencil or full-color paint, and gives them to the art director. The pose, setting, all the elements of the illustration are decided upon.

From model agency portfolios, the illustrator chooses models based not only on their resemblance to characters in the book, but also on their ability to act out the passionate poses. "They should be good actors," notes illustrator Elaine Gignilliat. The illustrator chooses and rents period costumes, if necessary, hires a photographer and supervises the shoot, directing the models through various poses and determining the lighting (some illustrators do their own photography in a rented studio). The art director may attend the shoot as well.

From the photos, the illustrator and art director pick one that will be used for the illustration. The artist then goes to work. The finished product goes to the publisher, where it is reviewed by art and editorial, and sales, if necessary. There may be some fine tuning, and then *voila!* It's ready to beckon to the customer, "Buy me!"

• XI. PACKAGING THE GOODS •

COVER STARS

You may swoon over Paul Newman on the big screen, but the handsome actor would never make it as a model for a romance cover. Not according to Milt Charles, vice president and art director of Pocket Books.

"Paul Newman would be absolutely ridiculous on a romance cover—he's too cute," says Milt, who is responsible for more than 400 Silhouette, Tapestry and Pocket Books romance covers a year (plus other books). "Debbie Reynolds, Lana Turner—same thing," he says. "We're dealing with a fantasy here, a sexual fantasy, and I understand it.

"I think women want to see two things on the cover, as far as characterizations are concerned: Gregory Peck and Katharine Hepburn, as they looked when they were in their twenties and thirties. Gregory Peck is spectacular looking. He's the epitome, the most perfect masculine male ever. Katharine Hepburn, even though she's not a sensual woman, with her bone structure, has a look that people respond to."

It doesn't matter, says Milt, if the hero is painted with blond hair or the woman with red hair, so long as their facial structure captures that unique Peck and Hepburn essence.

Sorry about that, Paul.

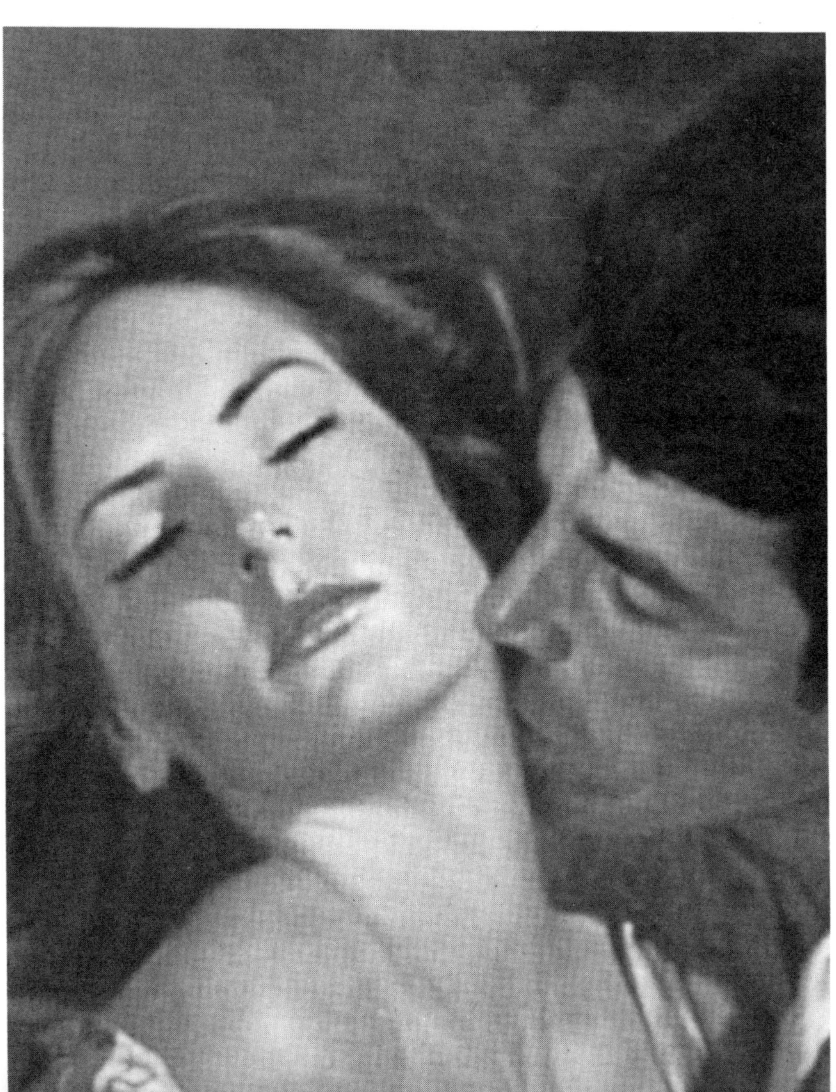

Meet seven illustrators whose work no doubt adorns the covers of some of your favorite romances:

HARRY BENNETT

He's one of the best-known romance cover illustrators, and author Jude Deveraux insists that he create the covers for all of her novels. Harry Bennett, whose work is distinguished by flowing movement, stays on top of his craft by constantly experimenting with new techniques.

One of his best covers, he says, uses a new approach, perhaps for the first time in romances. *Kindred Spirits* (Tapestry), by DeAnn Patrick, which shows two couples, one on the front and one on the back, and the women, not the men, are in the superior positions.

Harry, a native of South Salem, New York who now lives in Ridgefield, Connecticut, has always worked as a free-lance artist, beginning with Gothics in the 1960s. He did one of Fawcett's first reprints of Mary Stewart suspense novels, *Thunder on the Right,* which, in the booming market for romantic mysteries, led to more work on novels by Phyllis A. Whitney and Victoria Holt as well as Mary Stewart and others. "Then Gothics slid away and ran into historical romances, epics set in the nineteenth century," Harry says, and he followed the market.

While he's executed some contemporary romances for Pocket Books, most of his work—about 24 covers a year—is for historicals, especially Pocket Books' new line, Tapestry Romances. His cover for the introductory title, *Defiant Love* by Maura Seger, valued at $7,000, was given away in a consumer drawing held by the publisher as a promotion for the line.

Jude Deveraux spotted one of his historical covers for Richard Gallen, *The Silver Kiss,* and decided she wanted him to illustrate all her books. "His colors are beautiful," Jude comments. "I like his sense of anatomy. He's very creative, whereas other artists often use the same poses over again." For Jude, Harry has illustrated *The Velvet Promise* (Gallen) and *Highland Velvet, Velvet Song* and *Sweetbriar* (all Pocket Books).

Harry prefers historicals to contemporaries because of the period clothes. "The costumes for women lend themselves to romance," he says. "They come across better than a pair of straight jeans and a blouse." He often updates hairstyles to modern times, however, because it helps readers identify with the characters.

He works with egg tempera and oil, describing the latter as "the king of the medium—there seems to be no limit to what you can do with it." His method follows the ways of the old master artists; he mixes egg, pigment oil glaze, does an underpainting first in black and white and then adds glazed colors over it. Most of his colors are cool—blues, greens and violets—with high reds added in spots to attract attention, such as on a dress or a cape.

While Harry prefers to work directly from models, time constraints are such that he usually has to photograph models and work from prints. He handles the entire shoot himself, from renting a studio in Greenwich Village to hiring the models to taking pictures to printing and developing. He doesn't rent costumes—"They're usually replicas of replicas and the male models look silly in them"—but invents his own costumes, based on his knowledge and research, as he paints. During the shoots, women models are clothed in draped bolts of fabric.

Because so many romance covers look the same, embracing couples shown to the waist in profile or three-quarters view, Harry tries to vary his approach. Whole figures may be used on one cover and solely large heads on another, or a dress that dominates the picture on yet another. Illustrations will continue to prevail on romance covers, he says, because "photos don't allow identification with a fantasy—they're too real."

PINO DAENI

A mere few years ago (1978) Pino Daeni gave up his established career as a top illustrator in Milan, Italy and, with his wife and two children, immigrated to the United States. Unknown and unable to speak English, he spent a year trying to break into publishing, and almost gave up before he finally received a commission from Zebra Books. Today he's so much in demand that he's booked for months in advance, with sixteen or seventeen romance covers under contract at a time.

Pino achieves a romantic, almost dreamy effect in his oil-painted illustrations. His style, he says, is "like Fellini, whom I love so much, a fusion between realism and fantasy." Among his covers are *Palomino* by Danielle Steele; *Hidden Fires, The Court of the Flowering Peach* and *Vienna Dreams* by Janette Radcliffe; and *The Tiger's Woman* by Celeste de Blasis (all Dell).

Pino was born in Bari, a coastal city in southern Italy, in 1939. At an early age, he showed an aptitude for art, but his interest in pursuing it as a career caused conflicts with his father. "My dream was to become a fine arts artist," he says. Eventually he went to Milan in 1970 to attend art school, paint for galleries and illustrate for publishers such as Mondadori. For the galleries, he painted women and children and, for a period, old men. In 1975, he gave up fine arts to devote himself solely to illustration. His success as one of Milan's leading illustrators enabled him to enjoy a comfortable life.

However, Milan soon became too small a market for him, and he decided to follow another dream, migrating to America. "I didn't realize that America was not all like Hollywood movies, but I realized that in New York I could feel comfortable, even though I started with nothing. Finally, I am myself, to do what I want."

For Pino and his family, starting anew wasn't easy. A gallery in Boyleston, Massachusetts sponsored him by buying some of his fine arts paintings; he

sold more paintings, some for a mere $150, to a gallery in Manhattan. The owner of the Manhattan gallery predicted Pino would someday be famous.

Back then, however, predictions didn't put much food on the table. "I had such faith," Pino says. The family settled in Tenafly, New Jersey and got around on second-hand bicycles. Since he couldn't speak English at first, he had friends call and make appointments for him, and accompany him to translate.

Pino spent a year selling to galleries for modest amounts before his wife convinced him to try to break into illustrating for publishing houses. He took his paintings to an agency and was told he was good, but his style needed to be more "American." The agency referred him to Patty Pecoraro, associate art director at Dell. Patty referred him to Vincent Priore, art director of Zebra Books, who promised him a commission.

But the job was five months in the coming, and Pino almost gave up. When he finished the cover, he showed it first to Patty before delivering it to Vince. Patty was so impressed she gave him two book covers; Vince gave him another two. An elated Pino returned home with four new jobs. "I decided, now I want to show them what I can do," he recalls. He's hardly put down his paintbrush since.

Pino now works for Pocket Books, Harlequin, Bantam and Avon as well as Zebra and Dell; he is also doing religious illustrations for a Bible on a royalty basis. His success has enabled him to buy a new sports car—a Porsche 928—and build a new home in Englewood Cliffs, New Jersey. His family still comes first, he says. "Now I have everything."

ELAINE DUILLO

Success as a leading illustrator of paperback romances has a special sweetness for Elaine Duillo. She entered the publishing business in 1959, a time when paperbacks were scorned as second-rate books and there were few women in the field. Illustrators could make much more money in advertising. Today, the tables have turned—paperbacks are the mainstay of publishing, and there's more money to be made on romance covers than there is in advertising.

Elaine, a Pratt graduate, is a native of New York City who now lives in Hicksville, Long Island. She got her start in Gothics, mysteries and men's adventure novels. She distinguished herself with her different Gothic covers—large, beautiful girls in front of dark houses instead of the usual tiny girl fleeing the large house. Her style got her noticed and brought in repeat business.

As the romance market changed, Elaine moved from Gothics to historicals and contemporaries, working for such publishers as Warner Books, Avon Books, Dell, Harlequin, Zebra Books and Berkley-Jove. Each publisher is different, she says, some preferring sexy covers, like Warner, and others preferring romantic covers, like Dell. Whatever the publisher's style, Elaine tries to add her own style: "A strong impact between the man and the woman that shows the feeling between them and how they relate to each other." It's often difficult, she says, to follow a variety of publishers' styles while retaining her own stamp of individuality. She is particularly adept at shining, tempestuous waves of hair, says Lee Fishback, art director of Jove's Second Chance At Love, who often uses Elaine's work as a model for other illustrators.

Romances now comprise nearly all of Elaine's business. For Warner, she paints all of Valerie Sherwood's covers, such as *Bold Breathless Love, Rash Reckless Love* and *Wild Willful Love*. For Harlequin and its imprint, Worldwide Library, she does covers for the O'Hara Dynasty series, Superromances and Harlequin Historicals. Recent Avon titles include *Golden Roses* and *This Cruel Beauty*.

Romance covers have become increasingly sexy as competition among publishers has escalated, notes Elaine. "You've got to catch the customer's eye. Things are put on covers today that never would have been allowed ten to fifteen years ago, such as deep cleavages, very suggestive poses and people who appear to be nude."

Besides becoming sexier, the covers are more complex and detailed than they were even a few years ago, and many are wraparounds that extend from front to spine to back. Elaine spends an average of ten to fourteen days on a single cover, compared with the average five days she spent on a Gothic.

Unlike many major romance artists, Elaine works strictly in acrylics rather than oils. "Acrylics have a luminosity you can't get with oils," she says. "But they dry immediately so there's no room for mistakes. With oil, you can make changes and paint over."

She applies the acrylics in transparent washes, thin transparent layers of color; 100 to 200 washes may be needed to achieve a desired color, such as a peach tint on a face.

For theme colors, that is, the dominant color of a cover, Elaine favors the major colors of the genre: eye-catching purples and reds. Green can be used successfully, but yellow and brown are avoided, she says, especially brown. "It's not a color that women will pick up."

After publication, Elaine's paintings are sometimes sold to authors. She keeps the rest for future shows and perhaps a secondary market that might develop in the future. "I'll never part with a few, very special paintings," Elaine says. "They're really 'my children.' "

ELAINE GIGNILLIAT

Her romance illustrations have a distinctive, realistic style. She works slowly and meticulously, but for publishers, the wait is well worth it, for Elaine Gignilliat's book covers have helped sell many a major title.

"She's certainly a very big hitter," says Len Leone, art director of Bantam Books. "She's captured the imagination of many of the romance editors throughout the industry. She's doing a very nice job—she has exquisite taste, she uses the right kind of models. Her men and women have a look that is very appealing." Elaine, Len adds, has had a great influence on the state of the art of romance illustrations. Her influence was recognized at *Romantic Times*, 1983 Romantic Book Lovers Conference in New York City, where she was named Illustrator of the Year.

What is it that makes Elaine's covers so identifiable? Her embracing lovers are always idealized—"beautiful, brave and strong," as she describes them. "I try to capture the feeling that the man and woman are discovering each other and experiencing strong feelings, not that they're just attracted to each other," she says. "They're past the point of curiosity and being afraid of commitment, to where they're beginning to be swept away by being in love. The illustration has to set a romantic mood. It is doesn't reach the reader's

emotions, it won't appeal to her."

Elaine's appealing, swept-away look has appeared on such covers as Day Taylor's *The Black Swan* and *Moss Rose* (both by Dell); Catherine Coulter's *Devil's Embrace* (NAL/Signet); Lorena Dureau's *Iron Lace* (Pocket Books' Tapestry Romance); and Diane Dunaway's *Desert Hostage* (Dell). Fawcett Books commissioned her to illustrate the covers of 18 Victoria Holt novels, as well as the author's Plantagenet Series, written under her pseudonym Jean Plaidy. And New American Library commissioned her and fellow illustrator Pino Daeni to do the covers of its Scarlet Ribbons historical line; Elaine did the launch title, *Kimberly Flame* by Julia Grice.

While nearly all of her illustrations are for historical romances, Elaine has done some contemporary illustrations for Pocket Books as well as for one of Bantam's Loveswept launch titles, *Matching Wits* by Carla Neggers.

Elaine, a native of Atlanta, has built her reputation as a leading illustrator quickly. She entered the paperback field in late 1974, landing her first assignment from Pinnacle on her second day of prospecting. Her background is in fashion as an illustrator for department stores in Atlanta and New York. She also spent time in Paris, where she wrote and illustrated a review column on couturier fashion collections. A fellow artist in New York who illustrated book covers suggested she give it a try. She has done more than 150 paperback covers, working from her studio in her Manhattan apartment.

She devotes a great deal of time to research and details for each of her covers. If a reader's report summarizing a book is too vague, she reads the book herself. "It has to be right," she says. "Readers resent it when the cover doesn't fit the descriptions in the book, or if it looks too general. When you fake something, it usually looks it. The cover should fit the book." It should also indicate the degree of sensuality in the book, she adds, to help guide the buyer.

Elaine visits the library or consults her own voluminous files for her research. Thoroughly familiar with clothing, she can pinpoint a style within ten years throughout history. If a cover calls for a sunset, she researches photographs until she finds the right cloud formations or colors.

Elaine allows two weeks for the actual painting. Her work days tend to be long—ten to sixteen hours—and spill into weekends as well. She paints in oils and uses any colors, whichever seem best suited to the book. The illustration should look believable, she says, "but the artist has to breathe a little magic into it."

H. TOM HALL

Fans of Kathleen E. Woodiwiss are quite familiar with the work of H. Tom Hall, who created the covers for *Shanna, Ashes in the Wind,* and her fifth and most recent best-seller, *A Rose in Winter* (all published by Avon Books). *Shanna* was Tom's first major romance cover. "He's one of the best," says Barbara Bertoli, former Avon art director, who used a lot of his work.

A Rose in Winter, which is evocative of the style of certain Renaissance painters, is "extremely romantic," Tom says. He actually painted it for another Avon novel; it wasn't used and then Avon executives decided it was the perfect fit with Kathleen's 1982 release.

Tom, a native of Prospect Park, Pennsylvania, began his career as a free-lancer in 1958 with a children's book he wrote and illustrated with brush and ink drawings. The book, *The Golden Tombo,* was published by Alfred A. Knopf. Tom spent the next twelve years illustrating children's books and magazines, such as *Jack and Jill,* before he entered the paperback industry. He took his portfolio to Manhattan—he's never left Pennsylvania; today he lives in Pottstown, about 140 miles from New York City—and persisted until he got an appointment with Len Leone, art director of Bantam Books. Len commissioned him to illustrate the paperback cover for *Cup of Gold* by John Steinbeck.

More assignments came from National Geographic Books, Reader's Digest Books and other publishers. Mysteries comprised much of Tom's early paperback work, but with the publication of *Shanna* in 1977, he devoted nearly all of his time for several years to historical romances for Avon, Warner, Ballantine, Fawcett and others. One of his notable romance covers for Warner Books was Jennifer Wilde's *Love's Tender Fury,* and one of his most famous nonromance covers was for Avon's reprint of Colleen McCullough's *The Thorn Birds.*

Today he works almost exclusively for Ballantine Books, working on a range of titles that includes romances, epics and sagas. Those plus an occasional western "keep things interesting," he says.

Tom works with acrylics and sometimes sketches ideas for covers that are then fitted to books, rather than vice versa. Such was the case with *Lady Rogue* by Carole Nelson Douglas, a romance published by Ballantine. "I don't consciously do a style," Tom says, "though a lot of people seem to recognize my style. It's not photographic—I don't work much from photographs of models, and I suppose that makes my covers different. I usually work out of my head."

For romances, he says, it's difficult to come up with something different for each cover. "The clinch is the big thing for romances, and it has to be used more than you like. I've done just about every variation I can think of. But one of my most successful and favorite covers had a couple that wasn't touching at all, yet it implied that something passionate had just occurred." The cover was for *My Lord Monleigh* (Avon) by Jan Cox Speas. It showed a couple on a hillside: the woman, whose lace ties on her gown were loose, is combing her hair, while her lover is reclining near her playing a lute.

Two trends seem prevalent in romance covers today, Tom says: one, sexy but romantic, and two, just sexy. Of the two, he prefers the more romantic approach.

Tom paints one to two paperback covers a month, usually wraps that involve front to back artwork. He also does western paintings. Western art has enjoyed a boom market in the last few years (though the recession cooled it a bit), and it greatly appeals to him. "It's a halfway step between illustration and other forms of art," he says.

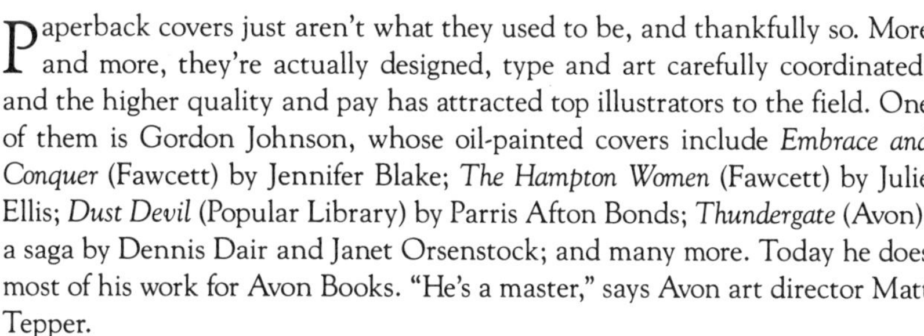

XI. PACKAGING THE GOODS

GORDON JOHNSON

Paperback covers just aren't what they used to be, and thankfully so. More and more, they're actually designed, type and art carefully coordinated, and the higher quality and pay has attracted top illustrators to the field. One of them is Gordon Johnson, whose oil-painted covers include *Embrace and Conquer* (Fawcett) by Jennifer Blake; *The Hampton Women* (Fawcett) by Julie Ellis; *Dust Devil* (Popular Library) by Parris Afton Bonds; *Thundergate* (Avon), a saga by Dennis Dair and Janet Orsenstock; and many more. Today he does most of his work for Avon Books. "He's a master," says Avon art director Matt Tepper.

"A good cover has an overall design, and the artist has to have a sense of the design element," says Gordon. "I spend more time designing than I do in the actual rendering.

"Years ago, you just did a painting and they slapped type on it; the illustration was on the bottom one-third of the cover and the type on the top. Now it's much more innovative. The art director and the illustrator work together on the total design, including the type.

"Cover designs," adds Gordon, "are much more flexible and flowing now. They used to have more of a stamped look."

He describes his own style as "painterly with a strong emphasis on the feeling of light. I'm intrigued by light effects, and I look for a pattern."

Before entering the paperback industry, Gordon, a native of Worcester, Massachusetts, illustrated posters for highway billboards, a background he says helped him later with book covers. In New York, he spent time with Dean Cornwell, a well-known mural painter. A poster contest he won got an agent's notice, and that led to assignments to illustrate covers for *American Magazine*, *American Weekly* and *Collier's* plus some advertising work. The highway billboard business dropped in the 1960s, and in the early 1970s, Gordon began to illustrate paperback covers, mostly young adult, adventure and detective novels. His first cover was for *Snowbound*, a Dell paperback by Harry Mazer. "I found my little niche," he says. "In advertising, everybody wants to get in on the act—it's all done by committee, then the client gets involved, and I don't feel like it's my own work. But in publishing, the deadlines are more comfortable, and it's my own concepts that I carry through."

With the growth of historical romances, Gordon began to do more covers for the genre, until it became his forte. He does most of his illustrating now for Avon Books, working out of his studio at his home in Lake Katonah, New York.

Once Gordon and an art director discuss a cover, he does whatever research is necessary for costumes, periods and locales. He then arranges a shoot. First he paints a preliminary sketch in acrylics, from which changes, if any, are decided. For the actual cover, Gordon paints on canvases, some as high as forty-eight inches, preferring to use warm colors for romances. Sagas get earthy colors, oranges and browns, which give the illustration a glow.

The clinch is a must for romance covers, which poses a problem of repetition. "There's a never-ending search for different ways to do a clinch," Gordon says. An embrace generates more heat if the heads are close together and the mouths slightly parted, while hair that's flying or a man's shirt that's partially undone conveys wildness. "You don't have to show skin," says Gordon. "Sometimes the suggestion that something is going to happen can be more provocative. There's a tightrope you walk, because these books appear in supermarkets." He adds, "It has to be tasteful if you're trying to push a class book."

The emphasis on design means more freedom for the illustrator and, in turn, more satisfying work. "I hope the business continues forever," says Gordon, "because I'm enjoying it."

BOB McGINNIS

"My favorite subject is women," sayd Bob McGinnis, and he paints them exceptionally well, with intelligence in their faces and a sensual, graceful beauty. He paints men well, too, including several stark naked heartbreakers for the covers of Johanna Lindsey's *Fires of Winter, Glorious Angel* and *So Speaks the Heart*, all published by Avon Books.

That's right, the fellows haven't got a stitch on, though you may have to look closely to tell, due to the strategic positioning of the heroines' bodies. "Bob achieves a wonderful feeling of sexuality," says former Avon art director Barbara Bertoli.

But the increasing sexiness of romance covers is a trend Bob is not sure is good for the genre. The books, he says, should focus more on quality writing—"the Bronte sort of tradition that's closer to love in its pure state. After all, demand for these novels arises from a society starved for romance. To have them reduced to the level of pornography would be self-defeating for publishers."

While the covers are showing characters in more advanced states of *deshabille*, there have been changes in quality and content. "The standards are getting higher and the art content is improving," Bob says. "There's more of a softness in them that's on the edge of a fantasy realm rather than looking hard-edged and graphic."

Bob has painted about 1,500 book covers since he got his first publishing assignments in the late 1950s. A native of Wyoming, Ohio, on the outskirts of Cincinnati, he first worked at Walt Disney Studios in Burbank, California as a traffic coordinator and apprentice animator. He returned to Ohio to attend Ohio State University, study art and work at assorted jobs (including advertising for Procter & Gamble) until ambition lured him to New York City.

Life as an illustrator in the big city was far from glamorous at first, however; Bob worked in a large studio that handled a wide variety of jobs, mostly advertising. Then an associate introduced him to an agent who took his samples to Dell, which hired him to illustrate Mike Shayne paperbacks. "That started the ball rolling," says Bob. He left the studio and took on more book covers, including many Gothics and romances as well as movie posters and illustrations for stories for *Saturday Evening Post, Guideposts* and *Good Housekeeping*.

Today romance covers take up about a third of his time, the rest of it going to other types of novels (he painted the inside cover of the Bantam paperback of Judith Krantz's *Princess Daisy*, for example, and the pencil illustration for the cover of *Banners of Silk*, published by NAL/Signet; movie posters; *Good Housekeeping, National Geographic*; limited edition prints sold throughout the country; and western paintings for galleries. After women, the West ranks as his second favorite subject; a painting of John Wayne, whom Bob greatly admires, brought $9,500 in 1980.

He also admires Andrew Wyeth, whom he describes at "the greatest artist of all time, a total master" and who has had a tremendous impact on art.

Like Wyeth, Bob usually works with egg tempera, a mixture of egg yolk and natural pigments, though he does some book covers in oil. "Art directors are used to oil now and almost insist on it," he says. "It has a greater range of hues, although you can get some marvelous results with tempera."

When romance covers were much simpler, Bob could produce six a month, but the detailed covers of today take up to two weeks each.

Whatever the illustration, it must be full of emotion, he says. "If the artist is not emotionally involved, it shows—it's dead." Romance readers who respond to his covers would definitely agree Bob's style is full of emotion.

XI. PACKAGING THE GOODS

Sometimes writing the copy for the cover—the "jacket blurb"—can be the most difficult part of publishing a romance. How does the editor or free-lancer distill the story into one or two paragraphs that give the meat of the plot yet still remain enough of a teaser to attract the book buyer?

Mary Ellen Cotter, editorial assistant at Dell Candlelight Ecstasy Romances, says that the copy chief has staff members who write the blurbs after reading the books. There's no real formula, Mary Ellen says, "they go by the book each time. They try to incorporate the essence of the story and make the copy teasing."

At Harlequin American Romances, all of the jacket blurb is written by one person, Hilari Cohen. Hilari reads each romance and tries to emphasize the one thing about the book that strikes her the most. "I want to be as dramatic as possible and capture the excitement of the book without saying too much," she says. "I want to grab the reader." Hilari also reads the jackets of other publishers' romances to see what they're saying about their books and how. "I want to see what everyone else is doing and then say something different," she says.

There is a big difference in writing copy for contemporary romances versus historicals, Hilari notes. "It's easier to write for the contemporaries, for I can use contemporary language. For historicals, I try to stay within the time period." She readily admits that words such as "passionate," "fiery" and "desire" are proven winners for jacket copy, but she tries to avoid them since they're overused. "I want the passionate, fiery tone of the book to be apparent without using buzzwords," she says.

Jacket copy for Silhouette romances is written by both staff editors and free-lancers. Editor Leslie Wainger has written copy for all five Silhouette lines: Silhouette Romance, Special Edition, Desire, First Love and Intimate Moments. She tries to approach the copy for each line a little differently. "Most jacket blurbs have used a conflict approach," Leslie says, "and I've tried to get away from that. For Silhouette Special Editions, I use the title as headline and then emphasize the 'promise.' I go into the plots and characterizations a little and set up the initial situation. Then I emphasize the happy ending—they all end happily because they're romances, so that's not giving anything away. I want the image, the promise.

"For Silhouette Desires, which are very sexy and sensuous, I emphasize the set-up," Leslie continues. "In general, I try to pick out a couple of intriguing plot elements—an unusual profession, locale or how they meet. Then the last half of the jacket copy is tailored to the particular line."

And titles? Do the major publishing houses come up with most of them, or do they rely on their authors to provide the catchy names? At Dell Candlelight Ecstasy, sometimes titles are provided by the authors and sometimes they're changed by the editors. "If a title is really horrible, we'll change it," says Mary Ellen.

Karen Solem, vice president and editor in chief of Silhouette Books, says that titles generally are provided by the authors unless they are inappropriate or bad. She also notes that many manuscripts reach her desk untitled.

And at Harlequin American Romances, Hilari says that the publisher nearly always sticks with the title provided by the author; changes are rare.

In this section: writer's groups, the award-winning cream of the crop on both sides of the Atlantic and where to find the absolute *latest* in romance news.

CHAPTER ONE

Hot Love By Cool Writers

You've read quite a few romance novels and now you've gotten the bug to write one. Maybe you've even prepared a manuscript, and you're ready to show the world your talent. But where do you go from here—to the publishing houses, to other romance writers, to your best friends? One place is a professional association of your peers. Even published writers need a network of professional people in their chosen field to keep them up to date about editorial requirements, contracts and what the readers are buying. It was from this need to know that the Houston-based Romance Writers of America was born in December 1980.

The RWA, like all good ideas, didn't just appear on the scene; it evolved gradually and with a lot of hard work. Vivian Stephens, senior editor of Harlequin American Romances, provided the catalyst to get the group started.

In 1979, while Vivian was editing the Dell Candlelight line, she was invited to speak at the Southwestern Writers Conference in Houston. The convention attracted quite a few attendees, many of whom were romance writers—or trying to be. "I was very popular," recalls Vivian. "I dispelled mysteries about romance writing. I told them exactly how much I paid writers, how long the manuscripts had to be, that I prefer the completed manuscript because I was not smart enough to really judge fifty pages, how many books I did a month, how far I bought in advance—how I had bought for the next year and so didn't have any slots for any books."

Because she was so candid, for months afterward Vivian, a native of Houston, received phone calls from authors and aspiring authors hoping to break into romantic fiction. Conference policy forbade her from speaking at the same conference the following year, but she continued to hear from people interested in romances. "Because I was getting so many calls," Vivian said, "I thought what they really needed [was] their own group."

In 1980 Vivian spoke to Rita Estrada, a published romance writer from Houston, and suggested getting interested writers together to meet and find answers to their questions. Vivian asked Rita to find a meeting place and invite writers from all over Texas.

About forty people attended the first meeting, which was held at the San Jacinto Savings branch in Houston's North Oaks Mall. Vivian had temporarily christened the group Romance Writers of America, and the name stuck. She was named founder and Rita was named president. There were only seventeen official members by February 1981, but by the time of the first RWA conference, outside of Houston, in June of that year 600 people had joined the organization.

The first conference was an organized bedlam of writers meeting editors, agents and each other. Author Janet Dailey gave the keynote address, proclaiming—in a borrow from a Loretta Lynn country and western song—"I was a romance writer before it was cool to be a romance writer." Workshops covered topics such as "How A Cover Is Born," "The Most Common Mistakes Writers Make" and "Quality Passion." Authors clutching manuscripts grabbed editors in hallways to sketch out plots and ask for pointers. Questions like "Must the hero and heroine be Americans?" floated around the conference rooms. Other problems under discussion were intriguing professions for the heroine, such as matador, and the constant search for new and exotic locales, such as Tampa, Florida. And always the questions returned to sex—or sensuality, as romance writers and editors prefer to call it—with queries like "Can the lovers have sex, even in the second chapter?" (yes, if there's the promise of marriage) and reminders that the heroine need not be a virgin, but she is not promiscuous, either.

Most of the attendees agreed that the conference was a great success—some seventy manuscripts were sold as a result of the contacts made there. Rita Estrada was re-elected president for 1981–82, and plans were made for the second annual conference, aboard the *Queen Mary* in Long Beach, California, in June 1982.

But RWA, like all new organizations, has experienced growing pains. Some of the members, principally the more experienced, published writers, have become dissatisfied with RWA and have formed their own groups.

The most significant group is the Society of Romance Novelists, based in New York, which has restricted voting membership to published writers. Agents and unpublished writers may be associate members. The SRN was still in the preliminary stages as of early 1983, but plans include a newsletter, a convention and annual awards. The group's goals include advisory support for romance writers and some kind of monitoring of contract negotiations. Steering committee members include agents/authors Irene Goodman and Alex Kamaroff and authors Rebecca Brandewyne, Serita Stevens and Angela Talias.

Although the RWA's membership has fallen a bit—it's now around 1,500—due to the formation of other groups, officers feel such splintering is healthy. "There is room for everybody," says Barbara "Bobbie" Jolly, RWA president for 1982–83. In fact, Rita Estrada says she is most proud of the outcropping of new groups. "If it hadn't been for RWA, these groups couldn't have gotten started. Now romance writers can find groups in their area—they have a place to go to help each other."

To "provide a place to help each other"—a network—is the most important function of RWA. Vivian Stephens says: "I really wanted RWA to be—and I still want it to be—a place where a writer, who is trying to break into the romance market, can come to listen to what every publishing house is looking for, so that she can match her work with a house, instead of sending it around to houses that won't want it. That is the purpose—a network for other writers so that you don't feel so alone, you have friends, you realize you're not the only one. It's a kinship."

The feeling of kinship is fostered by local chapter meetings, an annual national conference and a bimonthly newspaper, the *Romance Writer's Report*. "Some members feel that belonging to RWA is worth it just to receive the *Report*," says Bobbie, "especially if they can't attend the conference." Information about other writer's groups is made available to members via RWA's participation in the Council of Writers; the council reports on the success of other genres, such as mystery or science fiction, and what readers are looking for. "Everybody in RWA is willing to share whatever they know with anyone else," says Patricia Hudgins, executive secretary of RWA and editor of the *Report*.

RWA has between sixty and seventy chapters grouped into six regions. There are members in all states except Montana and in eleven foreign countries, including Australia, New Zealand, India, France and the Caribbean. Patricia notes that there are more members in the Southwest, Kansas, Missouri and Colorado because "those are the states where most of the romance writers are." Another characteristic of most members: their husbands are self-employed, often working at home as do their wives.

Bobbie says that RWA provides more than just moral support. The annual awards program gives recognition for published writers (Golden Medallion Awards) as well as unpublished (Golden Heart Awards).

Another support feature of the RWA is its grievance committee. The recession has pushed some publishers out of business, and the committee is working to help writers get paid for work published by those firms.

With all the trials and tribulations of starting a new group, Rita Estrada doesn't hesitate to say she'd do it all over again. "I have never seen so many people with genuine care for each other," she says. "Our conferences are all done by volunteers, and they do outstanding work. RWA members work hard and give good advice."

XII. LOVE NOTES

Two decades before American romance writers organized, English romance writers formed the Romantic Novelists Association, its purpose to raise the prestige of the romantic novel. The key organizers were authors Denise Robbins and Vivian Stewart, and today the association has about 300 members.

"It's a splendid organization that is of immense help to the authors who belong," says author and former chairwoman Nancy John. "In the early days it had teething problems due to the clash of personalities, but it has now settled down as a well-regarded professional association."

The RNA meets about eight times a year, mostly in London. Awards are given at an annual luncheon. A journal, *R.N.A. News*, is published four times a year.

Membership is open only to authors who have had published at least one romance novel or two full-length serials in magazines. ("The rules are designed to stop people who hang out on the fringes," explains Nancy.) Associate membership is open to publishers, editors, literary agents, booksellers, librarians and others who have "a close professional connection with novel writing and publishing."

Most of the members are women, and most are part-time writers. "English women don't take to writing at quite such a young age as they do in the States," comments Nancy. "There is not as much opportunity here to make a living out of it."

Mary Burchell, who has written for Mills & Boon/Harlequin for more than forty years and is one of their most successful novelists, has been president of the RNA since the mid-1960s. The presidency is a figurehead position; the association's chief executive officer is chairman, and that position changes hands every two years.

The most prestigious award given by the RNA is the Best Romantic Novel of the Year, which can be either historical (must be set prior to 1930) or contemporary. The Netta Muskett Award, named for the late and famous romantic novelist, is open to writers who are unpublished in novels or who have not had two full-length serials published.

At one time the association had an Elizabeth Goudge Historical Award, named in honor of the author who is well known for her sweet and gentle historicals. The award was instituted to give special recognition to historicals, which at one time were few in British publishing, but was dropped as they became more commonplace.

One of the most valuable benefits of the RNA is the contact it provides writers. “The writers get to know each other pretty well,” says Nancy, “and they have a good network. It helps them stay up with the trends. There’s nothing like personal contacts to get things going.”

Books Judged To Be The Best

ROMANCE WRITERS OF AMERICA

Golden Heart Awards 1981
Unpublished manuscripts

FIRST PLACE: *Man of Velvet, Man of Steel*, Dana Terrill
SECOND PLACE: *Race the Wind*, Barbara Cameron Smith
THIRD PLACE: *Weekend Affair*, Deborah Bryson

Golden Medallion Awards 1982
Novels published in 1981

CATEGORY HISTORICAL: *Rendezvous at Gramercy* (Dell), Constance Ravenlock (June Casey)
CATEGORY CONTEMPORARY: *Winner Take All* (Silhouette Romance), Brooke Hastings (Deborah Gordon)
MAINSTREAM HISTORICAL: *The Day Beyond Destiny* (Jove), Anna James (Shannon Harper and Madeleine Porter)
MAINSTREAM CONTEMPORARY: *The Sun Dancers* (Richard Gallen Books), Barbara Faith

Golden Heart Awards 1982
Unpublished manuscripts

FIRST PLACE: *Bittersweet*, Martha Gordon
SECOND PLACE: *Island of Love*, Phyllis Humphrey
THIRD PLACE: *Perfect Strangers*, Patsy Rutkauskas

ROMANTIC BOOKS LOVERS CONFERENCE

Sponsored by *Romantic Times* and Long Island University

1982
HISTORICAL AUTHOR: Jennifer Wilde (Tom Huff)
PUBLISHER: Mills & Boon/Harlequin
SERIES AND SAGAS: Lyle Kenyon Engel, packager
ILLUSTRATOR: H. Tom Hall
EDITOR: Nancy Coffey, formerly of Avon Books
ART DIRECTOR: Barbara Bertoli, formerly of Avon Books
AUTHOR: Rosemary Rogers
CRITIC: Ray Walters, *New York Times Book Review*
CLASSIC HISTORICAL AUTHOR: Anya Seton
CLASSIC CATEGORY AUTHOR: Elise Lee
PEARL AWARD (NEW AUTHOR): Alice Morgan

1983
SEXY HISTORICAL AUTHOR: Bertrice Small
HISTORICAL AUTHOR: Morgan Llywelyn
CONTEMPORARY AUTHOR: Jayne Castle (Jayne Krentz)
PUBLISHER: Ron Busch, president, Pocket Books
SERIES AUTHOR: Roberta Gellis
ILLUSTRATOR: Elaine Gignilliat
ART DIRECTOR: Milt Charles, Pocket Books/Silhouette
SAGA AUTHOR: Belva Plain
CLASSIC HISTORICAL AUTHOR: Barbara Cartland
CLASSIC CONTEMPORARY AUTHOR: Janet Dailey
PEARL AWARD (NEW AUTHOR): Lee Damon

ROMANTIC NOVELISTS ASSOCIATION, England

Best Romantic Novel of the Year

1961 *More Than Friendship* (Collins), Mary Howard
1962 *Witches' Sabbath* (Hodder & Stoughton), Paula Allardyce
1963 *Larksbrook* (Hurst & Blackett), Margaret Maddocks
1964 *House Divided* (Hurst & Blackett), Dorothy Cray
1965 *Journey from Yesterday* (Collins), Suzanne Ebel
1966 *The Silver Answer* (Hurst and Blackett), Margaret Maddocks
1967 *The Truth Game* (Hurst and Blackett), Anne Betteridge
1968 *The Future Is Forever* (Hurst & Blackett), Maynah Lewis
1969 *Comfort and Keep* (Ward Lock), Doris E. Smith
1970 *Thea* (Hurst & Blackett), Margaret Maddocks
Cat on a Broomstick (Herbert Jenkins), Joanne Marshall
Broken Tapestry (Hurst & Blackett), Rona Randall
1971 *Flower of Silence* (Mills & Boon), Joanne Marshall
1972 *The Pride of Innocence* (Hurst & Blackett), Maynah Lewis

1973 *The House of Kuragin* (Heinemann), Constance Heaven
1974 *The Burning Lamp* (Hodder & Stoughton), Frances Murray
1975 *Vote for a Silk Gown* (Troubador/Macdonald & Janes), Jay Allerton
1976 *The Look of Innocence* (Hodder & Stoughton), Anna Gilbert
1977 *Every Man a King* (Hodder & Stoughton), Anne Worboys
1978 *Merlin's Keep* (Souvenir Press), Madeleine Brent
1979 *Countess* (Macdonald & Janes), Josephine Edgar
1980 *The Red Staircase* (Collins), Gwendoline Butler
1981 *Zemindar* (Bodley Head), Valerie Fitzgerald

THE HISTORICAL NOVEL PRIZE,
England
Awarded annually by The Bodley Head and Transworld Publishers (Corgi Books) in memory of Georgette Heyer. Unpublished manuscripts only are considered; winners are published by the sponsors in hardcover and paperback.

1977 *Gallows Wedding*, Rhona Martin
1978 *Day of the Butterfly*, Norah Lofts
1979 *Children of Hachiman*, Lyn Guest
1980 *Zemindar*, Valerie Fitzgerald

1981 no award (no entry met standards)

A Directory of Romance Publications

AFFAIRE DE COEUR

5660 Roosevelt Place
Fremont, CA 94538
(415) 656-4804
Editor: Barbara Keenan
Established: August 1981
Frequency: Monthly
Circulation: 3,000
Cost: $15/year or $2/issue
Distribution: Mail, bookstores

Affaire de Coeur is a magazine that features publisher news and trends; reviews; author and agent profiles; lovelore—history of romantic traditions; and other news of interest to anyone who "is romantic at heart." *Affaire de Coeur* is written and edited for buyers, authors and publishers alike, providing each with current happenings in the world of romantic fiction. Advertising accepted. *Affair de Coeur* and Barbara Keenan Enterprises sponsor the annual West Coast Rom Con romance conference.

BARBRA CRITIQUES, LTD.

2710 R. D. Mize Road
Independence, MO 64057
(816) 373-4527
Editor: Barbra Wren
Established: February 1980
Frequency: Monthly
Circulation: U.S., Canada, South America
Cost: $60/year
Distribution: Mail

Barbra Critiques, Ltd. critiques from 75 to 85 current romance novels in each monthly newsletter, providing booksellers in the U.S., Canada and South America with the latest information on upcoming titles. The publication also includes information about romance trends, romance authors and the best romance buys of the month offered by the various publishers.

BOY MEETS GIRL

Rainy Day Books
2812 West 23rd St.
Fairway, KS 66205
(913) 384-3126

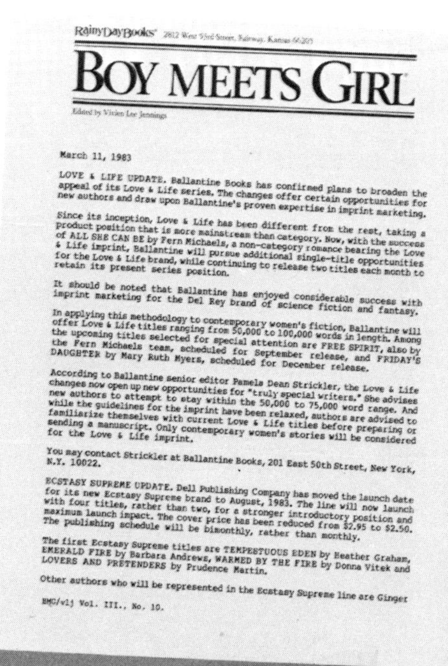

RainyDayBooks 2812 West 53rd Street, Fairway, Kansas 66205

BOY MEETS GIRL

Edited by Vivien Lee Jennings

March 11, 1983

LOVE & LIFE UPDATE. Ballantine Books has confirmed plans to broaden the appeal of its Love & Life series. The changes offer certain opportunities for new authors and draw upon Ballantine's proven expertise in imprint marketing.

Since its inception, Love & Life has been different from the rest, taking a product position that is more mainstream than category. Now, with the success of ALL SHE CAN BE by Fern Michaels, a non-category romance bearing the Love & Life imprint, Ballantine will pursue additional single-title opportunities for the Love & Life brand, while continuing to release two titles each month to retain its present series position.

It should be noted that Ballantine has enjoyed considerable success with imprint marketing for the Del Rey brand of science fiction and fantasy.

In applying this methodology to contemporary women's fiction, Ballantine will offer Love & Life titles ranging from 50,000 to 100,000 words in length. Among the upcoming titles selected for special attention are FREE SPIRIT, also by the Fern Michaels team, scheduled for September release, and FRIDAY'S DAUGHTER by Mary Ruth Myers, scheduled for December release.

According to Ballantine senior editor Pamela Dean Strickler, the Love & Life changes now open up new opportunities for "truly special writers." She advises new authors to attempt to stay within the 50,000 to 75,000 word range. And while the guidelines for the imprint have been relaxed, authors are advised to familiarize themselves with current Love & Life titles before preparing or sending a manuscript. Only contemporary women's stories will be considered for the Love & Life imprint.

You may contact Strickler at Ballantine Books, 201 East 50th Street, New York, N.Y. 10022.

ECSTASY SUPREME UPDATE. Dell Publishing Company has moved the launch date for its new Ecstasy Supreme brand to August, 1983. The line will now launch with four titles, rather than two, for a stronger introductory position and maximum launch impact. The cover price has been reduced from $2.95 to $2.50. The publishing schedule will be bimonthly, rather than monthly.

The first Ecstasy Supreme titles are TEMPESTUOUS EDEN by Heather Graham, EMERALD FIRE by Barbara Andrews, WARMED BY THE FIRE by Donna Vitek and LOVERS AND PRETENDERS by Prudence Martin.

Other authors who will be represented in the Ecstasy Supreme line are Ginger

BMG/vlj Vol. III., No. 10.

Publisher/editor: Vivien Lee Jennings
Established: March 7, 1981
Frequency: Weekly (48 issues/year)
Circulation: International
Cost: $125/year; $75/year for members of the American Booksellers Association and Romance Writers of America; $20 for 90-day trial subscription
Distribution: Mail

Boy Meets Girl is a trade-oriented newsletter aimed at those who work in the industry, offering analyses of news and trends in romantic fiction. Popular authors are featured, romance convention business is summarized and new and forthcoming books are reported but not reviewed. Data is gathered directly from publishers, authors and their associations, book wholesalers, regional and national bookseller associations, and the bookstore staff and customers of Rainy Day Books. A supplement, *Happily Ever After,* is published occasionally.

HEART LINE
PO Box 1131
Brookhaven, PA 19015
(215) 876-3718
Publisher: Bair Ray Enterprises
Editor: Terri C. Busch
Established: Spring 1982
Frequency: Bimonthly
Circulation: U.S.
Cost: $1.50/issue
Distribution: Bookstores

Each issue of *Heart Line,* the only glossy romance magazine on the market, contains some 100 previews of upcoming romance releases. These previews are both informative and entertaining and provide just enough of the storyline to help a prospective reader decide whether a particular title sounds interesting. *Heart Line* also includes author interviews, photos, articles written by authors, as well as information about upcoming events such as romance writers' conferences, special tours or autograph sessions.

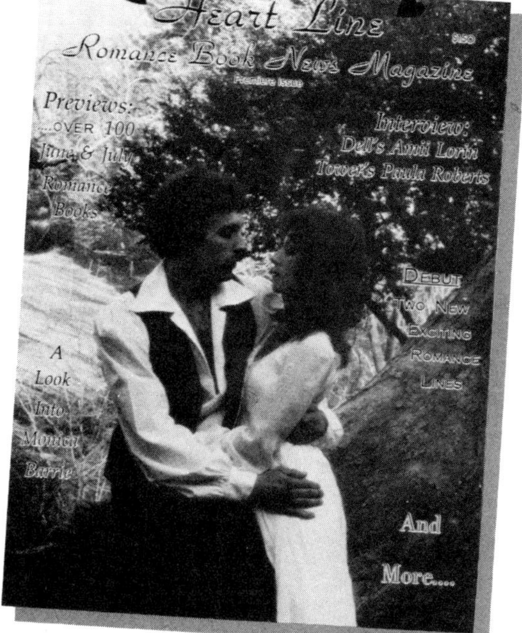

THE JANET DAILEY NEWSLETTER
Pocket Books
Dept. JDN
1230 Avenue of the Americas
New York, NY 10020

Established: 1980
Frequency: Quarterly
Circulation: 40,000
Cost: Free
Distribution: Mail

The Janet Dailey Newsletter keeps the fans of the prolific and popular author up to date on her major activities, such as her tours, the filming of her first movie, research aboard a cruise ship, and adventures filming commercials for Silhouette Books. Each issue has a warm, chatty letter from Janet, photos, news about her new and forthcoming books, reader comments, and anecdotes.

THE LOVE LINE
23 Kirby
Fort Leonard Wood, MO 65473
(314) 329-6012
Editor/Publisher: Linda Hamm Lucas
Established: October 1982
Frequency: Monthly
Circulation: 550
Cost: $30/year
Distribution: Mail subscription

This 20–24 page newsletter features author interviews, previews of upcoming releases, comments from bookstore owners, and releases from publishers. *The Love Line* also publishes short love stories, teen short love stories, and a column titled "Love Notes," miscellaneous news from the world of romantic fiction.

Ofelia

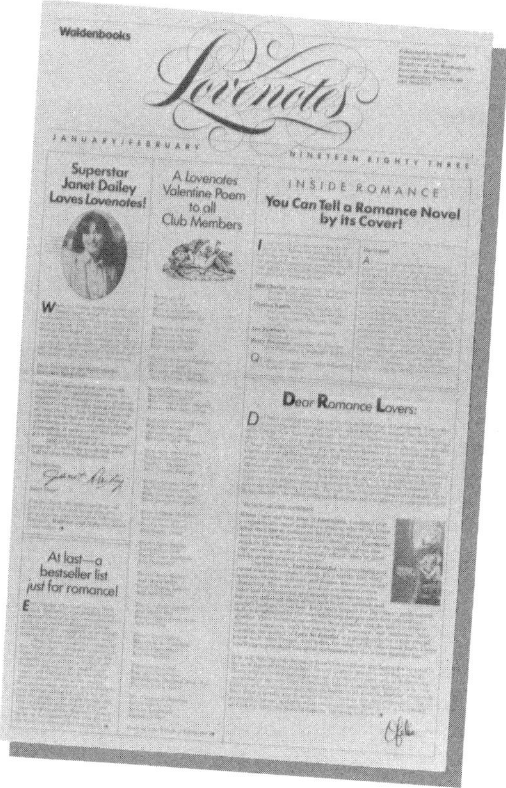

Waldenbooks
Lovenotes
JANUARY/FEBRUARY
NINETEEN EIGHTY THREE
Superstar Janet Dailey Loves Lovenotes!
A Lovenotes Valentine Poem to all Club Members
INSIDE ROMANCE
You Can Tell a Romance Novel by its Cover!
Dear Romance Lovers:
At last—a bestseller list just for romance!

LOVENOTES
Waldenbooks
PO Box 10218
Stamford, CT 06904
(203) 356-7530
Editor: Ofelia
Established: November 1982
Frequency: Monthly
Circulation: 80,000
Cost: Free to Waldenbooks Romance Book Club members
Distribution: Waldenbooks stores

Lovenotes contains listings of the latest romances from major publishers, author interviews, behind-the-scenes information about romance writing and publishing and special features, such as "How to be romantic on Valentine's Day." It also contains club announcements, for example, special purchases being offered to members, and reviews of other book clubs of interest to romance readers.

XII. LOVE NOTES

LOVE NOTES
c/o Book Communications System
Mail drop: 29-2
201 E. 50th St.
New York, NY 10022
Established: January 1983
Frequency: Quarterly
Circulation: N/A
Cost: Free
Distribution: Mail

Love Notes features news and tidbits about Ballantine/Fawcett/Columbine authors and their new and forthcoming titles, short profiles, photos, working habits and favorite recipes. Reader comments and questions are invited.

ROMANCE WRITERS REPORT
Romance Writers of America
5206 FM 1960 West, Suite 207
Houston, TX 77069
(713) 440-6885
Editor: Patricia Hudgins
Established: 1981
Frequency: Bimonthly
Circulation: 1,500 (RWA membership only)
Cost: Free with RWA membership, $35/year
Distribution: Mail

A tabloid newspaper, *Romance Writers Report*, keeps RWA members abreast of news in the industry and features items on editors, authors, bookseller reports, market news, writing tips and agent's columns. It also reports on activities in the organization, on national, regional and local levels.

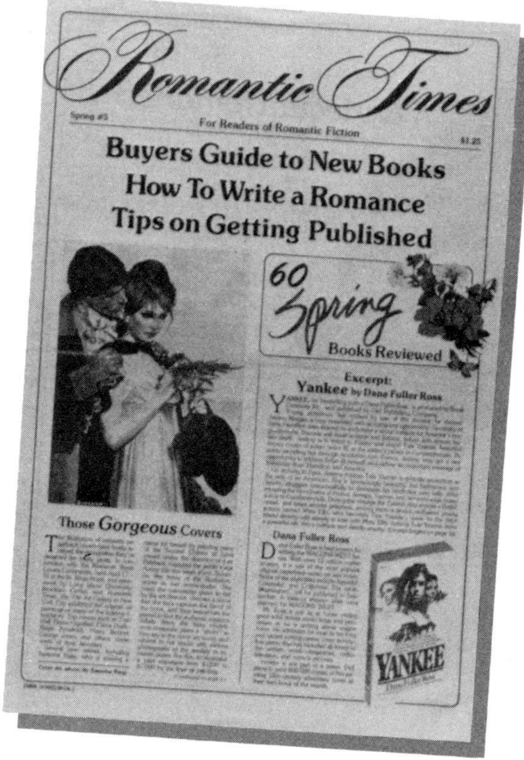
Romantic Times
For Readers of Romantic Fiction
Buyers Guide to New Books
How To Write a Romance
Tips on Getting Published
60 Spring Books Reviewed
Excerpt: Yankee by Dana Fuller Ross
Those Gorgeous Covers
Dana Fuller Ross
YANKEE

ROMANTIC TIMES
163 Joralemon St. #1234
Brooklyn Heights, NY 11201
(212) 599-2180
Publisher: Kathryn Falk
Established: July 1981
Frequency: Bimonthly
Circulation: 55,000
Cost: $9.95 for nine issues; Canada add $4.50, overseas add $8.00 for postage
Distribution: Mail subscription, book stores, libraries

Romantic Times, a 36-page tabloid, provides book reviews, news of forthcoming titles, book excerpts, industry news and gossip, author profiles, how-to tips for aspiring writers, lists of author's pseudonyms, a romance buyer's guide and articles and columns by leading editors, authors and others in the romantic fiction business. Reader comments and queries are printed and answered. *Romantic Times* sponsors the annual Romantic Book Lovers Conference, begun in 1982, held alternately in New York and London (following the British Book Fair).

BIBLIOGRAPHY

Adams, Cleve F. *No Wings on a Cop.* Harlequin, 1953.
Adams, Douglas. *The Hitchhiker's Guide to the Galaxy.* Pocket Books, 1981.
Andrews, V.C. *Flowers in the Attic.* Pocket Books, 1983.
Austen, Jane. *Pride and Prejudice.* Penguin, 1972.

Barrie, Monica. *By Invitation Only.* Richard Gallen Books, 1981.
——— *Cry Mercy, Cry Love.* Simon & Schuster, 1983.
——— *Island of Desire.* Simon & Schuster, 1983.
Blake, Jennifer. *Embrace and Conquer.* Fawcett, 1981.
——— *Golden Fancy.* Fawcett, 1980.
——— *Love's Wild Desire.* Popular Library, 1981.
de Blasis, Celeste. *The Tiger's Woman.* Dell, 1982.
Bonds, Parris Afton. *Deep Purple.* Fawcett, 1983.
——— *Dust Devil.* Popular Library, 1981.
——— *The Flash of the Firefly.* Popular Library, 1979.
——— *Made for Each Other.* Fawcett, 1983.
——— *Savage Enchantment.* Popular Library, 1982.
——— *Sweet Golden Sun.* Fawcett, 1976.
Bonner, Terry Nelson. *Free Woman.* Dell, 1983.
Brandewyne, Rebecca. *Forever My Love.* Warner, 1980.
——— *Love, Cherish Me.* Warner, 1983.
——— *No Gentle Love.* Warner, 1983.
Bronte, Charlotte. *Jane Eyre.* Bantam, 1981.
Bronte, Emily. *Wuthering Heights.* Penguin, 1965.
Brookes, Beth. *Untamed Desire.* Jove Publications, 1982.
Brown, Sandra. *Heaven's Price.* Bantam, 1983.
——— *Relentless Desire.* Bantam, 1983.
Bruff, Nancy. *The Manatee: Strange Loves of a Seaman.* Harlequin, 1950.
Burchell, Mary. *Wife to Christopher.* Harlequin, 1983.
Busbee, Shirlee. *Gypsy Lady.* Avon Books, 1977.
——— *Lady Vixen.* Avon Books, 1980.
——— *While Passion Sleeps.* Avon Books, 1983.

Calloway, Jo. *Dance the Skies.* Dell, 1982.
Cardwell, Ann. *Crazy to Kill.* Harlequin, 1949.
Cartland, Barbara. *Barbara Cartland Romances.* Quick Fox, 1981.
——— *The Flame Is Love.* Quick Fox, 1981.
Castle, Jayne. *Gentle Pirate.* Dell, 1980.
Chase, Elaine Raco. *Best Laid Plans.* Ballantine, 1981.
——— *Designing Woman.* Dell, 1982.
——— *Double Occupancy.* Dell, 1982.
——— *No Easy Way Out.* Dell, 1982.
——— *Rules of the Game.* Dell, 1980.
Coffman, Virginia. *Affair at Aklai.* Crown, 1960.
——— *Moura.* G.K. Hall, 1980.

BIBLIOGRAPHY

Collins, Susanna. *On Wings of Magic.* Jove Publications, 1982.
Conklin, Barbara. *P.S. I Love You.* Bantam, 1981.
Coombs, Nina. *Love So Fearful.* New American Library, 1983.
Cooper, Jilly. *Bella.* Fawcett, 1981.
—— *Emily.* Fawcett, 1981.
—— *Harriet.* Fawcett, 1981.
—— *Imogen.* Fawcett, 1982.
—— *Octavia.* Fawcett, 1982.
—— *Prudence.* Fawcett, 1981.
Coulter, Catherine. *The Autumn Countess.* New American Library, 1979.
—— *The Devil's Embrace.* New American Library, 1979.
—— *The Rebel Bride.* New American Library, 1979.

Dailey, Janet.* *Foxfire Light.* G.K. Hall, 1983.
—— *Night Way.* Pocket Books, 1981.
—— *No Quarter Asked.* Harlequin, 1976.
—— *Ride the Thunder.* Pocket Books, 1981.
—— *The Rogue.* Pocket Books, 1980.
—— *Stands a Calder Man.* Pocket Books, 1983.
—— *This Calder Range.* Pocket Books, 1981.
—— *This Calder Sky.* Pocket Books, 1981.
—— *Touch the Wind.* Pocket Books, 1981.
Dair, Dennis and Orenstock, Janet. *Thundergate.* Avon Books, 1983.
Dalton, Jennifer. *Run in the Wind.* Gallen/Dell, 1983.
Deveraux, Jude. *The Black Lyon.* Avon Books, 1980.
—— *Casa Grande.* Avon Books, 1982.
—— *The Enchanted Land.* Avon Books, 1978.
—— *Highland Velvet.* Pocket Books, 1983.
—— *The Velvet Promise.* Pocket Books, 1981.
—— *Velvet Song.* Pocket Books, 1983.
Douglas, Carole Nelson. *Lady Rogue.* Ballantine, 1983.
duMaurier, Daphne. *Rebecca.* Avon Books, 1971.
Dunaway, Diane. *Desert Hostage.* Dell, 1982.
Dureau, Lorena. *Iron Lace.* Pocket Books, 1983.

Ellis, Julie. *The Hampton Women.* Fawcett, 1981.
Ernest, Jeanette. *Lover's Lair.* New American Library, 1983.

Falk, Kathryn. *The Complete Dollhouse Building Book.* Bobbs & Merrill, 1981.
—— *How to Write a Romance and Get It Published.* Crown, 1983.
—— *Love's Leading Ladies.* Pinnacle, 1982.
—— *Miniature Needlepoint and Sewing Projects for Dollhouses.* Hawthorne, 1979.
Fletcher, Dorothy. *Whispers and Embraces.* Zebra Books, 1980.
Friday, Nancy. *My Secret Garden.* Pocket Books, 1981.

Gallagher, Patricia. *All for Love.* Avon Books, 1981.
—— *Castles in the Air.* Avon Books, 1976.
—— *Mystic Rose.* Avon Books, 1977.
—— *No Greater Love.* Avon Books, 1979.

*A complete list of Janet Dailey's books, as of 1983, appears on pp. 124-125.

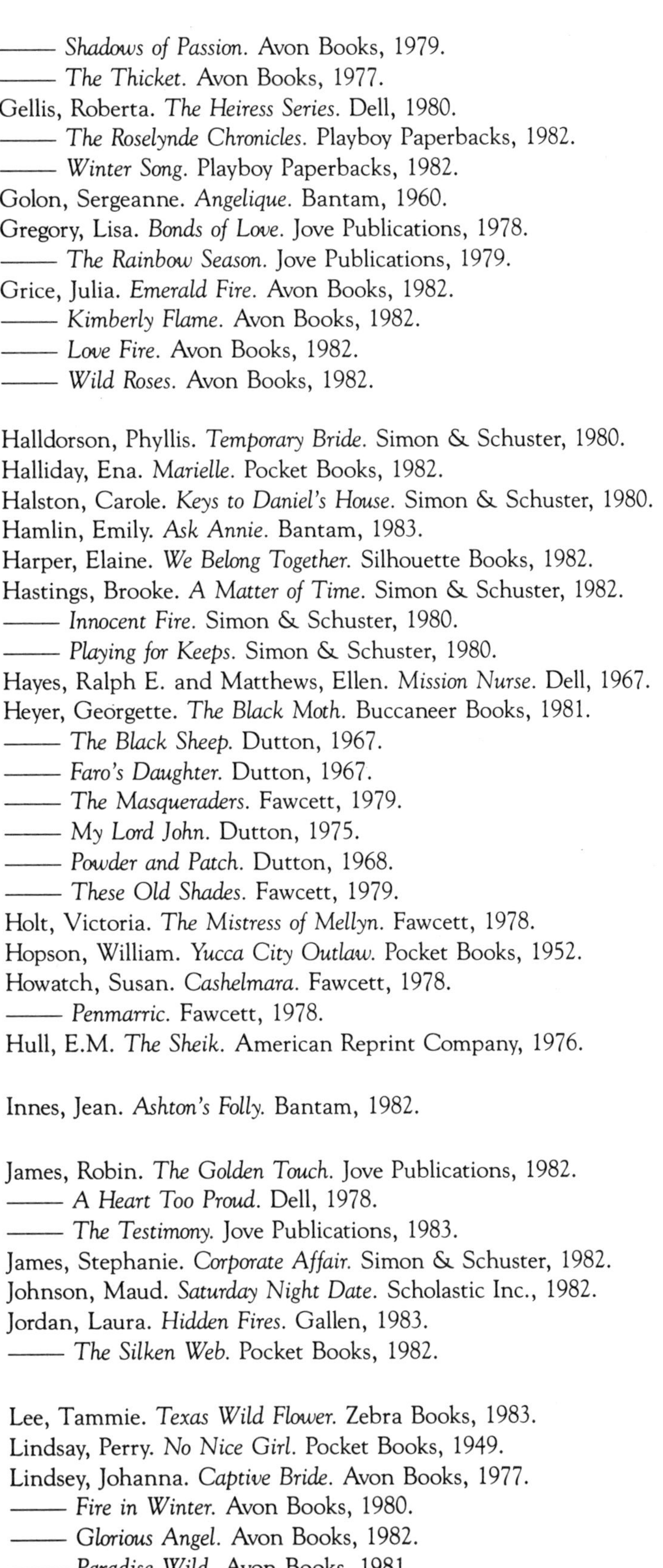

BIBLIOGRAPHY

—— *Shadows of Passion*. Avon Books, 1979.
—— *The Thicket*. Avon Books, 1977.
Gellis, Roberta. *The Heiress Series*. Dell, 1980.
—— *The Roselynde Chronicles*. Playboy Paperbacks, 1982.
—— *Winter Song*. Playboy Paperbacks, 1982.
Golon, Sergeanne. *Angelique*. Bantam, 1960.
Gregory, Lisa. *Bonds of Love*. Jove Publications, 1978.
—— *The Rainbow Season*. Jove Publications, 1979.
Grice, Julia. *Emerald Fire*. Avon Books, 1982.
—— *Kimberly Flame*. Avon Books, 1982.
—— *Love Fire*. Avon Books, 1982.
—— *Wild Roses*. Avon Books, 1982.

Halldorson, Phyllis. *Temporary Bride*. Simon & Schuster, 1980.
Halliday, Ena. *Marielle*. Pocket Books, 1982.
Halston, Carole. *Keys to Daniel's House*. Simon & Schuster, 1980.
Hamlin, Emily. *Ask Annie*. Bantam, 1983.
Harper, Elaine. *We Belong Together*. Silhouette Books, 1982.
Hastings, Brooke. *A Matter of Time*. Simon & Schuster, 1982.
—— *Innocent Fire*. Simon & Schuster, 1980.
—— *Playing for Keeps*. Simon & Schuster, 1980.
Hayes, Ralph E. and Matthews, Ellen. *Mission Nurse*. Dell, 1967.
Heyer, Georgette. *The Black Moth*. Buccaneer Books, 1981.
—— *The Black Sheep*. Dutton, 1967.
—— *Faro's Daughter*. Dutton, 1967.
—— *The Masqueraders*. Fawcett, 1979.
—— *My Lord John*. Dutton, 1975.
—— *Powder and Patch*. Dutton, 1968.
—— *These Old Shades*. Fawcett, 1979.
Holt, Victoria. *The Mistress of Mellyn*. Fawcett, 1978.
Hopson, William. *Yucca City Outlaw*. Pocket Books, 1952.
Howatch, Susan. *Cashelmara*. Fawcett, 1978.
—— *Penmarric*. Fawcett, 1978.
Hull, E.M. *The Sheik*. American Reprint Company, 1976.

Innes, Jean. *Ashton's Folly*. Bantam, 1982.

James, Robin. *The Golden Touch*. Jove Publications, 1982.
—— *A Heart Too Proud*. Dell, 1978.
—— *The Testimony*. Jove Publications, 1983.
James, Stephanie. *Corporate Affair*. Simon & Schuster, 1982.
Johnson, Maud. *Saturday Night Date*. Scholastic Inc., 1982.
Jordan, Laura. *Hidden Fires*. Gallen, 1983.
—— *The Silken Web*. Pocket Books, 1982.

Lee, Tammie. *Texas Wild Flower*. Zebra Books, 1983.
Lindsay, Perry. *No Nice Girl*. Pocket Books, 1949.
Lindsey, Johanna. *Captive Bride*. Avon Books, 1977.
—— *Fire in Winter*. Avon Books, 1980.
—— *Glorious Angel*. Avon Books, 1982.
—— *Paradise Wild*. Avon Books, 1981.

BIBLIOGRAPHY

—— *A Pirate's Love.* Avon Books, 1978.
—— *So Speaks the Heart.* Avon Books, 1983.
Long, Manning. *Here's Blood in Your Eye.* Harlequin, 1949.
Lorin, Amii. *The Tawny Gold Man.* Dell, 1980.

Mansfield, Elizabeth. *A Regency Match.* Jove Publications, 1980.
Mather, Anne. *Stormspell.* Harlequin, 1981.
Matthews, Laura. *Aim of a Lady.* Warner, 1981.
Matthews, Patricia. *Empire.* Pinnacle, 1977.
—— *Love's Avenging Heart.* Pinnacle, 1977.
McBain, Laurie. *Chance the Winds of Fortune.* Avon Books, 1980.
—— *Dark Before the Rising Sun.* Avon Books, 1982.
—— *Devil's Desire.* Avon Books, 1977.
—— *Moonstruck Madness.* Avon Books, 1977.
—— *Tears of Gold.* Avon Books, 1977.
McConnell. *River of Love.* New American Library, 1983.
Michaels, Fern. *Wild Honey.* Pocket Books, 1982.
Mitchell, Margaret. *Gone with the Wind.* Avon Books, 1974.
Morgan, Alice. *Masquerade of Love.* Dell, 1982.
—— *Mysterious Surrogate.* Dell, 1982.
—— *Sands of Malibu.* Dell, 1982.

Neggers, Carla. *Matching Wits.* Bantam, 1983.

Parker, Laura. *Emerald and Sapphire.* Pocket Books, 1982.
—— *Jim Bridger: Mountain Man.* Dell, 1983.
—— *Kit Carson: Trapper King.* Dell, 1983.
—— *Silks and Sabers.* Dell, 1980.
—— *Til Love is Enough.* Avon, 1983.
Patrick, De Ann. *Kindred Spirits.* Pocket Books, 1983.
Pelton, Sonya. *Passion's Paradise.* Zebra Books, 1980.
Powers, Tom. *Virgin with Butterflies.* Harlequin, 1949.

Radcliffe, Janette. *The Court of the Flowering Peach.* Dell, 1981.
—— *Hidden Fires.* Dell, 1982.
—— *Vienna Dreams.* Dell, 1982.
Richardson, Samuel. *Pamela.* Penguin, 1981.
Rogers, Rosemary. *The Crowd Pleasers.* Avon Books, 1978.
—— *Dark Fires.* Avon Books, 1975.
—— *The Insiders.* Avon Books, 1978.
—— *Lost Love, Last Love.* Avon Books, 1981.
—— *Love Play.* Avon Books, 1981.
—— *Surrender to Love.* Avon Books, 1978.
—— *Sweet Savage Love.* Avon Books, 1979.
—— *Wicked Loving Lies.* Avon Books, 1976.
—— *The Wildest Heart.* Avon Books, 1974.
Royall, Vanessa. *Come Faith, Come Fire.* Dell, 1979.
—— *Firebrand's Woman.* Dell, 1980.
—— *Flames of Desire.* Dell, 1978.
—— *Seize the Dawn.* Dell, 1983.
—— *Wild Wind Westward.* Dell, 1982.

BIBLIOGRAPHY

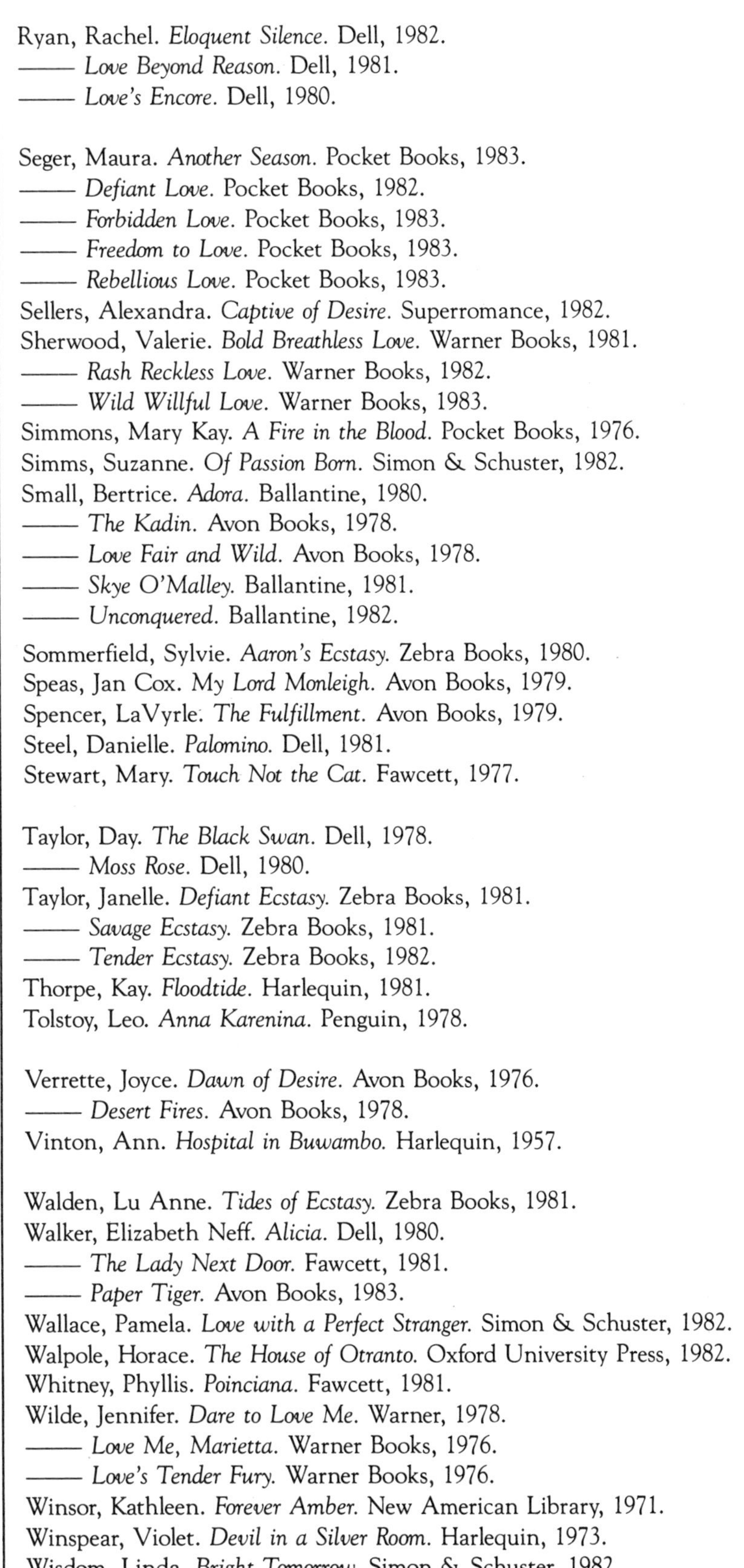

Ryan, Rachel. *Eloquent Silence.* Dell, 1982.
—— *Love Beyond Reason.* Dell, 1981.
—— *Love's Encore.* Dell, 1980.

Seger, Maura. *Another Season.* Pocket Books, 1983.
—— *Defiant Love.* Pocket Books, 1982.
—— *Forbidden Love.* Pocket Books, 1983.
—— *Freedom to Love.* Pocket Books, 1983.
—— *Rebellious Love.* Pocket Books, 1983.
Sellers, Alexandra. *Captive of Desire.* Superromance, 1982.
Sherwood, Valerie. *Bold Breathless Love.* Warner Books, 1981.
—— *Rash Reckless Love.* Warner Books, 1982.
—— *Wild Willful Love.* Warner Books, 1983.
Simmons, Mary Kay. *A Fire in the Blood.* Pocket Books, 1976.
Simms, Suzanne. *Of Passion Born.* Simon & Schuster, 1982.
Small, Bertrice. *Adora.* Ballantine, 1980.
—— *The Kadin.* Avon Books, 1978.
—— *Love Fair and Wild.* Avon Books, 1978.
—— *Skye O'Malley.* Ballantine, 1981.
—— *Unconquered.* Ballantine, 1982.
Sommerfield, Sylvie. *Aaron's Ecstasy.* Zebra Books, 1980.
Speas, Jan Cox. *My Lord Monleigh.* Avon Books, 1979.
Spencer, LaVyrle. *The Fulfillment.* Avon Books, 1979.
Steel, Danielle. *Palomino.* Dell, 1981.
Stewart, Mary. *Touch Not the Cat.* Fawcett, 1977.

Taylor, Day. *The Black Swan.* Dell, 1978.
—— *Moss Rose.* Dell, 1980.
Taylor, Janelle. *Defiant Ecstasy.* Zebra Books, 1981.
—— *Savage Ecstasy.* Zebra Books, 1981.
—— *Tender Ecstasy.* Zebra Books, 1982.
Thorpe, Kay. *Floodtide.* Harlequin, 1981.
Tolstoy, Leo. *Anna Karenina.* Penguin, 1978.

Verrette, Joyce. *Dawn of Desire.* Avon Books, 1976.
—— *Desert Fires.* Avon Books, 1978.
Vinton, Ann. *Hospital in Buwambo.* Harlequin, 1957.

Walden, Lu Anne. *Tides of Ecstasy.* Zebra Books, 1981.
Walker, Elizabeth Neff. *Alicia.* Dell, 1980.
—— *The Lady Next Door.* Fawcett, 1981.
—— *Paper Tiger.* Avon Books, 1983.
Wallace, Pamela. *Love with a Perfect Stranger.* Simon & Schuster, 1982.
Walpole, Horace. *The House of Otranto.* Oxford University Press, 1982.
Whitney, Phyllis. *Poinciana.* Fawcett, 1981.
Wilde, Jennifer. *Dare to Love Me.* Warner, 1978.
—— *Love Me, Marietta.* Warner Books, 1976.
—— *Love's Tender Fury.* Warner Books, 1976.
Winsor, Kathleen. *Forever Amber.* New American Library, 1971.
Winspear, Violet. *Devil in a Silver Room.* Harlequin, 1973.
Wisdom, Linda. *Bright Tomorrow.* Simon & Schuster, 1982.

BIBLIOGRAPHY

—— *Dancer in the Shadows*. Simon & Schuster, 1980.
—— *Fourteen Carat Beauty*. Simon & Schuster, 1981.
—— *A Man with Doubts*. Simon & Schuster, 1982.
Wisely, Charlotte. *Welcome Intruder*. New American Library, 1983.
Woodiwiss, Kathleen. *Ashes in the Wind*. Avon Books, 1979.
—— *The Flame and the Flower*. Avon Books, 1983.
—— *Shanna*. Avon Books, 1977.
—— *A Rose in Winter*. Avon Books, 1982.
—— *The Wolf and the Dove*. Avon Books, 1977.

INDEX

Abelard, Peter — 38, 39
Adora — 127
Advertising and promotion — 268-275
Affaire de Coeur — 311
Angelique — 97-98
Anna Karenina — 62-63
Aphrodisiacs — 44-45
Austen, Jane — 56
Autumn Countess, The — 136
Avon Books — 57, 65, 67-68
"Awakening of Cassey, The" — 24

Barbra Critiques, Ltd. — 311
Barrett, Elizabeth — *See* Browning, Elizabeth Barrett
Barrie, Monica — 239-240
Beauty and the Beast — 54
Beethoven, Ludwig van — 49
Bennett, Harry — 293-294
Black Moth, The — 56
Blake, Jennifer — 192-193
Bodice rippers — 99
Boleyn, Ann — 38-39, 46
Bonds, Parris Afton — 194-195
Boy Meets Girl — 4, 5, 12, 18, 311-312
Brandewyne, Rebecca — 195-196
Brand-name romances — 3, 4, 72
Brontë, Charlotte — 56, 89
Brontë, Emily — 56
Brothers, Joyce — 22
Brown, Sandra — 197-198
Browning, Elizabeth Barrett — 40-41
Browning, Robert — 40-41, 46
Burchell, Mary — 189

Camille — 62
Camp, Candace — 198-199
Candlelight Ecstacy Books — 11, 76, 173-175
Captive of Desire — 104
Cartland, Barbara — 200-201
Castle, Jayne — 201-203
Category romances — *See* Brand-name romances
Cinderella — 54
Circle of Love — 177-178
Charles (Prince of Wales) — 43

Chase, Elaine Raco — 203-204
Claire de Lune — 60
Clarissa — 56
Cleopatra (Queen of Egypt) — 36, 38
Coffman, Virginia — 89, 204-206
Cookson, Catherine — 189
Cooper, Jilly — 189
Coulter, Catherine — 206-207
Cruise ships — 33
Cupid — 48
Curial, Clementine — 49
Curtis, Tom and Sharon — 208
Cyrano de Bergerac — 63

Daeni, Pino — 294-295
Dailey, Bill — 25
Dailey, Janet — 25, 209-211
Defiant Love — 15, 100
Deveraux, Jude — 141, 142, 144, 211-212
Devil's Embrace — 136, 139
Doctor Zhivago — 64
Duillo, Elaine — 295-296

Edward VIII (King of England) — 42
Eros — *See* Cupid
"Escape to Love" — 24

Falk, Kathryn — 16-18
Faro's Daughter — 88
Fielding, Henry — 56
Films — *See* Motion Pictures and TV
Finding Mr. Right — 262-265
Fitzgerald, F. Scott — 41
Flame and the Flower, The — 57, 65, 67, 127
Flame Is Love, The — 20
Floodtide — 118
Forever Amber — 56, 127
Foxfire Light — 20, 25

Gellis, Roberta — 212-214
Gentle Pirate — 76
Gignilliat, Elaine — 296-297
Gone with the Wind — 56, 63-64
Gothic romances — 89-91
Greeting cards — 50

Hall, H. Tom — 297-298
Hamilton, Emma — 39, 46
Hampson, Anne — 189
Harlequin Books — 4, 9, 11, 57, 72, 75, 151, 154-160
Hastings, Brooke — 214-215
Heart Line — 312
Heaven's Price — 117
Helen of Troy — 58
Heloise — 38, 49
Henry VIII (King of England) — 38-39, 46
Heyer, Georgette — 56, 86, 88, 190-191
Historical romances — 80-91, 99
Holt, Victoria — 89-190

"Immortal Beloved" — 49

Jacket blurbs — 302
Jacket designs — 276-303
Jane Eyre — 56, 61-62, 89
Janet Dailey Newsletter, The — 312-313
Jennings, Vivien Lee — 18
Johnson, Gordon — 299-300
Joseph Andrews — 56
Josephine (Empress of France) — 49
Jourdan, Louis — 22

Kelly, Grace — 42-43
Keys to Daniel's House — 104
Kleist, Heinrich von — 46

Lamb, Charlotte — 190
Lee, Tammie — 240-242
Leopard in the Snow — 20
"Lights, Camera, Action, Love" — 24
Love, Wild & Fair — 139
Love American Style — 20
Love at first sight — 57-58
"Love at the Top" — 24
Love Boat — 20
Love letters — 46, 49, 50-52
Love & Life — 11
Love Line, The — 313
Lovenotes — 313-314
Love Notes — 314
Love's Leading Ladies — 16
Love's Philosophy (Shelley) — 132
Loveswept Books — 5, 178

INDEX

Mansfield, Elizabeth — 86
Mark Antony — 36, 38
Masquerade of Love — 118
Matching Wits — 118
Matter of Time, A — 105
Matthews, Patricia — 215-217
Maurier, Daphne du — 89
McGinnis, Bob — 300-301
Mills & Boon, Ltd. — 56, 72, 75, 183-189
Mistress of Mellyn, The — 89
Mitchell, Margaret — 56
Morgan, Alice — 217-218
Motion pictures and TV — 20-25
Moura — 89
Musset, Alfred de — 40
My Secret Garden — 14

Napoleon I (Napoleon Bonaparte) — 49
Nelson, Horatio — 39, 46
No Easy Way Out — 117
Normandie (ocean liner) — 31

Orpheus & Eurydice — 59-50
Ovid — 54

Pamela — 55, 56
Paper Tiger — 108
Parker, Laura — 218-220
Plots — 116-118
Poinciana — 91
Pride and Prejudice — 56
Pseudonyms
  of female authors — 230-235
  of male authors — 236-245

Queen Elizabeth (ocean liner) — 31
Queen Elizabeth II (ocean liner) — 32-33
Queen Mary (ocean liner) — 28-31

Ranier III (Prince of Monaco) — 42-43
Rainy Day Books — 12, 18
Rapture Romance — 9, 265-266
Rebecca — 89
Rebel Bride, The — 86, 136
Regency Match, A — 86
Regency romances — 81-84, 86-88, 136-137
Richard Gallen Books — 182
Richardson, Samuel — 55-56
River of Love — 118
Rogers, Rosemary — 65, 220-221
Romance publications — 311-314
Romance Theatre — 20, 22, 24
Romance Writers of America — 304-306
Romance Writers Report — 314
Romantic Book Lovers Conference — 16
Romantic fiction
  award-winning books — 309-310
  bibliography of — 69-70
  characters in — 115
  clothing in — 141-144
  contemporary — 72-78
  ethnic — 78
  guides for writing — 248-254
  history of — 54-57
  locales of — 119-125
  marriage in — 145-149
  quiz on — 34-35
  rape in — 139-140
  readers' comments on — 19
  sex in — 126-140
  statistics on — 2-10
  submitting a manuscript to a publisher — 255-257
  vs. soap operas — 26-27
  why people buy — 11-15.
    See also Advertising and promotion; Bodice rippers; Brand-name romances; Gothic romances; Historical romances; Jacket blurbs; Jacket designs; Plots; Regency romances; Teen romances
Romantic Novelists Association — 307-308
Romantic Times — 12-16
Romeo and Juliet — 61
Royall, Vanessa — 242-244

Sand, George — 40
Saunders, Jean — 190
Sayre, Zelda — 41
Scarlet Ribbons — 181-182
Second Chance At Love — 5, 175-176
Seger, Maura — 100, 221-223
She Walks in Beauty (Lord Byron) — 138
Silhouette Books — 4, 14, 24, 25, 75, 152-153, 162-172
Silhouette Romance Theatre — 20
Simpson, Wallis — 42
Small, Beatrice — 223-224, 246-247
Small, George — 246-247
Song of Roland — 55
Sonnett 116 (Shakespeare) — 134
Sonnetts From the Portuguese (Elizabeth Barrett Browning) — 47
Spencer, Diana — 43
Stendhal — 49
Stewart, Mary — 190
Sweet Savage Love — 65, 127
Swift, Jonathan — 49

Tapestry Romances — 153, 258-262
Tawny Gold Man, The — 76
Teen romances — 92-95
Tristan and Isolt — 60-61
Troyes, Chretien de — 54-55
TV — *See* Motion pictures and TV

United States (ocean liner) — 32

Valentine's Day — 9
Vanhomrigh, Esther (Vanessa) — 49
Virtue Rewarded — 55
Vogel, Henrietta — 46

Walker, Elizabeth Neff — 224-226
Wilde, Jennifer — 244-245
Winsor, Kathleen — 56, 127
Wisdom, Linda — 226-227
Women's liberation movement — 12, 14
Woodiwiss, Kathleen E. — 57, 65, 227-229
Wuthering Heights — 56

Zebra Books — 179-181

PHOTO CREDITS

PHOTO SUBJECT CREDIT

Roberta Gellis — Charles Gellis
Heart Throb cards — Ruby Street
Renishaw Hall — Reresby Sitwell
Prince Charles and Princess Diana — Central Office of Information, London
Castles of Coch, Bamburgh, Culzean, Windsor, and Harlech — British Tourist Authority
Rosemary Rogers — Francesco Scavullo
Jayne Castle — Stephen Castle
Pride and Prejudice, Rebecca, Jayne Eyre — British Broadcasting Corp.
Fred Kerner — Seattle Times
Kathleen E. Woodiwiss — Joan Bingham
Scott Fitzgerald Family — Associated Press
Duke and Duchess of Windsor — United Press International
Prince Rainier, Princess Grace and family — United Press International
Bertrice Small — George Sumner Small
Laura Parker — Chris Castoro
Kate Duffy — Robert Bonifeld
Joan Schulhafer — Robert Bonifield
Maura Seger — Leslie A. Beran
Page Cuddy and Tom Stanley — Ann C. McKeown

NOTES

NOTES

NOTES

NOTES

♥ NOTES ♥

Houston Public Libraries
FOR LIBRARY USE ONLY